Frank Lloyd Wright's Taliesin Fellowship

Frank Lloyd Wright's
Taliesin Fellowship

Myron A. Marty
Shirley L. Marty

TRUMAN STATE UNIVERSITY PRESS
KIRKSVILLE, MISSOURI

Library of Congress Cataloging-in-Publication Data

Marty, Myron A.
    Frank Lloyd Wright's Taliesin Fellowship / Myron A. Marty. Shirley
L. Marty.
      p.   cm.
    Includes bibliographical references and index.
    ISBN 0-943549-74-4 (cloth : alk. paper)
    ISBN 0-943549-73-6 (pbk. : alk. paper)
    1. Taliesin Fellowship.   2. Architecture—Study and
teaching—Wisconsin—Spring Green.   3. Architecture—Study and
teaching—Arizona—Scottsdale.   4. Taliesin Fellowship Interviews.
5. Wright, Frank Lloyd, 1867–1959—Friends and associates Interviews.
6. Wright, Olgivanna Lloyd—Friends and associates Interviews.
7. Architects—United States Interviews.   I. Marty, Shirley L.
II. Title.   III. Title: Taliesin Fellowship.
NA2127.S66M37   1999   99-34910
·720'.7'077576-dc21   CIP

Cover photo: John Engstead. Courtesy Frank Lloyd Wright Foundation.

Cover and dustjacket: Teresa Wheeler, Truman State University designer.

Printing: Sheridan Books, Ann Arbor, Michigan

Composition: BookComp, Inc.

For
Mildred Marty Burger
and
Martin E. Marty

Contents

Illustrations

Introduction

Coming to terms with Frank Lloyd Wright is not easy. In his long career, spanning more than seven decades, his designs defied one architectural tradition after another. In his personal life and manner he was similarly defiant. By the 1950s, as Neil Levine tells it in *The Architecture of Frank Lloyd Wright*, younger architects, critics, and historians

> came to regard [him] as a somewhat annoying—yet vaguely threatening—super-annuated folk hero, living out a mythic existence in a world of his own devising in rural Wisconsin and Arizona, totally divorced from the political, social, economic, philosophic and artistic problems of the real world. In his flowing cape and porkpie hat, he appeared terribly corny; and the kitschy quality attributed to his buildings and projects of the later years made them seem beyond the pale. Who should care, anyway, about someone who disdained all schools and professional organizations and took every opportunity to say so?

So they tried to ignore him. When that failed, they criticized or ridiculed him, even as he commanded their reluctant respect. Wright thus inspired a love-hate relationship that continues to this day. But modern architecture, Levine explains, has changed:

> Gone is the unquestioning moral belief in the historical validity of the machine aesthetic that at first deified and then dismissed Wright. A broader understanding of what constitutes the modern experience in architecture is being elaborated, and with that effort has come the demand for a more comprehensive and balanced account of its historical development.

And so, he continues, there exists a need for "another" book about Wright. Levine's impressive, thoroughly researched book approaches Wright's work afresh, and at the same time draws upon the exhaustive work of others. The book answers the need he has identified.[1]

But yet another need exists, for the full dimensions of Wright the man, the eccentric, the creative genius, remain blurred. Some writers portray him as a man of many masks; others denigrate the work of his students and followers.[2] Still others treat Wright with a mixture of curiosity and adulation.[3] Many studies of specific aspects of his work reflect the man but offer few insights into his personal life.[4] As far as the Fellowship is concerned, we have discovered that many who comment on it do not know as much about it or understand it as well as they think they do. We regard it as important to enter accounts into the record that will serve as correctives to mistaken impressions of both Wright and the Fellowship. In this respect, this work complements books by four persons who knew Wright well and worked closely with him. These books, cited below, provide insights into his personal life at several stages, but many avenues for coming to know him, particularly those that reveal Wright through his relationship with his third wife, remain untraveled.

This book travels some of those avenues. It tells the story of the Taliesin Fellowship, created by Frank and Olgivanna Lloyd Wright in 1932, in the words of men and women who joined the Fellowship, some of them as early as the 1930s, and have remained with it into the 1990s. Many of the storytellers worked side by side with Wright, who died in 1959, and almost all of them lived and worked with Olgivanna Lloyd Wright, who survived her husband by twenty-six years. The Taliesin fellows are joined by other storytellers who have been their partners in recent years and who know the Fellowship well. Myron Marty interviewed most of these storytellers.

Cornelia Brierly, one of the senior fellows whom we interviewed, has been with the Fellowship since 1934, except for the decade she practiced architecture in the Pittsburgh area (1946–56). In her recently published *Tales of Taliesin,* she has used her insider's perspective to recount interesting episodes in the Fellowship's life. Many among the hundreds of other men and women who came to the Fellowship through the years and then moved on attest to the profound influence their experiences with the Fellowship, and particularly with Mr. and Mrs. Wright, had on their lives. Two of them, Edgar Tafel and Curtis Besinger, have published books that describe their years with the Fellowship, and Pedro Guerrero has produced several excellent collections of photographs and reminiscences of experiences with the Wrights and the Fellowship.[5]

Many former apprentices are members of the Taliesin Fellows, now recognized as Taliesin's alumni organization. The mission of this organization is, among other things,

> to serve as a medium of exchange among apprentices from all the years, including the present; . . . to accumulate the personal remembrances that may be significant, amusing, or may simply illuminate daily workings of the Fellowship; . . . [and] to record personal interactions or conversations with Mr. Wright that would testify to the true nature or a more historically accurate picture of Frank Lloyd Wright the man.[6]

We had an opportunity to meet a number of the Taliesin Fellows at their annual meeting in September 1996 and again at the celebration of the sixtieth anniversary of the founding of Taliesin West in November 1997. On both occasions they provided insights reflected in this book. The quarterly *Journal of the Taliesin Fellows* offers interesting perspectives on the Fellowship's past.

In *Frank Lloyd Wright's Taliesin Fellowship* we construct the story almost entirely from the perspective of men and women who have committed their lives to the perpetuation of the ideals of community life and all that that entails in a fellowship based on organic architecture. Others, many of whom are mentioned in the stories told here, played critical roles in establishing the Fellowship and carrying it through trying times, but the Fellowship owes its survival to those whose voices are heard here.

Not surprisingly, the members of the Taliesin Fellowship heard in this book who knew Frank Lloyd Wright speak admiringly of him and his work. Similarly, most express reverence for Mrs. Wright. It should be noted, however, that they have not escaped criticism for their roles as perpetuators and protectors of the Wrights' legacy. Robert McCarter, for example, faults Wright for having taken too many commissions in the last twelve years of his life—nearly four hundred projects after reaching age eighty. He claims that Wright's apprentices "were rarely capable of effectively assuming responsibility for his designs." Consequently, Wright's work in this period "consisted either of repetitive schemes, often adapted to neither their sites nor programmes, or extravagant and overscaled forms, usually given only superficial design development." Further, McCarter asserts, the "increasingly isolated situation (physically, intellectually, socially)" and the "ritualistic daily life at Taliesin [that] had long been guided by Olgivanna Wright, who had effectively assumed the guise of high priestess," denied Wright the constructive criticism that is essential in producing architecture of quality.[7] McCarter's judgments are not shared by all architectural historians, of course, but the substantial studies of Wright's work on which he bases them should be taken into account when one examines the history of the Taliesin Fellowship.

In contemporary terminology, the Taliesin Fellowship is an "intentional community." How that term is defined is the subject of much discussion among members of the Fellowship of Intentional Community, but this definition by Dan Questenberry in the 1995 *Communities Directory* aptly describes the Taliesin Fellowship: "A group of people living cooperatively, dedicated by intent and commitment to specific communal values and goals."[8] What sets the Taliesin Fellowship apart is its distinctive dedication: to produce organic architecture. This architecture has been its economic lifeblood, and from its founding to the present day its identity has been synonymous with the accomplishments of Frank Lloyd Wright, whose name, in turn, is synonymous with organic architecture.

Our purpose in this book is to present the essential elements of a good story of that community: its origins, milestones in its history, dynamics that have shaped its progress, its character, and the general plot the story has followed. Occasionally we refer to the histories of other communities to better understand the distinctiveness of Taliesin. This is not intended to be a critical appraisal of the Fellowship's evolution, although there is a healthy measure of self-criticism in the words of the persons interviewed.

In carrying the story of the Taliesin Fellowship through the mid-1990s we do not attempt to anticipate its future. Nonetheless, because the Fellowship's future is much on the minds of its members, many of them have spoken freely of their concerns, and we include here what they had to say. The deaths since 1991 of five senior fellows (William Wesley Peters, Kenn Lockhart, John DeKoven Hill, Kay Rattenbury, and Richard Carney) have heightened the concern about the future.

Although this is not a biography of Frank Lloyd Wright or Olgivanna Lloyd Wright, it offers readers fresh and provocative insights into the genius and mystique of the Fellowship's creators. The accounts of the architects who worked with Wright help to explain his amazing productivity, particularly in the last decade of his life, and stories told by the men and women who knew him well implicitly debunk some of the common caricatures that are a part of his legacy.

Organizing the stories of the persons interviewed was much like assembling a jigsaw puzzle. Excerpts from the interviews provided the pieces, but some of those pieces contended for the same space, some pieces were missing, and some did not precisely fit into any space. Because the pieces of the puzzle did not come in a box with a picture on it, painting the picture itself was also our task.

To fit the pieces into the right places and to keep the book from becoming too long, we sometimes omitted words, sentences, and paragraphs. Omissions of words within sentences and sentences within paragraphs are usually indicated by ellipses. Words inserted to give a sentence clarity or meaning are typically enclosed within brackets. Questions raised in the interviews are frequently omitted when the responses make them unnecessary, and segments from the interviews do not always appear in the sequence in which they were spoken.

Readers will see that the fellows and staff members always refer to their mentors as Mr. Wright and Mrs. Wright, and except in the opening chapter we follow that custom here. For everyone else, given names are used, as they are in all conversations and even in the Taliesin telephone directories.

All of the persons interviewed had the opportunity to edit their own transcripts. In preparing portions of the transcripts for publication, we followed standard editing practices to eliminate redundancies, confusing digressions, crutch expressions, false starts, and some of the contractions. Occasionally we clarified the text by bringing consistency to matters of tense and number and making certain that the identity of persons referred to by pronouns was clear. The complete, literal transcripts as edited by the persons interviewed, along with the audio recordings of the interviews, will be placed in the Frank Lloyd Wright Foundation Archives in accordance with the terms of deposit agreements between the persons interviewed, the Archives, and us.

Taliesin, Spring Green, Wisconsin: Hillside, designed by Frank Lloyd Wright in 1902 for the "Home School" operated by his aunts, was remodeled in 1932 (and several times since then) to serve the needs of the Taliesin Fellowship. The living room on the main floor overlooks the dining room on the ground floor. A mezzanine at the upper level houses a library, and the kitchen is adjacent to the dining room.

Taliesin: Beyond the kitchen on the lower level of Hillside is the dining room, and beyond it the theater. This part of Hillside was rebuilt after a fire in 1952.

Some of the interviews occurred in Wisconsin, where the apprentices and the majority of the fellows are in residence from May to October, and some in Arizona, where they reside in the winter months. Readers will ordinarily be able to determine the location of "here" and "there" as they appear from the context. A roster of persons appears on pages following this Introduction. The roster also gives the date and location of each interview. Other persons are identified in the text, sometimes in brackets, or in footnotes at their first mention, which can ordinarily be located through the index. The notes also provide other clarifying information. The conversations include frequent references to buildings designed by Wright. Readers wishing to know more about them should consult one of the many well-illustrated works on the architecture of Frank Lloyd Wright.

Readers should bear in mind that the Taliesin Fellowship stands under the umbrella, so to speak, of the Frank Lloyd Wright Foundation, a nonprofit entity

Taliesin, Spring Green, Wisconsin: A hallway connects the Hillside living room with the drafting studio.

Taliesin: The first Taliesin, built in 1911, was rebuilt after a fire destroyed the living quarters in 1914, and again, following another fire in 1925. Since then it has been altered in many ways; the "bird walk" was added in the 1950s. It is now being gradually restored by the Taliesin Preservation Commission.

incorporated by Wright in 1940. (Interestingly, the Fellowship was also incorporated at the same time, but its corporate status was allowed to lapse in the 1980s.) The Foundation's bylaws provide that the "entire membership of the Foundation is known as the Taliesin Fellowship" and that the senior members of the Fellowship "shall be the sole voting members of the corporation." Consequently, it is the fellows who elect the members of the Board of Trustees. Half of the trustees must be senior fellows and half representatives of the public.

Also under the Foundation's umbrella are the Frank Lloyd Wright School of Architecture and the Frank Lloyd Wright Archives. The architectural firm, Taliesin

Taliesin West, Scottsdale, Arizona: The Taliesin West complex includes the drafting room at its northwest end. For more than a decade after its construction in 1937, its roof was made of stretched linen canvas, the same material that was drawn over window openings to protect against excessive sunshine and occasional rain.

Taliesin West: The center portion of the complex includes an office area, the kitchen and dining room, and, upstairs, guest rooms.

Taliesin West: At the southeast end is the living room, known as the garden room. Connected to it were Mr. and Mrs. Wright's living quarters, now used as offices.

Architects, is incorporated as a wholly owned subsidiary of the Foundation. Members of the Fellowship play essential roles in the School, the Archives, and the Taliesin Architects, as will be apparent throughout this book. Chapter 7 has separate sections on the evolution of the School, the Archives, and the firm.

The meaning of such terms as "fellow" and "apprentice" will become clear through their usage in the chapters that follow. Other terms are explained where necessary in footnotes in the chapters, with their locations noted in the index. Milestones in the life of Frank and Olgivanna Lloyd Wright and the Taliesin Fellowship are recorded in appendix A. To help readers understand references to locations, such as Hillside, Taliesin, Tan-y-deri, and Midway in Wisconsin, and the living areas, studio, and buildings in Arizona, we have included maps and building descriptions in appendix B.

Although we are familiar with the valuable oral history collection now being assembled by the Frank Lloyd Wright Foundation Archives, to have used it here would have drawn this work away from its specific purposes. Moreover, those wide-ranging interviews have as a principal purpose to establish the record of architectural projects in which the apprentices were engaged and the apprentices' relations with Wright.[9] Our focus is on the community in which the apprentices and fellows have lived—why they joined, how they worked, the nature of their relationships, their contributions, and the evolution of the community.

We have read the constitution and bylaws of the Frank Lloyd Wright Foundation and several other official documents, but we have not examined other possible sources of information—for example, minutes of meetings of the Fellowship; records of apprentices' applications or their accomplishments while at Taliesin and beyond; periodic internal documents concerning the Fellowship; or files of correspondence between and among fellows, apprentices, and former members of the Taliesin Fellowship. These materials, as well as the oral history collection, will be useful in what we envision as the second phase of work on the Taliesin Fellowship. We anticipate that phase will result in a comprehensive, critical history of this distinctive institution.

Notes

1. Neil Levine, *The Architecture of Frank Lloyd Wright* (Princeton: Princeton University Press, 1996), xiv–xv.

2. Brendan Gill, *Many Masks: A Life of Frank Lloyd Wright* (New York: G. P. Putnam's, 1987), provides the ammunition for the "many masks" school of critics, and Robert Twombly, *Frank Lloyd Wright: His Life and His Architecture* (New York: Wiley, 1979), exemplifies the attitude of the denigrators.

3. For example, Meryle Secrest, *Frank Lloyd Wright: A Biography* (New York: Alfred A. Knopf, 1992).

4. Examples are the excellent studies by Donald Hoffman: *Frank Lloyd Wright: Architecture*

and Nature; Frank Lloyd Wright's Fallingwater: The House and Its History; and *Understanding Frank Lloyd Wright's Architecture* (New York: Dover Publications, 1986, 1993, 1995).

5. Cornelia Brierly, *Tales of Taliesin: A Memoir of Friendship* (Tempe, AZ: The Herberger Center for Design Excellence, Arizona State University, 1999); Edgar Tafel, *Apprentice to Genius: Years with Frank Lloyd Wright* (New York: Dover Publications, 1979); Curtis Besinger, *Working with Mr. Wright: What It Was Like* (Cambridge: Cambridge University Press, 1995); Pedro E. Guerrero, *Picturing Wright: An Album From Frank Lloyd Wright's Photographer* (San Francisco: Pomegranate Artbooks, 1994); and Tafel was with the Fellowship from 1932 to 1941, Besinger from 1939 to 1955, and Guerrero from 1940 to 1941 (with frequent visits in subsequent years).

6. The mission statement appears on p. 2 of each issue of the *Journal of the Taliesin Fellows.*

7. Robert McCarter, *Frank Lloyd Wright–Architect* (London: Phaidon Press Ltd., 1997), 321–2.

8. *Communities Directory: A Guide to Cooperative Living* (Rutledge, MO: Fellowship of Intentional Community, 1996), 35.

9. See the note in the bibliography on these and other interviews.

Persons Interviewed

Portions of interviews with these persons appear in *Frank Lloyd Wright's Taliesin Fellowship.* They are listed in the alphabetical order of their given names, since those are the names by which they are identified in the text. Indicated in each instance are the date of their arrival at Taliesin; the person's principal responsibilities and expertise in the Frank Lloyd Wright Foundation, the School of Architecture, the Archives, the Taliesin Architects, and the Fellowship; and when and where the interviews occurred (*AZ*=Taliesin West, Scottsdale, Arizona; *WI*=Taliesin, Spring Green, Wisconsin; *HI*=Hawaii). Details about their lives appear in the interviews.[1]

Senior Fellows

Anneliese Dodge, 1976. Bookstore manager. *1 December 1994, AZ.*

Ari D. Georges, 1986. Assistant Dean for Curriculum; architecture, graphic design. *27 June 1996, WI.*

Arnold Roy, 1952. Registered Architect; Treasurer; Vice President for Facilities; architecture. *22 November 1994, AZ.*

Bruce Brooks Pfeiffer, 1949. Director of the Frank Lloyd Wright Archives; Vice President for Archives; architectural history. *28 November 1994, AZ.*

Charles Montooth (J. Charles), 1945. Registered Architect; architecture, planning, history. *21 June 1995, WI.*

Cornelia Brierly, 1934. Registered Landscape Architect; landscape architecture, interior design. *16 November 1994, AZ.*

David Dodge, 1951. Registered Architect; architecture, music. *17 November 1994, AZ.*

Dick Carney (Richard), 1948. Chairman of the Board of the Frank Lloyd Wright Foundation; formerly Managing Trustee and CEO. *15 November 1994, AZ; 21 June 1995, WI.* (Deceased, January 1998.)

Dori Roy (Doris), 1958. Administration. *30 November 1994, AZ.*

Dr. Joe Rorke (Joseph F.), 1956. Public access program; Fellowship publisher. *16 November 1994, AZ.*

Effi Maria Casey, 1966. Associate Dean for Assessment; nature patterns, music, painting. *22 November 1994, AZ; 25 March 1997, AZ (by telephone).*

Frances Nemtin (Mary Frances), 1946. Landscaping, pottery. *30 November 1994, AZ.*

Heloise Crista, 1949. Applied arts, sculpture, correlation. *24 November 1994, AZ.*

Indira Berndtson, 1962. Administrator of Historic Studies, Archives, *1 December 1994, AZ.*

Jay Jensen, 1991. Certified Construction Specifier; architecture, specifications. *21 June 1996, WI.*

Joe Fabris (Joseph R.), 1948. Construction, design, preservation. *21 November 1994, AZ.*

John Rattenbury (known as John R), 1950. Registered Architect; architectural design and professional practice. *16 November 1994, AZ.*

Johnny Hill (John de Koven). Honorary Chairman of the Board of the Frank Lloyd Wright Foundation, 1993–96. Design, interior design. *23 November 1994, AZ.* (Deceased, July 1996.)

Julie Nelson Kardatzke, 1991. Architecture, social work. *18 March 1997, AZ (by telephone).*

Kay Rattenbury, 1935. Painting, interior design. *19 November 1992 (by Indira Berndtson and Greg Williams), AZ.* (Deceased, December 1996.)

Ling Po, 1946. Design, drawing. *21 November 1994, AZ.* (On leave.)

Marian E. Kanouse, 1947. Assistant Treasurer. *1 December 1994, AZ.* (Deceased April 1999.)

Paul J. Kardatzke, 1991. Civil engineering, architecture. *27 June 1996, WI.*

Sarah Logue, 1957. English literature and applied arts. *23 November 1994, AZ.*

Shawn Rorke-Davis, 1983. Director of the Outreach Program; sociology, education. *2 July 1995, AZ (by telephone).* (On leave.)

Stephen M. Nemtin, 1959. Registered Architect; architecture, landscaping. *20 June 1995, WI.*

Susan Jacobs Lockhart, 1958. Art education, graphic design, decorative design. *17 November 1994, AZ; 26 March 1997, AZ (by telephone).*

Tom Casey (E. Thomas), 1950. Registered Architect; Registered Structural Engineer; Dean of Architecture; Vice President for Education. *28 November 1994, AZ; 25 March 1997, AZ (by telephone).*

Tony Puttnam (Anthony), 1954. Registered Architect; architecture, planning. *21 June 1995, Madison, WI.*

Non-resident Members of the Taliesin Community

Elizabeth Al-Hassam Dawsari, 1984. Dean of Libraries. *23 May 1996, AZ.*

Golnar Casey, daughter of Tom and Effi Casey, born into the Fellowship in 1973. *28 June 1996, WI.*

John Wyatt, School of Architecture, 1993. Academic Dean. *14 March 1997, HI (by telephone).*

June Hill, School of Architecture, 1985. Executive Assistant to the Deans. *20 June 1995, WI.*

Margo Stipe, Archives, 1990. Registrar. *15 March 1997, AZ (by telephone).*

Nick Muller (H. Nicholas Muller, III), Frank Lloyd Wright Foundation. President and CEO, 1996. *27 February 1997, AZ (by telephone).*

Oscar Muñoz, Archives, 1988. Assistant Director, Administrator of the Archives and Photographic Collections. *23 May 1996, AZ.*

Penny Fowler, Archives, 1986. Administrator of Fine Arts Collections. *13 March 1997, AZ (by telephone).*

Ryc Loope (R. Nicholas Loope), Taliesin Architects, 1992. Managing principal. *22 May 1996, AZ.*

Suzette Lucas, Frank Lloyd Wright Foundation, 1988. Director of External Affairs. *21 May 1996, AZ.*

Note

1. The sources for much of this information were the *1996 Bulletin of the Frank Lloyd Wright School of Architecture* and the *1997 Apprentice Handbook for the Frank Lloyd Wright School of Architecture.* For information in notes to the text about former apprentices, the main source was "1932–1982, The Taliesin Fellowship: A Directory of Members," prepared, privately printed fall 1981, and distributed by Elizabeth B. Kassler; also "A Supplement to 1932–1982, The Taliesin Fellowship: A Directory of Members," prepared, privately printed July 1982, and distributed by Elizabeth B. Kassler. Both were provided for our use by the Frank Lloyd Wright Archives. Dates for apprentices enrolled since 1982 were provided by various persons at Taliesin.

1

Taliesin: "The Whole Gamut of Human Experience"

In the eyes of those who knew Frank Lloyd Wright best, he was a genius. Admirers, including Wright himself, saw his genius in his architecture, his voluminous writings, and his legendary lifestyle. Many who knew Olgivanna Lloyd Wright, who is sometimes called a "partner to genius," regarded her as a genius in her own right. Detractors notwithstanding, these judgments were widely shared and remain so.

The genius that matters most in this book, however, is the "genius of Taliesin." In ancient times, "genius" did not refer to a human being, but rather to the god honored on each person's birthday to ensure continued prosperity and life. Genius so interpreted serves as nature's agent and protector, as society's wellspring of inventive ability and inspired talent. In today's terminology, the concept of genius encompasses the collection of distinctive, determinative, natural endowments peculiar to each society. It embodies a society's genesis, genealogy, and ingenuity. It is fitting, therefore, to speak of the spirit that has prevailed in the Taliesin Fellowship for more than sixty-five years as the genius of Taliesin.

Those who entered and remained with the Taliesin Fellowship during the lifetimes of Frank Lloyd Wright and Olgivanna Lloyd Wright credit them with making it a magical place. The genius of their legacies lingers, and with it some of the magic of their creation.

Origins. Great architect though he was, Frank Lloyd Wright faced hard times in the 1920s and into the 1930s. His architectural practice suffered from unfavorable publicity arising from scandals in his personal life. Leaving behind his wife Catherine and their six children in 1909 was bad enough. Traveling to Europe with Mamah Borthwick Cheney, the wife of a client, and then living with her at Taliesin (constructed

1

in 1911) in Spring Green upon their return damaged his reputation further. Wright was devastated when a house servant murdered Mrs. Cheney and two of her children and set the living quarters of Taliesin on fire in 1914.

Soon thereafter he began a relationship with Miriam Noel, and despite its stormy nature the two were married in 1923, when Catherine finally granted her estranged husband a divorce. The relationship with Miriam Noel soured quickly, however, and nasty, protracted divorce proceedings followed.

During the proceedings Wright was attracted to Olgivanna Lazovich Hinzenberg, who was also awaiting a divorce. In 1925 she and her daughter Svetlana came to live with him at Taliesin, and the same year she gave birth to their daughter Iovanna. That happy moment in their relationship apparently inspired Miriam Noel to make the divorce proceedings even nastier. Meanwhile, disaster struck again: faulty wiring started a fire that completely destroyed the living quarters of Taliesin. By the time Frank Lloyd Wright and Olgivanna Lazovich Hinzenberg were finally free to marry in 1928, they had been virtually homeless for several years.[1]

Although Mr. and Mrs. Wright found love, companionship, and stability in their relationship, the arrival of the Great Depression dampened prospects for a speedy recovery of Wright's architectural practice. "This was a terrible time in his life," Bruce Pfeiffer observed. "He had no work, and what work he had was not built. . . . His home was taken away from him. He had no place to work for a long period of time. Imagine [being] an architect with no place to put your own drawing board. He wrote to one of his clients: 'We are cutting up bedsheets for handkerchiefs because we haven't had new clothes in four years.'" "The poverty they were living in" Bruce said, "was dreadful." Were they doomed to perpetual poverty?

A realist might have considered turning to another career. For Wright, lecturing and writing held possibilities. He had been doing both as early as the 1890s. In 1927 and 1928 he published nine articles in *The Architectural Record,* separately subtitled but all titled "In the Cause of Architecture," a heading he had used as early as 1908. In 1931 he published "Modern Architecture: Being the Kahn Lectures," which he had delivered at Princeton University. The next year he produced a work he had begun five years earlier at Mrs. Wright's urging: books 1, 2, and 3 of *An Autobiography,* his most influential work. The same year, in *The Disappearing City,* he laid out plans for Broadacre City, his conception of an ideal community, and articles continued to flow from his mind and pen.[2]

He might also have considered retirement. After all, he turned sixty-five that year, and his amazingly productive life had assured him a prominent place in the history of American architecture. But retirement was unthinkable. Besides, Mrs. Wright was thirty years his junior. Neither of them was ready for an inactive life. Instead, they conceived a plan for working with young people—an apprenticeship program at Taliesin in rural Wisconsin, their home. In book 5 of *An Autobiography*[3] Wright recalled the origins of the Taliesin Fellowship in a section headed, quite romantically, "A Station for the Flight of the Soul":

Many times before, in desperate circumstances (perhaps because of them) came an Idea. I, too, can get a bad idea—but not this time. The now subjective promise came to its object as the idea? No buildings to build at the harrowing moment but, capitalizing thirty-five years of past experience, why not build the builders of buildings against the time when buildings might again be built?

"After talking the 'idea' over," Wright continues, "a son of Wisconsin Welsh pioneers and a daughter of Montenegrin dignitaries aiming to be educators" sent a circular letter in the summer of 1932 to a small list of friends. Frank Lloyd Wright and a number of competent assistants, the letter said, would be in residence at Taliesin and would lead the work of "a new Fellowship of Apprentices." This would be, he continued, a rational attempt to coordinate art and industry with everyday life. Such an attempt "must be *essential architecture* growing up by way of social, industrial, and economic processes natural to our way of life."

Organic architecture would be the basis, the integrating ideal of the new community. As the Wrights saw it, organic architecture incorporated "the very qualities most basic and worthwhile in Philosophy, Sculpture, Painting, Music, and the Industrial Crafts. Principles underlying life and the arts are the same. So it is the Architecture of Life itself that must be the fundamental and therefore first concern of any true culture anywhere if the world is to be made safe for Science."

To begin again at the beginning in the study of architecture, according to Wright, required what Taliesin had to offer: daily life, in the country rather than the city, in which all experiences and inspirations come together to produce learning—all directed toward creating "new forms needed by machine work and modern processes if we are to have any culture of our own worth having." The Fellowship, in other words, would be "a kind of daily work-life."

What would it be like? Life would be simple:

> Meals in common. Fixed hours for work, recreation, and sleep. Each worker will have his or her room for study and rest. Suitable toilet accommodations will be made convenient to all rooms. Entertainment too will be a feature of our life at home. . . . Fellowship work in its manifold branches will come directly under the influence of an organic philosophy: organic architecture for organic life. . . .
>
> *Apprenticeship* not *Scholarship* is to be the actual condition and should be the attitude of mind of the Fellowship. . . . There will be no age limit for apprentices but the qualifications of each will be decided finally by Mr. Wright after a month's trial in the Fellowship work. . . . The Fellowship . . . is not on trial. The apprentice is.

Each member of the Fellowship would be engaged in the daily work of necessary maintenance. No matter that the laboratories, machine shops, draughting room, studios, and galleries had yet to be built—building them would be the first experiments in architectural construction and design. There was more to come: the study of the philosophy of architecture and typographical design, the printing of a Fellowship publication, molding and casting, woodworking, the "collateral study of philosophy and the practice of sculpture, painting, drama and rhythm, . . . glass-making, pottery, weaving, modern reproduction processes in any form we may be able to establish."

How would they establish them? "We believe that businessmen in industry will find it worthwhile to cooperate with us in setting up these crafts."

There would be no diplomas, no degrees—only a "personal testimonial" to be given to each worker at the end of his or her apprenticeship.

And how would they pay for it? The "sustaining revenue of the Fellowship for the next several years must come mainly from apprenticeship fees and maintenance work, four hours each day, of the apprentices." There might be added architect's fees, compensation from industries for services rendered, the sale of complete art objects, and a Fellowship publication, and maybe there would be funds coming from "Friends of the Fellowship," not yet organized.

Then this: "A BUSINESS-LIKE ORGANIZATION will manage the affairs of the FELLOWSHIP. [Note: This was never established because not needed.]"[4] As those present at the creation testify, Wright handled the Fellowship's finances out of his pocket, which was apparently turned inside out much of the time.

A fantasy? Unrealistic? Too ambitious? According to Wright:

> No sooner was this ambitious scheme proposed than we abandoned it. After sending out the circular we decided we would do better to stick to what we already had than to go too far institutional or "educational." I had certain qualifications; Olgivanna had others to add to mine. So we put our heads, as well as our hearts, together, simplified it all to come within our immediate capacities, so we thought, and wisely cut down possible membership to twenty-three. But the foregoing text—text by no means simple enough—was nevertheless sent out. It had the effect we hoped for and intended. Twenty-three young men and women brought twenty-three times six hundred and fifty dollars—one year each—to work it out at Taliesin. And a fair cross-section of Young America assembled there October 1, 1932, eager to go to work at something—ill prepared for anything except academic study of some sort. Least of all for the Freedom Taliesin had to offer.[5]

How did it work?

> As the plan for the Taliesin Fellowship unfolded itself, I had hoped that apprentices—like the fingers on my hands—would increase not only my own interest and enthusiasm for my work as an architect, but would also widen my capacity to apply it in the field. The first came true. But the second, as yet, is a temporarily frustrated hope. We somewhat overshot the mark. But I have not yet given up hope. We are steadily improving.[6]

While work continued in the Taliesin studio, some of it devoted to designing and building the model for the Broadacre City project (characterized by Neil Levine as "a kind of private WPA program to provide work for the Taliesin Fellows during the

Cornelia Brierly
working on model of
Broadacre City.

Depression"[7]), the dearth of executed projects continued until 1934. That helps explain the excitement that came with the construction of the home for Edgar J. Kaufmann, Sr., at Bear Run, Pennsylvania, in 1935. Wright's apprentices played a large part in preparing the drawings and building it. Known as Fallingwater, this stunning home is on every list of architectural masterpieces in America. In 1936 came the administration building for the Johnson Wax Company in Racine, Wisconsin; the Paul R. Hanna residence in Palo Alto, California; the Herbert Jacobs residence (a low-cost structure with floor heating and prefabricated walls) near Madison, Wisconsin; and the Abby Beecher Roberts residence in Marquette, Michigan.[8]

From then until his death in 1959, Wright's studio, while not always overflowing with work, maintained a steady schedule of designs and executions. Several of his most notable designs—the Guggenheim Museum in New York, the Marin County Center in California, the Grady Gammage Auditorium at Arizona State University in Tempe, Arizona, and Monona Terrace in Madison, Wisconsin, for example—were completed after his death (the last of them in 1997). The men and women trained in his studio continue to produce designs based on principles of organic architecture. William Wesley Peters provided leadership in the studio and at project sites for more than three decades. His wife Svetlana, the Wrights' daughter, was killed, along with the younger of their two sons, in a tragic automobile accident in Spring Green in 1946.

More important, though, in perpetuating the romantics' dream were the extraordinary competence, character, charisma, and hard work of Olgivanna Wright. Because she lived until 1985, memories of experiences with her remain vivid among

Mr. and Mrs. Wright
with daughters Svetlana
and Iovanna, and
son-in-law Wes Peters.

many Taliesin Fellows, and, as their stories attest, her influence in their lives was immeasurable.

Mrs. Wright's role had of course been important from the beginning, for if the studio was Wright's domain, the Fellowship was hers. *An Autobiography* includes many references to her and the Fellowship. For example: "Olgivanna felt that the Fellowship—looking like the wrath of God during the week—should wash itself behind the ears, put on raiment for Sunday evenings and try to find its measure and its manners." Another reference cites her role in helping young people who were "suddenly dropped into a world of interior discipline, yet without a rule written down."[9]

Romantics though they were, the Wrights did not create the Fellowship out of mere imagination. Both had had experiences that prepared them for the discipline of living in a community and providing leadership in it. Mrs. Wright had been a disciple of Georgi Ivanovitch Gurdjieff, a mystic philosopher, the son of a Greek father and an Armenian mother. She met him in Russia at the beginning of the 1917 revolution there, and she and others migrated with Gurdjieff to Istanbul and from there to France.[10]

Gurdjieff promulgated his organic philosophy at the Institute for the Harmonious Development of Man in Fontainebleau, near Paris. The artists and intellectuals Gurdjieff attracted participated in the rigorous physical and mental activities of the Institute. Cooking, household duties, construction work, and gardening complemented their ritual exercises, called "Movements." These were dances Gurdjieff derived from Kashgar, Chitral, and Tibet during his travels and studies there.[11] Mrs. Wright studied and taught for four years at the Institute before coming to the United States.

Georgi Ivanovitch Gurdjieff

A Gurdjieff thread runs through the Taliesin story from the Fellowship's founding to the present, although usually it has been woven so subtly into the story's fabric as to make it virtually indiscernible to external observers. In our interviews, a number of the fellows referred to Gurdjieff's influence on Mrs. Wright and the Fellowship, but by the 1990s that influence seemed largely to be a memory rather than an active force. It was not always so.

Frank Lloyd Wright, recalling his initial encounter with Olgivanna, said that he had heard about Gurdjieff's Institute for the Harmonious Development of Man before the "Asiatic savant brought his group to New York . . . and performed remarkable studies in human correlation at Carnegie Hall." From Olgivanna he learned more about Gurdjieff's remarkable training methods. The Institute, Wright said, "took unrhythmical neurotic human beings in all the social stratas, took them apart, and put them together again better correlated, happier, more alive and useful to themselves and others." Olgivanna was one of the "star leaders in the teachings Gurdjieff had promulgated and was preaching." Olgivanna's description of experience with Gurdjieff, he noted, was a fascinating revelation, and "she seemed to approve and like what I had to say about it. Between us across that tea table went more from each to each than I can ever describe."[12]

One of Gurdjieff's visits to Taliesin during the Fellowship's early years prompted Wright to remark in an "At Taliesin" column that there is "only one Gurdjieff. . . . He rather impressed me as being something of a Walt Whitman in Oriental terms." The writer of another "At Taliesin" column in 1934 reported that "Taliesin was much honored last Sunday by the visit of Georgi Gurdjieff. . . . In the evening we heard some of his music and the introduction to the vast series of books which he has written. His powerful personality affected us all strangely. It seemed as though we had an oriental Buddha come to life in our midst."[13]

Who was he? Michel de Salzmann says that Gurdjieff, who was a near contemporary of Frank Lloyd Wright (1877?–1949) resembled "more the figure of a Zen patriarch or a Socrates than the familiar image of a Christian mystic." Those who knew Gurdjieff, he says, regarded him as "an incomparable 'awakener' of men" who brought to the West "a comprehensive model of esoteric knowledge and left behind him a school embodying a specific methodology for the development of consciousness." Such consciousness required a "harmonious blending of the distinctive energies of mind, feeling, and body." His teachings, no doubt made more appealing to some by his exceptional personal character and demeanor, attracted leading artists and intellectuals to the Institute, located at Fontainebleau after moving from Russia because of the revolution there. Gurdjieff had a genius, says de Salzmann, for "using every circumstance of life as a means for helping his pupils feel the whole truth about themselves."

Gurdjieff was a prolific writer and lecturer, as well as a designer of dances, known as "movements" or "correlations." He was also a composer, in collaboration with Thomas de Hartman; much of his music was used to accompany the dances. According to de Salzmann, misleading accounts of his work "overshadowed the integrity of his ideas, . . . [but his] teaching has emerged out of this background of rumor and innuendo to be recognized as one of the most penetrating spiritual teachings of modern times." Foundations and societies perpetuate his work in many cities around the world.[14] The Taliesin Fellowship is associated with none of them, and there are no references to the Wrights or Taliesin in Gurdjieff's writings.

Mrs. Wright shared her husband's view that learning and doing were inseparable. By living close to nature and learning by doing, apprentices would master not only architecture, but also farming and building and, perhaps most important, how to work hard in adverse conditions.

Wright had long held unconventional ideas on life and learning. In his home and studio in Oak Park, Illinois, apparently influenced by the English Arts and Crafts Movement at the turn of the century, he integrated work and family life in one dwelling, as he was to do also with the Taliesin Fellowship.[15] The Hillside Home School near Taliesin—operated by his aunts from 1886 to 1915 and for which he had designed buildings in 1902—provided an idea and a setting for a Hillside Home School of the Allied Arts, conceived by the Wrights in 1928 and proposed in 1931. The ambitious program they outlined was intended "to harmonize the spirit of art and the spirit of the machine" in a setting where students would "get their own living as far as possible from the ground itself."[16] Despite the conceptual appeal of the proposal and the illustrious teachers the school was to have, financial support failed to materialize. The proposal was abandoned, but not the idea behind it.[17]

The Taliesin Fellowship proposed in 1932 reflected Wright's antipathy to academic institutions and practices. His writings, laced with denunciations of policies and practices of colleges and universities, convey a sense that no good thing could come out of such institutions. His Fellowship would eschew all their iniquities. There would be no course of study, no advancement by grades, no grading of work done, no granting of credits, no transcripts, no professors, no students, no degrees. Even though he and Mrs. Wright were teachers in everything they did, teaching in any formal sense was not part of the plan.

A Taliesin Evening with the Wrights, guests, and apprentices (1938).

But theirs was no negative vision for Taliesin. Its positive elements are evident in Wright's summary of the "Fellowship's Assets" in book 5 of his *An Autobiography*:

    I. An honest ego in a healthy body—good correlation
    II. Love of truth and nature
    III. Sincerity and courage
    IV. Ability for action
    V. The esthetic sense
    VI. Appreciation of work as idea and idea as work
    VII. Fertility of imagination
    VIII. Capacity for faith and rebellion
    IX. Disregard for commonplace (inorganic) elegance
    X. Instinctive cooperation

These human attributes of the Fellowship when inspired by love will eventually evoke THE CREATIVE CONSCIENCE.[18]

While the Taliesin Fellowship was surely distinctive, the nature of fellowship life placed it in the tradition of American and worldwide experiments in community building. Although H. Darin-Drabkin focuses on kibutzim in Israel, his study titled *The Other Society* looks beyond them to discover the basic reasons accounting for communal enterprises.[19] Man, he says, is a cooperative animal in whom there exists a strong urge for social behavior and cooperation. Mr. and Mrs. Wright found ways to capitalize upon such urges, which they shared.

Further, says Darin-Drabkin, people have always wished for equality and for a society based on justice. No doubt this was an implicit motive of the Taliesin Fellowship's founders, although the two of them, as was so often the case with charismatic founders of communities, were intrinsically more equal than others.

Third, economic hardships compel people to come together. Founded as it was during the Depression, this no doubt played a part, but apprentices continued to be attracted to the Fellowship even in the years of national post war prosperity.

Fourth, communal life helps combat threats of physical extinction and lack of security. At the time of the Fellowship's founding, there was little prospect that architects would become extinct, but there was a considerable lack of economic security. Some who came to Taliesin were men and women of very limited means, and the Fellowship provided them with a haven from personal economic distress, although the Fellowship itself has always stood on the edge of poverty.

Milestones. To place the events mentioned in the stories that follow in their larger context, it is useful to be aware of milestones in the lives of the Wrights and the Fellowship, in addition to those already mentioned. A listing of such milestones appears in appendix A.

As the years passed, the romantic character that prevailed in the first decades quite naturally gave way to modern times, signs of which included not so much the installation of electricity and the telephone at Taliesin West as other matters in the list of milestones, particularly the quest for accreditation, adoption of the constitution and bylaws, the practice of holding regularly scheduled meetings, and employing persons from outside the Fellowship to direct essential parts of the Frank Lloyd Wright Foundation.

Dynamics. What has made the place run? The answer to this question for the Fellowship's first fifty years is not in doubt. "Mrs. Wright," says Tom Casey, "made the Fellowship run on a day-to-day basis. All of its organizational structure and all of the fine tuning of what we now have as the work list and how jobs are delegated and so on . . . is Mrs. Wright's work."

"Both Mr. and Mrs. Wright were benevolent dictators," remarked Richard Carney, who was to become her successor as the chief executive officer of the Frank Lloyd Wright Foundation, "and so if I had an idea or Mrs. Wright had an idea all Mrs. Wright had to do was say, 'Do it.' And then I could go and tell everybody that Mrs. Wright said we were going to do this. So we would do it."

Why would such authoritarian practices be tolerated? In part because Fellows and apprentices knew that without Mrs. Wright, the Fellowship would not have existed, so they were indebted to her. But admiration for her played a larger part. That admiration is evident in many of the interviews.

How has the situation changed? Since the death of Mrs. Wright, power and authority have been shared, and other changes, some that she had initiated before her death, have by now become a part of the place:

- Decisions are made by consensus or through voting.
- Responsibilities are assumed by members that might formerly have been suggested or delegated by Mr. or Mrs. Wright.
- Persons representing interests of the public play a part in the governance processes.
- External sanctions, such as those gained through accreditation, affect educational and other decisions.
- Economic necessities dictate other decisions, such as opening the gates to increased numbers of tourists, allowing facilities to be used by external groups, and licensing reproduction of Wright's designs.
- The nature of the Fellowship continues to evolve as a result of the aging and deaths of senior fellows and the arrival of apprentices with postmodern temperaments.
- This evolution makes it necessary to employ persons who are neither Fellows nor apprentices.
- The diminishing influence of the deceased founders compels those who bear their legacy to find new ways to sustain it.
- Concern for perpetuation of the work of Frank Lloyd Wright inspires publications, exhibitions, a design-licensing program, and public outreach efforts.

- Being surrounded by housing developments threatens to make Taliesin West a desert island, requiring new ways of dealing with the encroachment on the once-isolated environment.
- Costly maintenance of buildings at the two Taliesins requires intense efforts at fund-raising and makes collaboration with public entities attractive.
- Development of cordial relations between the Taliesin Fellows—now recognized as the Taliesin's alumni association—and the resident Fellows and apprentices makes possible cooperation and increases the base of support for the Frank Lloyd Wright Foundation. The sixtieth anniversary celebration in 1992 contributed substantially to the rapprochement between the parties, and the sixty-fifth in 1997 had similar effects.
- The president and chief executive officer of the Frank Lloyd Wright Foundation, who did not come up through the ranks of the Fellowship, bears responsibility for its administrative functions.

Arnold Roy, one of the fellows, put his finger on some of the magic of Taliesin's dynamics by recalling a talk Wright gave at Hillside about his interaction with the younger people in the Fellowship, how he [himself] got so much out of it. "Mr. Wright said, to this effect, 'I am nothing without you, and you are nothing without me, and we need one another.' He got an awful lot of energy out of young people."

Character. The character of Taliesin was shaped by Mr. and Mrs. Wright and perpetuated by Mrs. Wright for twenty-five years after her husband's death. Observers of the Fellowship must ask how the changes in recent years have affected the character of Taliesin. Indeed, what is the character of Taliesin, and how will new developments affect the reshaping of Taliesin's character? The Fellows offer a variety of answers to these questions in the interviews.

Plot. This book unfolds the plot of the Taliesin Fellowship, but only implicitly. If the story of the Taliesin Fellowship is ever told in full, it will emerge in more explicit terms. At the moment, the Fellowship is considering alternative scenarios for the future. In any event, its story will have either an interesting continuation or possibly a final act on the way to transformation into something new.[20]

"The whole gamut of human experience." Frank Lloyd Wright, according to Tom Casey,
"was someone whom you saw every day. He came to work in the studio virtually every day of his life. And there he was, working, and he'd come and sit at your desk to see what you were doing. . . . This was not the remote genius who walked in and threw it down on the table and said, 'Take it or leave it, this is it.' That's the characterization farthest away from the truth. . . . You know, if he was this remote person, how come so many people were attracted, and why did they come and stay? . . . This is not some cult of exotic, religious belief or something; it's a working organization, a day-to-day kind of thing. You have wonderful times; you have very lively, interesting times. You have sad times, you have happy times, you have the whole gamut of human experience."

Notes

1. Bruce Brooks Pfeiffer, ed., *Frank Lloyd Wright Collected Writings,* vol. 1 (New York: Rizzoli, in association with the Frank Lloyd Wright Foundation, 1992), 19, inter alia.

2. These writings and many others appear in the five volumes of *Frank Lloyd Wright Collected Writings,* ed. Bruce Brooks Pfeiffer (New York: Rizzoli, in association with the Frank Lloyd Wright Foundation, 1992–5). The classic 1943 edition of *Frank Lloyd Wright: An Autobiography* (New York: Barnes & Noble, 1998), was recently published as an authentic facsimile.

3. When Mr. Wright revised *An Autobiography* and added to it in 1943 he divided the original book 1 into two books, which explains why the first of the new books was numbered Five.

4. *Collected Writings,* vol. 4, 129–32. A description of Fellowship life continues to p. 177.

5. *Collected Writings,* vol. 4, 132. The fee was increased to $1,100 the following year. The full text of the 1932 Taliesin Fellowship brochure appears in Bruce Brooks Pfeiffer, ed., *Letters to Apprentices: Frank Lloyd Wright* (Fresno: California State University Press, 1982), 3–7. This volume also includes the brochure composed after Taliesin West was established and used until Mr. Wright's death in 1959 (38–9).

6. Pfeiffer, *Letters,* 134.

7. Neil Levine, *The Architecture of Frank Lloyd Wright* (Princeton: Princeton University Press, 1996), 220.

8. The bibliography includes the titles of a number of books containing information about buildings designed by Frank Lloyd Wright. The most comprehensive, featuring pictures and floor plans, is William Allin Storrer, *The Frank Lloyd Wright Companion* (Chicago: University of Chicago Press, 1993). A chronological listing of the buildings and projects of Frank Lloyd Wright appears in Robert McCarter, *Frank Lloyd Wright–Architect* (London: Phaidon Press Ltd., 1997).

9. *Collected Writings,* vol. 4, 146, 149.

10. Randolph C. Henning, *"At Taliesin": Newspaper Columns by Frank Lloyd Wright and the Taliesin Fellowship, 1934–1937* (Carbondale: Southern Illinois University Press, 1992), xii–xiii. For a detailed treatise of the Gurdjieffian influence on the Wrights and the Taliesin Fellowship, see Robert C. Twombly, "Organic Living: Frank Lloyd Wright's Taliesin Fellowship and Georgi Gurdjieff's Institute for the Harmonious Development of Man," *Wisconsin Magazine of History* (Winter, 1974–75).

11. *"At Taliesin,"* xiii.

12. "An Autobiography, Book Five: Form," *Collected Writings,* vol. 4, 205.

13. *"At Taliesin,"* 64–5.

14. Michel de Salzmann, in Mircea Eliade, editor-in-chief, *The Encyclopedia of Religion* (New York: Macmillan, 1987), 139–40. For a detailed treatise on the Gurdjieffian influence on the Wrights and the Taliesin Fellowship, see Twombly, "Organic Living," 126–39. See also Donald Leslie Johnson, *Frank Lloyd Wright versus America: The 1930s* (Cambridge: MIT Press, 1990), 5–9, 304–13. Anthony Alofsin identifies experiences earlier in Wright's life that revealed his susceptibility to the ideas of Gurdjieff and a Gurdjieff disciple. Wright and Mamah Borthwick Cheney, his mistress from 1909 until 1914, were attracted to the work of

the American dramatist Richard Hovey and the Swedish feminist Ellen Key, both of whose work bore mystical qualities. See Anthony Alofsin, "Taliesin: 'To Fashion Worlds in Little,'" *Wright Studies,* vol. 1: *Taliesin 1911–1914* (Carbondale: Southern Illinois University Press, 1992), 44–65.

15. Levine, *The Architecture,* 25.

16. Quoted by Levine, *The Architecture,* 218.

17. *Collected Writings,* vol. 3, 39ff.

18. *Collected Writings,* vol. 4, 176.

19. H. Darin-Drabkin, *The Other Society* (New York: Harcourt, Brace & World, 1962), 16–18.

20. See the foreword in Donald E. Pitzer, ed., *America's Communal Utopias* (Chapel Hill: University of North Carolina Press, 1997). The present work reflects what Pitzer, a leading historian of communal societies, calls "developmental communalism." It takes into account the evolution of the Taliesin Fellowship, from its idealistic yet practical origins to the gradual institutionalization of structures and practices that had existed informally during the lifetime of its charismatic founders. By making changes, many of them identified in these pages, the Fellowship has sought to avoid stagnation and to continue as a vital community. See also Pitzer's essay, "Developmental Communalism: An Alternative Approach to Communal Studies," in Dennis Hardy and Lorna Davidson, eds., *Utopian Thought and Communal Experience* (Middlesex Polytechnic: Geography and Planning Paper no. 24, 1989), 68–76.

2

Coming to Taliesin:
"A Place Designed for the Soul"

W*hy did you come to this community? That is frequently the first question visitors ask members of intentional communities, and it is a natural opener in conversations with members of the Taliesin Fellowship. They might all respond with a question in turn: Where else can you live and work in such distinctive buildings and commune daily with the genius who built them?*

Philip Johnson, speaking to other architects in 1957, paid an affectionate but candid tribute to Frank Lloyd Wright, a man with whom he had had a love-hate relationship. Johnson's talk, transcribed in his Writings, *takes readers on a vivid tour of Taliesin West. He captures its earthy majesty and the emotions it awakens in those walking through it. Johnson urged his listeners to visit there "before [Wright] is gone. He is as brilliant and cantankerous and magnificent as ever. But the spirit will go out of the place when he is gone."*

Earlier in his talk, Johnson sympathized with Wright's apprentices: "Have you ever heard him talk about his own disciples, those poor children who sweat over the garbage pails at Taliesin East and Taliesin West year in and year out? . . . I am second to none in those who admire his architecture in those two houses, but he treats them like slaves."[1]

Johnson was not the only one who mused over the mixed picture of Taliesin's attraction. Jenkin Lloyd Jones, the son of Mr. Wright's cousin Richard Lloyd-Jones and a visitor at Taliesin in its early days, wrote this in a letter to a Fellowship member several years ago:

> *Slave labor has been outlawed in the United States since 1863, and here was slave labor with refinements undreamed of by Simon Legree. Not only were the young laborers paid nothing for growing food crops and restoring buildings in advanced states of decay but they were charged for the privilege. . . . I saw them consume concentration camp cuisine. In spite of gross exploitation they gathered worshipfully around their two gurus, male and female, and the talk was not only stratospheric but often incomprehensible to me.[2]*

Many of those whom Mr. Wright allegedly treated as slaves have worked tirelessly to keep the spirit of the Taliesins alive. If they felt at times like slaves, it was voluntary servitude, something to joke about, and their admiration and respect for their master was in no sense diminished by the way he treated them. Their responses to the question, "Why did you come to Taliesin?" include similar themes, despite their distinctive personalities and circumstances.

John deKoven Hill came to Taliesin in 1937. I asked Johnny, as he was known, how he had learned about Taliesin.

JOHNNY: I can tell you quickly. I was in my senior year in high school, and I had enrolled at the University of Virginia. It was one of the good architectural schools. . . . Also, I had some good partying and drinking companions who were going there, too (it was supposed to be a good party school). And then Dad, who knew Hib Johnson in Racine, came home from a trip and told me that Frank Lloyd Wright was doing a building for Johnson Wax, and also he understood he took students. So I then decided that I would have to forget about classical architecture, which was really all I knew, and face a modern world; and I dreaded it because I thought it would be like the 1932 World's Fair in Chicago. But I thought, "This is the year I'm in, I'm going to have to like it—stainless steel and white formica and all of that—and I better just learn."

So I called Taliesin. I got Gene Masselink [Mr. Wright's secretary].[3] What I learned later [was that it was] the night he was leaving for Arizona, everybody else having gone, the water turned off and everything, so he forgot all about sending me anything. Dad was in Tucson that winter, and he came up to Jokake Inn here (which was across the valley) where Mr. and Mrs. Wright were staying, waiting until the Fellowship could recover from Christmas holidays and get down here.

My father was with the business department of the Curtis Publishing Company in Chicago. He . . . also worked with [Mortimer] Adler at the University of Chicago

John deKoven Hill

on the Great Books, and it's a long story there. . . . That was the kind of work he belonged in.

Then, after about a year of that, he realized there was no reason why he and Mother should be in Chicago at all, and they took an apartment down here. He gave up the Great Books thing and concentrated on building up some stocks and something to live on. Meantime, he went up to see Mr. Wright at Christmas time in '37, and he called me in the middle of the night and said, "I don't know whether you'll learn anything about how to conduct an architecture career, but a year or two with those people would be wonderful for anybody." This was Mr. and Mrs. Wright both, collectively. "And I've enrolled you," he said.

Mr. Wright couldn't see why I couldn't come right away, but Dad told him I was the editor of the high school newspaper, and Mr. Wright said, "Well, social obligations—that's different." So my arrival was postponed until high school graduation in May, and then when I came to Wisconsin Mr. and Mrs. Wright were in England. So I was there for a couple of weeks without having seen them yet. However, the place was so beautiful; I felt as though I had come home. I had no idea anything like that was in the world. It had all the loveliness of the Georgian mossy brick and all of that, plus something. It was ageless. It was falling down in places, but it was really . . . it's a place designed for the soul and the emotions, not for comfort. I cried. I just couldn't believe what I had gotten into.

You were eighteen years old at the time?

Seventeen. When Mr. and Mrs. Wright got back (they came on a midnight train, from Chicago to Spring Green), as a new one I hung around in the background, in the shadows, but everybody (that was maybe twenty-three, twenty-four people then) was in the little studio at Taliesin to greet them. And they came through. I have never seen anything in the theater as dramatic as that sight of them, beautifully dressed, full of vitality, good-looking beyond any understanding of the word (because of what was inside them, I guess). They came into the room and did all of the things . . . responded to everybody—except me who was hiding, and some got kissed . . . but it was very fast, and on through.

Kay Rattenbury, who came to the Fellowship in 1935, also had a passing acquaintance with Mr. and Mrs. Wright. In this excerpt from an interview conducted by Indira Berndtson and Greg Williams, she describes the unusual circumstances that brought her to Taliesin. Her father was an inventor who had come to the United States after World War I. Her mother remained in Europe and her father remarried. As she recalled recuperating from an automobile accident in which she was injured—she had been riding with another person from Taliesin—she explained why she liked the attention she received.

KAY: I'd never had that attention in my life because my mother and father ignored me since I was seven years old and I was on my own. My mother was traipsing around Europe; my father was in Annapolis designing the diesel engines, designing the submarine engines for the Navy. He'd fly home and I'd help him. If I was home—this was before I came to Taliesin—I was home alone out in the country (we always lived in the country). I would help him pack and I'd say, "You'll be late for the plane, you'll be late for the plane."

I learned to drive when I was twelve. . . . When I was thirteen I had the first car with an automatic transmission, which was my father's invention. All it had was a gas pedal, a brake, and a button for reverse. The gears were perfect; there were no gears to shift in the car. But the war came along. They were producing the transmission at Warner Gear, which was in Muncie, Indiana, and my father was negotiating with Henry Ford, Edsel Ford, Chrysler, and General Motors. General Motors had their own inventor; Ford stole all his inventions and Chrysler . . . I think he was going to buy my father's invention. He also had meetings with Henry Kaiser and Turner. But the war came along and his main job was building the submarine, then mass producing them. And for that he got $1,000 a day, which at that time (that was in the 40s and early 50s) was a lot of money.

But he forgot about me. Being a genius, as he was, he completely forgot about me. He never sent me any money. The only way I ever got any money was through Viva [his second wife] whom Mrs. Wright persuaded to send me an allowance of $25 a month. And she soon forgot that, so Mrs. Wright bought my clothes and supported me with her own small income. So, when I got money [later], all I could do was pay her back for everything she'd done for me all those years.

Do you have sisters?

Yes. . . . Viva had two children who lived with us before she married my father, which was a big scandal and they had to get out of town. Almost at the same time that John

Kay Rattenbury

[Rattenbury]'s family had also the big scandal because of his father's divorce and his second wife. Also, Mr. and Mrs. Wright's scandal was at about the same time. So at that time divorce was an unheard-of scandal, and everybody was put out of work, put out of town, just absolutely mistreated terribly. It was a terrible time—the conventions were so awful. And we all went through it practically at the same time.[4]

Viva brought me to Taliesin. Because she was A. D. German's daughter she had known Mr. Wright since she was seventeen. She had rescued me. I was home with the flu, and she had found me. My father was in Annapolis and my mother was in Europe, and I was home with a high fever. She took care of me and took me home to Richland Center. On the way back to Beloit where we had moved, where my father worked for Fairbanks Motors, she said, "Oh, Taliesin is just right on the road. Do you want to see it?" I said, "Oh, I certainly do." I'd heard Mr. Wright lecture when I was thirteen, and I had met Mr. and Mrs. Wright briefly through Viva, but I didn't know what Taliesin was or that Mr. Wright had a school. So we came to Taliesin and Mr. and Mrs. Wright were just coming out of the House. We came up the front steps and I fell in love with Taliesin. I thought, "This is my home!" Immediately.

I met Mr. and Mrs. Wright again [later], really for the first time at close proximity, where we talked. And I realized that Mr. Wright was a genius, because I'd grown up with a genius. They were very similar in their behavior; Mr. Wright also neglected his children and just devoted his life to his work.

All these things were familiar to me. Mrs. Wright was European; Svetlana [Mrs. Wright's daughter] was raised during the revolution in Russia. Her mother had to stand in line for oatmeal one day a week. I was raised in Germany during the revolution, with the Kaiser and the communists, with my father standing in line one day a week, in the German revolution. Because my father had been building U-boats in Germany in the First World War, he got caught. Although he was Swiss, we couldn't get out of Germany. So my mother and father were starving, and of course I was undernourished. I lived on tea and oatmeal once a week; that's all I lived on. Finally, we got a passport— my mother and I—to get out of Germany. They wouldn't let my father out, so we went to Switzerland and that's where I grew up.

Mention of Kay's arrival in an "At Taliesin" newspaper column provides an insight into how things happened there: "[A] new apprentice came to Taliesin from Beloit. Her name is Cornelia Schneider, but since we already have one Cornelia, we have adopted her as 'Kay.'" The writer was Cornelia Brierly.[5]

Susan Jacobs Lockhart also came to Taliesin as a result of experiences her family had had with Mr. Wright. She describes her entry into the Fellowship:

SUSAN: I am a daughter of clients of Frank Lloyd Wright. Frank Lloyd Wright has known me since I was three years old. I perhaps knew him at a much later date. My parents were always involved and included in all kinds of social activities and entertainments. My father was named by the Madison, Wisconsin, newspaper (*The Capital Times*) as *the* person to cover all Frank Lloyd Wright's activities. In fact, the day I was born my father was heading to Spring Green from Milwaukee, Wisconsin, where he was a new reporter with the *Milwaukee Journal*. He checked into the hospital to make sure that I wasn't going to appear and, being sure that I wasn't, headed to Spring Green to find out what was happening two years after the founding of the Taliesin Fellowship. Needless to say, I did not wait for him to get back. I appeared, and so, perhaps, the synchronicity of all that was the very beginning of my entering the Senior Fellowship.

I was invited by Mrs. Wright to spend some time during the summertimes and got to know the Fellowship's great diversity of activities. Obviously, I grew up in architecture; my parents made ends meet to support their architectural habit. They built two houses of Frank Lloyd Wright's.[6] My father was a journalist and always had minimal funds, so he wrote books, he wrote columns. We had hand-me-down clothes; we basically lived a life of architecture. So that part was very well developed.

The part of the actual community I got to know by coming and spending some time in it. I realized that all of those areas of the cultural arts, which, of course, were my sort of mainstream of interest, were alive and very active, as well as the architecture and the arts in an architectural context. When I had a chance [in 1958] to come back to Taliesin by invitation with my husband, I was working in New York. (I was married to David Wheatley at that time, who was also a fellow member.)[7] It was an opportunity to combine all those things that I was pursuing in single paths—like across the city to a civic chorus, to upstate New York piano lessons, and working uptown in a graphic publishing firm.

Susan Jacobs Lockhart

So, to come back to Taliesin was to come back to a holistic circumstance. That was my personal attachment; that was my personal entry point. I did everything that one does when one enters, because you don't enter simply and do only those things that you feel are your main interests in life.

Sometimes, as with Frances Nemtin, experiences in working with Mr. Wright and others from Taliesin provided the inducement to join the Fellowship.

FRANCES: I came here specifically as a result of an exhibition which I arranged for Mr. Wright's work in a museum in Milwaukee where I was director. I had the good fortune to become director of the Milwaukee Art Institute when I was very young; I came out to Milwaukee from the East as assistant to the director who left within four months of my arrival. To my utter dismay, he left for the Army or Navy, and I inherited the Art Institute, which was the predecessor of the present large art center.

When I had come from the East, Wisconsin to me had been synonymous with Mr. Wright, so one of the first things I suggested when I met with my exhibition committee, who helped me plan succeeding exhibitions, was to have a show of his. They were very encouraging, but the Board of Directors, who were stuffy businessmen but civic minded (that's why they were supporting the museum), were very discouraging, saying Mr. Wright wouldn't be interested. They didn't even think of proposing it. Of course, he had had unpleasant experiences in Milwaukee. But I persisted, and I had sufficient people who supported me. Finally, I was allowed to write him and ask his interest in having a show.

I was really dismayed when I had to sign my name to a letter that they composed, very pompous, long-winded (and I knew it wasn't his style). The upshot was that he responded in a three-sentence letter saying, "The idea interests me; we'll discuss it when we return to Wisconsin in the spring." That satisfied me but not them, of course. Anyhow, all subsequent exchanges with him confirmed my feeling about him. I felt more and more on his side, more than on the museum's side. Anyhow, finally the result was that we had a very beautiful big exhibition two years after I arrived. And it was so successful, bringing him commissions, bringing him lots of attention. He brought the whole Fellowship to Milwaukee to the large public lecture.

That would have been 1944 then, or 1945?

1945, November. And he sent four apprentices in to set it up for me. They were Kenn [Lockhart], whom I later married; Johnny Hill; Gene Masselink, a very gifted, wonderful person; and a fourth, Burt Goodrich.[8] They were all about the same age, from about the same time, and I was so impressed with their combination of artistic sensitivity, knowing how to arrange the show, as well as the fact they brought their hammers and nails and put it up for me. That combination of gifts I realized was integral to the Taliesin way of doing things.

In the meantime, I had spent Thanksgiving at Taliesin, as Mr. Wright's guest, and that was a wonderful experience. Snow was everywhere; icicles hung from the roofs; my room had a fireplace, and it was all very romantic, very beautiful. Previously, I had bicycled out from Madison to Spring Green with three friends that summer. That was my first glimpse of Taliesin.

Bicycled?

From Madison . . . two Madison friends, and a Milwaukee friend and I. That's a whole story in itself, how we walked in on a Saturday evening in our blue jeans and everyone was in formal clothes. Luckily we were not seen, because we were in the upstairs area of the theater and hid there until the guests left. And Gene was projecting the film that night. When he saw us he laughed and was very encouraging and said, "Come back in the morning and I'll show you all around."

But everything about my contact with Mr. Wright and Taliesin was an inevitable climax, the result of my previous life experience. And living here in this community was not a big adjustment for me, because I came from a large family, and we'd been very ingenious and flexible in our lives. We lived in India and had moved and had to adjust all the time and make our own entertainment.

You went to Bryn Mawr and majored in . . . ?

History of art, which, of course, gave me a lot of information on Mr. Wright from a very sympathetic professor.

Were you a Pennsylvanian?

No, after we came back from India we settled in Princeton. My family wanted to be in a university town, with all its advantages. My mother became known as the university

Frances Nemtin

mother; she took us to everything that was free, even if the lecture was in German. If it had slides on Dürer we went. We went to all the concerts, to everything, so we had wonderful exposure.

My father was a YMCA secretary, the international YMCA, and that was a wonderful childhood. In fact, my winter's project is putting my memories of our Kashmir summers in a formal little book for my siblings and my children.

Anyhow, I arrived here in February, in the middle of winter. One of my [museum] trustees was kind enough to arrange a ride west with his nieces who were driving to Phoenix. So I had a nice introduction to the West through them. And I arrived again in the middle of the night, again walking in on Saturday night in blue jeans. I remember the theater was that little room [known as the Kiva], and everyone was there at dinner sitting at stepped up rows of seats like bleachers, facing the movie screen, which was the space over the fireplace. I remember Mr. Wright always treated me very amusedly. He didn't like museums, but I guess he liked me. He was very kind to me about the fact I was from a museum.

[The exhibition] was an eye-opener to the city, and thousands of people came. More than had ever come to any show at that museum, and many people still remember that exhibition as very beautiful. It had many original drawings.

During the course of preparation for it, Mr. Wright called me several times with instructions. One time he said, "Ask Mrs. Boak (she's a client of mine) to lend you the rug I designed for her living room. It would look beautiful in the big gallery." And I gulped and called her, and she hesitated and said, "Just a minute, did Mr. Wright ask you to make this request?" I said, "Yes, he thought you might be willing to do it for him." She said, "Of course I will, but please have the rug cleaned before you return it." And so I sent out a man with a truck to get it and it was cream colored and very beautiful.

Another time he called to say, "Please call a florist shop and borrow or rent a cactus to decorate the part of the museum where you'll hang photographs of the western work, especially the Southwest." So I went out and got a cactus. Then he sent the trucks in—I think one was a semi full of the models and drawings. (I had previously gotten hold of the negatives from Gene and had large blowups made, 6'x8', 4'x6', of a lot of his buildings.) He also sent a pickup truck. Two other fellows drove in that, with a load of pine boughs and antimony to decorate the galleries.[9]

And just inside the front door he painted on the wall a red square with his initials across it, giving his approval. You know, whenever he finished a home he gave his clients a red tile with his initials. Long after the show we didn't paint that over; we were so pleased to have that. And he came to Milwaukee several times to lecture. I arranged to have two talks at the museum for the members and one talk downtown for the public. Those were all filled to capacity and so exciting.

. . . I think it was the first show he'd allowed for several years, so it was important to him. The most important result of that show (aside from my coming here) was not realized. It happened to coincide with the city starting to think of having a big art center and there would also be a war memorial. And I privately hoped that one result of this show would be that he'd be given that commission. And that was in his mind, too, and we were both very disappointed when subsequently it was announced that Saarinen would design that building. I found out later why Saarinen was chosen. One of the board members had been a resident of Detroit from the wealthy Booth family who had been the benefactors of Cranbrook where Saarinen was. So, she was influential in persuading the city fathers to go to Saarinen, her favorite. But that was one disappointment. . . . No one really likes [the design]. It's on the lakeshore, and it could have been a very great asset. It's not even very functional; it's very ugly. That was a big dismay to us.

So then, Mr. Wright invited you to come to be part of the Fellowship?

No, it was my idea. It occurred to me during the course of the show that I had become much more drawn to Taliesin as a place to live and work. I was a big fish in a big pond in a way. I had a very wonderful job for a young woman. I was probably the youngest museum director in the country and certainly one of very few women, but I more and more became attracted to the idea of [the Taliesin] way of life. And so, I tried to find a chance to speak to Mr. Wright and ask if it would be possible for me to come. And time slipped by. As he was putting this in the museum he was always besieged by people—reporters and clients and students and people asking questions.

But a chance didn't come till after he left the museum. I ran after him out into the street. It was snowy, and I just tugged on his sleeve and [said], "Mr. Wright, I have to speak to you. Can I join Taliesin?" He wheeled around and said, "Certainly, come along. We're leaving for Arizona in three weeks. I think you'd be a good addition." As simple as that. I was glad I had found the courage to be as direct as I knew he was.

I went back to the museum in the lobby where all my friends were gathered, and they said, "Where did you go?" I said, "I went to see Mr. Wright and I'm leaving Milwaukee." Most of them didn't believe it, and one of them said, "Why would you want to do that?" One understood, and he said, "Congratulations." And he has remained a very dear friend.

Anyhow, I wasn't able to leave, of course, in three weeks. I had to wait until my predecessor returned from the navy, which took about six weeks or two months. He tried to persuade me to stay, saying, "We'd be a great team; you can be my assistant again." And I said, "Bert, I've had too much fun. I could not be your assistant again. My life is set in a new direction now." So, I told him what I'd planned for the next year or two and left. And I've been here ever since.

Bruce Pfeiffer, another Easterner, was drawn to Taliesin by vicarious experiences with Mr. Wright. A 1946 article in Life *magazine led him to Mr. Wright's* An Autobiography. *Bruce is the founder and director of the Frank Lloyd Wright Foundation Archives, but that is not what he had in mind when he came to Taliesin. I asked him whether he had come to Taliesin with the expectation of becoming an architect.*

BRUCE: Yes, but also I came here with the expectation of spending my life here.

How could you know that at eighteen or nineteen?

I knew it at sixteen, when I read *An Autobiography*. I said, "That's the life I want." I didn't want to stay in New England. I couldn't stand the living and the temperament, the very enclosed colonial life. It was very charming, but it wasn't for me. But I knew when I read the autobiography that's where I wanted to be. My family thought I was crazy. They sent me to psychiatrists to get that idea out of my head—as far south as Baltimore and New York and Boston.

Were they ever reconciled to your being here?

My mother, no; my father, yes. After I was here for six months my father came and liked Mr. and Mrs. Wright very much. He was a little afraid of them; I think he was a little afraid of their influence on me. But he said at breakfast the next morning to Mr. Wright, "I've never seen Bruce so happy in his life." And Mr. Wright said, "Well, Mr. Pfeiffer, Bruce is natural for Taliesin and Taliesin is natural for Bruce. You support him, and Mrs. Wright and I will raise him." And my father agreed with that. For my mother, who had only known me ten years, it was a little hard to take. But she was a very, very strict disciplinarian, which I think was good, good for me. (My father adopted me when I was two weeks old, and my mother married him when I was eight.)

Bruce Pfeiffer and Geronimo, his Doberman

I remember one time, I think my first summer in Wisconsin, I came into the loggia and Mrs. Wright came in. We got talking and I said, "You know, Mrs. Wright, it was really quite a wonderful coincidence that I found that August 12, 1946, issue of *Life* magazine which opened my life to Frank Lloyd Wright." And she said, "It was no accident. It was planned in the stars long before you were born." I looked a little surprised, and she said, "You're an architect, aren't you? Everything is according to plan."

What was it about the autobiography that drew you?

It was such romance. Here was a man . . . well, first of all, when I saw the photographs of the buildings in the magazine—here I am born and raised in a colonial environment—and the photographs I saw were Taliesin West, a building with rock walls and canvas ceiling and sheepskins and furniture like I'd never seen before in my life. It all appealed to me as the right thing.

And the magazine had a picture of Fallingwater and the Imperial Hotel. It wasn't a well-written article. Mr. Wright hated it, but at least it brought me here. Then I mentioned it to a friend of mine at school, and he said, "Well you should read the man's autobiography." And I just read everything I could find for two years.

Arnold Roy, who came to Taliesin in 1952, also discovered Mr. Wright as a high school student in the Boston area. How did he make his entry? "Like everything else about Taliesin," he said, "it's very simple but very complex."

ARNOLD: When I was still in high school (I remember this very clearly as if it just happened yesterday) I had an art teacher in ninth grade who was a frustrated architect. This was in one of the suburbs of Boston, North Quincy. One day she was discussing different architects, and she showed some slides of Taliesin in Wisconsin. Needless to say, I had never in my life seen any architecture anything like that, and my eyes just popped, almost like having a revelation. At that point, you know, I thought "What is this?" After class I went up and asked, "What is this you showed us?"

And so she told me about the American architect Frank Lloyd Wright, and she said "You should read this." So I immediately went down to the library, got whatever books I could on Frank Lloyd Wright and read and read and read. They would mention Louis Sullivan, so I got the book on Louis Sullivan, *An Autobiography of an Idea*, and I read that. This continued (I was just in the ninth grade), and I would read the books all the time. And finally one day I noticed in [Mr. Wright's] autobiography there was a facsimile of the application form to join the Taliesin Fellowship, and all of a sudden it occurred to me that there was a school there. I could go to Taliesin. I could study with this great man.

I was working after school, and then I worked for about a year after I got out of school to earn enough money to come to Taliesin. When I had enough money, I wrote a letter to Taliesin—it was in December, I think, '51. Then correspondence

Arnold Roy

back and forth, and finally the last correspondence said that Mr. and Mrs. Wright would be in New York at the Plaza, and [I thought], "Why don't I just call and make an appointment?"

About a year after [I was out of high school], I had earned enough money to come to Taliesin. So I called the Plaza and, naturally, Frank Lloyd Wright answered the phone. He said, "Young man, how can I help you?" I explained my problem, and he said, "Come on down tomorrow."

I'd never been on an airplane in my life. I got on the plane, flew down to New York, went to the Plaza. The Plaza at that time, when Frank Lloyd Wright was in residence, was sort of a circus, because outside in the hallway was the waiting room since there was none inside. There were clients and friends and people waiting to see Mr. and Mrs. Wright. Every so often the door would open and Mrs. Wright would come out, and whoever was next would come in and whoever was left would stay in the hall.

One of Mr. Wright's clients was there waiting, and I was there. I went in and there were Mr. and Mrs. Wright. We talked for a while. "Young man, what's your background?" I told Mr. Wright about my background and family. He said, "Hmm, black sheep, eh?" He was looking for some kind of cultural background and there wasn't any. My father was just a laborer, construction, a very humble background. My father is French Canadian and my mother had French Canadian parents. She was born in America; my father was naturalized.

But [the Wrights] were very willing to take in anyone who was sincere. Mrs. Wright said, "Okay, when you go to Arizona you're going to be living in a canvas tent." Of course I was from Boston. I said, "Sure." I got on the plane, tidied up affairs in Boston and flew out to Taliesin and, sure enough, I was living in a canvas tent. I thought, "This is what Mrs. Wright meant." I lived in a tent out in the desert for eight years. I loved it.

Joe Fabris, who had no prior connection with Mr. Wright, joined the Fellowship in 1948. He had studied chemistry in Canada and began working in a research lab with a defense center in Montreal just as World War II began. He had worked there about seven years but needed a change.

JOE: I was becoming dissatisfied with the field I'd gotten into, and I wanted to do something more in the arts, more creative, and I started to study at night school. You know, drawing and painting.

Then I just happened to pick up Mr. Wright's autobiography one day. I was browsing in a bookstore and I read it. Immediately I felt a kinship, and I figured that would be a great place for me. So I wrote to inquire about the Taliesin Fellowship, and I got an answer back to come for an interview, which I did in the summer of '48. That was in Wisconsin. I took the train from Montreal to Spring Green. I was there for a day to meet Mr. Wright. In the afternoon Gene Masselink had seated me in his studio waiting for him to come in. He was outdoors somewhere. So Mr. Wright came in and Gene introduced us, and Mr. Wright said, "Can you work?" And I said, "Yes." He said, "Fine." And then he went off to have his afternoon tea.

That was my interview. Of course, I'd written a letter saying who I was and describing what my background was. So I asked Gene, "What does that mean?" He said, "Well, I guess you're in." So I went back to Montreal, packed up everything, sold everything to get enough money to come, and in September of that year, '48, I came and I've been here ever since. I had in mind that I would study architecture and someday I might become an architect, but I wasn't really bent on that particular

Joe Fabris

aim. I just was attracted to the whole idea of the Fellowship and the community and working with Frank Lloyd Wright.

I immediately sort of just fell into everything and committed myself to it, which was great for me. It resolved all those problems of "Am I going in the right direction? What are you doing with your life?" I just made a commitment and I never thought about that anymore. There were a lot of difficulties and hardships and everything, but I felt that I was on the right path, so nothing else mattered.

Do you remember your first day?

I joined in Wisconsin. Yes, partly . . . being taken to a little room I was given at Hillside, beside his [Mr. Wright's] Hillside studio there. That's my primary memory, just unpacking and getting there.

Another who had had no prior experience with Taliesin was Heloise Crista. She describes how it happened that she came to Taliesin in 1949:

HELOISE: I was so very attracted by Mr. Wright's work. I had to write a paper in school, and I couldn't find any material in the library. I had to write this paper called "Implications of Modern Philosophy on Modern Architecture," and I couldn't find any material, so I went to a bookstore and asked about it. They said well maybe you can [find some here]. And here were Mr. Wright's books: *An Autobiography, On Architecture* and *In the Nature of Materials.* I bought all of them and went home and started to read. I was so taken by the autobiography. I just loved that.

The idea of Taliesin was like paradise to me—the whole idea of it. And then his work, too—pictures of his houses and everything. I just loved it. I wasn't interested

Heloise Crista

in architecture before that point, but when I saw his work I thought, "Oh, this is so beautiful; there is so much depth and warmth to the buildings." It was not like anything I had ever seen before, and I was so taken by it.

I just wrote him a letter and said, "I haven't studied architecture at all, but I would like to come and be a part of the fellowship for a while, a year or whatever." I wrote this very long letter, which I finally tore up, and wrote a much shorter one, which I sent. . . . At the time I wrote, everybody was in Wisconsin, so I didn't hear for months until they got back here. And then they finally said to come over for an interview, so I came and talked to Mr. Wright. And he accepted me. That's how it all started.

Marian Kanouse came to Taliesin in 1947 through her dealings with the Fellowship at the Spring Green bank where she worked. In her taciturn manner, Marian guards confidential matters scrupulously, but her special relationship with Mr. and Mrs. Wright and how it developed is apparent. I asked her to speak a little bit about how she had met the Wrights.

MARIAN: Well, I have no idea how I met them. They knew my father, and so I just became acquainted with them, and we used to go there for social afternoons on Sundays—a heck of a long time ago.

And then how did you get connected with doing things with Taliesin? You worked in a bank . . .

Yes, and when they began to pay the people . . . in the early days when Mr. Wright had some money he would just pull a bill out of his pocket and give it to the fellows. So nothing was really certain. And then, eventually, when it worked into having a regular payroll—well, even before the payroll—some were paid contracts . . . it's so long ago, I've sort of forgotten. But in the early '60s they started a payroll and I was doing it. I've always done it. I'm still doing it.

Did you retire from a bank and then connect with the Fellowship?

Yes, Mrs. Wright called and said, "Why don't you come and live with us now?" So it sounded like a good idea. I have my own house [in Spring Green]. It's kind of fun, and it's only ten minutes to drive to Taliesin, and they're rather pressed for room there. *[At Taliesin West she has an apartment on campus.]*

I was always very much in awe of Mr. Wright, and it used to amuse him. He was a lot like my father, very quiet. But when he said something he really meant it. I didn't have as much contact, of course, with Mr. Wright as I did with Mrs., but he used to be amused and liked to introduce me as his banker. When I would come out to visit him he would introduce me that way, because I was considerably younger then than I am now and I imagine it did look rather strange.

How did you get to be the one at the bank who handled his affairs?

Oh, goodness, he was rather an eccentric customer, so when he walked in I got to handle him. I think he did ask for me a couple of times.

Marian Kanouse

The recent biography by Meryle Secrest makes a great deal of his financial problems.[10] *He did have them, didn't he? I mean lenders or people he owed money to?*

Well, I suppose. I don't think I thought too much about it, but he really wasn't the ogre that they liked to make of him. He found some of this rather amusing, but the people to whom he owed the money were not amused, and the fact that Mr. Wright was so famous called more attention to it. I think that I was probably about the only person in Spring Green who was able to live and have contact with all of the villagers and still be accepted as being part of Taliesin.

I was the officer cashier [at the bank]. The bank was founded in 1914, and Harry Gray was the first cashier that they hired. And I went in to the bank just to help out. Some woman was out on maternity leave, and at that time my aunt happened to work there. They needed somebody temporarily and she asked me to come. I got along well with everybody and caught on pretty rapidly. The woman decided not to come back so they asked me to stay permanently. It was just about the end of the war, so I did come home and live with my folks. My brother went into the service. One thing led to another and somehow or other it was the longest part-time job I ever had, because I stayed there.

I was assistant cashier first, then Mr. Gray thought that he would like to be president of the bank, and he thought that I had worked there long enough so I could be the cashier. I said, "No way." I didn't want all that responsibility, but he talked me into it. I retired in 1984. So, from 1914 to 1984, in 70 years that bank only had two cashiers. And in a small bank in those years the cashier was the ranking officer. It had a president, but he was not active. He was one of the leading farmers in the area there.

Did you go out on a limb sometimes in making loans to Mr. Wright?

Well, I'm not sure we ever made him any loans. I think when he had the money he spent it. I'm not too familiar with all of the finances when Mr. Wright was living. He didn't [only] deal with our bank; he had some in Madison and other advisors rather than just coming in and cashing a check. Prior to this I'm not too familiar with everything that was going on, only what I've read.

Have you had to perform some financial miracles for the Fellowship? Were there times when meeting the payroll was in question?

Oh, sometimes you have to work a few miracles.

How do you do that?

I'm not going to tell you. I was kind of a handy person to have in the bank. . . . When the Fellowship traveled back and forth from Wisconsin to Arizona and Arizona to Wisconsin . . . there again, I don't remember the number of years ago, but anyway we had this big semi which transported all the stuff. Now we rent a U-Haul. And Gene would call me to find out where the truck was, what location, because it would always break down, and then they would call me for money. I would have to wire money to them. And other people would check in with me. Sometimes they would have a breakdown, and I was always at the bank; sometimes they had trouble finding other people. And so people called me and asked me where so and so was, and if they needed money I'd make arrangements for them to have it.

I imagine there have been plenty of touch and go times with them, when they wondered whether they were going to make it.

True. But nobody made too much of that. It was just a part of living.

I think you have stored up a lot of secrets in your head for when you write your own book someday.

That will never be. I've enjoyed my life and my contact with these people, and just accepted it. I've not been swayed by it, I guess. It's just the way I like to live.

David Dodge was studying music at Oberlin College when he decided in 1951 to join the Fellowship. He is the grandson of one of the founders of the Dodge Motor Company. After his grandfather died, he said, his grandmother "built a French château in Detroit, a really incredible thing. And inside it wasn't just decorated with things that looked like Louis XV, it was Louis XV stuff." How would someone with such a background adapt to Taliesin?

DAVID: When I first came for my interview, Mr. Wright sort of set us straight on what we would be expected to do, and I had been warned even before I got anywhere near to even writing a letter to Mr. Wright that, "Well, you'll go to Taliesin, you'll arrange flowers," as though that was a degrading thing to tell somebody they would be doing. I was told by one of my professors, "Yeah, you go to Taliesin, you'll arrange flowers and have to clean and sweep." And I said, "Yes, but I would be working with a great architect." I said, "I don't care what I have to do there. I will be working with someone who is without a doubt the most active and creative architect alive. So what does it matter? I can only learn from him, and if I get tired of it I can leave."

Of course, as soon as I came to Taliesin, Mr. Wright in the interview told me exactly these very things. He says, "You'll take out the garbage for those who'll take the garbage out for you, and everybody rotates and takes the jobs. Everyone helps with all the work here, and all of the work is related to architecture. If you don't know how to live in a building, how can you design a building for someone else to live in?"

And, of course, every architect at Taliesin generally learns how to cook. There are a few that manage to sneak out of it—which is always an amazing thing to me. . . . And then, the most amazing thing is that those that were most loud about how they hated being in the kitchen, and that it was demeaning, and it was this and it was that, twenty years after they had left Taliesin . . . they would say, "The kitchen taught me more than the drafting room did." And it's quite true.

But it's architecture. You're learning about architecture. And so, as long as you're thinking about the whole process, thinking about how to make it better, how does it work, why, it doesn't matter what you're doing, it's productive. It's strengthening you; it's not weakening you. It's using your energies, but you're not losing, you're gaining from that expenditure of energy.

How did your family feel about your coming to Taliesin?

My mother had always told me that she thought that I should study with Mr. Wright, after college. But I left college and came here. My mother didn't have that strong an influence on me. I decided this at college, seeing Mr. Wright's work and just seeing for sure that it was hands down so much better than everything else the college could

David Dodge

show me. It was the first modern architecture. I could say, "Well, that certainly is as good as the Gothic cathedrals, as good as the great, old architecture. It's got something to it." So, they were all quite agreeable that I go and work with Mr. Wright. I was not aware of what Taliesin really was. It was still an unknown. I just wanted to simply go and work for him as an apprentice. But I had no idea what the arrangement would be.

Tony Puttnam, who joined in 1953, describes how his interest in architecture led him to Taliesin.

TONY: I had for years and years as a young person thought that I wanted to be an architect, and then after the war, in Chicago, Mies van der Rohe was the great rage of architectural circles. Finally, a few new buildings were built, which was a very big, big thing. After five years of war and ten years of depression there were very few new buildings built. Any new one was an enormous novelty. But when they finally were built, they were very disappointing and not inspiring. They just didn't have very much adventure to them.

Coming to Taliesin was like walking into a place and hearing music for the first time. Here was overwhelming experience about architecture and space, and the whole atmosphere to begin with was overwhelming: all the new things that you found in those buildings that you did not find in other buildings that I had experienced. It's still very difficult to describe or deal with in any kind of objective way. There are a lot of buildings that have space in them, but Taliesin was like having space as a kind of energetic force moving through the building and relating to various parts of the building in various ways. The materials that this pier or this wall or that window, the materials that you found in the building influenced the dynamics of that space . . . and that configuration speeded it up or made it rhythmical, or other things.

Tony Puttnam

So, it was a big revelation about what the possibilities were. And the works of art there which all related to this in a sort of mysterious fashion—Japanese prints and screens and ceramics and sculptures and all that sort of thing. The ensemble of the place was also quite overwhelming, along with the landscape and the whole way that the building managed to be both an expression of the landscape and be forceful enough almost to make the landscape an expression of it.

I decided, on the basis of that weekend that I went to Taliesin, that this was the place for me. And whether or not I would ever really be any good at design, I didn't feel like this was something I was going to deal with easily or ever become proficient with. The whole thing in total was the first experience I had ever had with someone who had made the world whole. It was the world that was as put together, as whole in one piece in any place, that I think it could have been.

With a great piece of synchronicity, I received a small inheritance totally unexpected from someone I had never heard of before. I didn't realize that I had a relative of that nature. And so I went to Mr. Wright and asked him if I could stay. He was not markedly enthusiastic about this, but I told him my Mies van der Rohe story, and that pleased him a good deal, and so I guess he figured that at least I knew the difference between this and that.

You're quoted in the Guggenheimer book as saying that Wright said that he respected Mies van der Rohe but he didn't like his work.[11]

Well, that was the feeling that one had, and I think Mr. Wright did because Mies certainly was extremely generous to him. He felt hurt later on when Mr. Wright criticized his work, because Mies would say freely at any time that Frank Lloyd Wright was the great oak under which all twentieth century architecture had found shelter and sprung up. There are many stories like that, that reinforce that idea of Mies' respect for Frank Lloyd Wright. I think Mr. Wright was terribly disappointed in him. Mies' early work was certainly very much more sympathetic and more romantic. . . .

Some who came to Taliesin were disillusioned by their experiences studying architecture elsewhere. In her Tales of Taliesin, *Cornelia Brierly writes that she came to Taliesin in 1934 from Carnegie Tech, where she had been studying architecture. She left there, she says, because she found the classical Beaux Arts system taught there to be uncreative. Her professors tried to discourage her from leaving. When she told Mr. Wright that they regarded her as "a young radical embarking upon a complete misadventure," he seemed to enjoy the idea that she had "rebelled against a stultifying situation."*

As with so many others, Cornelia's reading of Mr. Wright's autobiography convinced her that he was "a man who didn't copy the past, an architect who worked out new forms for a new age. He envisioned a different way of living and learning for the Taliesin Fellowship, an exciting holistic lifestyle for young aspiring architects." Her professors at Tech, she says, didn't seem to know about Mr. Wright or his work, despite his accomplishments by then. "By following my own intuition

Cornelia Brierly

or instinct," she says, "I went to Taliesin and discovered the treasures of a life devoted to creative architecture, a life where beauty is held to be 'the highest form of morality.' "[12]

John Rattenbury is another whose disillusionment with architectural studies elsewhere made Taliesin an attractive place:

> JOHN R: I came in 1950, from Vancouver, Canada. Architecture was in my blood, since my father was an architect. He was born in the same year as Mr. Wright, 1867. My mother was a musician and composer. We lived in Victoria and when I was a year old we moved to England. I lost my parents when I was five, and at the age of eleven I moved back to Vancouver.[13]
>
> I worked my way through the University of British Columbia. After two years of liberal arts and a year of engineering I qualified for the School of Architecture. Once there I quickly became disenchanted. It was a huge school and I was lost in the crowd. Most of the courses seemed irrelevant. I dropped out and took a year off to work in Alaska and earn some money. Then I enrolled in Oregon State College where they had just started a Department of Architecture. It consisted of two professors and about twenty-five students, a friendly size. While I was there I discovered Frank Lloyd Wright. I found a book about him in the library and stayed up all night reading. I was electrified. When I learned that he had a school of apprentices I headed east to Wisconsin.
>
> I was twenty-one at that time. Mr. Wright charged $1,000 a year for apprenticeship. This didn't begin to cover costs, but by contributing to the work effort we earned our education. From the day that I first set foot in Taliesin I have never wanted to be anywhere else. In college I knew instinctively that architecture could be something

John Rattenbury

much better than what was being fed to me, but I did not see it expressed until I came here. Walking into Taliesin was like coming home.

To this day I can remember the smell of dried antimony, tidewater cypress, and smoke from the oak logs burning in the fireplace. It was love at first sight, the excitement of Taliesin activities, the incredible beauty of the buildings, the people, the work—everything. There was a spirit to the place that touched me deeply. I found [that] the reverence for nature which permeated the architecture gave expression to my feelings of a divine force. When Mr. Wright said, "Nature is the only manifestation of God we will see on this earth," I agreed. I threw myself into life at Taliesin and never worried about a curriculum.

Stephen Nemtin describes his coming to Taliesin as "an interesting little saga":

STEPHEN: I had some training in architecture at McGill University for several years that was not a very satisfactory experience, and I was thinking of maybe transferring out to the University of British Columbia, since I am Canadian. I hopped on the train one summer, the cross-country domed train, and ended up in Vancouver. I was interviewed by a professor (I have no recollection of who it was) and came to the conclusion that my experience would be somewhat similar though possibly a better experience.

In any case, I just happened to ask him whether he knew where Taliesin was, and he said, "I think it's somewhere in Phoenix." And I hopped a plane to Phoenix. That was in the fall of '58. My previous knowledge of Frank Lloyd Wright was through his books. I remember going to New York and also trying to look for the exhibition building that was on the site of the present Guggenheim Museum. Of course, that had been torn down and that was all in the past, but I was growing in my—I wouldn't say knowledge—just really the feeling of the whole thing.

So, as I say, I hopped a plane and flew to Phoenix. I think I stayed at the YMCA. I inquired where Taliesin was and rented an old car and drove out there. The Fellowship hadn't arrived from Wisconsin. I remember being shown around by, I think, Bill Owen[14] and told approximately when Mr. Wright would be there. I think I passed somewhere under a week's time waiting for their arrival. I don't even recall who I called up to make the appointment, but an appointment was made and I came out and had a very short interview, because as it was starting Mr. Wright received several long-distance calls. There really wasn't much of an interview at all, but he did accept me.

Do you remember what he asked you?

The only thing I remember is whether I was sexually, emotionally involved at the time, which I wasn't. I think he asked me what my father did. My father was a custom's broker in Montreal. I really don't remember a lot else. We didn't really get into anything architectural at all. In any case, he accepted me; he called Gene in and accepted me. I stayed overnight. I remember the following day . . . it was the time that the roof of the studio at Taliesin West had been reconstructed, and on the low side of the roof there were some angled wood kickers. There was one in place that he was viewing to see whether he wanted them to be repeated because the structure no longer needed them. But visually, it needed it; the roof needed it. That he okayed and then he went on up to the pavilion—the pavilion was being constructed at that time. I remember him calling for his cape. I think one of the most notable things was that I always had the impression that Frank Lloyd Wright was taller than I am. I still have that impression today, so it's a question of stature, it's not a question of height.

Stephen Nemtin

Then I went over to him when he was looking at the studio later and said, "I want to say goodbye," and he just kind of shot out his hand from his hip. It sort of took me aback and I guess I shook it—I don't quite remember—and that was it. I went back to Montreal and heard of his death over the radio. I remember my father asking me whether I was still going to go there, and I said yes.

Between the time of your acceptance and your arrival is when he died?

Yes, the Fellowship, I think, was the highest in number at that time; there just physically wasn't any room. If it hadn't been that way I would have just stayed. So I never had the chance to see the man at work, but I have a sense of the man, certainly. Then, in the spring of '59 I joined the Fellowship, and I'm really the first apprentice following the death of Frank Lloyd Wright. I consider that important, because I consider that the beginning of another time at Taliesin, but at the same time, nothing really changed in the beginning. I had the whole sense of how the Fellowship functioned and . . . the way things were done, and then slowly changes began to occur under Mrs. Wright's direction. I'm the only one really that stayed on at the beginning of a changing era, an evolving era.

Joe Fabris, John Rattenbury, and Stephen Nemtin were all Canadians. Another senior fellow (now on leave) came from a much greater distance. Ling Po had graduated from college in China with a degree in architecture and worked for a Chinese architect before coming to the United States. His story:

LING PO: After the Second World War I spent a year in the United States learning architecture, but I had learned just about nothing. I visited Frank Lloyd Wright at Taliesin, Wisconsin, and asked to join the Fellowship, with no means to

Ling Po

pay the tuition. As Mr. Wright had a great kindness to Oriental students, he generously took me in. That was in 1946 that I first saw him.

Where did you spend the year before that, that you said was not worth anything?

In New York and Chicago, working for architects.

Another person who had studied architecture elsewhere is Tom Casey, who had earned a bachelor's degree in architecture at the University of California at Berkeley. Mr. Wright's visit to that campus and Tom's encounter with him there opened the way for Tom to join the Fellowship in 1949:

TOM: I was at the University of California, Berkeley, in the School of Architecture after World War II, and there was a neighbor of mine from our hometown who lived just three or four doors up the street from me who was a year ahead. He was in the Phi Delta Theta house. Frank Lloyd Wright had a connection with Phi Delta Theta in some way. (Naturally, they've always claimed him—very eloquently.) Jack Engle was his name, and Jack initiated a contact that when Frank Lloyd Wright was going to be in San Francisco he would come to Berkeley and have lunch with students of architecture. I was included. Frank Lloyd Wright accepted the invitation. He came to San Francisco all by himself. Wes [Peters] or somebody else may have been lurking around taking care of some other job or something, but Mr. Wright came by himself to Berkeley.

The School of Architecture resided on the north edge of the campus in an old wooden building . . . just across the street was a row of fraternity houses on Hearst Avenue. The School at that time consisted of many students who were World War II veterans who chose to join the fraternity across the street . . . so they would be living in close proximity to where they were going to spend their time.

. . . Jack Engle arranged to invite Mr. Wright, who came to lunch at the fraternity house. We all sat around the table sort of tongue-tied, because here was this great man sitting there surrounded by a bunch of kids. Mr. Wright didn't pay any attention to faculty at all. We walked through the building, he strolled through the corridors, he never stopped to look at anything. We ended up at a wonderful courtyard in between, with a little pergola around the edge; it was a spring day in Berkeley. We sat around the courtyard. A whole flock of other students sat around him and there was a question and answer session. We had a very nice time there, and he was very affable. . . . All of his attention was directed at the young people. He didn't ask to go see the dean of the school or anything like that. His connection just simply was with those who invited him to come.

There were a few of us in school who were quite enamored of his work in architecture, and it was being published. *In the Nature of Materials*, a fairly new book then, was a collection of his work. And there were the magazines. The '38 and the '48 *Architectural Forums* were available then. Some of us were very attracted by what he was doing, although we had instructors and professors in the school who told us we were absolutely going the wrong direction. That's not where architecture lay, they said. But, of course, being young we dismissed that attitude and went our own way.

Just as he was leaving, Mr. Wright threw out this general invitation, which I learned later he did anytime he was with a group of students. He would say as a sort of parting invitation, "Come and see us. Bring your sleeping bag." I took that very much to heart. We had spring break coming up within a month. I got in my car and drove down to Southern California, where I lived, put my sleeping bag in the car, and drove out to Taliesin West to see what was going on.

I was received very openly there. I remember I slept overnight on a chaise lounge out in the Apprentice Court.[15] I had a good chance to see what was going on. I had another opportunity the following summer to visit the upper midwest. I stopped at Taliesin and looked around there, at Hillside particularly. I came back and finished my program at midterm—at the end of 1949—and graduated. I still had considerable eligibility available from the GI Bill, because I had spent five years in the service and had used only about two and a half years to complete my course at Berkeley.

I started seeking employment. I went to San Francisco and tramped all around. It happened to be a very low period in professional activity, so there were no jobs anyplace. I thought, well, the best thing I can do—I have this GI Bill available—is to use it. So I decided I would go to Taliesin West (and I found out it was applicable there) and spend my time in what I would consider graduate school in the Taliesin Fellowship.

Again I drove out there. Taliesin West was quite inaccessible. The only thing you could do to get ahold of Frank Lloyd Wright was send a telegram. Paradise Inn was one of the early resorts established on the east end of Camelback Road. They had

Tom Casey

a telegraph there, and that was the place you had to send a telegram to reach Frank Lloyd Wright. Two or three times a week somebody [from Taliesin West] would stop by Paradise Inn and pick up any telegrams that happened to have come in.

I thought the best way to get in contact was to do what I did before, get in my car and drive out there. So I did that. I just walked in and said, "Here I am, I want to see Frank Lloyd Wright." Gene Masselink was in the office at the time and he said, "We'd be happy to have you hang around here. I think Mr. Wright will be down here in an hour or so; why don't you just stick around outside there." I went outside of the theater behind the office, the little Cabaret Theater at that time, and hung around there. There was some construction going on.

Sure enough, it was not long before Gene came out and said, "Well, Mr. Wright is here now. You can come and see him." So I simply went in and sat down, and I told him who I was and why I was there and what I wanted to do. He listened carefully and said, "You're in luck, because some people have just left." He explained to me that two or three people had gone. So there I was, bingo, I was accepted. I couldn't stay then, however; I had to go back home and get the registration for the GI Bill set up. I came back within two or three weeks, and there I was, part of the Taliesin Fellowship. That was very early in 1950.

After the death of his wife, Shirley,[16] *Tom Casey married Effi Maria Bantzer, who had come to the Fellowship by a most unusual route. On one of the Fellowship's sojourns in Europe (recounted in a later chapter), Effi had a chance encounter with Frances Nemtin.*

EFFI: I happened to be in Montagnola, Switzerland, which was the home of the Taliesin Fellowship for two summers. A trip was planned for the Fellowship to Switzerland in order to have a base from where they could take trips around Europe and really educate themselves. It so happened that the American school for the sons and daughters of foreign ministers in Switzerland was always vacant during the summer, so the Fellowship was able to reside there.

I cannot go into the details of this summer [1966]. It's a fascinating story in itself but too long. But I happened to make the connection through Frances who heard me practice the violin in my little hotel room, and she said, "We have a little musical group with whom you could play. Couldn't you come down; you play so wonderfully." That was my first connection, but I had really been waiting for the Fellowship to arrive in Switzerland. I had been working for a painter who was paralyzed, assisting him in carrying out his work. After he died the lady in the hotel I stayed in said, "If you don't want to return to your academy in Germany, why don't you wait for these people from the United States? They're just your cup of tea."

Even if I didn't quite know at the time what she meant by that, she was right, because in getting to know the people and then eventually also Mrs. Wright, I realized that I was attracted to the whole philosophical outlook of this group—not being held

Effi Casey

together by any "ism," or any religious sect, or any political group, but as a group of individuals who joined in the attempt to move an idea forward, the idea being all the principles of organic architecture as it pertains to your life, really. I found that very attractive, and I think I was actually prone to that because my schooling was in the school of Rudolph Steiner.[17]

Are you familiar with this Anthroposophical leader? I went for thirteen years to that school, which is a very meaningful, holistic way of education—philosophy, religion, everything plays a part in it, [also] the arts. . . . The teachers [were] extremely dedicated—again, also to an idea. So I think that was a good prerequisite for Taliesin, having had that kind of education.

Who asked you, then, to come back to the United States with them?

I asked them. Nobody asked me. Several people said, "Oh, it would be so wonderful." But nobody thought I would ever be serious about it, because it was not my intent to become an architect. But I could see myself as a contributing person from the point of view of music or painting. See, I came out of a painting background, actually.

To make things short, I joined with them after having an official interview with Mrs. Wright in which she, curiously enough, did not ask so much of what I could do in the realm of architecture but where did I come from, what did my family do, what were our activities at home. She wanted to, I think, get some [idea of my] greater cultural background—where I came from and what was it that attracted me.

Some who joined the Taliesin Fellowship already had college degrees in fields other than architecture. Charles Montooth describes how his coming to Taliesin in 1945 happened:

Charles Montooth

CHARLES: I went to the University of Chicago and walked daily past the Robie House. One day I was in Harper Library looking at different books, and I saw it pictured in a book and the date 1908 or 1909. I thought, "My god, this must have been the beginning of architecture." I was always interested in architecture. I used to do a lot of drawing when I was high school age, but I wasn't very good in math so I didn't go into it [architecture]. I was interested in music, and they didn't have architecture at the University.

But I had another friend from the same small town who went to IIT (Illinois Institute of Technology), and we used to make pilgrimages. Well, after seeing the Robie House and then getting into the books and having this eye-opening [experience] in the *Architectural Forum* of 1938 . . . we made pilgrimages around, from Chicago to Oak Park and the Auditorium, where at that time we'd go to concerts—[the] Sullivan theater.[18] Then we would go north searching out the houses. I went out to the Lloyd Lewis House once by myself, took the North Shore out. I phoned Mrs. Lewis, and she said, "I don't drive, so I can't come and get you, but you could walk down," which I did. And that was a revelation.

And then, of course, [there was] Johnson Wax. Finally, I got as far as Wisconsin (I think I did that on my own), and I went to the Pew House. I think I took a bus out there because we didn't have cars in those days, and I was walking along the road and looking at the house from the road. Then I saw this old 1933 Chevrolet come in and turn down the drive and drive in the carport, just like that. I thought, "That explains it all. He has this house—next century house—but he drives this old car. That's how he was able to do it; he made that kind of a choice." I guess I called them up; I usually did that. Mrs. Pew was very kind, showed me around, and then said, "You appear so interested, why don't you go out and see [Mr. Wright]?" This was in wartime, actually. So I said "Well, I was never very good in mathematics." And she said, "Oh, he doesn't care."

That gave me the courage and I did write. Then I did have an interview. I was in the Merchant Marines and I was about to go overseas; I met Mr. Wright here (at Hillside), and he accepted me after the war. He was really short of people, of course. His interview was very brief. I don't remember [what he asked me]. Strange, isn't it, because I remember so many things.

Charles's presence led to visits by others from his hometown, Rushville, Illinois. Included among them were twin sisters, Sarah and Minerva Houston. Back home, Sarah married Bill Logue and six months later Minerva became the wife of Charles Montooth, who, after studying with Frank Lloyd Wright started his own architectural practice in Scottsdale. Visits to Taliesin by both the Logues and the Montooths continued. Sarah describes what happened at the end of one of her visits.

SARAH: . . . I was talking to Mrs. Wright (by that time I had two children), and said, "I have to go back to Rushville, and it just breaks my heart." I burst into tears and Mrs. Wright—I will never forget that look she gave me. The next day I had tea with Mr. and Mrs. Wright and I could tell by the questions that Mrs. Wright was asking that she was trying to get Mr. Wright to see what sterling characters we would be in the Fellowship, although she never mentioned it to me. The next day, Bill went in to see Mr. and Mrs. Wright, and afterward he said, "Do you know that we are going to join the Fellowship?" As far as I was concerned, it was just like joining heaven. It was something that I had longed for all those years, but my path had gone a different way.

That was 1957. Mr. Wright at that time was having many commissions, and the apprentices could not do all the architectural work as well as the work on the farm. So we joined as farmers and full members of the Fellowship. We stayed in Wisconsin all year round in that capacity until 1967.

Bill and Sarah Logue

So you never went through an apprenticeship here yourself?

Everyone was an apprentice, not necessarily architectural. There were not staff members as such; they were called senior apprentices. I came in working in the domestic end of things—shopping, cooking, guest apartments, and that sort of thing.

Did you use your social work training and skills?

Mrs. Wright did not need a social worker involved because she was so skillful with people and managed everything beautifully. For instance, working a way for us to join the Fellowship with Mr. Wright and realizing that we would be loyal members of the Fellowship, contributors. She just saw things very clearly.

Occasionally the attraction to Taliesin is attributed to both Mr. and Mrs. Wright. Dori Roy describes the principal part Mrs. Wright played in her coming:

DORI: I came here for Mrs. Wright. I had wanted to come here for Mr. Wright when I was in college, but I thought at the time you had to be an architect to come to Taliesin. I had majored in art at college at Northwestern. I went to Stephens College for two years and then Northwestern for two years. One of the courses I took was an introduction to architecture. We took a field trip up to the Johnson Wax building [in Racine, Wisconsin]. I walked inside and I started to cry. I was so embarrassed. I had never had an experience like that before, but it was so beautiful and uplifting. And I thought, "This is what it must feel like to be in a cathedral." I had never been in a cathedral in my life. When I [later] went to a cathedral it was the same experience; it just hit me right there.

Then I wanted to be an architect, and I looked at all the things you had to do. Of course, I was two years behind. At Stephens I hadn't taken any of the subjects you're

Dori Roy

supposed to take as prerequisites for going into architecture. But I plunged in and tried to catch up on the physics, and I couldn't. It was just too much with all the other courses I had to take to make up for courses that wouldn't transfer.

So I gave that up and got married and had a child and divorced. Then a friend of mine told me about a Mrs. Wright who taught this philosophy, and the philosophy made just so much sense to me. I had been looking for something for a long time and had joined the Quakers, but I could not reconcile what I believed with the pacifism. I knew that when push came to shove, if anybody was hurting [my son] Marc I would kill him. That always bothered me.

Then I read *In Search of the Miraculous*, and learned about Gurdjieff and that to follow this path you have to have a teacher. You can't do it by yourself, in spite of the fact that there are groups trying to do [that], but that's all intellectual stimulation. Anyway, they said, "There's a Mrs. Wright who teaches [Gurdjieffian philosophy], and come spring she'll be in Wisconsin and we can go see her." I never connected *that* Mrs. Wright with Frank Lloyd Wright. So I always felt that I was meant to come here one way or another.

Dr. Joe Rorke, who became the personal physician to both Mr. and Mrs. Wright, entered the Taliesin Fellowship in an unusual way.

DR. JOE: From the outset, I was not involved with architecture or the school program. I was outside of that from the very beginning, and that was an exception to the normal rule of things. Originally, it was at my request and with Mr. Wright's and Mrs. Wright's approval. Mr. Wright insisted on two things: One was that if I did [join the Fellowship] that I not give up my profession; and number two, that if I did this and I took care of people here that I charge them, because professionals don't give away their services. Now those were the only two stipulations, and he said, "Come ahead." I had previously seen him before that and had accidental occasion to treat him.

How did you make your first contact with him? Frank Lloyd Wright doesn't just walk into a doctor's office.

Oh, no, no. I met him here, right here in '54, I believe it was. Cornelia [Brierly] and her family were patients of mine in Pennsylvania [while she worked with her husband as an architect there]. They lived ten miles from me; we all lived in the country in southwestern Pennsylvania, in the mountains. . . . Cornelia and Peter [Berndtson[19]] became patients of mine, and we got very friendly. I think it was '54, maybe Christmas '53, that we took a vacation out here together by train. Just about died on that ghastly ride.

Who is the "we"?

Cornelia's family—Peter, Cornelia, Anna and Indira, and my wife, myself and [our daughter] Shawn, seven of us. I wanted to fly out, but they couldn't afford to fly out, so we came on the train—worst trip of my life, sitting on the train for four days. Anyway, we got out here, and we stayed at Cornelia's sister's home, the Drakes', down in Phoenix. They had been apprentices here also. Peter and Cornelia always spent Christmases in Mexico at their home down there. So we stayed down there, too, and then Cornelia brought me out here for a visit. And right there between the pergola and the side entrance to the house came Mr. and Mrs. Wright.

That's when I met them. . . . I had a book under my arm which I was reading at the time. It was a thin Emerson with a deerhide cover, a real favorite of mine. Mr. Wright said, "What have you got there?" I showed him, and he said, "Oh, this looks interesting." And he walked into the house with it. Mrs. Wright laughed and said, "That's the last you'll ever see of that." A year or so after he died Mrs. Wright gave it back to me. . . . But that's how I met him.

And then I saw him again, I think I was in New York at a medical convention. Mr. and Mrs. Wright were at the Plaza [their New York residence] and I stopped by to pay my respects. Then I was invited to come to Wisconsin, and I did that, I think, the next spring or summer. On that occasion, Gene Masselink asked if I'd mind looking in on Mr. Wright. He thought he might need a minor checkup to see if there was anything wrong. And I did and that's how it started. Then, I had other business, and occasionally I would get a call from Gene: "Are you free this weekend? Can you come out? Time for a checkup." You know, that kind of call.

Had you moved to Phoenix by that time?

Not yet. But I made a couple of visits like that. Then I decided . . . my life in the boonies out there [in Pennsylvania] wasn't panning out too well. It was a good life, good fresh air and all that, but it was sort of a dull, boring life. We had gotten involved with Mrs. Wright after these visits. She was teaching philosophy in those days, and

Dr. Joseph Rorke

she had formed groups. There was a Chicago group and a Scottsdale group, and we formed—with Cornelia, my family, Bill and Annette (I can't think of their names . . . another family close by over there), and a fourth family who had a remote connection earlier with Mr. Wright when he built what we called the Dinky Diner for Mr. Wright.

Anyway, these four families formed this little group, and we were called the Pennsylvania Group. We would try to visit here or in Wisconsin at least once during the year. Mrs. Wright would assign us reading material. We would learn what we called "correlations" in those days, and we would practice [these stylized exercises] at home and have meetings and readings. She sent Steve Oyakawa[20] out one year to give us some additional hard work on the correlations theory. (At one time he was Kay's husband; he's dead now.) I think she also, if I remember correctly, sent Iovanna to Pennsylvania one time. And then we'd meet with Mrs. Wright at Taliesin or Taliesin West.

That's how that got cemented. Then I decided it was a good time to make a move, and I wrote to Mr. and Mrs. Wright with the idea of coming here and they approved. First I moved to Wisconsin, moved the family there, got settled in there. I sold my practice, put the house on the block, had an auction—I couldn't stay to watch that. We were the big shots in a small village, and it was too painful to watch hundreds of dollars worth of things going for a nickel. So I just left and let them sell it all. I didn't care if I got anything out of it or not. I was just ready to go.

A major factor in this decision was that my office had been devastated by heavy floods—twice within one year—that ruined nearly everything. The first time the water reached the second floor.

Were you by then absorbed with the Taliesin philosophy?

I was deeply involved with that idea, and I was sick and tired of living in the mountains of western Pennsylvania. It was about fifteen minutes from Fallingwater, beautiful country but still deadly, deadly, living the way we did. We had a few friends in a forty-mile radius and the rest were not quite hillbillies, but almost. Anyway, that's when I made the move and we got settled there.

Through the years, retaining the services of senior apprentices was essential to Taliesin's life and work. By the mid-1980s, when the status of "senior fellow" was created, it became apparent that conferring that status upon select apprentices would be necessary if the Fellowship was to have a future. An apprentice whose substantial contributions to community life made him a good prospect was Ari Georges, who was awarded an M.Arch. degree by the Frank Lloyd Wright School of Architecture in 1993. He then returned to Greece, his homeland, for the required two-year stint in the army. His election as a senior fellow occurred after his return from Greece. How and why did he come to Taliesin in the first place?

ARI: It was my destination coming from Italy; I was already at the University of Florence. I had heard about Frank Lloyd Wright for the first time when I was fourteen.

That was when I had a tutor architect teaching me at home who had seen some of my early sketches. I had started sketching what I thought were plans since I was twelve or so. It was a double game I was playing to escape reality. I would get into these imaginary places. When the tutor saw the drawings, he wanted to meet me; my father knew him. When he came over he had under his arm the *Wendingen* book, which is a very beautiful book that Frank Lloyd Wright himself thought was one of the best publications anybody had done on him. Incidentally, it's the one that's sitting open on his desk [in his Taliesin study]. That's something I put back there. I had read in his autobiography that he always liked that book in there, so I found an edition and put it on his desk. I always had it open at the plan of Taliesin, but I guess people go through and look at it.

So, that's when I first was acquainted with the work of Frank Lloyd Wright, and I studied a little bit of his work with the tutor. He had given me a magnifying glass and told me, "Copy as abundantly as you can." When you're fourteen it is not dangerous to do that, because by copying you got interested. I always was intrigued by Frank Lloyd Wright's work, because it had another dimension to it. It had some mystery not only in physical evidence of material standing without evident structure (you know, those cantilevers, this very free form that seems to defy gravity) but also the whole idea of ensemble that the buildings showed—the combination of materials together that seem to be so mysterious. I studied him on my own, making my own conclusions about how things were, having no idea that there was ever a school.

I went on to Florence and studied architecture at the University for two years, and it was a pretty bad time because, first of all, it was a difficult school with a very large number of students. It's a funnel, inverse funnel tactic. They have open admission and they graduate sixty every year, so from the fifteen hundred that entered with me to the School of Architecture alone [only] about fifty or sixty would graduate. The tactic,

Mr. Wright's desk at Taliesin.

especially the first two years, was to diminish the number as much as possible. The professors weren't bad, actually. I had so much love for it that I thought, "Why am I with a bunch of people who are not interested in this?" Since I had dedicated all my adolescent years to it, I had different aspirations about the university experience.

It was at the time that I met a lot of Americans in Florence, because they are easier to meet than the Florentines themselves. And when those friends returned to the U.S. [and] sent me some catalogs of schools of architecture, it was the American Catalog of Schools of Architecture (ACSA) of 1984 that had Taliesin in it. It was at the time when Taliesin didn't even offer a degree yet; it was a certificate program. As soon as I saw it, I thought, "What I really should do is take a break and go for a year and revisit my early love for Wright—it was like a filter to the source—and see what it was like."

Incidentally, my tutor, who introduced me to Frank Lloyd Wright and his work and got me so interested in him, when he heard I wanted to go to Taliesin he was very upset with me. He advised me not to. When I asked him why, thinking he should be happy because that's where it all started, he said, "No, the problem will be that they are all copiers there and you will not find people who will discuss critically those things that you're interested in about Frank Lloyd Wright's work. You will see them doing things without necessarily thinking, and you will be frustrated." I said, "Well, nonetheless, I think the place itself should be something of interest, and if the people are not up to my standards then I will have to deal with that. But the place itself is intriguing enough to bring me there."

So I came originally for a year. That was '86. When I sent my request for material, they sent me a packet of information, including John A's (Amarantides) address in Athens so that I would contact him. That was the first real Taliesin contact. I flew to

Ari Georges

Athens, and I went to his apartment and we spent a full day together. His apartment was very reminiscent of Frank Lloyd Wright's ideas about furniture layout. He had built-in furniture and nice couches with shelves behind—all of those characteristics that immediately are recognizable, and the atmosphere which was very fine. And John A is a very impressive person.[21] He is half Greek. He showed me a lot of photographs, he explained to me how Taliesin was, and we had a very good interview. Then he recommended me highly, and I was admitted in the spring of '86.

It took me about six months to be able to export the money and get it all together. At the time I was working in Greece with the architect/tutor of mine in his office, and I also did some of my own work. I was only twenty-two. Once I decided to fly to Taliesin, I left Florence. I thought it would be truer to this idea of following my bliss, rather than playing safe and staying in Florence until I hear from Taliesin. I decided to break from Florence, indifferent of the result of the application. I got here about ten years ago this fall. As I said, originally for a year, but as soon as I arrived I realized there is a lot more to discover than just a year would allow and I remained—the main reason being Wes Peters, who took me under his wing immediately. I worked with him the first four years of my apprenticeship.

Paul Kardatzke joined the Fellowship in 1991 and attained the status of senior fellow in 1996. He, too, had a long-standing interest in Frank Lloyd Wright and prior education and experience in architecture-related fields. I asked him how it happened that after he graduated from the Illinois Institute of Technology he decided to come to Taliesin.

PAUL: I decided I wanted to study at Taliesin. When I was in high school, I believe, is when I first became familiar with the work of Frank Lloyd Wright in a more academic way. I grew up in Chicago, so I was familiar with Frank Lloyd Wright. When I was in high school I read *A Testament*,[22] a Frank Lloyd Wright book (not the autobiography) describing his work. When I decided to go to college I wanted to study for an engineering degree, because I enjoy the sciences and made a decision at that time to focus on getting an engineering degree, getting drafting training and architectural training while I was receiving that.

I came up to visit Taliesin; I think it was my sophomore year. I came up here to Taliesin in Spring Green and just visited, took a tour and got information about the school. I didn't have an official interview at that point. Then when I got closer to getting my civil engineering degree, I came up for a shorter visit and set up a time for when I would go into the Fellowship. I actually spent six years working on my civil engineering degree and reading of Frank Lloyd Wright and his description of the way this school was. I worked and went to school. I ended up working part-time and eventually just taking six months off here and there and working in engineering firms in Chicago. So that extended the time I was in school and made a much richer experience. After I graduated, I worked for a year in Chicago and then joined the Fellowship.

Paul Kardatzke

Julie and Paul Kardatzke met, courted, and married at Taliesin. I asked Julie why, with her social work background, she came to Taliesin.

JULIE: It started back in high school. I was trying to decide between two different careers. I was interested in both psychology and in architecture at the time and trying to make the choice between the two different fields. Somehow, I decided that I would study psychology, which led me into the field of social work. I had nearly completed my degree. In my last year of college I had to do a field placement to get some real experience, and I discovered I didn't like actually practicing social work—that it was fascinating to study but I really didn't care for the actual doing of it.

So I finished my degree and worked for several years before deciding to go back to school and study architecture this time. That's how I decided to make the switch. At

Julie Kardatzke

the time I was planning to go to the University of Wisconsin in Milwaukee, because it was in my home state of Wisconsin. But then I met an apprentice who was in the program here at Taliesin, and the more I found out about it the more it sounded like just the sort of thing that I was looking for. So I also applied here and decided to come here instead.

Has it proven to be what you were looking for?

It has, yes. I can't imagine having gone anywhere else.

Many who came to Taliesin through the years found it a congenial place where they could experience what they wanted and needed and then move on. Some who came found it to their liking for a long time, but for one reason or another felt compelled to leave. Curtis Besinger, for example, was a valued member of the community from 1939 to 1955 (he was away from 1943 to 1946, doing "work of national importance" as a conscientious objector), before beginning a lengthy professorship in architecture at the University of Kansas. In Working with Mr. Wright: What It Was Like, *Besinger describes his growing frustrations over such things as the way the studio worked, the time and energy consumed by preparing for an elaborate summer party, the presence of the "Chicago group" that studied Gurdjieffian philosophy with Iovanna and Mrs. Wright, and apparent differences with Mrs. Wright as reasons for his decision to leave in 1955.[23] Although he is critical of the Fellowship, as he apparently was also while a member of it (current fellows simply say that "Curtis could be difficult") his book sheds valuable and frequently affectionate light on the Taliesin Fellowship during years when many of the fellows quoted in this book were joining.*

Notes

1. Philip-Johnson, *Writings* (New York: Oxford University Press, 1972), 194–8. Along the same lines, Robert C. Twombly, in *Frank Lloyd Wright: His Life and His Architecture* (John Wiley & Sons, 1979), writes: "With its rigid hierarchical structure, individualism at the Fellowship was reserved for the Master's inner circle, social equality for the lesser apprentices" (217). In the earlier version of this book, *Frank Lloyd Wright: An Interpretive Biography* (New York: Harper & Row, 1973), Twombly notes that in 1959 the Frank Lloyd Wright Foundation created the Taliesin Associated Architects and the Frank Lloyd Wright School of Architecture, while the Taliesin Fellowship, he says, "passed out of existence, but the name continued to be applied informally to the corps of student draftsman" (285). In the 1979 version, he writes disparagingly of the Taliesin Architects, the School of Architecture, and Mrs. Wright and pays scant attention to the Fellowship (401–9).

2. David Larkin and Bruce Brooks Pfeiffer, eds., *Frank Lloyd Wright: The Masterworks* (Rizzoli: New York, in association with the Frank Lloyd Wright Foundation, 1993), 290.

3. Gene Masselink was with the Fellowship from 1933 until his death in 1962. He is mentioned frequently in later chapters.

4. John's father, Francis Rattenbury, was a prominent Canadian architect who moved with his wife and young son to England, where both he and his wife met tragic deaths. See

Anthony A. Barrett and Rohdri Windsor Liscombe, *Francis Rattenbury and British Columbia: Architecture and Challenge in the Imperial Age* (Vancouver: University of British Columbia Press, 1983) and Terry Peksten, *Rattenbury* (Victoria: Sono Nis Press, 1978).

5. Randolph C. Henning, ed., *"At Taliesin": Newspaper Columns by Frank Lloyd Wright and the Taliesin Fellowship, 1934–1937* (Carbondale: Southern Illinois University Press, 1992), 159.

6. See Herbert Jacobs, with Katherine Jacobs, *Building with Frank Lloyd Wright: An Illustrated Memoir* (San Francisco: Chronicle Books, 1978; Southern Illinois University Press, 1986).

7. David Wheatley was with the Fellowship from 1953 to 1956 and 1958 to 1969.

8. Burton Goodrich was with the Fellowship from 1934 to 1942 and 1944 to 1946.

9. Antimony was the name used by the Lloyd-Jones family for old-field balsam.

10. Meryle Secrest, *Frank Lloyd Wright: A Biography* (New York: HarperCollins, 1993).

11. Tobias S. Guggenheimer, *A Taliesin Legacy: The Architecture of Frank Lloyd Wright's Apprentices* (New York: Van Nostrand Reinhold, 1995), 17.

12. Cornelia Brierly, *Tales of Taliesin* (Tempe, AZ: Herberger Design Center, Arizona State University, 1999), 5. Cornelia's experiences at Carnegie Tech are the subject of a 22 May 1935 newspaper column reprinted in *"At Taliesin,"* 125–6.

13. See Anthony A. Barrett and Rohdri Windsor Liscombe, *Francis Rattenbury and British Columbia: Architecture and Challenge in the Imperial Age* and Terry Peksten, *Rattenbury,* for accounts of the tragic deaths of his parents.

14. Bill Owen was with the Fellowship around 1958 to 1960.

15. The Apprentice Court is a courtyard surrounded on three sides by rooms originally intended for apprentices. The rooms have been converted into apartments for senior fellows, but the name of the courtyard remains the same.

16. Shirley Casey was with the Fellowship from 1951 until her death in 1968.

17. Rudolph Steiner (1861–1925) founded a spiritual teaching called Anthroposophy, meaning that it embodied "knowledge of man" and "human wisdom." A prolific author, lecturer, and teacher, Steiner addressed topics in the sciences, social sciences, the arts, religion, and education. His knowledge is sometimes described as esoteric and his teachings mystical. In any event, he attracted and influenced large numbers of followers, and his teachings enjoy adherents yet today. See chap. 11 for a brief reference to the Camphill movement based on Steiner's principles.

18. This refers to the Auditorium Building (1886–89), designed by Frank Lloyd Wright's mentor, Louis Sullivan. Working on the plans for this building was one of Wright's first assignments when Sullivan employed him as a draftsman in 1887.

19. Peter Berndtson was with the Fellowship from 1938 to 1940 and 1942 to 1946.

20. Steve Oyakawa was with the Fellowship from 1948 to 1961.

21. John Amarantides, known as John A, was with the Fellowship from 1951 to 1973.

22. *A Testament,* Mr. Wright's second-from-last book, was published in 1957. See *Collected Writings,* vol. 5, 155–225.

23. Curtis Besinger, *Working with Mr. Wright: What It Was Like* (Cambridge: Cambridge University Press, 1995), 260–1.

3

Working: "The Place Is Magic"

rank Lloyd Wright's interviews with prospective apprentices were typically brief and casual. Some who joined the Fellowship recall him as having seemed indifferent. In most instances he knew little about them. Perhaps he had seen letters they wrote, perhaps he had been briefed by his assistant, Gene Masselink. But mainly he relied on an instinctual sense concerning their fitness for satisfying the Fellowship's needs and demands. What apparently mattered to him was whether they would fit well into the community, not whether they had an impressive background or knew how to put their best foot forward in an interview. To discover what he needed to know, he put them to work as quickly as possible.

For most of the senior fellows, their first work experiences were unforgettable. Here in the sequence of their arrival we hear from Charles Montooth (1945), Joe Fabris (1948), Bruce Pfeiffer (1949), David Dodge (1951), Arnold Roy (1952), and Tony Puttnam (1954). Time and different experiences may account for their contrasting recollections of Mr. Wright working with them at their drawing boards.

CHARLES: Outside of going into my room, which was magic then (I've written about this part of it), and going right to work, I remember Gene Masselink saying (I brought my drafting tools), "You probably won't need those for a while." And, there were just endless lessons, because he [Mr. Wright] was all over the place. He would come in and sit down with you when you were working on drawings, things like that. I came in November, so it was just a very short time before Mr. Wright went with Mrs. Wright to New York to the Guggenheim. It was a snowy day, and I remember when they left they were dressed for the city. That was 1945.

When you arrived, if you had great dreams of sitting down right away with Mr. Wright at your elbow drawing plans for great house and other buildings, they didn't materialize?

Not right away. Because it was winter and cold, they were building a model for the Loeb house, and so pretty quick I got to work on that. No, the first job was shoveling coal for the boilers, and it was a lot of fun and a lot of hellish hard work. Wes Peters, who did everything, commandeered a dump truck and the green apprentices, and we went into town and unloaded a big gondola railroad car full of coal and brought it over here.

JOE: My first job was working with a group who was doing some plastering. They were plastering a new little apartment on the end of the Midway barn. I remember that very well, because it was sort of dismal. The weather happened to be wet and cold. And I immediately got into it; I guess I had an aptitude for construction. Certainly during Mr. Wright's lifetime I spent, I would say, maybe 75 percent of my time on construction work. I did do some work in the studio; I worked on different projects.

I've designed and built buildings. I built a lot of the buildings here, or rebuilt them. When I first came to Arizona, that first winter in '48, '49, we were working on construction of the little Cabaret Theater and I started with that. Very quickly I got to be in charge of projects; I guess I just had an aptitude for it. I guess Wes and Kenn had done a lot of that sort of thing, and Wes more and more was being needed in the studio. So it just happened that I got into the situation where someone was needed, and I was good at it.

BRUCE: I was standing outside the big kitchen here—it was a cold day in February, much like today—and there was a wood cover over the electrical outlet in the ground. It was made of mitered wood, a rather nice architectural feature. John Hill walked by and said, "Why don't you get a hammer and saw and repair that?" I looked positively horrified because I'd never seen a hammer and saw in my life. That was my first experience of participating in the Fellowship life.

And then a week or so later I was in the kitchen, and the cook was Elizabeth Mock,[1] a good writer and architectural historian. She was cooking. She had some leftovers and was trying to make a meal out of them. She had some mashed potatoes and some rice and some hamburger, and she said, "I haven't got enough potatoes or enough rice." I said, "Why don't you combine them and put some hamburger in?" "Oh," she said, "that's not a bad idea."

Later, as we shall see, Bruce became the founder and director of the Frank Lloyd Wright Archives. Before Mr. Wright died, he knew that Bruce was moving in that direction:

He always called me the Fellowship historian. And he loved the fact that I was a musician. And he showed . . . well, he actually complained to Mrs. Wright when he said, "Bruce is not going into the studio." Other people who were in the Fellowship even less time than I, such as say John R or Tom Casey, came in and very quickly moved up to a very high position because they were very fine draftsmen. Mr. Wright never would let me take another piece of paper after he'd drawn on it. He made me erase it and then draw. He would make his sketches over my sketches, and then he'd say, "Now, okay, erase it and put it in." He was very conservative; he hated to waste paper. We sat together on a long bench [covered] with sheepskin.

I got worried that I wasn't really doing what I should be doing for him. I didn't think I was serving him well enough, and I told Mrs. Wright that. I said, "I don't know if I'm really helping Mr. Wright, working on this house project." And Mrs. Wright said, "Do you notice something when Mr. Wright comes into the studio?" (He usually came in through the kitchen door. And as he went from desk to desk the apprentice got up and Mr. Wright sat down and drew.) "And did you notice that they all get up and he sits down and draws? But when he comes to your desk he says 'Move over.' He sits beside you and you work together and then he leaves. And I asked him, 'How's Bruce?' and Mr. Wright said, 'His drafting is terrible but he's very quick to pick up ideas.'"

Twice Mr. Wright told me that my house was the best of the Box Projects.[2] He said, "If you want to learn to draw you can always learn to draw, but having good ideas is something that cannot be taught. It comes from within."

DAVID: At home I was not asked to sweep things or do anything. I came from a very luxurious circumstance. Taliesin was really an enormous shock to me. The first thing Mr. Wright did, or whoever made out the work list (maybe Mrs. Wright), was to put me in the kitchen with the women . . . in the Hill kitchen in Wisconsin—canning tomatoes. And I was the only boy amongst them. And these women were all smoking

Joe Fabris and Bruce Pfeiffer in the drafting room at Taliesin West.

cigarettes, which was a complete and total taboo at Taliesin. If Mr. Wright walked in there, they would be all on the bus leaving Spring Green. That would be the end of them.

I was twenty-one. But I could barely lift these cases of tomatoes that they were canning at an ungodly speed up there. I had to cart them down the back steps and into the root cellar, and that was about all I could do—barely to lift them, you know. And the steps were all so uneven. Oh, it was just a hellish job to do that. But it was building up my strength, and then the next thing I knew I was helping the stone masons, and of course—huhhhhhh—lifting stones and helping them. Mr. Wright had me hauling the stone for the bird walk.[3] The bird walk had stone all over, the whole surface of it and the big terrace out there. We needed the stones up above to put them there, and Mr. Wright didn't even have a pulley. I mean, Mr. Wright was just poor; we didn't have a block and tackle; we didn't have a pulley. So, with a rope, hand over hand, I'm pulling up these big rocks, these big limestone flagstones, you know. Oh, God, it was tremendous physical work!

ARNOLD: We were working on the men's locker room. I remember Wes Peters was working out there. Wes was something else; you've probably heard stories about Wes. Here he was . . . he'd been at Taliesin for many, many years, and he was an architect and an engineer and had worked on the Guggenheim and was the engineer on it. Here he was putting in some plumbing in the future men's locker room up there. That was one of my assignments—to work on that, on construction. So I was working with Wes right away. I didn't understand; I didn't know who Wes was or what. Later I found out: here's a fellow who's an architect, an engineer, and Frank Lloyd Wright's right-hand man, and here we are installing some sewer lines. Right away I got a glimpse that this was a very unusual place. Everyone does whatever work has to be done.

TONY: I was to go out and get rid of the Canadian thistle on the property. Some of the farmers around the neighborhood were not good about [that]. They let their cattle overgraze and the Canadian thistle would take over, and they didn't seem to care much about that. Mr. Wright hated Canadian thistle. So, virtually the first assignment I ever had, he went into town and bought a sort of flame thrower and asked me to go around and burn Canadian thistle and all its seeds and make sure I got it right down, way down into the ground so it wouldn't sprout again. So I did that for a while. Then, the theater had burned the previous year, and I guess the second job I had was working on rebuilding the theater at Hillside. That was a long project, trying to get that done. We worked all day and early evening to try to get that done—everyone worked on it.

Did Mr. Wright make the point of teaching you about construction while you were doing this grunt work?

No, he had plasterers and carpenters—Cubby Koster was a plasterer, and so you would work with him for a while and learn about plastering. And then George Hass was the stonemason and you'd be kind of his apprentice. George Hass had been a stonemason in Europe before he came to this country. Mr. Wright hired him on to do that and very much admired him. George understood about Taliesin stone work and how to arrange the stones so they weren't either too messy, too random, or too perfect. He understood how to get it so it was sort of casual, you might say, without being too finished.

Another of Tony's stories reveals the financial circumstances of Taliesin throughout Mr. Wright's days and beyond them.

One of the first things I ever was asked to do at Taliesin was when Gene Masselink came along and explained to me about visitors and how much they were charged, and he said, "I want you to stand here, and the next car that comes up you take their five dollars for the tour and send them on in and they'll give them the tour. But you bring the five dollars directly to me. If you encounter Mr. Wright on the way and he asks you, 'Do you have any money?' you say no."

It took a while before Tony was able to move into more serious work, but as this exchange reveals, that did not matter much to him:

When did you sit down at a drafting board with Mr. Wright?

Oh, with Mr. Wright? I can't say that I ever sat at a drawing board with Frank Lloyd Wright. The amount of work that he had to do in the last years [was very little], although in the very, very last several years of his life it picked up. But really, four or five people could do all his work in those years. There just wasn't enough to go around. There was a great competition to do that. I don't really recall, but I think I was there a couple of years before I got into the studio at all. There was very, very little [work].

You mean you basically were a laborer there?

Yes, an apprentice. The point of being there, though, was that you were able to learn from both Mr. Wright and from the buildings. What Mr. Wright would do—I have no idea chronologically when any of these things happened—but, for example, Mr. Wright had a set of samples. Someone at Minnesota Mining was very interested in the idea of putting iridescent coating on thin pieces of plastic and folding it structurally and welding it in between two sheets of plastic, making it very stiff, sun reflecting. Glass was not as sophisticated as it is now, like you could get green if you wanted to reflect sun. It didn't have any particular properties to reflect light or any of the kind of engineered products that we have now.

So someone apparently was interested in trying to fuse a composite panel of plastic to do this, and they produced all kinds of configurations, in different colors. Mr. Wright had them lined up in a window—they were quite high in the office at Taliesin. He would come by and he would look at them every so often. One day I was coming one way and he was coming the other way, and he looked at all these things and said, "You know, I can imagine a house that would be like lacework, and some parts would be light and other parts would be dark but it would all be varied and it would all have these gradations." He was looking at this plastic, at the idea of—the then very novel idea—of being able to modify light coming in the walls with these various capacities, and he was thinking of how buildings could be formed this way and designing in his own mind a new kind of building.

The point of being there was more for the exposure to that kind of creative process. You could see his thinking as it went along. He would go out and find some new material or get interested in some particular thing. Five or more years before my time, [I've been told], Mr. Wright got very interested in spider webs, and he sent people out to find different kinds of geometries in spider webs. This was at the time when he started doing cable, being very interested in cable structures, which was very novel at that time, although he had done some before. He was very interested in the material. Nothing that I can recall that was ever built came of this, but there were quite a few designs based on cables. Nonetheless, people were participating in his process, in his creative process of trying to look at things and learn from [them]—in this case, learn from nature, learn from materials.

And then Mr. Wright would have Japanese print "parties." I have no recollection of anything that he ever said about a Japanese print, but I remember the way he treated them. I didn't know anything, absolutely zero, about Japanese prints. They were old, they were Japanese, they were woodblock; fine, that's all I knew. But in showing them, the way he would pick them up and handle them made them [very special]; compared to anything else you had seen picked up or handled, you knew that this was the most precious thing and most fragile thing. He was treating it in a way appropriate to that. It was the bodily motion of respect and love that he had for these prints which came through. That was the big impression. I suppose he said something about them— I don't remember what it was—but his attitude was vivid. There are many stories like these.

When did you get into the studio at a drafting table, and who were your mentors in doing that?

It was for the Box Projects. You had time in the evening or sometimes during the day to do things like that.

Do you remember your first Box Project?

Yes, it was a house. I can sort of see that it was an L-shaped-floor-plan house. I don't remember much else about it. There were some people who were quite competitive about Box Projects and who would do the most extraordinary thing that they could think of. I can't remember if it was the first one or a later one, but Mr. Wright irritated everyone terribly by coming down heavy on some of the more showy projects and saying if you have a simple landscape you should have a simple house, and things like that. I guess what I'm trying to say is he approached these things in more generalities. I remember the first Box Project that I was there, he was talking about simplicity, and he said, "You know, if I had really let myself go (or something to that effect), I could have really knocked their socks off. I could have done this, but I have always been kind of conservative."

Tony also described experiences with Mr. Wright when he was temporarily separated from the Fellowship.

Well, I was there off and on for a number of years before Mr. Wright passed away, and then the army got hold of me. I had an abbreviated experience with the army because they made a mistake on my physical and finally discovered it and threw me out, which was fine with me. I ended up in New York City at the time that Mr. Wright had the suite in the Plaza Hotel. And that was fun because he would come to town every six weeks or about, as I recall, and sometimes we'd go up there and help. There was one Sunday afternoon with drawings of the Guggenheim Museum rolled out on the floor and we were down there making corrections and fussing around with little things in the drawings.

Mr. Wright was really in his element in New York City, loved New York City. He loved having an elegant suite in the Plaza, and he enjoyed the entire thing. He loved looking out over Central Park in the twilight and seeing the little lights, the very wonderful little lights that came on in Central Park. And he loved, I think, knowing how to be a nineteenth century gentleman among people who still appreciated that you knew that sort of thing. He was a very charismatic figure. People would stop, even if they had no idea who he was. He had a sort of presence that was very dramatic. He

Frank Lloyd Wright posing with Hilla Rebay, curator, and Solomon R. Guggenheim at a model of the Guggenheim Museum in 1946.

could walk into almost any room and silence it just by walking in, any night of the week. He had that kind of presence. Those were extraordinary times.

His books were being published, and the publisher was there in New York. Ben Raeburn[4] was enormously caring and a very witty, intelligent, entertaining guy, and they had wonderful times together. And Bill Zeckendorf, who kept threatening to build some great project by Mr. Wright, was nonetheless a wonderful, delightful person, and I think that he probably supplied . . . I know that he would occasionally send money over to Mr. Wright, because he was simply broke then. Mr. Wright called up once and he said, "Zeck, I'm broke. I have to get out of town. Send over $500." It arrived by messenger very quickly.

Were you working with him at the time on the Guggenheim?

No, I had a job in New York. There certainly weren't any paying opportunities to work with him at my level of experience. If I'd had money it would have been delightful fun.

I asked Ling Po whether he remembered what he did the first years he was at Taliesin, maybe even the first day. His response reveals how much the Fellowship meant to him and how he got started.

LING PO: [I was] greatly excited by the early morning routine of after breakfast, everybody going to the vegetable garden and each taking their assignment of a patch of the vegetables and starting the weeding and doing all kinds of things to cultivate it. I was very, very excited. Being a city boy, I never knew anything about gardening. I only knew, from reading, the importance of working outdoors with nature, of manual laboring. So, I was naturally very excited to see this present-day American institution instituting this as an important part of training.

Were you able to speak good English when you came to the United States then? Had you studied English in China?

I could read and write better than I could talk. I had been very slow in understanding and articulating this speaking language.

Ling Po's excitement derived in large part from his respect for Mr. Wright.

Mr. Wright started his school in 1932 in the deep Depression of America, with no help except from his wife, no support, nobody that he could enlist as his professors, his staff members, and no money. Being a man of superior confidence in himself, he started anyway, felling his own trees, quarrying his own stone, even burning limestone into lime to make mortar for the stonework. Being the only teacher of the School and the only money earner, whatever he said was law in the community, and this one-man leadership gave character to this organization. And this was also the reason that his Fellowship stays to today, while so many utopian communities came and are gone, like summer flowers throughout the history.

If his community was ruled by a dictatorship, there was an ethical basis to it. For any member is free to quit. If he stays put, he should accept this leadership because he acknowledges him to be the wiser and braver leader. And he better submit his will and obey. To Mr. Wright this is true democracy—the ruling of the innate aristocrat—while so-called democracy, which is the ruling of the majority is most of the time mobocracy, for the majority is so often wrong. His community was a wonderful thing, don't you think?

What happens, though, when Frank Lloyd Wright dies?

Any organization has its life span, even as any individual. Under one-man leadership or majority ruling, our community has a reason to live on, so long as it does not outlive its usefulness. And if after a time of studying in a Buddhist community I still wish to come back to this group, for long or short periods, I should be thankful to the members here that have kept it going through thick and thin and benefiting young people who are attracted to Mr. Wright and his work as I had been almost fifty years ago from today.

Johnny Hill's remembrance is more detailed. Recall that he had come to Taliesin when he graduated from high school and Mr. and Mrs. Wright had been abroad when he began his apprenticeship. When they returned, they greeted everyone—except Johnny, who, shy and nervous, was in hiding. The story continues:

JOHNNY: The next morning I had been set all by myself to hoeing corn in a great big field over on the other side of the farm. I had been around for two weeks doing this sort of thing. But that's what I was doing, and Gene came in an open car and said, "Mr. Wright wants to see you." I was wearing, for then, a very small bikini and nothing else. I was barefoot and dusty and dirty, and I said, "Oh good. I'll go in and shower and get cleaned up." And he said, "There isn't any time. You have to go right now." So he ushered me into Mr. Wright's office over at Taliesin, and I was pretty scared. I felt so unprotected. Mr. Wright was writing, sitting absorbed in something he was writing. He had that way about him, whatever he was doing . . . anything could happen around him. But finally he finished and he looked up and said, "Well, you've got a nice flat belly." It was such a nice face.

He asked me how my father was and then he asked me what I was doing, and I told him I'd been hoeing corn. And he said, "Okay, let's go; I want to get out." So Gene drove us back [to the field], and Mr. Wright and I hoed corn for what seemed, at least, like an eternity to me because it was hot and I was already tired and I wasn't used to that kind of continuous labor.

[He was dressed] in a suit. He took his coat off. He wore his hat. He wore a hat outdoors all the time, really, and a good deal of time in the studio, too. But he explained the principle of the hoe to me. It didn't require strength; it was a skill, proper positioning. You were supposed to be severing the roots and not hacking the whole thing up. Well, I just fell in love with him; he was so wonderful, and it made it seem all the more as if I'd come home. He was not indulgent; he demanded a lot of people. He paid it back, very consciously, not necessarily with money but with what he had—good guidance, careful consideration for your own good, so that it was a very strong something or other to count on and to help.

Sometimes the first assignment led to subsequent ones as each apprentice found her or his niche. In John Rattenbury's case, that involved some special experiences with Mr. Wright:

JOHN R: I worked on the farm, driving a tractor, and when it was discovered that I could operate a bulldozer, I was assigned to the road grader. On my first day, Mr. Wright walked beside the grader, tapping the blade with his cane. "Let the road follow the slope of the land, John," he directed. "Don't try to change nature." A false move with the blade and I would have wiped him out, but he never gave it a thought. As I was to learn, he had both physical and moral courage, in great abundance. I poured concrete, repaired roofs, worked in the kitchen. . . .

Eventually I got a chance to work in the studio, on some of the many houses that Mr. Wright was designing. Twice a year we had an occasion called the Box, when we presented our own designs to Mr. Wright. My first project, a design for a house in Oregon, received his approbation. I was encouraged beyond words. I discovered that at Taliesin hard work was genuinely appreciated, that honest mistakes made in the course of an endeavor were not censured, but accepted. I found that the best way to relax was not to lie around but to find another form of work. . . .

After I had been here a year I went to see Mr. Wright in his room. "Mr. Wright, I would like to stay another year," I said, "but I don't have enough money. This is all I have left." I handed it to him, my last $300. He put it in his pocket. "Thank you, John," he smiled, "Come on, let's go and plant a tree." So I picked up a shovel and started digging and not a word more was ever said on the subject. But I sensed that as long as I kept faith with him, kept working and kept learning, I could stay.

I worked on many different things. Some were surprises. For example, one day I was cleaning the living room when Kay, who was Mrs. Wright's administrative assistant, came out of Mrs. Wright's room carrying a radio. She saw me and said, "John, could you take Mrs. Wright's radio into Spring Green and have it repaired? It doesn't work." When she left I plugged it in and turned it on. Nothing happened so I gave it a whack and out came some music. Back around the corner came Kay. She grabbed it from my hand, exclaimed, "Oh, thank you," and disappeared back into Mrs. Wright's room. A moment later she reappeared with another radio, dropped it in my arms, asked me to fix it, and was off. Well, my fate was sealed because I applied the same scientific technique, the radio began to play, Kay returned, snatched it up, and as she ran into Mrs. Wright's room I heard her say, "Isn't it wonderful, Mrs. Wright, John knows all about electricity." For the next eight years I was the electrician at Taliesin, learning by doing, barely one step ahead but highly motivated. I eventually built the electronic control system for our theater lighting.

Shortly after I came, there was a fire at Hillside, which burned down the Taliesin Playhouse, the Fellowship dining room, the weaving gallery, and several apprentice rooms (including mine). Mr. Wright, undismayed and always the optimist, immediately drew a new design and we started rebuilding. So I added to my skills daily. I was doing carpentry, masonry, concrete work, roofing, plastering, and plumbing. I helped make jam and preserves. I became a breakfast cook, brought in the hay, cleaned the studio, started a rose garden, joined the Taliesin chorus.

One week in every six I was the family server, serving meals to Mr. and Mrs. Wright and their guests. Sometimes in the evenings, when everybody had gone to bed and I was still washing dishes in the Little Kitchen, Mr. Wright, in pajamas and robe would come for a late snack, usually a bowl of cornflakes. He always had some humorous story to share or some words of wisdom. "Listen to this," he said one such night, reading from a book in hand, "He hadn't an enemy in the world but his friends couldn't stand him. Did you ever hear such a devastating description of anybody?" Any feeling of tiredness I might have would vanish. Treasured moments.

Another interesting experience John had with Mr. Wright seems humorous now but was not so then.

I had been here about six years when I got some problems with my teeth, and I had a big dental bill coming up. I didn't know what to do about it; I knew I had to get my teeth fixed because it was my front two lower teeth. I had made some friends in town, and they asked me if I would design and build a super doghouse. They had two police dogs. I agreed, and they said, "How much will it cost?" And I figured, "This is how I'm going to pay for my dental bills." So I made the price what was equal to my dental bill, which was a few hundred dollars. For me it was a staggering amount of money since I didn't have any.

I had gone to Mrs. Wright and said, "Mrs. Wright, I have this opportunity. Would it be all right for me to do that?" And she said, "Well, I think that's all right, John. I understand you need something." She knew I was a hard worker—dedicated and everything. She felt it wasn't the kind of thing I could really go to Mr. Wright to ask.

So I designed a clapboard, mahogany doghouse for two dogs, with radiant heating. I made it down in the shop; I did it on Sunday afternoons. One Sunday afternoon Mr. Wright came down with Mrs. Wright. I was just finishing it off, and I heard him coming in. Well, he came in, saw this thing, and tapped on it with his cane and said to one of the other apprentices who was down there, . . . "Jerry, what is this?" And to my absolute horror I heard Jerry say, "Oh, that's something that John R is doing, Mr. Wright. It's something he's doing on his own, and I'm sure he's using up all of your lumber and wasting your time."

I thought, "Oh no, I'm not hearing this." Mr. Wright was furious and he said, "That's it. Out with that boy." He turned to Mrs. Wright and the two of them went out. I thought, "Oh, my God." I wanted to strangle Jerry. I said, "How could you say such a thing?" He hadn't realized I was just around the corner, and he was embarrassed about it all. About an hour later, Kay called and said, "Go and see Mrs. Wright, and don't worry, she's taken care of the situation for you."

. . . Mrs. Wright had taken all the rap. She hadn't been able to say that I had come to her, but she had explained something, I don't know what. Anyway, Mr. Wright said, "What are you doing down there?" I said, "Well, I'm making a doghouse for somebody and it's because I have this dental bill." And he said, "While you're here, if you have a need for a dentist or doctor, you come to me and I'll take care of it for you. I'm glad to do that. But," he said, "while you're here you don't have clients and you don't do houses on your own." I kind of meekly responded, "Well, it was only a doghouse, Mr. Wright." He looked at me and that twinkle was in his eye but he didn't dare smile. He saw the humor in it, but he said, "It doesn't matter, John, it's a house. Now don't you do it again."

"What was the first thing you did when you arrived at Taliesin?" was a rather standard question in the interviews. Here is Tom Casey's response:

TOM: Go to work in that same place where they were building a theater that I had just visited. We happened to be digging this hole where the orchestra pit is. There's a geologic form around here called caliche; you may be familiar with it; it's absolutely like concrete. If you study it geologically, you find out it's made just about like concrete is made. It's a combination of a matrix and a lot of gravel and stuff, and it's so hard. So, we were down in this pit slugging away at this stuff. We already had the roof on. Wes, of course, was anxious to bring some dynamite in to do this, but we said, "No, no, we're liable to blow the roof off. We don't have that much skill." So we were down there shoveling and picking. . . . We were actually doing it with a sledgehammer and wooden wedges. You could get a purchase, and you would wedge it out of there in small chunks.

Here you were, a new degree holder in architecture from Berkeley.

Yes, digging a hole. That's at least construction, so you're learning a lot about construction. I had participated in some construction anyway, so I was familiar with some of the tools and some of the activities, and I was enjoying it enormously. You know, the place is magic. I couldn't believe when I first drove up here, these colors on the face of the rocks. I thought, "My God, somebody must be painting these things or something." But you discover where this comes from and what effect it is and how that effect is achieved. There is a quality of magic about Taliesin West that, in my view, has always been here. And I continue to see it throughout all this time. It still seems magic to me.

You were not married at the time?

No, I was not. In any case, that summer when we all went to Taliesin, I ended up working on the farm, and I took care of all the pigs that year. Then people would ask me, "Well, let's see, you've gone to Taliesin to go to school for architecture; what are you doing raising pigs?" Well, as a matter of fact, again in retrospect, that's one of the key experiences in learning, working on the farm that summer. I just learned an awful lot about life and what it's all about and what architecture has to do with it.

Yes, I had thirteen sows and 130 pigs and took them all the way through until they went off to market in the fall. And, I met the people in Spring Green who ran the gristmill and took care of the animals. There was a lot of human contact. I got acquainted with people who had vast stores of knowledge about all kinds of things that I learned there. I enjoyed that, and I was the garbage man all summer long because we were separating paper from wet garbage, and I had a huge cast-iron pot—it was about three feet in diameter inside—and put all this wet garbage in there. About three times a week it would get filled up, and you'd build a big fire under it and fill it up with water and feed it to the pigs. You learn an awful lot about farming and animal husbandry and everything else on the farm.

Before long, however, Tom found himself engaged in many notable projects. In describing them, he also offers astute insights into the character of Frank Lloyd Wright, which he sees in sharp contrast to what he regards as the caricatures that persist to this day.

I got to work in architecture on most all the major buildings that Frank Lloyd Wright did in the last decade of his life. The Guggenheim Museum, the Greek church in the Milwaukee area, the Marin County buildings in California, some of the buildings at Florida Southern College. You can hardly name any major building that was done in the last decade of Frank Lloyd Wright's life that I didn't play a really significant role in, especially in terms of its structure.

I was always fascinated by structure, because in my mind the structure of something and the architectural expression of it in true organic architecture cannot be separated.

Pig shelters at Midway Barn, Taliesin. Affectionately called "Pork Avenue."

They are integral. The architectural expression of a building grows out of how the thing is put together. Frank Lloyd Wright had incredible imagination about how you can use structural circumstances to give architectural expression. He really analyzed those buildings—like the Guggenheim Museum or the synagogue in Philadelphia or the Greek church in the Milwaukee area. You will see that the structure of those buildings is absolutely integral, or essential, in their expression as a piece of architecture. That always fascinated me, that connection, and I found . . . it was going on here.

Wes Peters was doing it all, with the help of Mendel Glickman. From those two people, especially Mendel, I learned all I know about structural engineering. I had basics in school—it's coming back a little bit now, it was divorced for a long time, the idea of structure was gradually pushed aside—but when I was going through school it was a big part of the program. We actually took courses in the engineering school and learned the basic structural theory that then got applied to the major materials of concrete, steel, and wood. So you had some capability; you understood the physics of the whole circumstance. I simply . . . was attracted toward that here at Taliesin.

It was in the last decade of Frank Lloyd Wright's lifetime that some of those particular buildings were finally realized. So I just gravitated toward Wes and Mendel and ended up working together with them, learning from them and, therefore, participating in the realization of most all of those major buildings. To me that's great satisfaction.

Mendel was a structural engineer who was attracted and joined the Fellowship. He brought his wife and children in the very early years (1932–33) into the Fellowship. They had four or five children. Mendel was a young engineer in Milwaukee, and he came and worked with Frank Lloyd Wright on the Johnson buildings, on Fallingwater, and so on. Well, his family situation didn't in the end . . . Mrs. Glickman wasn't happy there, and I guess the children were struggling . . . anyway, they left.

Mendel went to Russia to help and got involved in building tractor factories in Russia (consequently he spoke fluent Russian). He spent a few years there, then came back to this country because it didn't take him long to get disenchanted about . . . the Soviet system when he was actually there experiencing it.[5]

Do you have any recollection of particularly significant experiences with Frank Lloyd Wright?

Well, it concerned these things, but also significant experiences in terms of activities in the Fellowship. What always astonished me, and what I appreciated, was the fact that Frank Lloyd Wright was someone whom you saw every day. He came to work in the studio virtually every day of his life. And there he was working, and he'd come and sit at your desk to see what you were doing. Not, say, every single day, but from time to time. We were working on some project or other and he would come and ask you what you were doing. And then maybe sit down at your desk and sometimes, much to the trial of somebody like Jack Howe[6] who was trying to organize all this stuff, Mr. Wright would sit down . . . and say, "Oh, let's look at this." He would begin to change things, you know, which Jack was always concerned about because it meant an interruption in the flow of work. . . . I guess the most significant things were those kinds of experiences.

I remember one time in the summer there was a local plumber who . . . you know, Mr. Wright did that, he employed elder people who had construction skills to come and work at Taliesin when they were beyond their years of working in the trade. So, Joe Krogman was the local plumber in Spring Green and he came out and worked all the time. And apprentices would be assigned to help him from time to time. So I was working with Joe Krogman, which was a revelation, because you learned what was underneath Taliesin—all the tunnels and pipes and everything else, where they were. Joe had this habit of going around the place and picking up tools he would see here and there that somebody might put down and carrying them home, because he felt they had just been neglected, somebody had thrown them down. Well, when I observed this for a while I got very upset about it. The guy was just taking all this stuff away, and I went to Mr. Wright and made a big fuss about it. I said, "We gotta get rid of this guy." Mr. Wright then sat me down and gave me a lesson in what value this person had to Taliesin and surely it was worth you losing a couple of shovels and picks, you had to see the bigger picture. That was also a good experience.

But it was more than, let's say, just something to do with the specifics of architecture. It was interaction. There was a group of us who served them [Mr. and Mrs. Wright] meals quite a lot, and I was part of that group for years. There again, it was another kind of encounter. We used to cook their breakfast; we had breakfast right here in this fire cove. And Mr. and Mrs. Wright would come. Often Brandoch[7] would come—he was just seven, eight, ten years old at that time—and have breakfast with them. And so, there was another level of interaction when you were there first thing in the morning, exchanging greetings and talking.

Even though you served them, they evidently didn't treat you as menials.

Oh, that's very true. Well, Mrs. Wright really . . . I'm sure you probably have heard, Mrs. Wright made the Fellowship run on a day-to-day basis. All of its organizational structure and all of the fine tuning of what we now have as the work list and how jobs are delegated and so on is all Mrs. Wright's, basically Mrs. Wright's work. The struggles, as a matter of fact, that Mr. and Mrs. Wright often had were just about that, about who was going to do what. Because he wanted people to come out and build this wall or tear down that something or other. And Mrs. Wright would say, "Well, it's his turn to go in the kitchen." "Well, by God, how is he going to help me?" They would have pretty stiff arguments sometimes about people doing something or how they were going to be assigned one place or another.

I mean, [the disagreements] would all get resolved, but there was a definite contest of wills, to a degree, about who was going to do what, especially when somebody was a key person pursuing some construction change that Mr. Wright was wanting to do . . . and he had this group of young people out there working away, and suddenly she wanted to come and take somebody away from that job because they were going to go do something else. He would get very upset about that, and they would argue about this sort of thing. Sometimes he won and sometimes she won.

So you had a lot of interaction with both Mr. and Mrs. Wright on a whole variety of levels concerning not only architecture but just life in general, on a day-to-day basis. Here was somebody who was available every day. This was not the remote genius who walked in, threw it down on the table and said, "Take it or leave it, this is it." That's the characterization farthest away from the truth about this man that's persistently carried on by the media. That's my biggest complaint about the media, that they fasten onto idiosyncrasies and characterize someone by a few of the idiosyncrasies that they're able to pick out of the tremendous span of activity and say, "This is the characteristic of this person." I think that's so misguided; I think it's terribly misguided about Frank Lloyd Wright.

You know, if he was this remote person, how come so many people were attracted, and why did they come and stay? And the very fact that there was this large—I mean, the group was fifty people, for heaven's sake, who were attracted and stayed and carried on a lively daily life. That doesn't fit with the characteristic that is being described. I mean, people don't stick around somebody who isn't fun to be with. Forget it, they won't stay around. You know, this is not some cult of exotic, religious belief or something; it's a working organization, a day-to-day kind of thing.

Mr. Wright overseeing
work at Taliesin West.

You have wonderful times; you have very lively, interesting times. You have sad times, you have happy times, you have the whole gamut of human experience. Well, that doesn't occur where people are antisocial, for God's sake. It's just the opposite. That's always been disturbing to me that these characterizations are carried on in that fashion. And then they get broadcast abroad and you read them in the paper and everybody begins to believe that, and it's not true.

The stories that have yet to be told. Bruce has got a roomful of boxes full, let's say, just about architecture, about projects, about how they got there, who did them, how were they realized—all these things. Those stories all have yet to be told. [Much] of the material is uncataloged so far. There's an enormous amount there. . . . Well, maybe it's not the tip of the iceberg, but there still remains an enormous amount there that has yet to be uncovered and made evident. It's just story after story about building after building after building and how they came from being a germ of an idea to a realization of something that's standing there. Frank Lloyd Wright didn't do that by himself. There was an enormous cadre of people who had to be there to make that sort of thing happen.

I think Mendel Glickman, to get back to Mendel, was a very key person. In later life—he had a heart condition; the doctor told his wife, "Look, you get out of Milwaukee. You get down to some other climate if you think Mendel's going to live longer." So they left the Milwaukee area and moved to Oklahoma, and he taught there at the University of Oklahoma at Norman. But he would come [back] to Taliesin. By then their children were all grown up, all gone; they'd come and spend virtually every summer at Taliesin and Mendel would work on these projects.

They came to Wisconsin and stayed there on a regular basis. Mendel used to come [to Arizona] when school was out and would spend a week. . . . Or he'd come over a long weekend to help out on all these major projects that were going on in that final decade of Frank Lloyd Wright's life. Who knows what a key figure Mendel Glickman was in all this? Nobody knows that yet. I know it; I'm the one that's still living. Mendel's gone, Wes is gone. Wes knew it. There is still plenty to do yet.

Susan Lockhart's story also shows how roles of the fellows evolved:

SUSAN: The first week was getting ready and living in a single sheepherder's tent. Two people . . . we built a bed that was a single bed during the daytime and folded out into a double bed. We built a planter; we had a little built-in cabinet work around two sides of the tent. A tent slab is basically, what, maybe 9'x9'? So we made our way.

Then I was assigned to help in the office because I had typing skills (I put myself through school that way); I worked in the drafting room. I was very much involved immediately in the dance work, which was very active at that time, directed by Iovanna Wright, Mr. and Mrs. Wright's daughter. And so I worked pretty intensely in the dance program for a period of almost ten years. At the same time, I was taking my own art training [with Gene Masselink and then Vern Swaback[8]], which was in fine arts and education, and adding to that the component of seeing in the abstract and making that seeing in the abstract applicable to the decorative arts, which we look at as that abstraction process applied to furniture, furnishings, decorative items, plans, elevations.

I also had the opportunity to learn graphic arts, particularly in the context of when we were working at the Biltmore Hotel. And so I started my graphic training there with hands on, and since then I have pretty much directed the graphics program.

For Dori Roy, too, the work responsibilities evolved. The changes in her role dictated by health problems show the sensitivity of the Fellowship to such concerns.

DORI: I was in the Chicago group [studying Gurdjieff] and we would come up on weekends in Wisconsin and just do anything that needed to be done. I cooked; I was doing just whatever anybody else did. I did a lot of sewing for a performance that we had that spring. Then . . . the girl that had been doing Mrs. Wright's sewing left, and so that's what my first assignment was—it was to alter clothes for Mrs. Wright. My first regular job. I liked to do anything that would give me contact with Mrs. Wright, because she was very busy, you know, and you didn't get to see her often, but sewing itself bored me.

What do you do primarily now?

I became Wes's secretary and was the only secretary in the annex. . . . In the annex you have pressure constantly. If there wasn't a deadline for one architect it would be a deadline for another one, so you were always under deadline pressure. [When the doctor took me off cortisone], I couldn't do that.

I was very much interested in starting our library, and I was fascinated with computers. We had the first computer here to type Mrs. Wright's autobiography. So Minerva[9] and I used that one; we were the first ones. And then I got a computer to put the library books on. Elizabeth [Dawsari] coded them all. So that's what I did, and little things like the architects' Christmas list—I would coordinate that with Mrs. Wright's so there wouldn't be duplicates. Now everybody more or less does their own thing, and I just give them their lists. But I used to be very careful not to duplicate Mrs. Wright's.

And [now] I pass out telephone bills. Everybody has a code . . . not everybody, not the younger students. I was astounded. I thought, "I just can't understand these bills. Nobody has been doing it, and we're losing thousands of dollars in personal phone calls and calls to clients that we could get reimbursed for." So I volunteered to do it a couple of years ago, and I thought, "I'll just pass these out, everybody will give me their checks, and I'll mark it off." People don't, and students, wow!

Well, this postmodern age . . . these kids don't write letters, they call. The whole thing has been an eye-opener.

Indira Berndtson, daughter of Cornelia Brierly, returned to Taliesin in 1962 after having lived with her parents in Pittsburgh and attending college. I asked her about the kinds of things she has done through the years.

INDIRA: The first thing I did was help Iovanna, Mrs. Wright's daughter. She was a writer and a choreographer, so I just basically helped do her typing, filing, taking care of her little daughter, Eve, who at that time was about two years old. Eve's father was Andrew Binnie who had left the Fellowship.[10] They had been divorced, I think, only about a year after Eve was born. He went back to Canada.

I helped take care of the Sun Cottage, so that's why I still to this day help take care of [it]. I've had a long history with it. . . . I also participated in the cooking and the chorus and then the dance performances. Iovanna was very lovely, and she could be really fun and inspiring, but as the years went on she began to be more and more irrational and erratic and very difficult, very cruel in her words to people.

You were quite a bit younger than she, were you not?

She was born in 1925. I was born in 1942. It became more and more difficult, so sometime in the '70s I asked if I could switch jobs. I started working for the architectural firm in the annex, and I was doing filing, secretarial work and continuing to cook for the group and also for Mrs. Wright. Then I became Wes Peters' personal secretary. My sister had done that before me, and then she became Dick Carney's personal secretary for a while.

All the time I really enjoyed Bruce. I admired him as a personality and for his intellect, so when he started putting together the Archives I wanted to be part of that. Whenever he had letters to type I volunteered to type them. But it wasn't until 1982 that I actually became his assistant; at that time there were just two of us working in the Archives. So from 1982 until now I've been working there.

Indira Berndtson

But you have other jobs assigned to you as well.

Right. I still participate in the cooking and the chorus, and my maintenance is the guest apartments. I try to be some sort of a mentor to the young apprentices, but none of them have asked me to be their actual counselor except one girl in her work in English. That's kind of sad, but I guess it's because I really don't have that architectural background that most of them want.

Sarah Logue says that Iovanna "was a large part of my life at one time." In fact, from 1970 to 1980 Sarah was Iovanna's companion much of the time, but Iovanna's "emotional roller coaster" made it impossible for the companionship to continue. Yet, Sarah speaks admiringly of Iovanna:

SARAH: Iovanna is a wonderful person. I can't tell you how inspiring she is. She is full of love and intelligence and leadership and sensitivity in every way. But she is too sensitive to stay with the Fellowship. There is too much excitement as well as a lot of disappointment. I went with her for a month to Paris one time, and it was obvious that Paris was too exciting and stimulating. . . . She is an extremely complicated person. With her parents she was loving and struggling at the same time. Perhaps she is that way in all her relationships.

I asked Sarah how she spends her days now.

I spend a lot of time keeping the routines of Fellowship life running smoothly—ordering of household items and doing the shopping. I work with the social committee and so forth. I am also on the education committee. I am in constant contact with people. Minerva and I do graphics on some of the publications. . . .

She also described her husband Bill's role in the Fellowship. He remains in Wisconsin year-round.

Bill does the gardening. For many years he has supplied the Fellowship with quantities of fresh vegetables all during the summer season. He is blessed now with the friendship of our young Chinese architect, Lang Yue. She has been in the Fellowship [since 1991], and is very interested in the garden. She knew nothing about gardening when she came, but she has worked with Bill, until now he says that she is a good enough gardener that he could walk off and she could do the whole thing.[11] Bill works also with a different apprentice each week and teaches them gardening for an hour a day every day all summer.

In the Fellowship's early years, the women did most of the cooking. Kay Rattenbury describes her experiences in the kitchen:

KAY: When I was cooking, there were only four cooks, and we cooked one week every month. I cooked nine years for the Fellowship, then I taught cooking for twenty years and supervised the kitchen. [Of] the nine years I cooked, for about six years I had every holiday because it came in the same time of month. I really learned how to cook turkey! I helped Mrs. Wright, who was in charge of Baba [Easter bread]. I was her

Apprentices preparing a meal.

main assistant, and then I was in charge of Baba until it was turned over to Arnold, Kenn, and Tom Casey.

The ones who were cooking were Cornelia, Svetlana, myself, and Frances Fritz. We all had children within a few years of each other, and we were nursing our children, getting up to cook breakfast, [fixing] lunch and dinner. Gene [Masselink] finally realized that we were trying to nurse our children and cook breakfast for the Fellowship, at the same time practically. We had to get up about 4:00 or 5:00 in the morning besides getting up in the middle of the night [with our babies]. And so he volunteered to be a breakfast cook, and Davy volunteered. Johnny volunteered. Later when Svet stopped cooking Kenn started cooking. That's all I remember of the first volunteers. So they cooked breakfast for us so we could take care of our babies.

As senior fellows recall their work experiences, one or both of the Wrights almost always play a part. Frances Nemtin describes how Mr. Wright called upon her and her then-husband Kenn Lockhart to run the farm at Taliesin. They had been in Lakeland, Florida, to supervise the construction of Florida Southern College, designed by Mr. Wright.

FRANCES: We came back after two years or so for a holiday, for part of a summer in Wisconsin, and Mr. Wright kept us hostage because Dr. Spivey, the college president, had not paid all his fees and Mr. Wright thought if we stayed here Dr. Spivey would realize he couldn't build without Kenn's presence so he would pay up. And ultimately he did. . . . He and Mr. Wright were very similar and got on very well. When the project started, Dr. Spivey didn't have all the money to finish the building. Mr. Wright appreciated his spirit, the fact that he wanted it so much. And he gave him lots of credit.

. . . Rather soon Mr. Wright had the idea that it would be interesting if the Fellowship ran the farm. He had been disappointed with the succession of tenant farmers he'd had, so he asked part of us, as an experiment, to be the farmers—Kenn and I, Johnny Hill, and Morton Delson,[12] who was a new apprentice, had been there a little while. And Mr. Wright said, "Morton, you can earn your tuition if you stay on the farm this year." And Eric Lloyd Wright, his grandson who was eighteen.[13]

So we moved into Midway. I think Eric lived at Taliesin and someone lived in the farm apartment at the end of the barn, and we occupied the cottage. And then started a really arduous experience, because it was a desperate winter. It got down to 52 below and snowed every day, and we were not equipped for the winter. The house wasn't really tight, and we didn't have enough winter clothes. Kenn was the only one who had had some farm experience of the five of us.

At another point in the conversation, I asked Frances about Kenn's background, reminding her that someone had heard Mrs. Wright say of him, "This is my right-hand lieutenant."

Well, she depended on Kenn for all kinds of information. Someone in the kitchen had a burn, or the tractor broke down, or a child was sick, or some plumbing needed something, or . . . he was just so knowledgeable for all these practical things, and he helped many people in a very kindly and quiet way. In the kitchen he'd go through and see the cook was having trouble chopping. He'd say, "Is your knife sharp? Let me show you how to sharpen it, how to cut." He was just very deft.

He came from one year of art school in Minneapolis. I don't know what precipitated his coming here. I think he always had a slight inferiority complex about not having the creative gifts that he perceived in Johnny, Wes, and Gene. They were four very close friends, but he didn't have that same design ability. And I think not till he found this CSI [Construction Specifications Institute] work did he come into his own.

When I was here in 1992 they spoke of how indispensable Kenn was to virtually every project in doing the specifications.

He was, absolutely. Stephen always introduced him right away to his new clients. He said, "This is Kenn and he'll be working with us." He wanted him to be recognized and appreciated for his invaluable technical gifts. . . . He was very important and very essential in the construction aspects of our work. He was always doing repairs. He was very versatile . . . and achieved a lot of prominence and awards from the Specifications Institute. He filled a very unique niche. He was central to all our jobs, but he never became a designing architect. I think that was a source of some frustration and disappointment to him.

What sorts of things did you do when the farm experiment was past?

One year stretched to two years, not just one winter but one full year and then a second full year. The personnel changed a bit. Johnny went to *House Beautiful* magazine. It was quite a switch, when you think he was for ten years assistant editor of *House Beautiful* living in Manhattan, and before that he was taking care of calves on the farm in Wisconsin. Eric also made quite a switch, going to the Korean War. Morton, who was there just the one winter, was a very good sport. He was a boy from Brooklyn, unused to the country. . . . A lot of effort and time in those years was spent sustaining ourselves. We canned a lot of food before the days of the freezer, and we had regular crews every week in the canning kitchen, putting up tomatoes and beans, pickles, corn, making great jars, vats of sauerkraut, making jam by the gallon.

That was a big effort. And we did all our own laundry then. I mean all the table linens and guest towels and sheets, everything. There was a lot of work just in maintaining our life. We didn't hire very many people then. In fact, Fellowship wives did the secretarial work after Gene died. And so, it was much more modest, more informal . . . the tone was relaxed but the work was intense. And we had time to do many things I regret we don't now.

To someone outside the Fellowship, Mr. Wright's age would have been a matter of concern, for he reached his eightieth birthday in 1947. The apprentices did not seem to be concerned about this, however, perhaps because they so deeply respected the master. I asked Charles Montooth to summarize what he regarded as the real genius of Mr. Wright.

CHARLES: I guess I'd lean on what Mrs. Wright said.[14] He had that gift of genius, the same way that Bernard Shaw described it. He had the ability to absorb from every kind of possible source and all kinds of ideas. And then he reconstituted them and put them back in ways that were beneficial to mankind. I think another thing about Mr. Wright—I think he was the personification of integrity.

Now somebody like Brendan Gill, a very charming guy who wrote his book [*Many Masks*], sort of comes with a different viewpoint.[15] Although Mr. Wright was a showman, I've never known anybody who thought he carried it into his work. It's evident in his architecture, just the fact that what you see here, that's the building. It is not what you see so much today in houses because of the economy and all kinds of things, but integrity in living by his principles, not going for fashion or sham. . . . He didn't do things for sham. The publicity, and whatever came naturally, came detrimentally a lot of times. He could say shocking statements, but still, you know, he lived and worked without a telephone. Here he had one pay phone and in Arizona no phone at all.

Johnny Hill provided an interesting perspective on working with Mr. Wright when I asked whether it ever occurred to him that this thing he was entering might not last all that long.

JOHNNY: No, he seemed as though he was going to go on forever. When I first came, there were just a couple of jobs. That's why I could do so much farmwork and things, because there wasn't enough studio work. And then, it kept building and building and building until, during those years when I was running the drafting room, we were turning out Usonian houses at a tremendous pace.

He would come in . . . I kept his desk set up for him, all clean, and I claimed I could affect the future of architecture by whether I gave him a 60-degree, 30-degree, or a 45-degree triangle. He wasn't fussy, you know; he fit himself into whatever was happening. But anyway, he would come in to the studio, and if there was a house or whatever, he would come in with the design pretty well defined in his mind. He didn't do it the minute the job came in; he let things cook. And then when he sat down and drew, he had this thing completely in his head—the simplest little house or even the Guggenheim Museum. Every floor was in there on one drawing, the sections and floor plans. It was hard to read, but the whole thing was there.

And then the draftsmen would take that and refine it all?

Yes, we would take it and work it out. You had to be very careful. For instance, on those very simple Usonian houses, he didn't always indicate dimensions, but you had to scale it very carefully. Sometimes he drew on the plot plan and it was even smaller scale. But you didn't guess, you measured very carefully because the proportions were terribly important. Sometimes it would be a nine-inch board fascia, sometimes it would be ten or twelve, but that was all in that first sketch. Things weren't right if you didn't preserve this very carefully.

Mr. Wright surrounded by apprentices in the Hillside drafting room, 1955, nine of whom are heard or cited in this book: Seated are John Howe, Eric Lloyd Wright, and Wesley Peters; standing to his right is Gene Masselink and to his left Ling Po, David Dodge, and Tom Casey; surrounding Peters, left to right, are Stephen Oyakawa, Kenn Lockhart, and John Amarantides.

He did so much that it's natural to ask whether any of the buildings that went up or any of the plans that were drawn under or over the name of Frank Lloyd Wright were done by other people.

Well, the drawing, of course, was, and many of the perspectives were laid out by other people and then he put the magic in them. I was working on a little house for Kenneth Laurent. He was in a wheelchair. It was a charming house; it was unlike anything Mr. Wright had done up to that point. It was all on arcs so that the chair could move easily. I wasn't happy because the perspective was obviously not the right angle. It wasn't explanatory, but I went ahead and started putting some trees over on the side. I showed it to him roughed in and I said, "I'll do this over a little higher."

"Oh, no," he said, and he took it and spent probably twenty minutes making a charming drawing out of it. It was just lovely. It was one of the nicest ones you'd ever see. It's not me. It's what he could do, especially in the circumstances when the client was coming that afternoon.

Was he a good draftsman himself?

Yes, he had an elegant touch. When he got into the flowers and things, he was an artist. But he didn't have much respect for just plain good drafting. He had respect for beautiful drafting in the sense of draftsmanship the way he would have had for craftsmanship in woodwork or something, but he didn't put it in on the level of creative work. He had this tremendous gift; he had to exercise it. He needed people to help him do it.

You apprenticed then, as an architect?

Yes. Along the way. Once Mr. Wright got to really know what was in me, he put a lot of faith in me to understand what he was doing, There were a few years there when Wes was tied up in Florida and Jack Howe was away, and Davy.[16] I was heading, really, all of the work. The work list of studio assignments and the work out of the studio were my responsibility. And arranging the parties and the music programs and doing the general work lists. Bit by bit these things fell to me.

I had studied piano beginning at six years old. I wasn't terribly good because I never would practice, but I could read wonderfully easily so I could do accompaniments and ensemble playing with some competence. For a few years we had a really professional pianist, Carol Robinson, who had been with Mrs. Wright in the Gurdjieff Institute. She was one of the resident musicians, and she took me in hand and got me so that I had some really good performing pieces. But I was too self-conscious to be a solo performer. Mr. Wright really pushed me into directing the chorus and doing all these things, thinking it would help, but I don't believe it ever did. Performing publicly was a nightmare.

John Rattenbury comments on Mr. Wright's manner and his relationship with others in the Fellowship in later years.

JOHN R: In the studio, Mr. Wright dealt with the client and designed the buildings. We were pencils in his hand, glad to be involved in such creative endeavors. Wes Peters and Mendel Glickman did the structural engineering, much of which broke new ground. Engineering for the spiral forms of the Guggenheim Museum was not found in a textbook. I made many of the construction drawings, drew structural details, and worked out formulas for dimensioning spiral shapes.

Jack Howe was the senior apprentice in charge of the studio. From Mr. Wright's conceptual sketches he drew presentation plans and three-dimensional perspectives. Jack had no equal in terms of speed; he was faster than any computer that we have today. Mr. Wright would work in the morning for several hours on a project, sometimes on several projects. Before he put pencil to paper, he had the entire three-dimensional concept in his mind. When he sat down at the drafting table, he rapidly drew plans, sections, and elevations. Jack would take these sketches and draw an accurate perspective of the building, usually having a beautifully colored rendering ready to show Mr. Wright that afternoon.

In the last ten years of his life, Mr. Wright designed 269 new projects. In addition, there were many commissions already in the office, either in the drawing stage or under construction. Besides Jack and Wes, there was a group of about ten senior apprentices . . . who were responsible for preparing the working drawings. Whenever the opportunity arose, Mr. Wright would send one of them out to supervise construction.

When I came, the group included seventy-five apprentices. Many, like myself, came from other countries. This international mix has always been a dynamic element of Taliesin. Our skills varied from novice up to a high level of technical and artistic competence. Mr. Wright was more interested in our spirit, our potential for learning, and our appreciation of organic philosophy than for our academic achievements. Whenever we became good at whatever job we were doing he would put us to work at something new. His definition of an expert was a person who had stopped learning. As a result, we grew in resourcefulness. . . .

We realized learning was a lifelong process. Somebody asked Mr. Wright one time who was his best student. His reply was, "I am going to have to give that honor to myself." He said he wasn't a teacher, meaning in the academic sense, but we learned from him every moment. The Wrights were our living heroes. They put up with no nonsense, nor did they ever talk down to us. They were interested in everything. Mrs. Wright described Mr. Wright's genius as his capacity for absorption. He was a great sponge, soaking up ideas from people, from nature, from events, from every source, transmuting them into creative ideas. And that is the way we learned, surrounded by the vitality and beauty of Taliesin, through a process of osmosis.

Mr. Wright would make the rounds of the studio, stopping at an apprentice's desk to see what he or she was working on, spending time going over their drawing. We designed many of the details but every drawing that left the office came under his watchful eyes and had his signature, FLLW. If it wasn't right, it was thrown out and we started all over again. Mr. Wright was often a great problem because he kept seeing ways to improve his designs. Once Wes said to Mrs. Wright that we would never make the deadline on the [Guggenheim] museum because Mr. Wright changed it every day. Mrs. Wright went for a walk with Mr. Wright. "Frank," she said, "if Beethoven had kept on making improvements to his first symphony how many more would he have written?" "All right, mother," he replied, "I get the message." The drawings went out the next day.

I participated in almost a hundred projects. Some of the most memorable were the Unitarian Church, the Guggenheim Museum, the Price Tower, Monona Terrace, the Dallas Theater, Lenkurt Electric Factory, the Oasis State Capital, the Greek Orthodox Church, the Beth Sholom Synagogue, Gammage Auditorium, Baghdad University and the Post and Telegraph Building, the Freund Department Store, and the Cultural Center at the University of Wichita, and many houses all over the country. After some years I took over the specification writing from Wes. I also did most of the lighting designs.

It is astonishing that Mr. Wright could continue to be so creative and energetic. What an exciting event it was to see him come into the studio and after an hour or two of concentration at the drafting board, throw down his pencil, stand up and say, "Well, there it is, boys." And we would gather around and see before us his beautiful design, a structure quite unlike anything ever seen before on the face of the earth. On one memorable day he designed the Mile High building in the morning and the Greek Orthodox Church in the afternoon.

Building a model of Price Tower.

Each apprentice had a different working relationship with Mr. Wright. Joe Fabris describes his:

JOE: Our relationship was pretty much a working, nuts and bolts, sort of thing. I did see a lot of him, but it was largely just to discuss what we were going to do here and there. Mr. Wright always kept in touch with all the work, a lot of it in the studio on the commissioned projects but also on the construction work. He'd always come around to see what was going on.

He respected your ability to get the job done.

Yes, and as I said, I was committed to that, and if Mr. Wright wanted it that was my aim to do it just the way he wanted it. So, yes, I'm sure he did get to trust me, because more and more he would leave things to me. One project was to convert a chicken coop in Wisconsin into dormitory rooms. He never came up once, and we just had a little discussion at the beginning on what to do . . . it was a lot larger than just a remodeling. I don't think he even saw the thing finished, because it was near the end of his life. It was finished before he died but he never came out there. There was a wonderful thing I heard later—that Mr. Wright was asking for "Joe." And he said, "I don't mean the doctor, I mean *my* Joe." I've really treasured that all my life.

Here are some recollections by Arnold Roy:

ARNOLD: Of course, Mr. Wright was still quite active [when I arrived], much more so than in later years. But he was active right up until the end. I remember working in Wisconsin and trying to do some painting. I was not much of a painter, of course—not much of anything, really. Mr. Wright was always immaculately dressed, and he saw I was having trouble. [He said,] "Young man, this is the way you do it." He took the paintbrush and showed me how. When you have somebody like that showing you how to paint . . . to this day I can paint in my tuxedo and not get any paint on me. Prior to that I'd get paint all over everything. Many times Frank Lloyd Wright would come along and just take whatever instrument I had in my hand and show me: "This is the way to do it."

Did he seem to know how to do just about everything?

He could do anything; it was unbelievable. Another time in Wisconsin we were working on the farm. Mr. Wright would drive around with Mrs. Wright and stop to see what was going on. He was great for taking his cane, pointing, and saying, I want such and such. One of the older apprentices was there and Mr. Wright said, "We need a road back here." And the cane went like that.

I happened to be standing there, and a senior apprentice jumped on the little bulldozer, the little caterpillar, and behind it was a grader and he said, "You get on that." I didn't know what a grader was, and he said, "Move these wheels so the blade . . ." (or something like that). And then he started off and I was supposed to be blading in a road. Well, I didn't know what I was doing, and Mr. Wright was standing there and he was yelling. We'd come around and he'd yell at me and the apprentice would yell back [to me], "Do something." So we'd keep going around in circles, and finally we put a road in. You learned very fast in situations like that.

And by Dori Roy:

DORI: I remember Kamal said when Mr. Wright died, "I will never, ever, know if what I did was right in the way of design"—because he wouldn't have Mr. Wright to tell him. You see, Mr. Wright would say, "Oh no, this has to be here to make the design work."[17]

I was too in awe of Mr. Wright to be close to him, but he was always very kind to me. I remember that first Christmas. He liked capes, so I made one. A dark navy wool cape with a leather collar. And oh my goodness, I had many tears over sewing on leather because I had never done it before. But after many skins I finally got it, and he called me in on Christmas Day, and I gave him the cape. And he said to me, "Doris, this is the nicest present I received." Well, [it lifted me] about two feet off the ground.

Did he wear it a lot?

Yes, he did. I don't know who got it after he died.

Dick Carney, who became the chief executive officer and managing trustee of the Frank Lloyd Wright Foundation after Mrs. Wright's death, enjoyed a very close working relationship with both Mr. and Mrs. Wright. Here he describes experiences with Mr. Wright:

DICK: Mr. Wright's secretary, Gene Masselink, had to have his hip replaced, and having your hip replaced in 1950 was quite different than having it replaced now. It incapacitated him for about a year and half, and while he could still be Mr. Wright's secretary, he couldn't go with Mr. Wright and be with him most of the day the way he had been in the past. So Mrs. Wright asked me if I wouldn't like to become his aide.

I would say, at that point I sort of became Mr. Wright's aide-de-camp, and I was with him from early in the morning until the end of the day. I would help him get dressed, and I would drive him wherever he wanted to go. In other words, I was just continually with him, and I learned a great deal. Those were the most fascinating ten years of my life, I would say. And that's why I got so close to Mrs. Wright, because she was very interested in Mr. Wright's well-being.

While I was Mr. Wright's aide I was expected to see to his well-being each day. That meant that if the doctor said he should take a pill at ten o'clock that didn't mean at five minutes till ten or at two minutes after ten; it meant at ten o'clock. [I had to] follow those rules and see to it that he did exactly what he was supposed to do.

Dick Carney

But then . . . just to be with Mr. Wright and see that he had a totally different viewpoint about everything than anybody else does. If he got started at something, there was absolutely nothing that was going to make him stop. He was going to move forward with whatever he had started. If he was on his way to the airport, we were going to get to the airport; we were going to get on the plane and go. We even got to the airport once when the plane had taxied away, and I had to go in and persuade them to bring the plane back, which they did. I simply learned that I could do a lot of things that I would never have dreamed of doing myself. [When we were] driving in traffic so thick you couldn't move, I would get over on the outside of the traffic and go around and keep right on going.

Or go shopping with Mr. Wright at Sears Roebuck. He would feel that he wanted to go through Sears Roebuck in about thirty minutes, gather all the things he felt the Fellowship needed, and give them a check at the end of the thirty minutes. But that's not the way Sears Roebuck works. You know, you go to each department and you write a separate check. So I would have to get the manager of Sears Roebuck, let him come with us to keep track of everything Mr. Wright was buying, be ready to write out a check for Mr. Wright to sign at the end of the thirty minutes, get in the car and leave, and then go back later in the day with the truck and get everything we had bought. That teaches you an entirely different way of operating.

Indeed, the Fellowship itself had an entirely different way of operating. Members of the Fellowship readily grant that the Wrights were benevolent dictators. The charisma of both made their style of leadership acceptable to those who stayed. Johnny Hill's comments help one understand how it worked:

JOHNNY: I think that the whole basis was very much Mr. Wright's theory that democracy was the highest form of aristocracy that the world had ever devised. And we were to be living a life that included all of the arts, much music, some performing, lots of reading. He himself, probably monthly, took an evening to read Whitman to us, or sometimes Emerson. And he spent several times during the summer for an evening of Japanese prints where he would show some of the collection and explain them to us. He got a lot of inspiration out of them early on—the simplification in them, the depth of the message that was got across with so few lines. There was a very conscious effort on their parts to be molding everybody.

Of course, there were people who wouldn't take it and didn't last. But there were those who did and in various ways were grateful. But there were rules. You did your part. You took your turn in the kitchen, you took your turn at serving, you helped in the garden. I did a lot of farmwork, partly because—Evanston isn't city, but it's not country—I loved it. I loved to be out, so I had to be dragged practically by the collar into the studio to learn to draft.

If the Taliesin Fellowship depended so fully on the Wrights' charismatic leadership, how could it continue after they were gone? Cornelia Brierly provides an explanation.

CORNELIA: The Fellowship was started in an experimental way. Both Mr. and Mrs. Wright tried to find ways to deal with each problem as it arose. The nature of the Fellowship has always been to solve problems as they arise. As things change, people say, "You'll never be able to continue." We've always continued. People thought the Fellowship would end after Mr. Wright died and it didn't. They said the same after Mrs. Wright died and the Fellowship continued. It's in the nature of this group to try to solve disruptive problems. That's what keeps the group active and creative.

Notes

1. Elizabeth Mock (later Elizabeth Mock Kassler) was with the Fellowship 1932 and 1933 as well as 1948 and 1949.

2. The 1997 Handbook of the Frank Lloyd Wright School of Architecture describes the place of Box Projects in the Taliesin tradition: "The Box Project is rooted in the early history of the Fellowship. Apprentices prepared their designs and compiled them in an elaborately crafted box to present them to Frank Lloyd Wright on his birthday and Christmas. It was a 'gift' of ideas, which he regarded greatly and affectionately. The apprentices would take turns in removing each project from the box and presenting it to Frank Lloyd Wright, who in turn would give them feedback. Over the years the Box Project has evolved into being the primary demonstration of a learner's total architectural development and has become the tool for comprehensive design evaluation" (64).

3. The bird walk is the cantilevered extension over the hillside from the living room at Taliesin.

4. Ben Raeburn published books by both Mr. and Mrs. Wright at Horizon Press.

5. Mendel Glickman maintained an association with Taliesin from 1932 until his death in 1967.

6. Jack Howe was with the Fellowship 1932–64. For many years he was the head draftsman in the studio; he left to establish his own practice.

7. Brandoch Peters is the son of Wes Peters and his late wife Svetlana Wright Peters; he survived the automobile accident near Taliesin in which his mother and younger brother died in 1946, when Brandoch was five years old.

8. Vern Swaback was with the Fellowship 1957–78; he left to establish his own practice.

9. Minerva Montooth has been a member of the Fellowship since 1952.

10. Andrew Binnie was with the Fellowship in the late 1950s.

11. Lang Yue was elected to senior fellowship status in 1997.

12. Morton Delson was with the Fellowship from 1950 to 1959.

13. Eric Lloyd Wright was with the Fellowship from 1948 to 1956.

14. In *The Roots of Life* (New York: Horizon Press, 1963), Olgivanna Lloyd Wright wrote, "His power of observation, together with simultaneous absorption, was phenomenal. A form which left an imprint upon him, he abstracted perhaps ten, twenty or thirty years later. He missed and wasted nothing of what he saw" (55–56). Wright himself described a genius as "a man who understands what others only know about." He also cited an old Welsh definition of genius: "A man who sees nature. Has a heart for nature. The courage to follow nature," in "A Testament," *Collected Writings,* vol. 5, 157, 174.

15. Brendan Gill, *Many Masks: A Life of Frank Lloyd Wright* (New York: G. P. Putnam's Sons, 1987), portrays Mr. Wright essentially as a habitual, superfluous, self-promoting showman.

16. Davy (Allen) Davison was with the Fellowship from 1938 until his death in 1974.

17. Kamal Amin was with the Fellowship from 1951 to 1977.

4

Mrs. Wright:
"Such A Remarkable Person"

T he Taliesin Fellowship's vitality from the very beginning and throughout Frank Lloyd
Wright's life depended to a great extent on Olgivanna Lloyd Wright. While her husband
reigned supreme in the studio, the rest of the Taliesin domain was largely hers, subject, of
course, to Mr. Wright's sometimes reluctant approval.

Almost everyone associated with the Taliesin Fellowship credits Mrs. Wright with having
been a charismatic force in shaping its character and direction. She held things together in difficult
times, gave the Fellowship the discipline it needed, and served as a counselor and exemplar for
many—and she did so on her own terms. Consequently, she was a divider as well as a unifier.
Those who did not satisfy her standards met with rebuke or felt her sting. Some would call it an
imperial sting. If they did not respond, they were invited to leave or made to feel so unwelcome
that they left voluntarily. Consequently, those who remained with the Fellowship—the persons
whose voices are heard in this book—largely admired her.

Olgivanna Lloyd Wright had been conditioned for this role, according to Edgar Tafel, one of
the first apprentices, by her experiences with Georgi Gurdjieff. From him "she learned the patterns
of living in a closed society run on a strict routine by a master with a powerful philosophy"; this
enabled her "to bring another dimension to life in the Fellowship." Mrs. Wright, Tafel says, "was
the force that kept the Fellowship in working order, from the very start. A remarkable woman."
He adds that in the early days Gurdjieff's philosophy was never one of the major currents in
the Fellowship's life, since "the architectural core had neither time nor inclination for an outside
philosophy." Tafel believes, however, that Gurdjieff's philosophical influence grew after Iovanna
Wright went to Paris to study with him.[1]

Visits by Gurdjieff to Taliesin in the early years also helped Mrs. Wright weave his ideas into
the fabric of the Fellowship.

Olgivanna Lloyd Wright

The Taliesin fellows we interviewed had many years of experience with Mrs. Wright to draw upon in shaping their convictions about her. Three of them traced their relationship with her back to the 1930s, eleven to the 1940s, and eight to the 1950s. All of these persons would have been acquainted with Mr. Wright, too, but the longer association with Mrs. Wright left at least the younger ones with more vivid impressions of her.

Because Mrs. Wright was so influential in managing the Fellowship and inducing men, women, and children to commit themselves to life together on the Fellowship's terms, we begin with the fellows' recollections about her.

Johnny Hill remembers her fondly.

JOHNNY: Mrs. Wright was still the most beautiful woman I've ever seen—everything [about her]. Her features were lovely; her eyes were so alive; and her movements (which had come from years of studying with Gurdjieff, the dancing and so on) weren't self-conscious. . . . One of the things that could drive Mr. Wright crazy [was that] he couldn't stand to watch people doing awkward things. He would worry about their feet if they were sprawled in some way—sitting with their feet not together. Visual things mattered an awful lot to him. He really was an artist—primarily an artist—with an uncanny sense of everything else. But, in any case, Mrs. Wright felt that it was her position to fit us to associate with him. She said so, at least to me, and she worked at it very hard. And she shook a lot of things out of us.

I remember one dinner party, a formidable one, for eight or ten people in the living room at Taliesin. I think Senator and Mrs. Benton were there. They weren't formidable because I had met them, but still, and some others . . . and I was probably there because Iovanna probably was there and we were close to the same age. In any case, we went through the whole meal—a very formal meal—and then Mrs. Wright said, "Now that he's eaten, perhaps Johnny will say something," because I hadn't said a word. Well, I'll tell you, I never since have gone through a meal with somebody without making conversation. It was a terrible thing, but it worked. And that was her method. She could either put on a complete demonstration of fury or deliver a shock like that that was unforgettable.

Did you ever have a private rebuke from her?

Yes, because I was very close to them. I was in the house a lot. I took care of Mr. Wright's room and his clothes, and I arranged the flowers. He loved to, for relaxation, work around in there—move the furniture a little or rearrange the art objects or add new things. I helped him a lot with that—"eye music" he called it, and he considered it very important.

Well, being younger than the others, I think they were sort of keeping me from what might be the bad influence of some of the older apprentices. Their affection was always there through thick and thin. Mrs. Wright was awfully good at sizing up people, understanding them, seeing what they would need to get along with Mr. Wright—to get along anywhere they would have to go in the future, the White House for dinner or whatever, that they knew how to dress, etc.

Almost all of the longtime fellows recall having been "called on the carpet" by Mrs. Wright. In this exchange, Cornelia Brierly places such experiences in context:

CORNELIA: Everybody was called on the carpet. Mrs. Wright was trying to train everybody. She really helped me a great deal even though some tasks were very difficult at the time. She changed the course of my life. The fact that she started Taliesin and carried it on is a remarkable thing in itself. I would not be here if it were not for Mrs. Wright, . . . but she did start this wonderful group of people and I was able to participate.

What do you think it was about her that made her such a strong figure and effective leader?

She had infinite, incredible energy; she had incredible insight into the nature of people; and she had charm. She could be very severe. She could be a real general if necessary. Usually she was extremely kind to people. There were so many facets of her being, it's hard to count them. . . . Mrs. Wright was a genius in her [own] way. Not only was she good with people, but she worked out all those musical programs for the dance dramas and helped with the costuming and staging of all the programs. She could paint; in the early days she did very nice painting. She had a tremendous capacity for creativity. I think in one of the parts in my book I talk about the creative parties that we gave, and they always had some deep significance even though they were lighthearted, interesting, and fun.

Did she and Mr. Wright regularly join in the meals that are in common here?

To a certain extent, but there came a time when they needed different food because of their health. Then they always dined separately, except when we had formal evenings or went on picnics. Then they always participated. Mr. and Mrs. Wright were always at tea at 4:30 in the afternoon, where usually we had wonderful talks by both of them, mostly about architecture, of course.

Here is Bruce Pfeiffer's response to my request that he describe Mrs. Wright:

BRUCE: You cannot describe a person like that. She was such a remarkable person. One thing I remember, though. When I was sixteen and learned about Frank Lloyd Wright, I went [over] to Harvard—they had a wonderful architectural library at Harvard, which is not too far from where I lived. The librarian, or someone there, pointed out the sections of the autobiography that Mrs. Wright wrote, and it just so happened that those were some of the parts that moved me the most.

So I knew I was coming to Taliesin as much for her as for him. It was no surprise to me to find her as powerful a driving force as he was. My first day at Taliesin I met and talked with her for an hour and a half. It was a cold day, and we went into one of the apprentice's rooms in the apprentice court. There was a little kerosene heater, and we talked for maybe an hour and a half or two hours. Later on, when I met Kay, who happened to be my first friend in the Fellowship, she said Mrs. Wright was talking to her about me. Kay said to her, "He talks, he certainly talks." Mrs. Wright said, "Yes, but he knows what he's talking about." So we had that rapport, and Mrs. Wright was sort of like a mother to me, a very strong family figure.

Afternoon tea under the big oak at Taliesin. (The 200-year-old oak fell victim to a storm in 1998.)

Later in the conversation Bruce spoke about Mrs. Wright's background.

I . . . would like to see Mrs. Wright's autobiography published. It can't be published the way it is, because it's overedited. But I think if we can get back to some of the early transcripts and get back to her way of phrasing things [it could be published].

I worked a great deal with her on her autobiography. I was especially trying to get [stories] about her early life in Russia. She knew Aleksei Tolstoy and Alexandre de Salzmann—the stage designer. Her brother-in-law was a patron of Leo Tolstoy. She knew all those people; she knew the whole intellectual life of Russia at the turn of the century, especially theater. That was her fascination, drama, and she said the Russian theater before the revolution was way ahead of any theater in the world in its experimental, revolutionary concepts. But then, later in her life as we were working [on her autobiography] and she was tiring out, she said, "Nobody's going to care about this. All they're going to care about is 1924 when I met Frank Lloyd Wright."

I said, "Mrs. Wright, you're one of the few persons alive who went through the Russian Revolution. You knew both sides of it." It is very important to have that book. It can't be done the way she's done it, because she ended it in 1931. . . . My editor suggests that we go back to her writings and make it like an autobiography/biography.

When I asked Tony Puttnam if any interesting experiences with Mrs. Wright stood out in his mind, he described the way she worked.

TONY: Mrs. Wright cared about people. When you go to Yugoslavia or to Montenegro you understand exactly where she came from. And so she could be a very difficult person and a very demanding person, because in her world there was no gray, in-between position. In America there are a lot of things that are okay and they're accepted as okay but not enthusiastically. Well, in her world there was good and there was bad. I never heard of anything that was "okay," that was on the knife-edge that was so sharp. I think partially it's a cultural thing, partially because she worked with Gurdjieff for so long.

She had a knack of being able to precisely put her finger on where some of our problems lay. People would come out from having an interview [with her]; sometimes it wasn't so much fun, but it could only be amusing when other people would come out and say, "Do you really think I'm such and such?" It was absolutely obvious. She was absolutely right. And the kind of thing that stood in someone's way was the least obvious to them and the most difficult for them to accept. You saw this all the time, so finally you would get around to [realizing], with very keen appreciation, that everyone's strengths [are also] their greatest weaknesses. That is the great curse of the way things are. To a certain extent, there wasn't anything you could do about it, you just had to kind of accept it and say, "You can't be this way, you can't be everything, and so you are going to have some of those problems."

The kinds of experiences that I had with Mrs. Wright—the ones that I have great feeling about—were more kind of quiet understandings. It was not some circumstantial, dramatic event.

She came along and said [to me] one day, "What you have is a kind of inner poise, so this kind of tumult doesn't affect you." Or some words to that effect. So we had an understanding of sorts.

Sometimes fellows' memories of Mr. and Mrs. Wright are inseparable, as is evident in Ling Po's recollection:

LING PO: Mr. Wright was so very important to me that to think about him is just like to think about somebody who saved my life. Mrs. Wright is the person responsible for the School. If not for her, there won't be the Fellowship, because Mr. Wright was an artistic, poetic master, having no wish nor patience to deal with personal problems. Mrs. Wright took up the very difficult job of keeping the Fellowship going, holding it together. If not for her, there wouldn't be able for us to live with Mr. Wright, so I'm surely very thankful to her.

Arnold Roy responded similarly when I asked him about a one-to-one experience with either Mr. or Mrs. Wright:

ARNOLD: There was a talk that Frank Lloyd Wright gave us at Hillside. I'd say it was the Fall of 1958, just before he passed away. He talked to us over at the Hillside dining room about the interaction he had with the younger people at Taliesin and how he got so much out of it. As he went on, he started thinking more and more about it and said something to the effect: "I'm nothing without you, and you are nothing without me. We need one other." He got an awful lot of energy out of the young people. That was sort of the basis of the talk that morning. We have a tape of it. (That was another thing I did: I recorded Mr. Wright giving all of his talks. There are about three or four hundred of them, and they're in the Archives here.)

That particular day a group of us was working on Mrs. Wright's room. Whenever you were doing anything for Mr. or Mrs. Wright it had to be done the day before yesterday—boom. So, I rushed back to my room, put my work clothes on and ran over to Taliesin. I got there just a few minutes after Mr. Wright did, and he heard the noise—his room was right next door. . . . Just unbelievable energy was in the air whenever they were anywhere within the area.

So, Mr. Wright was in his room; he heard the noise and came in. And, of course, everybody stopped, and he started talking. It was a continuation of what he had been talking about before, about how important we were to him and how important he was to us. Of course, there was no tape recorder. I remember that moment so well, to have this great man say that we actually meant something to him. We certainly realized what he was doing for us.

Were you ever called on the carpet by either him or Mrs. Wright?

Mrs. Wright more often. Mr. Wright . . . I don't remember. Mrs. Wright, of course, had that great background of philosophy she had studied with Gurdjieff, and she was trying to mold us into something. The way she did it was, yes, by calling you on the carpet and telling you what a no-good you are. And by the time she was done with you, you didn't have to open the door; you just slid through the crack under the door. And then she'd feel so bad about having done that that she'd turn around and do something very nice for you.

Right away or later?

Yes, right away usually or very soon. You'd go way down, thinking: "Oh, God, I'm such a useless clod."

Occasionally Mrs. Wright played the role of matchmaker, as Dori Roy recalls fondly in describing what happened to her after time away.

DORI: . . . Mrs. Wright said, "Well, who shall I send to meet you?"—in her cute way. Oh, I wish you would have known her. I said, "I don't know. Maybe Cornelia," because Cornelia would always do anything for people. And she said, "Well, I'll think of someone." So when I got to the airport, who meets me but Arnold. Well, of course, I knew Arnold from being here before, but I hadn't expected him of all people, because when I left he was going with Kay. And the instructions were I was to go right in to see Mrs. Wright the minute I got here. There was a mix-up in planes and then one plane was canceled, and it was quite late when I got to the airport. Anyway, I went right in. Mrs. Wright was having tea, afternoon tea, and she said, "Oh, it's good to see you. Welcome home," and all this. And then she said, "You know, Arnold isn't going with Kay anymore."

Earlier I had asked Dori if she remembered any particular experiences with Mrs. Wright that stand out in her mind.

Oh, so many, so many. You can never second-guess Mr. or Mrs. Wright. You can't say, "Well, if Mr. Wright were alive he would do this," because nobody knew what he would do. It would be something that we mortals couldn't think of, the same with Mrs. Wright. Once on Christmas we had a Christmas Eve party here, for example, with Mrs. Wright and that was when "Hair" came out. And we were playing that very loudly; we had a very raucous party. The next morning Mrs. Wright called me in, and I thought, "Oh, wow, I'm going to hear it now," because, you know, we had carried on. And she said, "Well, that sounds like a very nice party you had last night." You see, you can't second-guess her. And Mr. Wright the same.

Dr. Joe Rorke and Mrs. Wright

Did Mrs. Wright have a sense of humor? Here is Dr. Joe Rorke's response to that question:

DR. JOE: Oh, yes, she sure did. She had a wonderful sense of humor. She was such an expert with people, you can't believe it. When any of us did anything out of line, whether in her ethics it was out of line, whether it was a personal thing or a physical thing or illegal thing—whatever it was, mostly personal—boy, she'd call you on the carpet and she'd rake you over the coals in no uncertain terms, and you'd feel lower than you could imagine. But she wouldn't let you go until she'd brought you out. You couldn't leave the room where she did all this without a smile on your face. She'd bring you right out.

Powerful figures like Mrs. Wright rarely enjoy unalloyed admiration, as is evident in the comments of Indira Berndtson, who spent some growing-up years at Taliesin. Her experiences with Iovanna Wright and Mrs. Wright's way of dealing with them left her with mixed feelings.

INDIRA: I have a very deep love for her. She was very kind to me over the years. She gave me lots of both advice and presents, like jewelry and clothing and books. Dr. Joe would go out and get her the latest books, both novels and scientific things, all types of books and magazines . . . and she tried to keep up with all of that. Whenever she really liked a book, she would get thirty copies of it and give it to everybody. She really shared. She was very inspiring; you really wanted to do your best for her. And she was very beautiful. I loved her voice, the way she talked and the way she looked and moved. But also, she could be very hard on you.

Were you ever the object of her wrath?

Yes, I was, and sometimes I didn't think it was justified and sometimes I did. But one of the things was that I felt in later years Iovanna was becoming, as I said, more irrational [in her behavior] and Mrs. Wright had to deal with that.[2]

Sometimes in dealing with that in the best way she thought one could, she would advise turning the other cheek and just going back up there to the Sun Cottage—even after you had been called bad names and reviled by Iovanna terribly. I questioned whether it was really the right thing to do, for either Iovanna or me. I don't know, I just began to have less faith in some of these ways of handling things, and this caused a lot of internal turmoil. Some things just didn't seem fair or just.

Susan Lockhart had known Mrs. Wright since her childhood days in Madison, Wisconsin. Her comments about aspects of Mrs. Wright's legacy reflect the feelings also of some others:

SUSAN: I think one of the things, and I'm very candid about that, is that during Mrs. Wright's lifetime the practicing of governance did not really happen among many people, and I think it should have happened a little bit more. But for whatever reason, and for her own way of governing and leadership, that was not something that she did. She did train and groom people, but more in the style of how she governed versus simply allowing others to practice some of that.

I think we're going through a kind of a learning mode of governance. You know, simply serving on the board of a nonprofit organization is a whole education in itself. I've served on other boards in the community, so I had a little bit of that to help me and to give me some perspective on how you do that and how those kinds of things work. I think we're still learning that.

Not everyone developed a close personal relationship with Mrs. Wright. Here is Joe Fabris' response to my question about her:

JOE: I was never as close as some of the people here with Mrs. Wright. I suppose a lot of people depended on her for advice in their personal affairs, but I never did. But I always respected her, and after Mr. Wright died, I carried on overseeing the construction work and worked with her a lot. Again, mainly on that basis, but also in the dance drama performances which she, of course, was very much involved in.

To Stephen Nemtin, who joined the Fellowship right after Mr. Wright's death, experiences with Mrs. Wright were "a very delicate area."

STEPHEN: I'm somewhat reluctant to talk about that area. I would say in the large framework the initial years were extremely vital years with Mrs. Wright, and I can't give you a length of time. It may be ten, it may be fifteen years. She imparted that sense of everything being beautiful, that that's the driving force behind your work. That for me was the most important gift that I received from her. It was not all a rosy relationship, and I'm not going to talk about the parts that were not a rosy relationship.

Effi Casey and Anneliese Dodge entered the Fellowship after Frank Lloyd Wright's death; both are married to fellows. It took them a while to establish a relationship with Mrs. Wright, partly because they regarded her with awe. Did Effi come to know Mrs. Wright very well?

EFFI: Yes, in the later years in particular. She was initially, to me, a very distant person, very powerful, and I had very, very high respect for her. But you didn't just sit around and really talk to each other like you and I do right now. She had that aura of unapproachableness, and I found out later that it wasn't really so. It was just that, well, that stature that she projected . . . and also some degree of protection of her . . . of the people surrounding her to not tire her. She was very active in writing her own autobiography until the late years. And she had these Sunday morning talks she prepared. I found out later that they were very difficult for her. That didn't come easy to her; she was very nervous about it. I recall these Sunday mornings as a wonderful time of reflection and always a moment after which you would walk away with an instilled feeling of wanting to discover, inquire, and go further. I think that's an element that I search for in our vision of today, because I think vision has to have an element of transcendence. So, I think there has to be always that degree in it. Otherwise, whatever you do in the group remains in the realm of personal opinion.

Later in our interview Effi added:

You asked me about Mrs. Wright and my connection to her. . . . I had a chance to cook for her in her later years, which then really gave me the opportunity to get to know her much more, simply because sometimes she would just walk into the kitchen. We would really then talk just like this about certain things. I have to say I love taking care of older people; I have real respect for seniority. Maybe that's a European thing. I have a real struggle when people don't get up when an older person comes into the room and things like that. And she was really very, very warm and personal and had a wonderful sense of humor also. I just admired her intellect, extremely stimulating to me.

Then the other deep connection I have with her, and that's what maybe prompts my getting emotional over it, is the music. Because Bruce and I performed her music, which she wrote—the violin sonatas. And so we worked on that often. . . . The music was really a wonderful connection with her.

An experience Anneliese Dodge had with Mrs. Wright is unforgettable to her.

ANNELIESE: It was always very exciting to work out the menu, and, of course, at that time Mrs. Wright always wanted to see the menu to make sure it was balanced and not so expensive—with meat. And I liked that very much.

There was one little incident. Mrs. Wright called me in [because] I changed a recipe. We had chili con carne, and that day she said she would like to have the lunch from the big kitchen, and I did not take that recipe from "the holy book," what I

Anneliese Dodge

would call Taliesin's cookbook. I had used a magazine recipe for a pot of chili con carne with little cheese cubes on it, and that was not Taliesin's original recipe. So Mrs. Wright called me in, and I thought, "Oh boy, I'm going to get it." And then, I did not have the time to explain that this was not in the Taliesin cookbook, it was just from a magazine. No way. I went home crying.

What did she say to you?

She said, "How dare you change Taliesin's recipes? Every recipe is developed so very carefully, and you have no business. . . ." I said, "I'm sorry, Mrs. Wright." But she would not listen. I could keep on saying, "I'm sorry, Mrs. Wright. I did not change the recipe," and on and on and on. And then we just said goodbye, and she said, "In the future you know about the last sentence. 'You must not change our recipes.' They have been developed very, very carefully." I said, "Yes, that's fine. I understand about that." And I went home crying and I said to David, "The end, the end, I can't take it anymore. I don't know. I tried so hard and I got so many compliments from the young people. They loved that melted cheese over my chili."

And then, in the afternoon David said, "You wait, one way or another Mrs. Wright will call you, and she will not bring it up again, but she will say sorry with something nice." Believe it or not, at three o'clock the phone rang: "Anneliese, I'd like to have you for tea. Just you, not David."

David said, "Now you make sure you do not bring it up. Don't bring up the chili, not even to say you're sorry." She was so charming, "Oh, Anneliese, I'm so glad you can come, and I will prepare some tea." Well, I did not even think . . . I thought I would try to say something again about the chili, but "No," David said, "Don't say anything." And so we just had a wonderful afternoon, and she was a wonderful host and she always liked to talk about so many wonderful things. And she said, "Anneliese, I respect you very much [for] what you do here, and we love to have you here." And with all this I knew immediately this was to say sorry. It was wonderful.

Anneliese also recalled Mrs. Wright's entertaining:

I wish I had met Mr. Wright, but, like I said, I liked Mrs. Wright really very, very much. She was a great lady. She loved to entertain, and almost every night she would have eight to ten people in the Swan Cove for dinner. She loved especially when David would remember stories of Mr. Wright or his experiences. She sat there like a little girl who could listen for hours and hours. She liked that very much. On Saturdays, when we had our formal evenings in the theater, in the back there was a big round table they called the family table, and she would invite guests from outside. But she always [also] would invite one or two of the Fellowship (different ones each week). In that respect she was very correct.

Mrs. Wright's Sunday morning talks provided a special connection with Sarah Logue, who says that "absolutely my relationship with Mrs. Wright was the mainstay of my life."

SARAH: She was really an incredible person. Among her many talents, she was a writer. For instance, I transcribed a lot of her tapes from Sunday morning talks, and you could tell the precision of her vocabulary and her way of expression. In transcribing you couldn't just guess at a word. She had a strong accent and sometimes would turn her head away from the microphone, and you would think, "Now what was that word?" And you would think and think and suddenly it would hit you what it was and you knew that there couldn't have been anything else that would substitute. She was articulate. She was loving. She had a flaring anger when [incidents provoked her]. After she would give you a lecture . . . she always turned it around and made it something happy, either a funny story or warmth of some kind, and when you left there was always a smile on your face.

Some of the senior fellows, such as John Rattenbury, never lost sight of the fact that the Wrights were a team, that each of them needed the other.

JOHN R: As I demonstrated my willingness to work at anything at all, I was given more and more responsibility. Everything was wonderfully informal in those days. There was a great sense of freedom, although the self-discipline we needed to make it all work was much harder to acquire than any technical knowledge. In this regard, we had Mrs. Wright to teach and inspire us, and to work with us on an individual basis. Mr. Wright was the master architect, but it was Mrs. Wright who had the idea of the Taliesin Fellowship and who conceived of community life as a way to immerse us in a living culture while giving us the opportunity to develop ourselves. Theirs was a fifty-fifty partnership.

There is no doubt that Mrs. Wright and the young members of the Fellowship were instrumental in nourishing Mr. Wright's creative genius. How else could you explain how he could produce, in the last ten years of his life, such an abundance of astounding original designs. Mr. Wright told us that the Fellowship would only work as long as he was an inspiration to us and we were an inspiration to him.

Every Sunday morning he would talk to us after breakfast. He talked about architecture and he talked about life—to him, one and the same thing. He talked from his wonderful intellect and he talked from his heart. And we believed him because he spoke from absolute conviction. In 1957, at the age of ninety, he said, "I love life and I want to bring the Kingdom of Heaven to Earth. It is too cumbersome to take Earth to Heaven."

. . . Mr. Wright was the inspiration. Mrs. Wright was the glue that held us all together. She was always there to help us with personal problems. She opened our eyes to an internal life as well as an external one. She enlightened us to the need of every individual to engage in a conscious inner struggle. She helped us to see ourselves and seek true values in life.

One of the Taliesin fellows who had a special relationship with Mrs. Wright, particularly in later years, was Dick Carney. He came to Taliesin in 1948, but rather than become an architect he found himself increasingly in management roles. Here he describes how his role and responsibilities evolved.

DICK: By the time I had been here ten years I felt like I wanted to be here forever, . . . and I think that the thing that made me want to be at Taliesin more than anything else was a sense of being needed. . . . I personally needed both Mr. and Mrs. Wright and what they contributed to me. I felt that they needed in return certain things from somebody who would be devoted to providing those things to them that I could do. And so it was this sense of being needed by both Mr. and Mrs. Wright that really brought me to becoming a member of Taliesin.

I remember once, when I had been here maybe five or six years (both Bruce and I were involved in this), we walked into the living room, and Mrs. Wright was there with Kenn Lockhart. And Mrs. Wright said to Bruce and me, "This is one of my right-hand men here, and he's somebody that I depend on all the time" (talking about Kenn). "You two have not attained that status yet, but I would hope that someday you might learn what Kenn has to offer, and then possibly you can be one of my lieutenants, too." At that moment I really wanted to see when I was going to attain that status, and it took me a long time to think that maybe I was attaining that status.

When did you feel that you had attained it?

Well, I think that I was always striving toward it, right up to the moment Mrs. Wright died, because I felt that I had never really reached the point that I was doing everything that could be done in order to help move forward with what Mrs. Wright was trying to achieve, which was to keep the Fellowship together.

What do you think were your main contributions during the years that you worked so closely with Mrs. Wright?

I think I brought a sense of organization. Mrs. Wright could say to me, "This needs to be done," and I would then go out and get it done. For instance, I became treasurer in 1962, and at that point I really became part of the management of Taliesin. I would have an idea and bring it to Mrs. Wright, and Mrs. Wright would say, "Fine, that sounds like a good idea. Go out and do it." So I would go out and do it.

Were you seen by the Fellowship as something of a gatekeeper . . . or did everybody have access to Mrs. Wright?

Well, anyone could ask to go in and see her. Kay and Minerva were Mrs. Wright's secretaries, and to a certain extent they were the gatekeepers, but I was also seen as . . . I mean, if you wanted to have an appointment with Mrs. Wright you could see Kay or Minerva, but if you wanted to do business with Mrs. Wright you probably came to see me. If Mrs. Wright was going to conduct business, she would call me in. So, I was more or less the person who ran the Fellowship for her.

Evidently, you were among the people who were in her good favor. She had it in her power to exile those who she thought didn't fit, did she not?

That's correct. Yes, those who remained at Taliesin had qualities that Mrs. Wright would like to see in the future of Taliesin.

Some of them must have left, then, with hard feelings.

Some did. When we had the reunion in 1987, we invited everyone who had ever been at Taliesin to join us in a three-day event. Many of those who came back had not been

Dick Carney and Mrs. Wright

at Taliesin since they left. It's amazing how many of the alumni felt that they left in bad graces and were not welcome to come back. But we began at that time to try to erase any hard feelings that people had. The majority of apprentices left with Mr. and Mrs. Wright's blessings, but many people left feeling that they had disappointed Mr. or Mrs. Wright and that they were not welcome to return to Taliesin.

At what point did you become CEO?

I became CEO about two weeks before Mrs. Wright died. She was the CEO up until that time. Mrs. Wright was sick. She wasn't sick very long before she died, and we certainly didn't know she was sick enough that she was going to die. The Board of Directors met and decided that Mrs. Wright could no longer perform that function, so they made me the CEO at that point.

I thought it was an awesome responsibility, but on the other hand, I felt that because I had been Mrs. Wright's administrator so many years that I already knew how to do it. . . . [Now, though], I couldn't go and say that *I* decided we were going to do this so we were going to do it. Both Mr. and Mrs. Wright were benevolent dictators, and so if I had an idea or if Mrs. Wright had an idea all she had to do was say, "Do it." And then I could go and tell everybody that Mrs. Wright said we were going to do this. So we would do it.

The death of Mrs. Wright brought back memories of her husband's departure almost twenty-six years earlier. I asked Dick Carney about the mood at Taliesin when the word of Mr. Wright's death occurred.

Well, I don't think anybody expected Mr. Wright's death. He almost, you would say, died accidentally. I mean, there was nothing . . . he was sick three or four days and he had an operation, and there was something about the operation he wasn't able to survive. But his health up until that point . . . everybody would have anticipated that he would have lived at least another ten years. He was a very vigorous man; he looked about fifty years old. So it was quite a shock and it took a long time to get over it. There were several students who left immediately when Mr. Wright died; they just felt that was the end of the Fellowship. But . . . Mrs. Wright somehow created a mood in which you felt that Mr. Wright hadn't died. You felt that he was still here and that maybe he was in the next room and would appear any moment.

Mr. Wright died on April the 9th (1959), and he had, of course, a funeral in Wisconsin and was buried. But the main ceremony took place on his birthday on June 8. Mrs. Wright invited probably 150 people to come and celebrate his birthday, and that was the real ceremony ending Mr. Wright's life. And that whole evening you kept feeling that he was in the next room and that he was going to show up. There was no sense of his not being there. I think that sense of his still being there and still going on lasted for a long time and just very gradually faded away. So, in other words, it wasn't a shock of loss, because somehow you still felt the presence.

What does Dr. Joe Rorke, Mr. Wright's personal physician, recall about the circumstances surrounding his patient's death?

DR. JOE: Well, the only [biographer] I ever read [quoted a nurse as saying], "It's a tragedy he died alone. I was the only person with him when he died." Now, that's an out-and-out lie. The room was filled. I don't remember exactly [who was there], but I was there, a couple of other doctors were, his surgeons were there, there were several nurses there. And I brought in Mrs. Wright before he died. She had been there for hours and was resting just outside for a while.

Had you remained his principal doctor?

No, no. Well, I was his family doctor. But this was an emergency surgery. Really, he was under the surgeon's care; I had nothing to do with that.

Did you do the referral to the surgeons?

Yes. Well, he had known these people before, but yes, I had arranged for that. I'm not sure, Dr. Flynn might been there, too. He was Mrs. Wright's heart doctor. Again, whereas I was sort of an in-house family doctor here, on specialized matters [Mrs. Wright] had been going to Flynn for years and years and years and still went to him. Usually I drove her down when it was time to see Dr. Flynn, and she'd take her dog with her and Dr. Flynn would welcome the dog in his office and spend more time with the dog than with Mrs. Wright—the only time he ever let a dog in his office, of course. But anyway, there were a lot of people there, including Mrs. Wright.

Was there some sort of rallying on Mr. Wright's part, or was he unconscious?

He never really recovered. He was not able to speak. There were no last words. It was a death vigil. And Mrs. Wright was there for hours.

Although Mr. Wright was in his ninety-second year, his sudden death, according to John Rattenbury, "was a terrible shock because he was so full of life." John also describes how Mrs. Wright carried on as the Fellowship now faced many new challenges and its members took on new roles.

JOHN R: Mrs. Wright, although devastated inside by the loss of Mr. Wright, threw herself heart and soul into keeping the legacy alive and the Fellowship flourishing. She talked to the Fellowship every Sunday morning on a great variety of subjects. She gave lectures around the country and overseas. For five years she wrote biweekly columns for the *Capital Times*. She wrote several books. She encouraged our interest in art and culture. She composed music for the Taliesin Festival of Music and Dance, which was the annual dance and drama performance, which we gave for the public.

Iovanna, their daughter, wrote the drama and choreographed the dance. Members of the Fellowship performed on stage. We designed and made the costumes, did the stagecraft and theatrical lighting. We gave performances in Chicago, Dallas, and San

Iovanna at an elaborate party in 1955.

Francisco. The creative effort that we applied on these occasions translated into our being ever more creative in our exploration of organic architecture. It also had a direct effect on our work. At that time we were designing performing art centers in many parts of the country. Our hands-on experience in running our own theater gave us special insight into theatrical design as well as a rapport with our clients and a depth of understanding of their needs.[3]

Mrs. Wright was not only the spiritual leader of Taliesin but the moving force behind so many of the innovative things that kept our lives creative and interesting. It was her idea to take the group to Europe, which we did for three summers in a row. Under her leadership we not only survived but flourished. In addition to the cultural side of Taliesin, which she constantly encouraged, our social life grew. She invited all sorts of interesting people to dinner and special events at Taliesin. She gave personal counsel to many of us. The daily decisions, which she had to make about work, life, and community activities were always wise and objective.

Did Mrs. Wright want the Fellowship to stay the way it was, or was she ready to face change? Here is Cornelia's answer to that question:

CORNELIA: She had to change to meet new conditions that made it impossible to just maintain what we'd been doing. For one thing, we owed a tremendous amount of taxes. Paying that took a whole different approach. I can't tell you the exact details of how much tax we owed at that time, but it was a tremendous sum. And it was necessary to sell off many of the art objects Mr. Wright had. That was very wrenching, to have to get rid of a lot of art objects that were so highly prized by everyone—the print collection being among them. Dick can tell you more about this, but when we finally paid off all that tax, the tax people wrote us a letter saying that we had done a wonderful thing and that very few people ever accomplished what we had accomplished. That was rewarding.

It must have been a strong commitment by Mrs. Wright not to try to bargain that down the way some people with big tax debts do.

She was very much for getting every cent paid, whereas Mr. Wright used to be very careless about paying bills. Of course, he had some reason for it because he had so many people he was feeding and clothing. There are very few people that can carry so many people. Very often he didn't have the money to pay for necessities. But Mrs. Wright made a big point of seeing that every bill was paid; she didn't keep anything in arrears.

Although Mrs. Wright remained a vigorous leader for many years, according to Dr. Joe, she began to suffer from failing health in the mid–1980s.

DR. JOE: Hers was a much more gradual decline [than Mr. Wright's], a matter of months to a year, slow, multiple small strokes, basically. You could see it coming both physically and mentally, and you could just see her slip down, down, down.

Dick Carney did not perceive her decline the same way:

DICK: To me, [Mrs. Wright's death] was more of a shock than Mr. Wright's, because I didn't expect her to die either. And when she died that sort of ended the regime of both Mr. and Mrs. Wright who, as I said, were benevolent dictators. They really ran the place. And so, I think it was almost harder to adjust to Mrs. Wright's death than to Mr. Wright's death.

I asked Bruce Pfeiffer, who had remained very close to Mrs. Wright through the years whether she remained intimately involved in the affairs of the Fellowship.

BRUCE: Well, she couldn't be because she went blind and she went deaf, which cut her off. But when she was going blind she would occasionally come in and have lunch with the Fellowship. I remember she was talking, I think it was to Larry Heiny;[4] he was at the table. She said, "Yes, I'm going blind, but I've lived a long life and I've seen a great deal, so I have nothing to regret." But then, about a year later I came in to announce lunch to her, and she was sitting in the sun and just sort of dozing or whatever. I tapped her and I said, "Mrs. Wright, it's time for lunch," and she said, "Lunch, dinner, it doesn't matter. It's all darkness now." I knew then that she really felt bad.

I would drive her in the car and point out things in the desert. But she receded from us, I would say, for a period of six or eight months. It was a great tragedy to see her, a person who was philosophically so very strong. She couldn't stand having me talk about anybody who had died. I couldn't mention Mr. Wright's name. It was as though she was terrified of death, and yet, one of the first things she ever said to me when I was nineteen and first met her . . . she said, "You should walk through life as though it's divided right down the center—half life and half death—so that when you come to that bridge the passage is very simple. It's no obstacle."

But it was hard for her when the time came.

Yes, but who knows what happens to the mind when it begins to go like that? To see a mind which is so brilliant slip. Or maybe it was just going somewhere else, you know. Like that one letter Mr. Wright wrote to Mrs. Martin when he discovered that his friend had had a stroke. He was still living in the house but he didn't know anybody, and Mr. Wright said, "It is good to know that he does not suffer . . . and that he still haunts the familiar scenes and is a physical presence still although his mind has gone away from him. Perhaps ahead of him, waiting for him." And yet after Mr. Wright died, Mrs. Wright said that when she met God she was going to confront Him about His poor design about death. She said it should be a slow receding; the transition should be a slow moving from one room to another, not a sudden one. So, in a way, maybe that's the way she went.

James Auer, producer and narrator of "Partner to Genius," concludes his Wisconsin Public Television documentary by recalling a poignant comment Mrs. Wright had made to him: "'When I see my husband again,' she said in that intense, melodic, Serbian-accented whisper of hers, 'I will be able to look him in the eye because I will have kept his name alive.'"[5]

The decade following Mrs. Wright's death brought many changes to the Taliesin Fellowship, as Dick Carney explained.

DICK: The role of the CEO changed considerably at that point. There had to be much more of a consensus. Up until that point the Foundation and the Fellowship were controlled by the Board of Directors. A year or so after Mrs. Wright died, we changed the bylaws and created the Senior Fellowship who became the membership of the Foundation. They elected the Board, and the Board elected officers. So it became a membership organization, which it hadn't been before, and since that time we've worked a great deal by consensus. Working by consensus really slows down the forward movement a great deal. You have to get everybody to agree to something, and in the past you didn't have to get anybody to agree to it, you just simply went ahead and did it. So it's a totally different way of doing things.

The transition to the new times that followed Mrs. Wright's death is the subject of chapter 9.

Notes

1. Edgar Tafel, *Apprentice to Genius: Years with Frank Lloyd Wright* (New York: Dover, 1979), 138–9.

2. See the characterization by Sarah Logue, chap. 3.

3. John Rattenbury supervised the construction of the Grady Gammage Auditorium at Arizona State University, one of Frank Lloyd Wright's last designs, built after his death.

4. Larry Heiny was with the Fellowship from 1977 to 1984 and subsequently worked on projects for the Taliesin Architects.

5. See James Auer, "Partner to Genius," *Frank Lloyd Wright Quarterly,* vol. 4, no. 4 (Fall 1993): 14–16.

5

The Fellowship:
"An Extraordinary Way of Life"

*T*he Taliesin Fellowship has never denied its members lives of their own. Granted, they work together, cook for one another, and eat in a common dining room. They live next door to one another. They have picnics and parties, and they welcome visitors to their community. But they also live independently. Throughout the Fellowship's history there have been courtships, marriages, and divorces. Parents have raised children in nuclear families within the larger Taliesin family. They send the children to public schools. Those with personal wealth are free to enjoy its benefits. The mixture of interdependence and independence produces an extraordinary way of life.

How did Frances Nemtin maintain a nuclear family in the midst of an extended family and integrate her family into the larger community?

FRANCES: Because of our two children (and perhaps I had more interest in spending time with them), I became the surrogate mother for several others who congregated at the cottage every afternoon. I took them down to the river to swim.

Mrs. Wright and I had the idea . . . it was really her idea, but I was very enthusiastic about it . . . of the children working in the vegetable gardens for three hours every morning, starting at age five. That first summer my son Brian was eight and my daughter Leslie was six, and Mrs. Wright appointed Brian to be in charge of the other children. Ling Po at that time was in charge of all the vegetable gardens, and so they reported to him right after breakfast and he'd take them out . . . three or four or five children, and several visiting ones that summer.

Maybe they would first hoe beans or they would weed beets or whatever, and Brian, being in charge of them, unknown to me, kept careful account of what they did each day: "Leslie, two rows; Brian, three rows; Ronnie, half a row." They'd work for

A picnic in the desert.

about three hours. I'd take lemonade or something out in the middle of the time, and we'd sit under a tree and cool off. This was hard. They also had to pick the vegetables that were for the kitchen, bring them into the kitchen and wash them for the cook. They didn't have to chop and peel, but they had to scrub them.

When we found sand in the spinach we'd let them know, and if the beets were especially good we'd let them know, but they knew they were contributing something. It was very important, and every Wednesday Mrs. Wright would have them in to tea in the loggia of the house and she discussed the week's work. "How did it go? Is Brian a good leader?" She'd consult him, "Were they good workers?" And they were very frank with each other, and then she'd give them a treat . . . chocolate, and then they'd see TV for a half hour, a big treat.

Did they become fond of her?

Oh, sure. They all scrubbed up and took her flowers. And the last Wednesday of the year, before school started, she announced they'd all be going to Spring Green and she gave them each five dollars to spend as they pleased. Great excitement, and that was sort of the culmination of the summer, the reward. Although I think just the experience was wonderful, because the next spring, the night we arrived here from Arizona, I overheard Brian saying to Leslie, "Let's set the alarm. We'd better get up early and get to the garden." I said, "Brian, we haven't even unpacked. I'm sure Mrs. Wright wouldn't expect you to go straightaway. Let's get settled first." And, as it happened, they were the first children there and they worked for about three weeks alone before any of the others arrived.

Where did you live with the children in Taliesin West?

We had what now is Heloise's apartment, and when Brian was six he wanted his own tent . . . which was where the swimming pool is now. He had concrete block walls up about three feet and the tent was on that. And then he graduated to one a little bit more primitive, a little bit farther away. And Leslie wanted her tent when she was eight, so both of them were nearby but private. At night I'd go out with them with a lantern, and if it was cold I would make a fire and sit down and watch the stars. That was a very important part of their growing up here, and I really regret that many of the Taliesin children haven't had that experience, especially recently. And also the fact they were so involved in the work, so they learned how to work well and learned many skills.

When Leslie left as a young bride at eighteen and went to Hawaii, she said, "Mother, I could get a job as a secretary" (she knew how to type), "I can cook" (she had learned how to cook for sixty people . . . they both could, they were very good cooks, so cooking for a family is a cinch for her now). She'd learned how to dance here; she sang in the chorus; she learned to design; she knew how to draft. Those are all skills that stood her in good stead.

How did you handle it when they got to high school years?

In high school they had unbroken school years here. They'd come early in the Fall from Wisconsin with an apprentice. Mrs. Wright arranged an apprentice to bring them if I wasn't coming out early. But until then, they liked having two sets of friends, and they made the adjustment back and forth to schools [in Wisconsin and Arizona] perfectly all right in grammar school.

Later, Frances explained how she balanced family life with communal life.

At the end of every day I'd look back on the day and say, "What have I done for myself?" . . . even if it was just write a poem, make a flower arrangement for myself. "What have I done for my family? What have I done for the Fellowship?" And I tried to make that balance. I was very conscious of that, and in some ways incurred displeasure sometimes because I didn't show enough, perhaps, loyalty (or whatever the word was that Mrs. Wright used), devotion to her. You know, to give more to her. On the other hand, when my children were a little older I gave her a lot of time, and willingly. I cooked her breakfast for a whole winter. Another two summers I always cooked afternoon tea for her, ran from Midway, ran from Tan-y-deri to be there in time. I served her in ways that I could, but my family came ahead, so that I didn't sacrifice them. I knew that was very, very important.

Where are your children now?

Well, my son is an architect in southeast Arizona, Bisbee. . . . He's been the architect in that area for quite a while. Most of his work has been at Sierra Vista, a city to the west, which is larger and has more money. And my daughter is in California outside Sacramento; for many years she was an architectural designer doing houses that her husband, a contractor, built.

They both grew up here. They had many fathers and mothers, and they learned everything here. My daughter did go to Hawaii University for a little while during her first marriage. And my son went for two years to Beloit but not to study architecture. He came back after two years to concentrate on architecture. . . . Everyone here knows them, and they visit as often as they can. And their children do, too. For both of them it's very important that their children have Taliesin in their blood. So it continues.

Accounts by others show further that rearing children has always been an integral part of community life at Taliesin. Anneliese Dodge describes a role Mrs. Wright played with children. Anneliese and David lived in Europe in the early years of their marriage, and their son Alexander was born and spent his early childhood there.

ANNELIESE: That's what we wanted very much, because it was a little bit difficult at Taliesin at that time . . . it was not so welcome to have families and lots of children. Alexander was our first child, and we really wanted to enjoy him while he was small. And so we said when he starts school, first grade, we will return back to America.

[When] I came to Taliesin I must say I was a little bit scared. I had already met Mrs. Wright in Montagnola; I had great respect for her and I thought, "To come to Taliesin, I have to do something in architecture." And David said, "Don't you worry about that. You don't have to do anything in architecture."

[Mrs. Wright] loved the children and once she arranged a wonderful children's party. At that time [the Fellowship] had about three, four, more children. Alexander and Golnar were about the same [age]. . . . Alexander, our son, is one year older. And so she arranged a little party with fairy tales that some of our staff put together, the

Apprentices' children at play. Left to right: Margaret Montooth, Marc Welt, Walter Logue, Susan Montooth, Andrew Montooth, Remington Logue, and Derice Pfefferkorn.

Children enjoying a ride with Mrs. Wright in her golf cart.

young girls. And she invited all [the children] out to the tent, and they had a little party there.

What was it like to rear a child in the Taliesin Fellowship? Effi Casey describes her experiences:

EFFI: That was difficult. I think I was lucky from the point of view that I was married to somebody who was considered a senior. So I had a little different clout than a young couple might have today. We didn't have a child by accident; we wanted one. . . . Tom was almost fifty years old when we had Golnar, our only child . . . so it was maybe the most meaningful event in his life and certainly in mine also. Therefore, we would do anything to hold onto that gift of having this child. That means in our daily life here that we were very concerned that we were able to establish some nucleus of family within the greater family.

It had its traumatic moments . . . you know, where requests were made, "Well, don't worry if your child cries, she'll settle down eventually, and you just do what needs to be done here in the community." I would then rather take the playpen near the kitchen so I could do my kitchen duty, and she was part [of it]. . . . The child knew what I was doing, could see it from a distance. So Golnar was actually always very much a part of the Taliesin family.

I was going to ask whether some of the senior fellows and apprentices took a special shine to her. Did she grow up with multiple parents?

I'm not sure how much parents, but real love and care from a great, great many people. I mean up to the day of today. And students likewise. She in return felt always, and still does today, very much part of this family. . . . I think that's the wonderful advantage of children growing up here. They have a sense of what their parents are

Wes Peters with godchild Golnar Casey.

doing, what they're involved in, rather than Dad goes off in the morning to some office that they hardly ever connect with and then comes back at night. She could walk up anytime during the day to Tom's desk, or even to any other.

Wes Peters was her godfather. We have this wonderful picture of her and Wes sitting in the drafting room, she in her little sunsuit. It was very, very hot; it was June, late June. And only [she and] Wes Peters [were there], only those two people. She was about four or so, drawing at a desk, and in the forefront is Wes Peters drawing. There is this whole atmosphere of absolute peace and quiet, these two individuals working. And that describes really a little bit that togetherness and intimacy. Absolutely wonderful. We would take meals home in order to have discussions with her when she was in school and had problems she wanted to talk about. I think it's possible, but definitely you needed to work for that, and we still do.

The reflections of persons who grew up in the Fellowship also shed light on the nature of the community. Shawn Rorke-Davis spent part of her childhood at Taliesin. She left for her college years and beyond, but returned as a single parent with two daughters, ages eight and thirteen, in 1983. As a fellow, she established Taliesin's Outreach Program (described in chapter 7). Although she is now on leave from the Fellowship, she continues to conduct this program.

SHAWN: We started visiting when I was four and moved here permanently when I was seven. Then I left instantaneously when I got out of high school and expected not ever to come back.

Were there children of other fellows around?

Five of us. There were three girls the same age and two brothers of the other two girls who were two years older.

Shawn Rorke-Davis

Who were they?

Leslie and Brian Lockhart, and Celeste was there some of the time and Tal was there some of the time, and Christopher was much younger than us . . . Christopher deKoven Hill. And then myself.

What are your memories of those years? What kinds of experiences did you have in the Fellowship? Did you eat meals in the common dining room?

My mother was mostly not here, and my father always was very closely connected with whatever was going on in the house, basically with the Wrights. He took his meals with them, especially later with Mrs. Wright. Most of my older childhood she would eat separate from the large group. Yes, I took my meals there. [I lived] in a tent at first, and then when I got in high school I lived up in the Carousel. We didn't have so many work tasks in the summer. We would work in the garden in Wisconsin, but we weren't on the work list when we were little because we were going to school. I was fully, although fairly independently, a part of the larger group. . . .

[Mrs. Wright] took on the role of mother in a lot of ways, and I always definitely considered her family. She had a lot to do with choices in my upbringing . . . where I went to school . . . and [with] discipline. I was kind of a mischievous child. Yes, she was involved on a daily basis with my life.

How has it worked for your daughters, living here?

They like the apprentices. They've made friends over the years with the apprentices, but they don't like growing up here.

There were a lot of things about the community part that I didn't like, [either]. The other two kids, especially the Lockharts, had more of a "family" life. Their parents

Mrs. Wright and Shawn Rorke

were married, they would go on vacations, they would do things together as a family. And I was . . . at least my memory of it is that I was . . . pretty much on my own because my father's first priority (I guess I could say) was the Wrights.

As [my daughters] grow older they like it less. When they were really little they thought it was so cool . . . things that I remember liking, too. There's the wood shop, the pottery studio. You can go, make, do. Just like in Wisconsin you can run around like crazy. We had horses . . . there were a lot more animals when I was little. But they went to camp every summer for a number of years to Hilltop with the Fritzes.[1] I never did that when I was a child, but they enjoyed that a lot in Wisconsin.

What prompted you to come back?

I had gotten into some real internal difficulties in California, and I didn't feel like I was going to be able to straighten them out at all if I stayed in that environment, that I really needed a complete break. And this was the place that I . . . somebody said to me the other day, "You must think of Taliesin as home," and I don't. California seems like home, I don't know why that is; but I felt that if I were allowed to come back [here] I knew that there would be an underpinning, a safety net for some of the economic situations. I would have a place to live, I would have food to feed my children, and then I could rebuild. And that's absolutely what happened. I came back for Easter . . . I guess it was in '83 . . . and asked Gana [Mrs. Wright] if I could move back and bring the girls. She said, "Absolutely. You're always welcome."

Indira Berndtson is also a product of Taliesin and has lifelong connections with it. I asked her to recount her years with the Fellowship.

INDIRA: I was born in 1942, so my parents were not actually here at Taliesin at the time; it was during the war years. But my mother had been here since 1934, and in 1938 my father came. I was a year in Spokane, I guess, and then we came back to Taliesin, and I really don't remember anything much as a child. My parents moved to Pittsburgh around 1946. . . . In '57 my parents were divorced, but in the interim we would continue to come back here [from Pennsylvania] for vacations. Either to Arizona or Wisconsin and spend some time, and I remember riding ponies in Wisconsin and just playing with the other children. There was Brandoch [Peters], who was approximately my age, and Tal [Davison], and my sister, who was a year and a half older, and a few other children along the way. I just remember pleasant memories; I don't have any specific memories. But also, you know, my mother remembers times when I was beating Brandoch over the head with a rock, and things like that (which somehow have been blotted out from my memory) when we were about four years old.

But then, when my parents were divorced in 1957, I had just graduated from eighth grade. It was a very big shock to me because I didn't know that was going on. So they sent us . . . to live with my aunt and uncle who lived in Phoenix. And by the following year my mother had rejoined the Fellowship, so I stayed here a year in my sophomore year. . . . I came here and lived in a tent.

The children were taken to school by one of the apprentices. They were driven into Phoenix every day. We went to Camelback High School. The only thing I really remember about that is doing my homework in the drafting room and one of the architects helping me with geometry. But then, the following two years I spent in Pittsburgh with my father. Then I went to the University of Chicago for one year, because my sister had gone there, and I thought it would be really great to follow whatever she did. So I got a scholarship from the American Daughters of Sweden, one of those little obscure scholarships.

When I was at the University, even though I enjoyed some of it . . . I'm not a city person, I guess. I missed the beauty of the buildings and the countryside both of Taliesin and Taliesin West. So I asked to return, and I did spend the summer at Taliesin. I guess I was so kind of intellectual, or whatever, that after my year at the University Mrs. Wright said, "Go away for awhile." And I was sort of dismissed. I don't really remember exactly much about it. My mother would probably remember more, but I guess I was rather insufferable.

So, I went back to Pittsburgh for about a year and then Mrs. Wright let me rejoin the Fellowship. I've been here since about 1962. I was not interested in architecture but more in the way of life and was very attracted to Mrs. Wright's philosophy. . . . My parents had been doing the movements and studying the philosophic concepts of both Gurdjieff and Mrs. Wright for years. I remember doing them from the time I was twelve or so on. That was my main aim in coming to Taliesin . . . for the way of life and for my love of Mrs. Wright.

When did they tell you that you were a senior fellow?

I came, as I said, in 1962. My father would give me a small stipend; I think he sent about $35 a month. I didn't have to pay from the very first time I came, because I was, I guess, earning my keep by helping Iovanna. So, around 1964 I started getting a stipend, which, as far as I know, was as big as the check Iovanna herself was getting. It was pretty heady; it was pretty incredible. Maybe it was only $60 or something a month; I can't remember what it was, but I was pretty overwhelmed. I guess [it was] because of my long association with the group.

How does it work, having grown up within the Fellowship, having been a child here, being yet the daughter of a very influential senior fellow . . . are you able to claim your own place in the Fellowship?

I think it took a while. I remember one time feeling quite inferior to both my mother and father because they were both artistic and I was not an architect or really had much interest in that whole thing except appreciating it as an observer. So I think, basically, I'm just coming into my own in the last five or six years.

Golnar Casey, daughter of Effi and Tom Casey, provides detailed recollections. Born in 1973, Golnar is much younger than Shawn and Indira. Her name, which means "pomegranate blossom," was given to her by Princess Shams of the Pahlavi Dynasty (sister of the Shah of Iran), for whom the Taliesin architects designed a palace and other buildings in Iran. Tom and Effi Casey, Golnar's parents, were working there when she was born. What are her earliest memories of life here and in Arizona?

GOLNAR: Probably Easter time, because Easter is always a huge celebration. Actually, one of my earliest memories, outside of my memories from Iran, is hunting for Easter eggs with my Dad. We would always dye the Easter eggs . . . the kids would always be in on that. Easter is always a really big celebration, with lots of people, and it was and still is one of my favorite things. As I grew up, it became a tradition that I would blow up the balloons with Joe Fabris and with other students. I always enjoyed that and I still do it. And I still dye eggs.

Easter at Taliesin West brings children together to dye hundreds of eggs.

Did you eat with your parents most of the time, or as you got older did you just go where you felt like going in the dining room?

I guess I just kind of shifted around, but I spent a lot of time with the students at Taliesin, especially when I got older . . . like when I was in middle school and up. I always liked being around them; they were like my brothers and sisters. Since I'm an only child in our nuclear family, they kind of filled in as my brothers and sisters.

I always felt older than I was, which in high school became a problem for me. I didn't always hang out with my peers in high school; I sometimes got a little tired of hanging out with them because I was used to being with older people. Sometimes it was more enjoyable to hang out with the students.

I grew up with Alexander Dodge and with Nina and Ari, Dick's stepchildren. Then Nina and Ari left (I forget how many years later), but there was a little time when it was just Alexander and me. Then Shawn's children, Jenny and Rachel, came. I grew up with all of those kids. We always played together, and we had a good time.

We played all around, but one of our favorite spots was in the orchard in Arizona. We would play war in the orchard. There are big pits dug out there, and we would split up into pairs and throw old lemons that were on the ground . . . or oranges . . . into each other's "dugouts." Nothing too serious, just fun. Another thing we did a lot, we got the old cardboard boxes that bulk paper towels come in and we would build houses and things like that. One of our best memories is when we put together an air band and performed for our parents.

Did you live in the trailer the whole time you were out there?

No, we lived in the East Wing for a long time. It's next to the Atrium. I think they're all student rooms now. We had all of the rooms on the south side. I think that's four

Alexander Dodge and Golnar Casey

rooms. We had a living room, and one was my parents' room and one was my room and one was storage. We went in and out; we always kind of complained about having to go in and out of the rooms instead of just walking through. But I have good memories of living there, too.

What about going to school?

I would start school up here in Wisconsin [in the Fall] and then after about a month would transfer to a school in Arizona. I didn't really like that. Up until seventh grade it worked okay. As far as my classes [were concerned], they were pretty much similar and I could always work that out.

I always finished [the year] in Arizona. Spring Green is such a small town that everybody knows everybody, and so I was always the very new kid [each Fall]. They would kind of forget me through the year, and then I would come back. They would wonder who this person was and then kind of remember me from the last year. But I did meet one girl, Holly Elmer, who is still one of my very, very best friends. . . . I met her in the third grade; we always did everything together when I was up here in Wisconsin.

In Arizona, where did the school bus pick you up?

It came all the way up the hill to the visitors' parking lot. I was thinking about that when you asked me for the interview. You asked me before how my friends at school viewed me living at Taliesin. On the school bus in the earlier grades the rowdy kids in the back of the bus would always complain that they had to drive all the way up this hill and drop one girl off and then come all the way back down. It added about ten minutes to their bus ride.

After seventh grade, did you go out to Arizona in the Fall before your parents and live there?

Yes, I just stayed in one of the guest rooms. There were people who stayed down in the desert, so there were all of these people to go to if I needed something.

What are your best memories of being in the Taliesin Fellowship?

I realized coming to Wisconsin this summer that it's only now, when I am older, that I appreciate everything that I grew up with here. I haven't come up to Wisconsin now for two years. That's a long time, because usually I've been up here every summer. It kind of made me realize, being away for two years, even though I've visited the Fellowship in Arizona since then, that the sense of community . . . the people here . . . is the most important thing. All the senior members are extensions of my family, like aunts and uncles. Everyone is like family. Just recently, since I've graduated [from college], I realize that I have quite a unique family with whom I have a long history. I have a lot of people who I am very close to, who know me quite well and I know them quite well. Not everybody has that. As I get older, I've come to realize that that is a thing to cherish.

At what age did you start participating in Saturday evening events?

Since I was little I just always went. Then I started playing the flute . . . probably sixth grade . . . I started taking lessons. That's when I became serious about it. And then I would always do chorus and ensemble when I was playing the flute. We did larger productions . . . "Fiddler on the Roof" in which my Dad played Tevye. He was great. My Mom was the fiddler, among many other things. That was a big production; we worked a lot on that. That was at Taliesin West; I was in that. I did [the Gurdjieff] correlations when I was smaller, too. I was always doing things. I was always on maintenance; actually, the kids had jobs as a group, like washing windows or cleaning the pool.

The title of Paul Engle's childhood memoir is: A Lucky American Childhood. *Do you think that could be the title of your autobiography someday?*

Yes, I guess it could. "Lucky" would definitely be in there. I keep saying that I'm only realizing things now. . . . When I grew up I didn't always notice that there was such a difference between my home environment and my friends' home environment. I knew it was different, but that just seemed natural to me somehow.

This might be obvious, but I want to stress that the Fellowship is very much family. Growing up I always felt, and still do feel, embraced and supported by the Fellowship, especially by the senior members. Most of them have watched me grow up since I was born and have been mentors to me in many ways.

I haven't mentioned too much specifically about my parents, but we are a very, very close family. They have always been my greatest support in life, and I have learned so much from them in their lifelong dedication to Taliesin. We have many good times

Tom, Golnar, and Effi Casey

together as a happy threesome but also many good times with our larger family here. For a long time, the three of us have been able to participate together in the musical programs, since we each play an instrument and sing. That has always been very special . . . that we can play together, along with many others, and have fun.

The reference to the trailer and the Eastwing suggests the modest nature of the fellows' living quarters. The trailer, designed by Frank Lloyd Wright, succumbed to termites and bees in November 1994, and the Eastwing now houses apprentices. In Arizona, three of the fellows live in their own homes—David and Anneliese Dodge in one David designed, located adjacent to the Taliesin property, and Bruce Pfeiffer in one designed by Frank Lloyd Wright. Most of the fellows, however, live in modest apartments of one to three rooms. No matter the size of the living spaces, most exhibit the special Taliesin touch that creates a sense of beauty and warmth.

The situation is similar in Wisconsin. Some fellows and apprentices prefer one location over the other, sometimes for the space they have and sometimes for the environment. When I interviewed Stephen Nemtin after visiting the tastefully decorated cottage he and Frances occupy on the hill behind the Midway barn at Taliesin in Spring Green, I mentioned that they seem to have better living quarters in Wisconsin than at Taliesin West.

STEPHEN: Well, we have more expansive quarters here. For me, I have better living quarters here because the countryside has not been destroyed as the Sonoran desert has in Arizona. So, it's not the fact that I have a small room there, it's the fact that I have more contact with a kind of ugliness and impersonal surrounding community that I don't really want in my life.

Although Stephen began building an imaginative desert shelter some years ago, the encroachment of surrounding housing is making completion of it less attractive. The idea of a desert shelter recalls the first experiences of many of the fellows, something of which they speak matter-of-factly. Richard Carney, for example, says that he lived happily in a desert shelter, a tent, for more than fifteen years and would have stayed there longer if Mrs. Wright had not wanted him in an apartment near hers after Mr. Wright's death.

I asked Ari Georges, who came in 1986, whether he had lived in a desert shelter.

ARI: I started in a tent for two years. I found the tent to be extremely spiritual. It reminded me of the ascetic character of finding yourself and finding the best of you. That's where I read a lot by candlelight. And also, I liked the limitations of not having a lot of clutter. It makes you feel a little more liberated as a young man. Just a locker in a locker room for your clothes and a tent, and you don't need to worry about furniture and stuff and storage. So, it was very interesting.

I moved into a shelter that I remodeled a little bit. Then I moved to another shelter that I had planned to remodel extensively, but I never was given the time to. At the time when I was an apprentice, there was no concept of having your own

Victor Sidy at his first desert shelter.

time frame. Everything was a very rigorous, service-oriented experience. And they wouldn't give me resources. I was expected to do it on weekends, and without the continuity you cannot accomplish such work. So I had those plans, and they developed by very lengthy contemplations on the spot, because you're out there without water, electricity, no means, no tools and you want to do something and you have to do it in a very rudimentary way. The design evolved out of thoughts like: "If I get a cordless drill, how many holes can I drill in the steel and then walk back and recharge it and figure out time for all of this?" You realize it is not worth it doing that. Up until I graduated, I really lived in the desert, because I enjoyed it. It was a very soothing environment.

What were Jay Jensen's first experiences when he came in 1991?

JAY: The first experience is always getting a place to stay at Taliesin. You have to make your space. That's an ordeal, because usually you don't have anything to begin with. You start searching for answers with day one.

I went to Taliesin West and I was given a tent out of the storage room, the root cellar, and put that on my back and had a senior apprentice with me. We walked out into the desert and tried to find a spot for me to live. That first spot didn't turn out too well. Also, the tent leaked a lot and it happened to rain for weeks after that. I was really motivated to have something better very quickly. So I did. I worked hard on making a better space.

What was your feeling as you walked across the desert with a tent?

I didn't know what I had gotten myself into. I really didn't. I just couldn't believe that I didn't have a place to even live. I was amazed. I knew I had ended up somewhere that was going to be really unique, really an experience.

Jay Jensen

Earlier I had asked Jay about his experiences before coming to Taliesin, wondering if any of them had prepared him for life there.

I did some miscellaneous things first. I graduated [from high school] in '76, worked as a carpenter, and then went back to school. I was back in school for about three years when I got a job for an architect.

I started out at a community college in Wausau, Wisconsin, and transferred my credits up to Stout [University of Wisconsin–Stout in Menomonie] and was working on a bachelor's in construction management. I had a job with an architect and let school fall aside and continued working in architecture in Wisconsin and in Iowa and Illinois for the next five years. Then I came to Taliesin in November of '91. I received both my bachelor's and my master's degrees here.

I also asked Jay about life in the Fellowship . . . the communal society, the meals together, the Saturday nights together, the clean-up crews, kitchen work, and so on.

The community situation for me was really good. It was the thing about learning about how to be responsible and how to contribute to a group and being forced into it as in this case. It's not a voluntary system; you have to participate in it. You end up depending on other people to do their bit to make this whole thing work. It was a really good thing for me to understand that, and should I leave Taliesin I think that would be one strong thing I would take with me . . . how to participate in a community.

This is a natural question for what the scholarly world calls "participant observers" like we have been: What kind of future do you see for yourself in the Fellowship, a young person surrounded by quite a few "senior seniors"?

Well, it's a hard question, because I didn't come here for the Fellowship. I came here for the school, and I didn't really understand what the Fellowship was nor was I too interested. It's just something that's sort of grown within me, and I've become a part of it without ever thinking I would be. So I haven't really given a whole lot of thought to your question, about what the future is. I just find myself here at this point after completing school and deciding to work with the architecture firm here. . . . I do enjoy the community, but that is not my binding [reason for staying].

What have been the best things that have happened to you since coming to Taliesin?

The best things . . . well, the community was probably the best thing that ever happened for me. That was for me to become part of a group of people; to be in the Fellowship really was a big thing for me. It added a lot to my personal growth. It enlightened me about different people and cultures. Just the working together with a mixed group of people, ages and cultures.

What have been your worst experiences?

I've always said you could have your best and your worst day in the same day at Taliesin. You would go from an evening of sitting across the table from the Governor [of Wisconsin] (something I would never think I would do in my life) and then go out to your rainy, leaky tent. Just think about that as a contrast. Also, there are a lot of people within the Fellowship and it is difficult to do everything right. I think most of the people feel the criticism as they pass through a day as an apprentice: from somebody wanting your best in the flower arrangement for the table, to the architect up in the studio, to every little task. I found it a challenging thing to do; it's a lot to expect out of somebody who is trying to attend college and then maybe wants to have a sloppy room or not eat or something. You can't do that. You have to do it all.

Paul Kardatzke recalls his experiences when he came to Taliesin in 1991.

PAUL: I guess my first experiences were with the first tour [of Taliesin at Spring Green] I went on, which was very magical, Camelotesque. I remember working with Bill Schoettker on construction, working with a whole crew of people on one of Stephen's Alzheimer buildings.[2] I have strong memories, which I feel really anchored the rest of my time at Taliesin. That first summer was very, very important.

You didn't have the same experiences that some people have . . . they are here three months or six months and don't do anything architectural.

No. I think, like most people, when they get here everything's not quite ready for them. I was put in Tan-y-deri for a weekend while another apprentice was leaving, so as he left I took over his room, his desk, things like that. The first week I was in transition. I was working on landscaping with Frances, but before that week was out Stephen grabbed me. He was on a big push, and he found out that I knew something about computers, so he got me working on details for the Alzheimer building. It's just on the order of relativity. I knew something about computers and CAD drafting but actually very little about the type of CAD drafting they were doing here. But I learned quickly.

It was a wonderful crew: Tom Payton, Michael Standish, Bill Schoettker and Arno Luthje.[3] That was fantastic; it was exactly what I imagined. It was what I wanted when I came here, to be completely immersed in putting out architecture. It was building like I had never seen before, never imagined architecture being done that way. I now realize that architecture is rarely done that way. It was a wonderful effort and it lasted a couple of months . . . really pushing to get these construction documents out.

I probably learned more in that single period . . . I may have been aware of learning more in that period . . . than for the rest of the time I was at Taliesin. But it certainly set work ethic. Thrown into the middle of that was also the Box Project; and Wes passed away in July. There was just a wonderful community experience at the same time, meeting people . . . whom I had [previously] heard about . . . at the time of the funeral and setting up for the funeral. I had just joined the chorus and we sang at St. John's chapel. That was really wonderful.

When you went to Arizona, did you construct a desert shelter?

I worked on a tent. I was given a tent base and the idea. The tent base had been poured the year before. It was a concrete base about two feet high, eight inches thick, and there were anchor bolts out the top and ties coming out of the sides. The concept was to have desert masonry put on the side of the tent. Tom Payton was in charge of the shelters at that point, describing what the concept was, that they just wanted basic setups that people could make there, so I did the desert masonry. I lived there for three years. I enjoyed the desert.

The same tent during that time?

Yes, you get very attached to it. I built a fireplace. It was sort of nestled in one of the washes. I sort of miss it, but now I have a room.

And a roommate.

Yes, my wife Julie.

I wondered aloud whether Julie remembered the first thing she had done when she came to the Fellowship.

JULIE: I don't remember the very first thing, but I remember construction being the first experience that I had. That was the addition to the Archives building. There were two rooms that were built on that are used for office space right now. Tom Payton was the supervisor of that construction experience, and there were about five or six apprentices working on the project. It made quite an impression on me. I still have pretty strong memories about doing that and the things I learned about construction from that project.

It helps you as an architect to be in on the construction?

I think, if anything, I could have used more construction experience, and I think that's something that all architecture students should be required to do during the course of their studies, because it is really important.

One of the interesting features of life at Taliesin is the way in which the fellows simply assume responsibility for tasks that need to be done. Elsewhere in this book John Rattenbury explains how he assumed a larger role in managing the Taliesin Architects, as Wes Peters had taken over direction of the studio following Mr. Wright's death. Also, Dick Carney describes how he became the CEO. Sarah Logue and Minerva Montooth oversee the day-to-day operations of the very large Taliesin Fellowship household, and Minerva is responsible for arranging housing for guests. In the case of Arnold Roy, no one assigned the role of facilities manager to him, at least not initially. But now, what are his principal roles?

ARNOLD: You name it, I do it. I'm an officer of the Foundation, on the Foundation Board. I'm the vice president in charge of facilities, so I've got the responsibility of the whole place. I'm also secretary of the Foundation, but that doesn't take very much time. But all of these administrative duties [together] do take a lot of time.

I represent the Foundation, like if there's anything happening in Scottsdale I'm the representative for the Foundation . . . zoning or public hearings of the Planning Commission or City Council, anything like that. I represented the Foundation on the construction of Frank Lloyd Wright Boulevard. I attended all of the construction meetings every week just to make sure our interests were well represented. I'm in charge of master planning, chair of the master plan committee of Taliesin West.

Who is responsible for security?

I guess my name's on that list, too.

Maintenance?

Yes, well, facilities.

Tom Casey explains how he became the one to develop and execute plans for the Frank Lloyd Wright School of Architecture.

TOM: We have [an understanding] among us in the Fellowship, that no one appoints people to a position. People make a position, so to speak. It just seemed to me that if we were going to be successful in preserving what's here in regard to an apprenticeship-learning program, that somebody had to start going out there and pursuing that goal, making their way into this arena of higher education so that people would begin to recognize that it was still going on. I just simply started doing that. Dick couldn't do it; he already had his hands full. So somebody else needed to do it, to step in. I said to myself, "You've got to do this; somebody's got to do it. You can do it; go and do it." So I did it, and that's how we find ourselves sitting across this table.

Sometimes fellows are asked to take on new roles even though they lack applicable experience. Anneliese Dodge explains how she came to be the bookstore manager and how she has enlarged the role.

ANNELIESE: The day came that Dick's ex-wife was leaving Taliesin, and she had run the bookstore, which was only the entrance in the theater [at that time]. We had a little wagon on wheels and a few books and a few T-shirts. . . . So Dick came to me and said, "Anneliese, would you like to take this over?" I said, "Well, I'd like to give it a try. This is very interesting."

And so, this began to grow. More and more people and more books and stuff and we realized that this all gets too small. So two years later we started building in place of the old pottery shop this bookstore. It's eight years old now. [Previously] it was a pottery shop and an outside space. Even now it gets too small. You know, now we need a bigger place. Since then, I have really enjoyed this very much. I was thrilled doing cooking [in the past], but three years ago I had a heart condition and I had to stop that, because the cooking is big . . . it doesn't matter, even if you have only three days, this is a very great effort. You have to really think and prepare and have the meal ready in time. I'm now so busy in the bookstore, you know, and up till now I really enjoyed [the cooking] very much.

Did you have any experience in retail management?

No, I really learned it all here. Like I said, I enjoy it. When you build up a wonderful business relationship with publishers, it's really fantastic. When new books come out, people call you. Also, I get new publication information from the Archives and Oscar [Muñoz]. When I travel in Europe I go right into big bookstores and look [at] what they have in Frank Lloyd Wright books. When we go to Switzerland I enjoy doing designs of T-shirts and sweatshirts.

I wondered if you were the designer of the sweatshirts that they sell there.

Yes, [for the ones with the] abstraction, I use Mr. Wright's square. The red and blue one I call "energy," and the black one with the red squares I call "the slide." I designed them; I let David look them over and then we get them ready for printing. I really enjoy this work.

How about the cups?

I only did the red cup, but the other ones are all Mr. Wright's designs. One day there were two ladies [here]. One lady said, "I tell you, don't argue with me, this is one of Frank Lloyd Wright's designs." So I had to step in and explain this to her [that it was my design]. And then she said, "Oh, are you allowed to do this?" And I said, "Oh, yes, we are allowed to do this. "But," I said, "you don't have to buy it." This is great fun.

I also want to explain, we don't know how long we will still have this bookstore here. When the day comes that the new visitor center is built with its own bookstore, this one will close.

Will you want to manage it?

No, no. Then I will start something else, because that will be really very, very big and then we need so many outside people. But here, this really belongs to the Fellowship. We're still on campus, and that's why I enjoy it very much.

Assuming responsibilities in this manner reflects the casual nature of so many of the Fellowship's operations. Many of the persons cannot recall when they discovered their own designations as senior fellows. As Tony Puttnam said, "Like a lot of other things at Taliesin, it just sort of would happen. Everybody would recognize that it was appropriate, but it was a funny thing."

When did Cornelia Brierly discover she was a senior fellow?

CORNELIA: Well, that's a hard question. I paid tuition for many years. After I got married, which was in 1939, my husband was working in the studio doing a lot of very serious work for Mr. Wright. Mr. Wright began to pay us at that point. Then we left for about ten years, and after I returned I became a senior staff member.

Another for whom the transition was similarly incidental in his life at Taliesin is Joe Fabris.

JOE: There was no official ceremony or anything like that. I had enough money to pay for my first year. [After that] I went to Mr. Wright and said I didn't have money to pay another year, and he said, "That's fine, just stay on. You earn your way." That was it. And then, I think maybe a year or so later, I was given a stipend which all of the so-called senior apprentices got, which was $30 a month, which at that time was enough. It took care of your clothes and your toothpaste and that sort of thing.

Similarly with Dori Roy:

DORI: We were in Switzerland, Montagnola, and I was working with Shirley Casey (Tom's first wife, who died of cancer) in the drafting room that was set up there because there was lots of work to-ing and fro-ing from the United States, and one month I got a paycheck. I was just thrilled. I'd been here seven years, and my aunt had paid my tuition all that time.

And with Effi Casey:

EFFI: You know, I've tried to remember how that happened. I think, because I . . . was engaged in all these questions of the future, particularly . . . Dick said one day, "I think you should begin to come to Senior Fellowship meetings." That's just about it.

He wanted me to become involved in the process, but there was no official initiation or anything.

I asked Ling Po if there was ever a line drawn between apprentices and fellows.

LING PO: There wasn't any hard line drawn.

Did you ever get a letter from them saying, "Congratulations, the Senior Fellowship voted and decided you should be a senior fellow"?

It was up to the Master of the school to say so, and the seniors would naturally all agree to it. And you kind of know it yourself.

David Dodge's recollection helps to explain why the situation was somewhat unclear, but also why it did not really matter.

DAVID: I knew about it about six years after I had already been transferred. . . . There was never any really sharp dividing line with it. And, of course, since there were no degrees, there were no ceremonies about it. So, one developed into being a senior, and one was a senior in some things and not in others. So, you see, it wasn't just all of a sudden now you are a senior. So you're supposed to know about everything? No, you don't. Some seniors never know about some things that young apprentices may know almost immediately, and so it doesn't matter.

. . . The only thing I have in my files is a letter from Mrs. Wright . . . "To whom it may concern" . . . when I left to stay in Switzerland, to work in Switzerland. Then she gave me a letter of . . . a certificate, you know, saying how many years I had been here, how accomplished I was or what I could do. But that was all there was.

Susan Lockhart's comments shed more light on the casual nature of status determination when I asked her whether one could be a senior fellow in some things and an apprentice in others.

SUSAN: Everything that I have done since coming here has been adding on to what I started out with . . . in new ways, always.

There never was a moment, though, when they had a party welcoming you into the Senior Fellowship?

No, I begged . . . both David [Wheatley] and I begged . . . to be given some kind of stipend so that we could be allowed to stay on, because our own money had run out after a year. And we basically came in as reentering into the group, both of us working in the organization, but outside of our room and board there was no remuneration. So, at that point I remember begging pretty furiously to get that status. The Senior Fellowship at that point was not necessarily designated as senior versus junior versus associate. That's all a very recent phenomenon.

Changes begun after Mrs. Wright's death continued and by the 1990s the fellows' status was more rigidly defined, not always happily so. Ari Georges was among the first to come in under the more definitive structure. He recalls having had job offers in Greece when he was released after completing two years in the army there. In fact, he accepted a job with an architect while he was yet in the army.

ARI: I worked two months there, and whenever I had free time from the army all I did was go back to the office and work. He [the Greek architect] would slip cash to me as a reward for two or three hours of work, and he was very generous. So after I got out of the army he wanted me to get heavily involved in the office. He increased my salary, he asked me what I was planning to do, and I said, "I really need to return and pay a visit to see how things are."

Honestly, one of the things that happens when you leave Taliesin, even if you are the most beloved person here, is they forget you. They are so self-involved as a group that it's very hard to keep in touch. So I came back to see what was going on, if there was any way I could return. They did want me to return. I had conversations with Dick and Tom and Ryc. But when I arrived here I saw the climate being very, very strange. For one, there was a big controversy with TA [Taliesin Architects]. . . . There was also a lot of sentiment about insiders and outsiders. It didn't seem to be the same place. I also saw that a lot of seniors had lost the level of energy that they had when I was here. They had started to be reclusive. So it was very, very strange.

I asked them, "Is it possible for me to go back [to Greece], work, complete my obligation to the office and then maybe in six months or so at the end of the season return and become a senior fellow?" The answer was very iffy, like, "Well, if you are interested in being a senior fellow why would you want to go back?" It is this expectation that you have to put your whole life on the altar. Nothing else matters. I realized if I really wanted to become a senior fellow or be at all interested in Taliesin I couldn't leave there. So, I had to stay.

When I spoke to them before the vote I told them that my interest here is the ethic of service; I consider this a public place; I'm not really in agreement with this whole idea of a closed fellowship community.

Something in the Taliesin lifestyle allows the fellows and apprentices to take in stride events and circumstances in their community life that might be a major concern to others. Perhaps that explains why several important aspects of their lives together were treated matter-of-factly in our conversations, particularly relations between the sexes and religious beliefs. Nonetheless, these represent significant elements in the lives of fellows and apprentices.

Concerning relations between the sexes, there has always been pairing off among the apprentices. That's only natural, their elders say. Through the years and yet today, the romantic and sexual relationships have no doubt paralleled those on a typical college campus. And there have been romances, courtships, marriages, divorces, and remarriages among the senior fellows, too. About such matters, the typical comment was, "We are a whole lot like the rest of the world, aren't we?"

In late 1994, when we recorded the first conversations leading to this book, there were seven married couples in the membership of twenty-seven senior fellows. All of the marriages were of relatively long duration and they appeared to be happy ones. [Paul and Julie Kardatzke, who became senior fellows later, are apparently the first married couple in many years in which both are architects.] In several instances one spouse or the other had been married years earlier to a departed or deceased member of the Fellowship, but nothing in their divorces and remarriage was regarded as scandalous. In others, as with Minerva and Charles Montooth, the marriage, encouraged by the Wrights, brought Minerva into the Fellowship. Charles commented briefly on their marriage:

> CHARLES: [Mr. Wright] liked Minerva when she came to visit, and he said, "You ought to marry her, and just to show you, I'll give you the wedding." He liked her because when she came she plunged right in. She had one of the messiest jobs. We used to carry all the food from here down to Arizona, and it [eventually] would begin to spoil. We had a root cellar. One of her jobs was working with Steven Oyakawa, and they were down there throwing out all the spoiled potatoes and things. And also, she did roofing with an English count. They were working up there on the roof with tar, everything else. Mr. Wright loved that when women actually did [such work].

You were married at Taliesin West, weren't you? The only wedding in the Pavilion or theater?

> We were married at Taliesin West, right. It was in the theater. We were the first to be married in the theater, but there was another couple later . . . John Oppenheimer . . . and then lately there have been several. . . .

In 1957, Minerva's twin sister Sarah and her husband Bill Logue also entered the Fellowship. In the foursome, Charles is the only architect, but all have played significant roles in the operation of the Fellowship.

In this conversation, Tom Casey describes his first marriage, the subsequent death of his wife, and his second marriage.

> TOM: We met here. Shirley was married to an apprentice [Kelly Oliver[4]] and came here and was part of the Fellowship. . . . But that marriage didn't last; they split up. . . . Shirley by then was well ensconced as a member of the Fellowship, and she stayed here. Then we got involved, and later we were married after they were divorced. . . . We eloped and had a nice honeymoon in Mazatlan in Mexico. We then stayed here and were married for twelve years. We did not have any children.
>
> Shirley became very involved with Mrs. Wright. She traveled with her, had a lot of personal connection with her, but at one point turned up with breast cancer. . . . [Despite apparently successful surgery], it reappeared within a couple of years. Actually, by the time it was really diagnosed, it was just all through her system. Once that really got going, poor Shirley didn't last very long . . . just a matter of a couple of months. . . .

This was in late spring, 1968, and she died in early July. I, of course, stayed with her here. Everybody else went [to Wisconsin]. Then we carried her casket to Wisconsin and she was buried next to the chapel there. We had had wonderful times together. It was the early part of the '60s when Mrs. Wright took the whole crowd during the summertime to Switzerland. And, actually, that's where we met Effi. We were all acquainted. She knew Shirley very well, Effi did.

Within the year or so after Shirley died . . . Mrs. Wright asked me if I would go [to Iran], pointing out that I was eminently qualified to do the work that needed to be done; I was now single and was free to go. . . . I worked very closely with Wes in those years, and poor Wes in the beginning just was having fits because I was going to go and leave him behind. Nevertheless, he basically had to accept it.

By then I was licensed. I had the capability, I had the opportunity, and so I should go. I thought it was a great idea . . . And so I went to Iran. In the course of being there, in order to supply the job, especially with things that were going to be in the interiors, the Princess wanted a lot of stuff that was available in Europe. So I started making trips to Europe to seek these things out, to arrange them . . . I went to Italy, and Germany and so forth.

Effi was here in 1967 and then she went home [to Germany], but she kept up quite a nice correspondence with Susan, Kenn, and several others she knew quite well. So I thought, "Well, I think I'm going to go visit." I wrote to her and arranged a visit. She was living in Hamburg then with her brother. I went to visit. We began corresponding, and our mutual attraction grew.

After I was there for several months, Princess Shams began to get worried that I was in Iran by myself. She asked me if I wouldn't like to bring my mother for a visit. Bless her heart, she was wonderful . . . I liked her very much. She was a person who operated intuitively, at extraordinarily sensitive levels. She was always extremely kind to me . . . and to us . . . and had concern about that sort of thing, enough concern to want to do something about it. . . . So, I told her that rather than bring my mother I had another idea, there was a young lady. Finally she said, "Bring her out here." I arranged then for Effi to come for a visit. Well, she and the Princess just hit it off perfectly. That worked out very nicely. That was just the other piece of the puzzle to put together. We were married then in the middle of 1971.

Then Effi came out to live with me in Iran, and we spent most of the '70s there. We went back and forth a little bit. It took us four years to build that first building, and we were there solidly through that time. And then . . . Stephen and Frances came out as an exchange. In the end, though, the Princess just asked us please to come back, which we did. And we ended up staying there until the latter part of 1978; that's when the revolution started. . . .

In hindsight, that was a very propitious time to have another reason to leave. We didn't leave because of the revolution, we left because we had finished . . . by that time we were also building another building for Damavand College, and we came to completion of a phase there and a phase of work we were doing for Princess Shams up on the Caspian Sea coast in a little town called Chalus.

There came a time for a recess, and . . . the Princess said we should go now for awhile until they decided to do something else. So we left and arranged to take most everything we had and ship it home, because it was unsure whether we might come back. As it turned out, shortly after we left the revolution occurred, and so we never went back. As a matter of fact, Nezam Amery, who brought us there, had [also] left the country.[5] The whole rationale for our being connected there at all was now gone.

Effi Casey remembers her first years of marriage spent in Iran.

EFFI: We married in '71, and we stayed there for the better part of the '70s. . . . That, I think, was a very important, in some respects difficult, beginning for us, because it was such a cultural desert [compared to] the culture we were accustomed to. And we really literally lived out in the desert away from Teheran, about forty miles. Because of the very intense work for Tom, we just really had to build a very good foundation between us. Otherwise I would have run home or something. I always felt if you make it in the bush like that together you can weather quite a few trials and tribulations.

Frances Nemtin, who had formerly been married to Kenn Lockhart, spoke briefly about her situation:

FRANCES: [Stephen and I] met here in 1959, the year that Kenn and I parted. Kenn and I both remarried happily. It's one of those nice situations where you can live amicably together in the same atmosphere.

What happens in a fellowship like this when there is that sort of remarriage—you are still eating in the same dining room and going to the same events?

Well, we were probably unique in that way, although there have been other remarriages here. It meant our children didn't have to choose between us. The family was more intact, which was wonderful. They didn't feel split. I was grateful for that. My eastern friends whom I see once in awhile don't believe it. They don't think it's possible. They regard me as a curiosity. Also, I think they regard me as a curiosity for staying here so long. I think they're condescending once in awhile. "Oh, you're still there" kind of thing. But when I've seen them more recently . . . the most recent time at my college reunion . . . their interest was genuine, and I think they're admiring of the fact that I've found something to believe in, to stay with and work for.

As Frances said, Kenn Lockhart remained with the Fellowship after their divorce. Susan Lockhart, his second wife, says more about Kenn:

SUSAN: I came to Taliesin with my husband [David Wheatley] and later divorced, and then Kenn and I were married in 1964. We would have been married thirty years this Fall. In the tributes [to Kenn after he died] there were hundreds and hundreds and hundreds of letters that came from over the world. The tributes to him were things like: "I came to study with Frank Lloyd Wright, and then I discovered that there was much to learn besides that that Frank Lloyd Wright had to give."

Kenn was particularly strong in the area of construction and the action plans and in his love of architecture. Frank Lloyd Wright saw that and would always take him out of the drafting room, much to his consternation, and put him on "now we're going to do the architecture" projects. Finally, in the '60s after Mr. Wright's death, he took on the technical writing of documents, which became then a very powerful part of the organization, and he achieved a lot of national recognition as well.

But people characterized him as simply a man of incredible service. If you wanted to know how to do anything . . . or anything about anything . . . you went first to Kenn Lockhart or Wes Peters. Those were the two people who sort of . . . in the original core group Gene Masselink took care of a lot of the people in the inner relationship areas, but Kenn and Wes were the kind of people who could always take the action plan to fruition. And so, for fifty-plus years that was their role, and they were looked to [for] that as their strength. [Sometimes when] visitors came late to the visitor program, he would stop and show them around personally. Kenn would take anyone who had a problem and he could solve it.

Did he play a leadership role in the Fellowship, like with the Board of Directors?

No, he didn't. He did not achieve that; I think it was a sadness for him, but he did not . . . for all [his] wonderful qualities, his vision of the future was, I think, not that vision of change and inclusion. It was in his personal life, but he was so dedicated to how Frank Lloyd Wright lived and what his experience had been that he couldn't quite separate himself in that particular subject to expand it out and see it as an unfolding, changing way.

Kenn Lockhart

As far as religion is concerned, the fellowship perpetuates the legacy of Frank Lloyd Wright, whose formal religious affiliation, to the extent that there was one, can perhaps be described as inactive Unitarian. At Taliesin, individuals are free to put into practice their personal religious beliefs, and there are no religious elements in the Fellowship's routines . . . no prayer before meals and no worship services, for example, and no invocations or benedictions at special events. Symbols of religious faith are absent, although many pictures of Mrs. Wright show her wearing a cross. From the founding of the Fellowship, the Easter celebration has been the most festive annual event with sacred music performed, but other religious elements are few. In his speeches and writings, Mr. Wright frequently identified God with Nature, to be spelled with a capital N.

Arnold Roy expressed sentiments that are widely shared in the Fellowship:

ARNOLD: When I came here, my parents were very strongly Catholic . . . Roman Catholic and French Canadian . . . and I'd been brought up Catholic, very strong. I went to Sunday school and Bible [classes] after school and all of that. So when I came out here, my mother naturally expected I would keep my religion and go to church.

All of a sudden I was confronted by Frank Lloyd Wright telling us that nature with a capital N is the only face of God any of us will ever see. Talk about an eye-opening experience. And all of a sudden you started looking, and there's something bigger here than simply going to church. My parents were very strongly Catholic, I mean really strongly Catholic. So I said, "Mom, I've got to explain something to you." I did, and she said, "You believe in it, don't you?" And I said, "Yes." That was all she needed.

So you didn't maintain any of your Catholic ties all through the years?

No, I found something bigger, something you really put yourself into, something that fulfilled me.

Ling Po saw Mr. Wright's views of religion similarly, but his background and experiences eventually took him in a different direction. Here he describes how his religious commitment evolved.

LING PO: I went to a missionary high school in Peking, China, now called Beijing, and in my late teens I tried to get myself converted into fundamentalist Christianity, but lacking the faith I got terribly frustrated. When I came to Taliesin I found that Frank Lloyd Wright was a deep religious man but not a churchgoer. He called Jesus the master poet, and he thought Jesus' teaching touched about every aspect of the human spirit. Having studied a little Buddhism, the more I see the greatness of Jesus. He is greatly misunderstood by so many churches of Christianity.

When we went on a desert hike, the guide pointed to a place where you have been planning to build a Usonian house. Are you still going to go ahead with that?

No, I'm going to give it up. [I started working on it] about five years ago. Off and on I workcd on the foundation and finished it. Then I borrowed a set of molds for casting the blocks. Now I've decided I'm going to send back those molds and not go on with the building.

Why did you decide that?

I've become a Buddhist.

I see, and why does that make you change?

[It] kind of awakened [me] to the fact that I wanted to build such a house because of my eagerness to be somebody who can build, who can not only design a place for himself, but with his own hand achieve that, perform it, make it come true. Now that's good, but the drawback is that it's from egoistic impulse, and that egoistic impulse is doing me harm for long time and got to be rid of.

How did you become a Buddhist?

As I [am] getting older and older, I find I'm angrier and angrier, and that points to a dead end. I also find other people of my generation going into the same exasperating tendency of getting more and more dissatisfied, angry, complaining. That is mainly because as one is getting older he finds that he is no longer lovable. Well, at least I am dependable, he thinks, at least I am somebody. But the world doesn't respect age, so you find people are ignoring you. And you become angrier and angrier as you get older and older. But Buddhism teaches that the ego is an illusion . . . that I have been deluded to think that this body, this set of personality and ability and these achievements is me. But when I die, it all disappears, like a movie is over, and it leaves the screen blank. Since ego is illusionary, one has to hold on to something more substantial. To hold on to the ego tighter is exactly like a person putting all his earnings into a bank that he knows is going to collapse. This is utter ignorance and extremely pitiful.

Have you joined a Buddhist community?

Well, there are people for learning Buddhism in Phoenix and also our friends of other states. Now and then we get together and study Buddhism together.

Do you find yourself, then, drifting away from the Taliesin Fellowship, or do you still feel like a central part of it? In other words, can you be both a Taliesin fellow and a Buddhist? Or are they in conflict?

One can be both because the Taliesin Fellowship has room for different religious beliefs. But one may have to be away from the group, for a time, in order to pursue the learning more intensely.

Will you continue to live at Taliesin?

That I do not know.

You've been here almost fifty years.

Fifty years.

It would be hard to leave, but if the call of Buddhism is such that it makes you do that, I guess you could do it. Do you know where you might go to live?

I still do not know.

Since our conversation, Ling Po has moved to a Buddhist monastery in California. He returns to Taliesin for visits and maintains a good relationship with the Fellowship.

The migration to Wisconsin each year in May and the return to Arizona in October is another example of taking things in stride. In early years the fellows and apprentices traveled in caravans, relied on the supply truck for provisions, and camped out along the way. Tales of adventures en route are abundant.[6] In more recent times, the migrants travel by their own arrangements, following different routes and in their own automobiles, although a rented truck transports essential goods for the community as well as for individuals. Moreover, the home base for the architectural firm, Taliesin Architects, remains at Taliesin West and the Frank Lloyd Wright Foundation Archives operates there year around. Fellows and apprentices involved in these operations, as well as some who prefer the southwest for reasons of health, no longer join the moves back and forth. Because there is work to be done year-round in Wisconsin, too, and because the buildings there must be maintained through the winter, several fellows and usually a couple of apprentices remain all year.

Even so, some who remain in one location today, such as John Rattenbury, recall past migrations fondly:

JOHN R: In Arizona I lived in a desert tent and was happier there than in a mansion. The trips across country twice a year, between Arizona and Wisconsin, were great adventures. We had the opportunity to explore the United States and spent a week crossing the country, camping out, taking a different route each time. In those days there were no interstate highways and driving was fun. We drove in a caravan of red two-seater Crosley Hotshots, the little sports cars that Mr. Wright bought for the senior apprentices. Across the country people would stare at what they thought must be a circus coming to town.

Others speak of the exhilaration of the move, despite its difficulty. Many share the sentiments expressed by Cornelia Brierly, who has been going back and forth between the two locations for more than fifty years.

CORNELIA: Moving is a very difficult thing, as you well know. To keep moving back and forth causes a lot of headaches, but just to have that wonderful sense of the whole atmosphere changing from desert to lush vegetation in Wisconsin is such a pleasure, and the architecture is totally different there, as a house of the north.

Mr. and Mrs. Wright in their Crosley Hotshot (1953).

Ask those who make the semiannual move which location they prefer, and you are likely to receive an answer like the one from Victor Sidy, an apprentice: "That is like asking whether you love your father or your mother more. You love them differently, for different reasons." Some, though, such as Frances Nemtim, have a preference.

FRANCES: [I prefer] Wisconsin. Because of the changing character here [Arizona], I don't feel there is the same sense of respect for the beauty of the environment. And I don't have the same sense of neighborliness that exists up there simply because of different scale, and people who have moved into those hills were attracted by the beauty, by the proximity to us, and by respect for what they have, so they want to preserve that. Here in Arizona you don't have that same feeling at all.

One other important aspect of Fellowship life received only passing attention. Perhaps that is because it is such a natural occurrence that the fellows felt no reason to talk about it. More likely it is because I did not raise the subject as I might have. I refer to the steady flow of visitors at the two Taliesin locations. In the mid-1980s, the Frank Lloyd Wright Foundation began to conduct tours to accommodate persons with general or specific interests in Frank Lloyd Wright and the settings in which he worked. By the mid-1990s, the tour program provided an important source of funds for maintenance of the facilities and some of the Foundation's other activities. When Mr. Wright was alive, Taliesin welcomed many distinguished guests and often provided special programs for them. In a written addendum to the interview transcript, John Rattenbury recalls some of the famous visitors and the occasions that brought them to Taliesin.

JOHN R: Such interesting people came to Taliesin. I remember Henry Luce and Clare Boothe Luce; the Baroness von Rebay (Solomon Guggenheim's mistress); Dorothy Liebes, the textile designer for DuPont, and her husband, Pat Morin, a correspondent for the Associated Press; Ray Rubicam and Bill Barton, moguls of the advertising world; Buckminster Fuller, the inventor; Philip Johnson, the architect; Elizabeth Gordon, editor of *House Beautiful* magazine; Harold and Mary Lou Price, our clients; Oscar Stonorov, Philadelphia architect; Alicia Patterson Guggenheim, editor of *Newsday*; Phil and Helen Wrigley; Senator and Mrs. William Benton. There was Carl Sandburg, Charles Laughton, Mike Todd and Elizabeth Taylor, Anthony Quinn, Charlton Heston, Anne Baxter (Mr. Wright's granddaughter), Andre Kostelanetz, Leonard Rose, Allen Dulles, Edward Teller, Eugene Ormandy, Margaret Sanger, Adlai Stevenson, and many, many more. What stimulating dialogue between them and the Wrights at breakfast on Sunday morning! Famous musicians would give recitals for us and in return the Fellowship would entertain them, sometimes with our chorus and ensemble, sometimes with humorous skits and satires that we would improvise.

In addition to tourists and persons with name recognition like that enjoyed by the ones John recalled, every social event at Taliesin draws many friends and relatives of the Fellowship, rather like celebrations of an extended family. Holidays, particularly Easter and Thanksgiving, are festive occasions, with attractive and abundant decorations, special foods, and entertainment. Family albums are filled with photographs of such occasions, and the Frank Lloyd Wright Foundation Archives also have photographs and other documents that reveal the importance of holiday celebrations in the Fellowship's life.

The Archives, of course, attract yet another kind of visitor. Year around there is a steady flow of architects, scholars, and film crews who are researching and recording the life and work of Frank Lloyd Wright. Others visit the Archives simply because they are curious about Taliesin, the luminaries of its past, and those who maintain it today.

The Taliesin Fellowship has lasted much longer than most intentional communities. How to explain that? The fellows spoke freely of the elements that hold the Fellowship together. Here is Tony Puttnam's response to my question, "What has it meant to you to be a leading member of this communal body?"

TONY: It's very unique compared to other communal societies that I know about, because I think it was formed for two reasons: of course, for the sake of the people who would come there, but it was also very much formed as a way that Mr. Wright could go on with his work. To some extent, it was an instrument that allowed him to be able to keep his creative adventure alive and to have a foundation both in land and in human resources so that if this job didn't come along or if no job came along you wouldn't die. This way you could do things. We were extraordinarily poor.

One of the first things we ever did in the desert . . . we were building a building and there was absolutely no money. We were pouring concrete, so the second morning we had to straighten the nails that we pulled out of the forms and put in the new form. By the third morning we took up a collection and sent someone into town to buy some new nails, but Gene said, "Don't even think about it. There's no money. We will not buy nails."

The Fellowship made an extraordinary way of life possible, which under any other circumstances would have been impossible. And I think it was Mr. Wright's feeling that in a real democracy it was what people did, not what they had, that determined their standing or their position of leadership and so forth within a community. In a way, from his point of view, it was a very democratic kind of thing, because the most energetic, the most creative people would rise to the top inevitably. And the people who were not interested particularly in the inspiration of the place would sift out rather quickly. I think it was, seriously, that kind of thing.

Johnny Hill offered this explanation:

JOHNNY: There is something strong here that holds the group together. I think it can easily continue. It's going through lots of adjustments because of all kinds of changes . . . one of the main ones is the fact that it takes so much money to support these buildings, which we considered just houses before. But, my feeling is it's a place for creative work, and it might someday be more productive in sculpture or painting or writing or some other art, not always necessarily architecture. There needs to be production here; it's a place for people who are creating things and in no sense a place for people who want a common, community kind of an existence. It's a place for people who want to get to the heights of what's available. And that would be my conclusion . . . music, painting, films, anything that is valuable in the way of knowledge.

I asked Cornelia Brierly what she considered to be the forces that hold the Fellowship together.

CORNELIA: Well, I think the original ideals were so strong they gave us strength to work together. I think that that's what's held it together . . . being very cooperative, being very understanding of each other, and realizing that everybody has certain flaws in their makeup. You go along with that. Each one does what he's best suited for.

Dori Roy responded to the same question.

DORI: The seniors. We have gone through so much together. We are a cohesive body. We fight, but let anybody else say something bad about us and one of us will be there. It's a very close community. Unfortunately, we haven't been able to draw many younger people into this community. The first people came after the First World War: Johnny,

Cornelia, Wes, and Kay. Tom and Arnold and John R and myself were another level down from the senior ones. And we came after the Second World War, so I often think that out of all the hard times and grief and everything, maybe, we were looking for something more, and these kids just haven't had that kind of experience.

What does Frances Nemtin see as the magic of Taliesin?

FRANCES: [The magic of Taliesin] brought us all together in the first place. Devotion to the ideal of an organic way of life and designing architecture according to organic principles. Not trying to imitate Mr. Wright but to absorb those basic ideas. And each one's work is quite different. Some is more obviously derivative of Mr. Wright or dependent on his grammar. For instance, with Stephen, I feel he is extremely free of that powerful, overriding influence. He has absorbed the principles and is himself very original.

Susan Lockhart and Effi Casey offered these contrasting perspectives:

SUSAN: I think what makes Taliesin work has had different definitions at different times. I think what makes it work now is ultimately people dedicated to the place which represents the architectural element, that tradition which, of course, comes with the place, which is the heritage of Frank Lloyd Wright and Mrs. Wright, of the idea that one does need to contribute as much as one takes away. Those parts that don't work are when we start dividing things and saying, "Well, I only get to do this much," and "You only get to do this much."

I'm trying to remember the name of the author, someone who studied communities, who was very articulate about how leaders must always be servants and vice versa. You could never stop being a servant while in a leadership role, and I think that, certainly in the best sense and in the best actions of this Fellowship, that is what happens.

EFFI: I think the secret was a degree of hardship, discipline . . . even though it was based on an authoritarian leadership, it wasn't always self-imposed discipline . . . coupled with real sense of joy, beauty, respect of beauty, nature and celebrating life. Sometimes it seems contradictory, and then on the other [hand] it is not. I recall that Mrs. Wright, for instance, would say, "You'd better join chorus." And you wouldn't answer, "Well, I just sing in the shower," like people say today. You did it, you'd better do it. Maybe it was a fear factor, but what it did is it planted you within an experience and didn't allow you to prejudge whether it's good for you or not, whether you would enjoy it or not. You were planted into those circumstances, and from within you discovered . . . wow . . . it just opens a whole new world to you. And I think that was important in her mechanism of how to run the place.

Arnold Roy explains what, in his view, made the Fellowship work initially and has perpetuated it even after the death of the two founders:

> ARNOLD: My view of it is very simple. On Frank Lloyd Wright's grave in Wisconsin (of course he is no longer there; the marker is still there) . . . "Love of an idea is love of God."[7] That's pretty simple. But when you think of all these diverse personalities . . . artists, architects . . . really diverse personalities, there has to be something holding them together. I say it's the commonality of it; we all love and respect the ideas espoused by these two people. And we use that to bridge the differences that we have.

Notes

1. The Fritzes ran a summer camp near Taliesin. Herb Fritz was with the Fellowship from 1937 to 1941.

2. See chap. 7.

3. Tom Payton was with the Fellowship from 1987 to 1995; Michael Standish, 1986 to the present; Bill Schoettker, 1988 to 1994; and Arno Luthje, 1983 to 1993.

4. Kelly Oliver was with the Fellowship from 1949 to 1956.

5. Nezam Amery was with the Fellowship from 1953 to 1957.

6. Cornelia Brierly describes some of them in *Tales of Taliesen.*

7. The grave marker remains in Wisconsin, but in response to wishes expressed by Mrs. Wright before her death, Mr. Wright's body was exhumed and cremated in 1985. His ashes were immured with hers at an unmarked location at Taliesin West.

6

The Arts:
"Creativity Is of the Soul"

Music, art, theater, and dance have always been important elements in the Taliesin Fellowship's character and mission. The visual arts are apparent in the architecture of Mr. Wright and his apprentices, and now in that of the Taliesin Architects. The buildings at both Taliesin locations are masterpieces, and the landscapes around them artistic enhancements. Mr. Wright's collection of Japanese prints and his respect for their beauty and delicacy are cited by fellows in several chapters in this book; Japanese art is prominent at both the Wisconsin and Arizona locations. The sculptures of Heloise Crista grace the sculpture garden, and works in glass by Susan Lockhart and others are on display at Taliesin West.

Cornelia Brierly, commenting on Taliesin's climate of creativity, spoke of Albert Schweitzer's ability to dream "on a different level," noting that he and others "thought . . . in another dimension." Mr. Wright's thought, she added, was also "always in that other dimension. We used to be very aware of it when he started talking." I asked whether that was what had attracted her to Taliesin.

CORNELIA: I hope so. As a matter of fact, a few years ago when I was doing yarn designs, I had the idea that the Fellowship could do so many things, that we should start having a show of Fellowship art. That's when we really started, with Susan making stained glass designs and Heloise doing her sculpture, and many others crafting interesting creations. We had a show; I think there's a brochure down in the visitor center that tells about our attempt. That's how we got started, and maybe I'm in a position now of being able to help to start things . . . just as we had that "Walk through the Woods" in Wisconsin with the public to get them more acquainted with Mr. Wright and nature.

As Cornelia describes the walk, the close relationship between nature, art, and artistic traditions at Taliesin is apparent.

> We have [in Spring Green] a new hotel—The Springs—that Charles designed, and the girl who's in charge of the activities [there] became our friend [when] we were going there to swim every day. Johnny told her that when he was young Mr. Wright sent the apprentices out in the dew of the morning to see if they could find an asymmetrical cobweb, which of course they couldn't because cobwebs are symmetrical. However, this fired her imagination to such an extent that she decided the hotel should have a benefit for our school—a walk in the woods where Fellowship people talked to the participants about Mr. Wright and his beliefs.
>
> It was a five-mile walk with four stations. At each station something was discussed about the life at Taliesin and how Mr. Wright regarded nature and how he incorporated those thoughts into his life. . . . People could have taken a three-mile walk or a five-mile walk, but they all decided on the five-mile walk. They left at quarter after eleven, and they didn't get back till four or four-thirty. They all came in stimulated by the experience. The hotel prepared a wonderful table of hors d'oeuvres. People sat around and talked about what they'd heard and seen. Our people were there to talk with them and acquaint them with the Fellowship. The hotel plans to make that a yearly event. . . . It was a very successful undertaking.

Performing arts play an important part in Fellowship life. Performances occur most frequently on the occasions known as "Saturday Evening at Taliesin." After spending the week in work clothes, women don formal dresses and men tuxedos for a social hour, dinner, and entertainment provided by the Fellowship's chorus, music and dance ensembles, and actors. Sometimes friends of the Fellowship participate, and guest performers appear occasionally.

In addition to the Saturday evening festivities, the Fellowship has for years produced plays, musicals, and other theatrical events. Browsing through pictures in the Archives and family albums (particularly Kay and John Rattenbury's and Tom and Effi Casey's), one gains the sense that such productions played a vital role in the life of the community. They have also produced tensions, however, particularly while Mr. and Mrs. Wright were alive. Curtis Besinger, for example, describes with disdain the Gurdjieff dance exercises that, in his view, consumed too much time and energy. As a gifted pianist and conductor he played a big part in the cultural life of the Fellowship and it fell to him to accompany rehearsals and performances of the dances known as "movements."

Writing to a Taliesin colleague in 1953, Besinger remarked that a mutual acquaintance had "about had his fill of the 'soul searching' establishment we are turning into—via 'movements' etc." Nor did he himself go along with it, "in spite of the fact that I am useful to it. And since 'soul-searching' is waxing here and 'Architecture' is waning, I wonder just what my status is going to be." He continued, "You see Mr. Wright's philosophy and Mrs. Wright's do not mix. As near as I can tell they are in direct opposition."[1] Two years later Besinger left the Fellowship. In citing his discontentment, however, it should also be noted that his book is filled with many happy memories and favorable and insightful accounts of life at Taliesin in the 1940s and early 1950s.

I asked Tom Casey about his involvement in music and the arts since he came to Taliesin in 1950, particularly about the Gurdjieff movements.

TOM: I was involved with those exercises from their inception at Taliesin; they started in about 1950. I participated in nearly all of the presentations that were made. In my view, the value of all those movements was the development of coordination and discipline. That's what, fundamentally, they were all about. They were in dance form, and . . . in practicing them you developed a higher degree of physical coordination.

I think they were started because their daughter, Iovanna, had spent a year in Paris with Gurdjieff and returned in 1949. She brought with her a young French woman she had met there and befriended; her name was Lisa Tracol. Lisa was also studying with Gurdjieff. When the two of them came, that's when classes started.

Did you enjoy doing the movements?

Oh yes, I did. I found them very beneficial. . . . You have to realize that as time went by, Iovanna Wright added her own dance interpretations in addition to Gurdjieff exercises. The series that Gurdjieff called the "obligatories," meaning they were a series of exercises in the form of dance, really did develop and require an extraordinary amount of physical coordination. Different limbs were doing different movements—feet one rhythm, legs another, arms a third rhythm, and head another movement pattern, different from the other three! As an outcome, we really did develop quite a lot of physical coordination.

Apprentices performing Gurdjieffian "movements" in the desert.

I think that most of the people who did them enjoyed them. I know some people have the idea that everyone was coerced into that, but nobody has ever been coerced into staying at Taliesin or doing anything at Taliesin. I think that's a view of a few people who were very badly coordinated, so they didn't do them very well and they felt they were dividing or taking away from their attention to other things which they felt more important. But I did them quite well, I enjoyed them, I developed coordination.

Also, as I said, I learned a great deal of interior discipline, which I have always considered has stood me in great stead. The ability to concentrate on what you're doing as a task is a thing which I've ranked as greatly needed, especially with young people I come in contact with today. They have a very difficult time really concentrating on things; they always have to have noise in the background; they're fearful of quiet and concentration. From that point of view, I think the movements were extremely valuable.

One of the current fellows, who joined the Fellowship before Besinger's departure, expresses greater concern about the place of dance and other arts after Mr. Wright's death in 1959. In our conversation, David Dodge describes how, in his view, things changed.

DAVID: I think after Mr. Wright's death there was a major change, because Iovanna was interested in developing young people that were to become dancers of "the movements"—"correlations," as they later became known. And Mrs. Wright was always interested in the development of the individual. Of course, that doesn't put the aim of Taliesin out of line. The fact that it was the development of the individual who was trying to be an architect, where everything in this whole community locks together, everything makes sense—there is no service, there is no menial job—everything is all part of this growing experience at becoming a better architect. But as soon as the thing began, we started then to accept people who came here for the philosophy rather than for becoming an architect.

That's when things started to get a little bit fragmented. It weakened the spirit, and "them" and "us" started to happen. And then, you know, we get people that are coming in just for an education, are coming for music, are coming for painting. Well, you know, the work for them is harder and more difficult than it is for those who came as architects, because it's easier to see the relationship with . . . everything. You need to know everything if you're going to be an architect. But what does a painter have to know about cleaning the floor? Not anything, really. I mean, he can look at the floor and look at the texture and look at how the light hits it and all that sort of stuff, but it really doesn't have quite that same significance.

Now, Mr. Wright did have people who came to Taliesin during his lifetime that came for other reasons than architecture. Gene Masselink came to be a painter and studied with Mr. Wright, but Gene wanted to be a painter in connection with the architecture. It was not just studying painting to make paintings and stick them in a museum; it was painting that would be design and add a spatial dimension that painting can do to an architectural space.

Given his background and interests, it was natural for David to help with the music for the festivals—"an incredible experience," he says. I asked whether he was referring to the Easter celebrations.

No, to the Festival of Music in May. You have to realize that was not a minor effort at Taliesin. The drafting room shut down almost for three months while rehearsals went on.

Well, it really didn't completely shut down, but for the amount of work that got done during that time it might as well have been shut down. Leave it open for two weeks and that would have been enough. But, basically, the three months were wiped out. Everybody who was in the Festival was rehearsing all night long; they were worthless in the daytime. The drafting room was empty most of the time, and even if you were working in there Iovanna would call a rehearsal for this or that. People had to disappear and they had to go there.

So, it was only those who were not in that program who were able to help. I wasn't in the dance part of the program, so I didn't have those rehearsals to go to, but I was involved with the music. Mrs. Wright started to write her own music, and Bruce would transcribe it. We'd have a piano score out of it and then from the piano score we were trying to make orchestra parts. So we were doing all these crazy things. Then I would end up by playing something in the orchestra—playing the percussion, or piano, or organ, or harmonium, or whatever, or singing in the chorus that was part of that Festival. I was really involved a lot with that.

How many years were those festivals presented?

They went from . . . really, from about '57 to about '77, I would say. I think '77 was the last one; I conducted that one.

Did you draw a lot of people from the community?

Yes, oh yes. We sold out. We had five performances, to sold-out houses. So that was five times 150 people. That was a lot of people for us in those days.

That was a Fellowship builder, wasn't it?

Oh, it certainly built the Fellowship. It also broke it up, in a way, because it put the concentration not on the architecture. It was definitely a major effort in a totally separate direction.

Anneliese Dodge, on the other hand, remembered the big productions fondly and expressed regret that they were a thing of the past.

ANNELIESE: Now we have so few people I don't think we can sing at the moment. And performances, . . . we did "Fiddler on the Roof." We were just talking [about

Kenn Lockhart, Kay Rattenbury, and Johnny Hill in costume at one of the many Taliesin parties.

that] yesterday when Sharon was here. She is one of our previous students.[2] She lived here for seven years. And she said, "Oh, Anneliese, I remember that was the best." And "Carmina Burana" we did in beautiful robes; that was a time Bruce was still conducting. Oh, that was so powerful.

Did you hire an orchestra, or did you do it with the people from here?

No, no, we just sang, with Bruce conducting with our own ensemble. But it was a big difference to have rented robes from a church so we all looked in uniform. And then Bruce made us to move on stage and do different movements while we were singing, to turn around sideways . . . oh, that was so powerful, I wish we could perform it again. That was in the '80s, but I can't tell you exactly the year. That was very beautiful. And "Fiddler on the Roof," that was all Effi's doing. And that was so much fun, oh, I wish we could do that again, too. We had fun, fun. That was great, but of course we do not have enough people, you know, not enough young apprentices. Effi is also now so involved in the accreditation program. Everyone has something different to do, even though we hire so many people from outside. But it is still everyone's wish that the Fellowship come closer together again. . . . Oh, years back, we would have cocktail parties. That's not so much anymore. Or we would invite other guests in the evening.

But, I must say, Christmas open house, that is still beautiful. We have it at our home earlier, and then Christmas Eve there are many Fellowship parties.

Arnold Roy remembered the festivals and dances with mixed feelings.

ARNOLD: I don't know if any of the other people have told you, but the reason for the Pavilion was to perform dance. And we did Gurdjieff dances, sacred dances. We had the Taliesin Festival of Music and Dance in the spring. It was just an unbelievable effort. We had to put on a professional performance, and everything else here had to go on [as usual]—the work in the drafting room, the community work, and then we put this on on top of it. It was just an unbelievable experience. All of us who went through it profited from it. It's something you wouldn't want to do again, but you're glad you went through the agony of it.

Although the festivals David, Anneliese, and Arnold described were eventually discontinued, the arts still claim a prominent place in the Fellowship's life. Effi Casey, who is trained in painting as well as music, directs the chorus and instrumental ensembles that perform at Taliesin. I spoke with her about her leadership role in the arts.

EFFI: I think that we at Taliesin still celebrate that kind of engagement in the arts as an integral part of this culture and today's curriculum. I have tried to help create an environment by involving young people in the cultural activities, particularly in music—just like Heloise in sculpture, Susan in the decorative arts, among others. I have also participated and continue to help conduct workshops in the so-called "Nature Patterns," in which we pursue the study of nature as the underlying source of design. These exercises also include the study and analysis of Mr. Wright's work.

I have participated in the Taliesin chorus and instrumental ensemble since I came in 1966. At that time, however, John Amarantides was the music director. He's living in Athens now, but he was for many years a major contributor to all the music activities at Taliesin. When John A, as we call him, left, I think Vern Swaback conducted the chorus, and after him, Bruce. Eventually Bruce got so overwhelmed with writing and editing Frank Lloyd Wright books that he passed the leadership on to me. It started really kind of informally. He said, "Couldn't you conduct the chorus for a while, and then when the pressure of the books eases off I'll take it back over." But that never happened. I saw the need for a chorus director and stepped in and did it. You know, I think this is how leadership develops at Taliesin quite often if you have any kind of talent. Instead of assigning "positions," people take on responsibilities. At least that's how I see it. So I've been conducting the chorus since the early 1980s.

The chorus has always consisted of both apprentices and fellows?

Yes, and that's the other wonderful aspect of our musical activity. We work together— faculty and apprentices, even sometimes children. Golnar, our daughter, sang in

Chorus in the Taliesin theater.

the chorus and used to play the flute—and still does sometimes—when we needed instruments with the chorus. She will play this Easter again, too. You just realize that together, as a group, you can affect so much more than by yourself. It is very rewarding to engage together in learning something and pursuing it and perhaps being able to perform, like at our Easter, to bring it to a high point.

What are some of the most popular compositions the chorus has sung?

What we do program-wise, or study, is music from the twelfth century all the way up to contemporary. It includes sacred and popular music. Since I took over I feel I have tended to focus possibly too much on Bach or Palestrina or composers like that. When I ask myself why that is, I think it is because they ultimately bring you to the source of not only design but order—structure and order. It's so architectural. I think there is a very, very powerful relationship to architecture in Bach's music, or Vivaldi's, for that matter.

But you have also done contemporary composers. Who are some of them?

Carl Orff, Hindemith, Bartók, Benjamin Britten, and living composers. I find repeatedly that the interest of our singers (and myself) fades rather quickly with many compositions of current composers because the spiritual content seems so shallow. Of course there are exceptions; for example, an *Alleluia* by Ralph Manuel, which is very uplifting and nourishing. We love it. I have also enjoyed the introduction of foreign languages. We sing folk songs, even in their native language. We sing Russian hymns, we sing African peace songs in Zulu, and we have always sung Latin, German, French, and Italian songs.

It is a wonderful activity, and I think for many people it has become the single most powerful language of what the Taliesin experience entails. It's almost like weaving something, like building a mosaic of emotions, of experiences together. Then later you reflect on what you experienced here at Taliesin, and music becomes a very meaningful part of that memory. I say that because music has been the voice for the greatest joy of our community's life and also the expression for deepest sorrow when we lost a community member, a Fellowship member. Music becomes the ultimate expression of that. It is a very, very powerful element in our community's life.

Have you been the leader of the instrumental ensemble too, through the years?

Yes. There is a little more difficulty with it now, because I think we are experiencing the effect of the high school system whereby not as many people as used to be are involved in music. They can't read music when they come here or they have just never been exposed to it.

We have something going every year. It's just that when people leave that really hampers what you can do, but then somebody else comes along and it picks up again. It's just a little difficult to maintain an ongoing successful program sometimes.

Tell me about some of the visiting groups that you have had.

We have had, for instance, Bill and Mona Schoen from Chicago, professional musicians. Bill Schoen was the assistant principal violist of the Chicago Symphony for many, many years. And Mona Schoen is part of the Lyric Opera in Chicago. They came originally on a tour, and when they heard about our musical activities they were very interested and fascinated. Eventually they joined us several times; for a while they came every summer. Bill gave lectures on music and always performed with the group, and really challenged us and helped individually. So that was highly motivating.

We also played together with members of the Phoenix Symphony; currently also with Bill Lutz and Martha Fisher. Bill Lutz is the musical director for the public radio station in Madison, an excellent pianist and singer. So is Martha. So, this is a great stimulus for us, to share.

Are you involved with the dance at all?

I used to be. That was in '66, when I was an apprentice, and then later on in performances. In 1966 we still had larger dance performances in which all members of the Fellowship participated one way or another. Yes, I loved those very, very much; I was very involved in it.

Who leads it now?

We don't have dance performances to that extent anymore. It has shifted more to drama currently. Heloise still carries on some of the Gurdjieff movements, and also she has introduced her own choreography, which is based on the Gurdjieff concept of movement. Well, you know the background of Gurdjieff movements. Having done this for a long time, it has really taught us self-discipline, incredible concentration power. You just learn to be absolutely focused, and that in turn really helps you to correlate the mind and the body.

What are some of the big productions you have done in recent years?

We have done "Candide" by Voltaire, adapted and directed by Terry Kerr;[3] and last summer "Three Works upon the Soul," by Thornton Wilder. Chekov was done in '95, the Chekov "Wedding." There again, a large group of senior members, faculty, and apprentices worked together. Everyone from Bruce to Noah [Terry's eleven-year-old son].

In years past, the large productions were an important part of Fellowship life, were they not, and that's diminished somewhat?

It has diminished because the demands of the profession are such . . . it's such incredible time pressure. Everything has to be done faster. The computer didn't really help you to do your work faster and have the rest of the time for yourself; it just moved up the deadlines. So, consequently, all jobs have to go out much, much quicker than they used to. That has seriously limited our time, the availability of people to rejuvenate and reenergize themselves through other activities. That is kind of sad, because it is a very unifying activity to be involved in cultural activities.

I wanted to also mention that Terry Kerr, Karen Holden,[4] and I, along with Heloise, worked on a statement about the humanities and the performance of the arts here, and we came across a quotation by Tolstoy, which is very correct, I think, for our situation: "Art is a human activity, having for its purpose the transmission to others of the highest and best feelings to which men have risen." . . . It goes also together with "learning by doing"; you discover from within and not by just looking at.

It was involvement in the arts that opened the way for Susan Lockhart to come to Taliesin, and her role as an artist has evolved through nearly four decades there. Here is how her involvement in the arts at Taliesin began:

SUSAN: Mr. and Mrs. Wright came often to New York City, because the Guggenheim Museum was being finished, and I was living there. David Wheatley, to whom I was married at that time, had been a former apprentice, and he was working for Edgar Tafel, one of the original apprentices of Frank Lloyd Wright. We saw the Wrights periodically. We were also using the apartment in New York sometimes for some of the Gurdjieff dance movements. One Easter, I remember, we did sort of a traditional Taliesin Easter breakfast in the apartment of the Plaza hotel. . . . That was when there was the invitation from Frank Lloyd Wright that "If you wish, you'd be welcome to come back." I had never been there as a permanent member.

When I came back, I entered very seriously the dance work, which was ongoing. The Pavilion had been finished two years before and was built for the dance and

Chamber ensemble
performing around a
music stand designed by
Mr. Wright.

music festival that was prepared for spring production every year beginning in '57. I
was there in '58, so beginning in '58 I began preparations and learning. I had studied
the Gurdjieff movements prior to that in New York with some of the members of the
Fellowship who were living in the area at the time. So, I was a very serious member
of that performance group. We prepared from November through April for a public
performance every year.

At the time of Mr. Wright's death in '59 we had had only two performances. I
continued to work in dance, which meant learning and teaching my part to others. I
did a lot of solo work. Heloise did the primary costume designing with Iovanna and
Mrs. Wright, but we did a lot of construction sewing on our costumes. The stage
sets, of course, were made on-site. The preparation for those performances would
last a good three or four months, and along with that I also had a major part in our
music program. At that time I was the only pianist, and so I would accompany John
Amarantides and any visitor who was the performer. For soloists, vocal or instrumental,
I was the piano player.

Bruce's primary musical work was performing and, of course, initially working
as arranger with Mrs. Wright. He really became a major element in bringing her
music to completion. She sang into a tape recorder—a single line; he brought it to
life through all of the orchestration of it. Primarily he performed those things that
had to do with Mrs. Wright's music. She was composing dance at that time, so a lot
of that started from dance music pieces and then worked its way into other things
which, of course, John Amarantides and various other people played and performed

with Bruce on the piano. Bruce didn't sight-read classical music per se, as I did, or do accompaniment work.

How did you move then into the visual arts?

Gene Masselink taught a class which was offered by Arizona State University, but it was held at Taliesin West, in the work of abstraction, that is, seeing in the abstract. That was the work that he did with Frank Lloyd Wright, as the primary person in many of the buildings that Frank Lloyd Wright designed. Gene was responsible for the abstract designs that appeared primarily in screens and doors and wall murals and a lot of graphic things that were printed. So I became a student initially of Gene Masselink's until he died in the early '60s.

From then on one of my peers, who had studied a little bit longer with Gene and worked very seriously, Vern Swaback, became my mentor. So in the '60s I was primarily a student, working in abstract designs on paper; however, my creative contribution was to appliqué fabric—tablecloths for our big, six-foot-diameter Saturday evening tables which Mrs. Wright used for guests. And then in the '70s I became also an apprentice to the graphic design department, and that was, again, with Vern Swaback. Subsequently he became a staff member and then in the late '70s went to begin his own work.

Beginning in '70 with the Biltmore I started doing graphic design, and then for another ten years was a major person within that work of doing design and production for Taliesin in-house materials or outside clients—logotypes, marketing pieces, all kinds of printed graphic designs. . . .

I think the first abstractions I did were in the appliqué fabric areas. Then I went to designs on paper, and then some of it applied to printed pieces—logotypes, of course, in the graphic design element of the '70s. And in the '80s I started doing some commission work. My first piece of glass was for a house that John Hill did in the Fort Worth area in the mid-'80s. That was the beginning of doing commission work in stained glass.

I subsequently then took a small workshop in glass just to know more hands-on because there was no one doing glass. John Rattenbury and Bruce Pfeiffer were doing serious glass mosaics designs, which were small glass pessere mostly embedded in tabletop pieces. No one was actually doing cut leaded glass at that time, so I went back and got some technical training and built little pieces myself. I started doing commission work at that time. In the late '80s, early '90s, I was asked by a couple of galleries if I would have work in their galleries, so I then had to go from commissions to creating a body of work that could be sold in editions in galleries.

Are you involved in any of the design work Taliesin Architects are doing now?

Periodically, yes. I've done some work for our architectural firm. One of the things that happens, which is a very understandable thing, is that most of the people who were trained at Taliesin—either by Frank Lloyd Wright or by the next generation—worked

Susan Lockhart at drawing table. Works of her glass sculpture are nearby.

in the area of abstraction design or what we call nature patterns. So when it comes to works of art like John Rattenbury's or anyone else's, Vern's certainly, within their own architectural design work, if there's an opportunity to do either graphics or decorative design in the way of glass or furniture or any of those other things, [turning to someone else is] sort of like giving someone else the maraschino cherry and whipped cream. Because that aspect of the design work is sort of the créme de la créme of the project. You may admire and love your co-artist peer, but you really want to do that work yourself.

So most of what you're doing now is commission and gallery work.

Yes, and it's through people who are not necessarily connected with any of our architectural work. I always wish for that to change, and periodically I do have that opportunity. I do have an opportunity in the Manila project.[5] It always has to be put forth and lobbied for by the architect. They always put those things in that go beyond the base budget, so it's a matter of being there and being able to get those things accepted. . . .

At one point when the Biltmore [remodeling] started, I think it was in '71, Vern said, "Would you like to work on the graphics for the hotel?" The first thing I did was to help design the little brochure that accompanied the opening of the hotel. I designed everything for those things—restaurant menu covers, lettering. I did not do the logotype. I did a number of those things for the Biltmore project and then went from there to actually being the main person who designed all of the firm's client graphics; I did the Grady Gammage Auditorium twenty-five-year logo. They had never had a logo before.

Do you still do a lot of piano playing?

I do. At this moment I don't practice, because I had to start giving up some things . . . in all the performing arts . . . you know how much practicing it takes to do artistic work. Well, if you're a pianist, if you're a singer, if you're a dancer, if you're a visual artist—if you're doing all these simultaneously there are just so many hours in the day for practicing all those arts. I was talking about this and someone said, "Well, do you want to be mediocre at this—an artist at this and an artist at that—or do you really want to be good and focused?" So I gave up dance in the last part of the '70s; I don't do any more dance work.

At this point, one of the exciting things that I am able to do is to have a couple of things going that would be parallel to our licensing program of the Frank Lloyd Wright designs. I have three venues, three different products which are . . . being designed for manufacture under a license, under contract with the Foundation, and we will get a royalty on them. They will go out under my ID as a member of either Taliesin Architects or the Frank Lloyd Wright Foundation. I'm sort of the first of that idea of licensing products designed by Taliesin. John Rattenbury's house for *Life* magazine will be a little bit of that.[6] That will go into a commercial release plan design.

Although visitors to Taliesin West come there to see Frank Lloyd Wright's architecture, the sculpture of Heloise Crista on display around the camp, particularly in the garden at the entrance to the Pavilion, always captures their attention. On the beautiful morning of Thanksgiving Day during our residency, we accompanied Heloise on a walking tour of the garden at Taliesin West, tape recorder in hand. As we looked at her artistic work, our conversation wove together three topics: how she came to be a sculptor, the way she works as a sculptor, and the significance and character of the pieces we viewed.

After describing her reasons for coming to Taliesin (recorded in chap. 2), Heloise talked about the first thing she did after arriving at Taliesin with a B.A. degree from UCLA.

HELOISE: I think I was mixing mortar and filling in cracks in the studio walls.

Did Mr. Wright set you in the direction of sculpture, then?

No, no he didn't. It was very accidental. Well, he did have a part in it, because there was a man from Temple University in Pennsylvania who wrote Mr. Wright and said that he would like to come and do a portrait head of him. Mr. Wright finally said, "All right, come on." So then he came here—his name was Dean Boris Blai—and they set up in what is now the annex. That was just a beautiful room at that time, it wasn't used for anything in particular. There was a fireplace and wonderful view. It was originally a dining room.

So they set up there to do the work, and several other people went in to work at the same time on sculptures of Mr. Wright's head. But I didn't do that. I mean, why *would* I do that? I was very timid about any of that, and I didn't think of doing Mr.

Wright's head at that time. There were two Italians here at the time—Franco D'Ayala Valva did the head of Frank Lloyd Wright . . . the green one toward the far end of the living room. . . . Giovanni del Drago was a prince, and he was doing another one. Franco was a marquis and Giovanni was a prince, and they were having a little hard time serving each other sometimes. Why should the prince serve the marquis?

Anyway, I used to go in and watch Franco do his work. I was a little bit attracted to Franco. I used to go in and watch what he did, and he would talk to me about it. Even after Mr. Wright left and Dean Blai left and everybody [was gone], Franco was the only one that kept working on his piece. He had a photograph of Mr. Wright, maybe 10"x12". I used to go and watch him, and he would tell me how to read a photograph. He said, "Don't pay attention to lines. Every time it gets lighter or darker that means there's something going on in the contour, and that's what you have to look for."

Then later Giovanni said to me, "Heloise, why weren't you there? Mr. Wright said, 'Where's Heloise?'" I think he was just kidding me, you know. I'm sure he was, but I thought, "Oh, my God, why would he ask that?" Anyway, Giovanni said, "Why don't you do a head of somebody?" And I said, "Well, Giovanni, I don't know how to do any sculpture." He said, "Oh, come on."

He was irritating me to the point where I finally said, "All right, I will." He said, "Why don't you do a head of Kenn Lockhart? He's got a good sculptural head." I said, "Okay." So I asked Kenn, and Kenn very nicely said yes, he would sit for me. And that's how it all started. The minute I started working on that head I got so fascinated by the process. I just loved it. I thought, "This is something I feel some affinity for," because painting I never did have an affinity for somehow. But sculpture, yes, it felt good and I got very interested in it. So that was kind of the beginning.

Then I did a few portrait heads of different people here. Once every two, three years or so something would come up and I would do a head. I did a head of Brandoch in Wisconsin when he was about sixteen.

Did Mr. Wright see [the head of himself]?

Yes, he did. You know, I think he really liked Franco's head better than he did mine, but Mrs. Wright liked mine. . . . I don't know where it is; it's just a plaster head.

Oh, it wasn't even cast?

Not in bronze. It wasn't that good; it was just my first thing. I never ever thought about putting it in bronze. But then Mrs. Wright asked me to do Mr. Wright's head one time in Wisconsin one summer. She was trying to get everyone going on lots of different kinds of work because the tax people were coming to assess us, to see whether we should pay taxes or not. Mr. Wright always said we were a school and we shouldn't have to pay taxes. Mrs. Wright was getting people to start up the weaving and she said to Joe Fabris, "You fix up the looms and start the weaving. She said to me, "You do a head of Mr. Wright." She was directing people to do things.

So, I said, "Okay." But it would never have occurred to me myself to go and do a head of Frank Lloyd Wright, you know, never. But anyway, because she told me to I just did it. I was lucky; I was just lucky. Other forces were working with me.

When you look at that head today, do you think there's any way you could improve on it? I think it's just perfect.

No, probably not. No.

Are you entirely self-taught in sculpture?

Yes. I didn't study sculpture anywhere. I had no mentor. I was doing a lot of dance work with Iovanna and I was doing costume designs and recording dances and things like that. I was also doing some work in the drafting room but not as much as I might have. I didn't aspire to be an architect. . . . It was 1978 when I made my decision to be a sculptor.

How does your being part of the Fellowship affect the way you do these kinds of things? Is it different than if you were off in a studio in San Francisco?

Well, I'm sure it is. Partly because I'm so free here. I'm given tremendous freedom to do this. . . . I have a few commissions but not very many, so I do what I want to, what comes out of myself. My work is not confined by what some client will want in particular. So living here and not having to worry about how I'm going to pay for the food and lodging and having to have money is so great for me.

Sculpture of Mr. Wright by Heloise Crista.

Have you had some apprentices in sculpture here?

No, that's too difficult to do, and everyone comes here with an architectural bent. In fact, I don't even have a studio here. I just have a very small room. It's just stuffed full of models and materials and tools; I can barely walk in and out of it myself, much less have anybody else in there. In Wisconsin I have a really nice space to work—big and high. It used to be the old ice house.

Do you find yourself pursuing a theme after reading a book, and then do you do several things on that same theme?

No, not necessarily several things on the same theme, but I am interested in general in the idea of evolution, individual evolution and the struggle to work and try to put in effort to become more conscious in your life, and all that. That general theme is going through a lot of my things lately. Not my early pieces, but my later pieces, yes.

In describing the way she works, Heloise explained that she sometimes conceptualizes a piece of sculpture on paper first, and sometimes she makes a maquette, a small model, just to see how it's going to work. She starts with an interior armature, a structure that holds the clay or plastiline or any other material she is going to work with in place. Typically she casts ten pieces, although of smaller ones she may make fifteen or twenty. Only one mold is needed for each casting.

I asked her how she attached the parts as they come out of the casting. Using a sculpture as an example, she explains the complicated technical nature of her work.

This one, "Call of the Soul," would be in two parts. . . . They weld it and grind it; that's called chasing. I go to the foundry and work on the wax, because for bronze casting you start with a wax replica. That gets cleaned and refined if you want it to. You can go as far as you want to with the wax. Then they put gates on it and sprues and then it goes into the shell room where it gets covered with a ceramic shell.

"Call of the Soul"

Tell us about "Call of the Soul."

The idea for this one came right after I read a book by Gary Zukav called *Seat of the Soul*. I read it here and then when I went to Wisconsin in the summer I was thinking, "I'd like to do a sculpture that would express an idea that was in this book, about not forgetting your soul and not being absorbed only with life that's on the outside."

This is supposed to be a person looking up and seeing the soul appearing like an arc above, almost like a rainbow materializing momentarily. It might be saying, "Don't forget about me. This is the reason you're here on this earth." Some people read it totally differently. But it doesn't matter how they read it; if they get some idea from it, that's good.

We looked at many pieces of Heloise's work. Excerpts from conversations about some of them show the intellectual and emotional depth of her creative expressions.

I got the idea to do this piece, called "Awakening," one day when thinking about the S-curve. I got the idea to have a face on one side of the curve and have another face on the other side to show totally different aspects of the same person. The more I worked on it, the idea got much deeper. This often happens. This could be the side of suffering humanity. I was reading recently that one of the times you suffer the most is when you are awakening and beginning to see yourself not in an illusory way but more as you really are. That's a terrible suffering—to realize that you're not what you thought you were.

So, that side is suffering, but this other side is of someone more enlightened, already more awakened and becoming more in tune with the universe and connected to higher powers. The blue area above indicates heaven. The fact that these lines

"Awakening"

"Archetype"

from heaven are connected with her sight and with her mouth, with her speech, shows she's working on the higher level. She is hearing, speaking, and seeing everything differently now than she did, and on a higher level. She has ascended to a new state.

On the suffering side, this person simply doesn't know what to do or how to get out of his suffering. There's so much suffering in this world that is unnecessary and useless. You're wasting energy suffering when you don't have to. People who react in hatred, jealousy, greed—all those negative emotions—are suffering. The results can be very bad for you, but it's hard to get out of it once it gets hold of you. Of course, there is real suffering, too, but this sculpture is not about that particularly.

This one I call "Archetype." It has to do with the family unit. I did this in Wisconsin one summer when I was thinking I would like to do the family because it's a vanishing thing now almost, that family unit and that togetherness, the nurturing and the love, everything that should be going on within the family. . . . I just wanted to show that within my own family, too, I felt the lack of the nurturing. I didn't have the connection with my mother or my father. We lived in Japan. We had servants looking after the children. My father was very noncommunicative. He didn't know how to talk to us; he just didn't know. It wasn't in his blood. . . .

My mother was born in Japan, too. We all, on my mother's side, have a little Japanese blood. I think I'm one-eighth. My grandmother was born there. My father went over there from the United States. He was sent over as a representative for his company. Anyway, I just felt the lack of love and nurturing in my own life, and I wanted to emphasize the idea of the family.

Is the figure in the sculpture holding something?

Yes, this is like the new baby to come. I call it the negative baby.

A negative image . . .

Yes, a negative image is a much better way to put it.

"Ascending Horizons" is one that has really captured me.

I don't know what it means to you, but for me, what I'm trying to show here [stroking the sculpture] . . . this represents the past, this is the present and this is the future. And all these little knobs are like new souls that are going to be born eventually, or new ideas that are coming into the world. What I was trying to show here is that we have to leave the past behind. We can't just carry the past with us all the time. We have to look to the future, we have to go with some new ideas, we have to go with global unity instead of war and chaos, and look after the environment and all those ideas that are coming now. We have to do that; otherwise we are going to self-destruct. . . . We've got to look to the future and not carry on the old obsolete ideas of the past.

But then, on a personal level, too, I was thinking some people maybe have a very bad background that they can't get rid of in their lives—some kind of abuse or whatever in their past—but they can't give it up, you know. They carry it with them, this old baggage, for the rest of their lives and they're blaming something or someone back there. Unfortunate as it is, we have to let it go and go on with the future. But it's not easy to do. It's not at all easy, because we're all so habituated to ways of thinking and feeling, all of those things. And so, to give that up is very difficult. Actually, it started on a personal level and then it went to the world level. These things can go into a psychological level as well. It depends on one's understanding.

"Ascending Horizons"

"Ring of Wisdom"

This one is called "Ring of Wisdom," and this also came from a book that I read a long time ago. . . . It said that a ring of wisdom exists around the planet earth that contains a lot of knowledge—not just factual knowledge, but real wisdom. And if you can tune into this, if you have the power to tune into it (and I'm sure that Mr. Wright did—I think he had that ability) this kind of wisdom is accessible to you. Now this is the planet earth. At first I just had one circle around here; then I had a circle going this way. And I thought, "No, no, no, it isn't working. It doesn't look good . . . it's too static." Then I started putting in more rings, and then even after I finished with that it was still sort of boring. And I thought, "I've got to put people in here," because you have to connect it with people.

So I put in these faces of higher beings that are looking down on the earth to see how we're doing. One of these faces sort of looks like Christ to me. And then I had this little lump of clay that was sitting here on my sculpture stand. I picked it up, looked at it and thought, "Hmm, looks like a monk." So I put it up here and made it look a little more like a person. Now he's walking on the path here.

Let's go over to that one. That's one that I find so intriguing.

This one is called "Path to Infinity." Here again I wanted to show a man's struggle from total ignorance, being asleep in the beginning, and then gradually starting to wake up and realize what he's about and what is possible for man, but with great effort. Gradually he becomes more and more awakened and more conscious. I wanted to show infinity on the other side. I wanted to show brilliant light. I wondered, "How am I going to show this side as being brilliant light?" So this is what I came

"Path to Infinity"

up with, the light as rays streaming forth, and the man is looking with awe at something that he's seeing there. The extent, the possibilities that exist for human beings, are limitless.

Earlier in this chapter we heard Cornelia Brierly speak of the climate for creativity at Taliesin. Later she reflected on Taliesin's past and present and concluded with a poignant thought on creativity.

CORNELIA: When the Fellowship was first started, it was during the depths of the Depression, and because at that time everybody was more or less leveled to the same economic circumstance, people began to help one another. They realized that they needed to be dependent on one another—to get together for accomplishment. It was a possible way for a lot of people to survive. I think at that time people were imbued with the idea of trying to work out a good life for everybody instead of concentrating on personal gain. Certainly, thinking people like Mr. Wright were trying to figure out ways to make a better life for everybody. That all became a part of the Fellowship idea.

Now we have come through an era where economy has been flourishing. People have become more absorbed in doing their own thing. Also, things are so expensive that people, in a way, have had to start thinking about making more money. But, the whole idea of anything creative, the whole thought behind creativity, has nothing to do with money. Creativity is of the soul.

Notes

1. *Working with Mr. Wright: What It Was Like* (New York: Cambridge University Press, 1995), 261.

2. Sharon Paty Monar was with the Fellowship from 1987 to 1994.

3. Terry Kerr has been a member of the curriculum faculty of the School of Architecture since 1994; she provides leadership in theater and other arts activities. She has acting experience at the University of Wisconsin, the Wisconsin Mime Company, and the American Players Theatre.

4. As a member of the curriculum faculty, Karen Holden teaches poetry and creative writing. She is a graduate of Scripps College and studied further at the University of Illinois.

5. One of the current projects of Taliesin Architects in the Philippines—a twenty-five-story Union Bank building.

6. Featured in the May 1997 *Life* magazine.

7

The School, the Archives, the Firm: "Taliesin Is Their Wellspring"

The Taliesin Fellowship's current transition to new times is partly human in character and partly institutional. The human parts of the transition have both dictated and followed the institutional aspects. To make sense of the big picture, it is helpful to consider the transition's institutional aspects first, although separating the human from the institutional is both artificial and, in the end, impossible.

The Architectural Program Report submitted to the National Architectural Accrediting Board in June 1995 aptly summarizes the purpose and structure of the Taliesin Fellowship, identifying its four essential elements. The Fellowship, it says, "consists of architects and artists, masters and apprentices, teachers and students residing at Taliesin and Taliesin West. Fellowship members are dedicated to the philosophy of life as architecture and architecture as life." The Fellowship, it continues, "carries out the mission of the Frank Lloyd Wright Foundation through its operating divisions: the Frank Lloyd Wright School of Architecture, Taliesin Architects, and the Frank Lloyd Wright Archives." The heart of Taliesin, says the report, is the Senior Fellowship.[1]

In this chapter we hear the fellows speak about the School of Architecture, the Frank Lloyd Wright Archives, and the Taliesin Architects, as well as a corollary to these essential elements, the Outreach Program for children.

The Frank Lloyd Wright School of Architecture

The Frank Lloyd Wright School of Architecture traces its origins to the founding of the Fellowship in 1932. When Mr. Wright died in 1959, the senior members of the Fellowship formed Taliesin Associated Architects and the apprenticeship program continued without interruption. Formal *structures remained minimal for some twenty-five years. In 1985 the State of Arizona chartered the Fellowship's learning program as the Frank Lloyd Wright School of Architecture. Two years later the School was granted accreditation by the Commission on Institutions of Higher Education of the North Central Association. In 1996 the School gained accreditation by the National Association of Architectural Accrediting Boards.*

To have developed a formal structure and to be accredited by the state and two independent agencies seems to be at odds with the convictions and practices of Frank Lloyd Wright. Although he had left high school in Madison without a diploma, Frank Lloyd Wright enrolled in the University of Wisconsin in 1885 to study engineering. But as he wrote in his autobiography, his heart was never in the "Education" the university offered. Rather, this "Education" meant "nothing so much as a vague sort of emotional distress. . . . [T]he inner meaning of anything never came clear." The rules and regulations were oppressive and threatening, hampering him. He was "being doctored in a big crowd and the doses never seemed to produce any visible effect at any vital spot whatever; and anyway, he didn't feel sick." Work as a junior draftsman for Professor Allen Conover, however, "was a great good" for him. Writing in the third person, he continues,

> But in the university, notwithstanding certain appearances, he was and remained outsider, yearning all the while for the active contact with the soil or for the tests of a free life of action—waiting for something to happen that never happened. Now he realizes that it never could have happened for "they" were all there to see that it did not happen. . . . The gestures were here and they were fine enough but—how about *work*? [2]

So he left the university, moved to Chicago, and began his career as a draftsman on his way to becoming an architect. But the feeling of unhappiness with university education, perhaps of a seeming futility or betrayal, he says, lingered. Perhaps there was "resentment against the mass product." [3]

Judgments regarding the futility of higher education remained a theme in Mr. Wright's speaking and writing. From among its many expressions, it seems appropriate to cite several that appeared in the Wisconsin Alumni Magazine *in 1934. An article titled "The Taliesin Fellowship" begins with a caustic critique of "textbook and classroom education by way of 'credits' and 'degrees.'" Such education, he says, "has inflated utterly commonplace intelligence far beyond its merits. And this mass production of the candidate for the white-collar job somewhere, somehow, is more serious than we imagine. . . . There is only one net result of the gamble of education—more impotence. And as a result of the economic gamble—more poverty."*

Taliesin, he wrote, "is concerned with the impotence that is [a] consequence of the gamble in education, believing young America over-educated and under-cultured." If "the salt and savor of life that is joy in work runs stale in our academic formula and in our moded 'institutions,'" a "stale sap is the consequence."

> Well, Taliesin believes the day has come for Art to take the lead in "education"; believes the time ripe for rejection of the too many minor traditions in favor of great elemental Tradition; sees needed decentralization as going forward in new spirit with new forces to old ground, free above artificial anxieties and all vicarious powers, man able and willing

to work again as the first condition of true gentility. Taliesin sees work, where something is growing and living in it, as not only the salt and savor of existence but opportunity for bringing 'heaven' decently back to earth where it belongs. Taliesin sees art as the needed expression of a way of life in this machine age if civilization is to live. . . . By new standards of success Taliesin expects to measure the man for a nobler environment and beget in him a better correlation of sense and factor. Not a back-to-the-land movement. No. Nor is Taliesin interested in art for art's sake. It is interested in practical appreciation of the gift of life by putting the man's sense of it into the things he makes to live with and in the way he lives with them. . . .

As for the young men and women who are voluntary apprentices: a group of volunteers; no courses, no credits, no examinations, no teaching. A work in progress and many refugees from "Education" doing all they can to help it forward wherever the work lies and whatever it may be. Meantime they are being as natural and kind as is possible to intelligent social human beings designing and creating a new integrity in the atmosphere of environment. . . . here is building, painting, music, sculpture and motion as good work, in a great correlation toward an end dimly foreseen, it is true. So Taliesin is a way of life, a "road," perhaps "better than the Inn." At any rate action is a form of idea and idea is, as surely, a form of action in that life.

But the action known at Taliesin is unthinkable as "academic." . . .[4]

Tom Casey, Dean of Architecture, spoke about the difficulties encountered in perpetuating Wright's ideals in times when degrees matter and the Frank Lloyd Wright School of Architecture grants them. As the dean of architecture in the School, Tom has been an instrumental figure in its development and has perhaps the most complete memory of when, how, and why things happened as they did. I asked Tom, first, how he divided his time among his various duties.

TOM: Recently, because of major efforts to increase the recognition of the School at Taliesin, I've devoted quite a lot of time to supporting the School. . . . Formerly, I spent a major amount of time as a professional with Taliesin Architects. That time now is reduced to about a third, or even a little less.

The rest of my time is divided pretty equally between the Frank Lloyd Wright Foundation and School kinds of activities. . . . Since Mrs. Wright is gone, there just needs to be a lot more energy put into administering the Foundation. She was more of a singular head of the whole organization. But also, since she's gone, the Foundation has expanded enormously in its range of activities, quite a bit more rapidly than during the latter part of her lifetime.

That was probably a function of changing times.

Yes, changing times, but also I think there were a lot of things that were, if I can say so, somewhat constricted because of everything having to pass through one channel in order for it to happen—especially when you recognize her as someone whose health was becoming more fragile and who was advancing in age. You put all those things together, and there forms kind of a natural, almost . . . I don't know if "constriction" is the right word. . . . Within a few months after she was gone, all sorts of things started happening. As a matter of fact, this very accreditation thing . . . although Mrs. Wright really initiated the impetus in that direction, it really got serious after her death.

Did she lay down any guidelines, or did she give you a master plan for the future? Did she say I want so and so to do this and so and so not to do that?

No, I don't think she ever did that. My understanding was that she simply recognized that if [the School] were going to survive it needed some other level of recognition beyond the people who started it. So she set us off in that direction a couple years before she died. We aimed ourselves at national architectural accrediting.

First of all, Mrs. Wright did, I think, a very wise thing. She invited an architect [Don Schlegel] whom we know from New Mexico who had been involved in the National Architectural Accrediting Board [NAAB] to come for a visit. Her question to him, in explaining the reason for the invitation, was—if he would observe the kinds of things that were going on here in the learning program for architects—what was his idea about the possibility of this being an accredited program?

Don was a very enthusiastic fellow, and after these visits he confirmed in a very enthusiastic way to Mrs. Wright that surely it was [possible]. So, with his positive response, we set out very seriously on the path toward broader recognition. And, of course, we aimed ourselves at NAAB. They had a board meeting in Scottsdale. She invited them to come to Taliesin one Saturday afternoon. . . . During that visit they were very cordial. They had tea Mrs. Wright had arranged for them. It was very pleasant, and they were very supportive.

They asked if Dick Carney and Charles Montooth and I would come on Sunday morning and have breakfast with them at the hotel, which we did. Whereupon, they proceeded in the kindest way possible to tell us that, for one thing, we would have to find institutional accreditation before advancing ourselves to program accreditation. . . . The other thing they observed about the program is that they didn't see how progress was measured.

So then we set about institutional accreditation and, of course, it didn't take us too long to find out that North Central Association was the association that covered us here [in Arizona] as well as Wisconsin. We learned a lot about North Central. Patsy Thrash was assigned as our staff contact, and she has been extremely helpful to us all along, even in her position now as executive director of the whole Association.

[After several visits back and forth between us and North Central], Patsy knew a little bit more about what we were and where we were coming from. . . . She was very deliberate and very direct with us, pointing right at us and saying, "Okay, the thing has been established now," and with a very direct announcement, "it's up to *you* to see that it survives. That's your task. You who have benefited by this thing, it's up to you to see that it survives."

Of course, she was dead right, and we took her very seriously. . . . She said, "You should know a few people . . . I'm going to write down a list down of people you should get to know who would be helpful to you." . . . The first name on the list was Austin Doherty. Patsy was somewhat enigmatic about this. She said, "Just you find these people. Here's this list. Go on your way, get started." So it was up to us to discover our way through the list of people, to find out who they were, where they were, what they might be, what their value to us would be, and so on. . . .

So we set out to find out who this person was. Yes, she was connected with Alverno College. Where is that? Well, we found that it's right up there in Milwaukee. Next, of course, we found out she was not only a woman, she was a nun. Our first contact was simply a cold call. Pick up the phone, call Alverno College, say you wanted to talk to Austin Doherty, and make an appointment to go in and see her.

Effi and I were shepherding a group of students down to Racine to visit the Johnson building[5]—this was in early Fall, not long before we were getting ready to come back to Arizona. We had arranged beforehand that if we would come at five o'clock in the afternoon we could have twenty minutes with Dean Doherty.

We found Alverno College, went in, and sat nervously in the outer office. We had Golnar with us. In a few minutes she came out and said, "Well, Mr. Casey, you can go in and see Dean Doherty now." So I go into the office; I leave Golnar and Effi sitting in the outer office, because we were somewhat tentative in this whole approach. Well, lo and behold, pretty soon someone spots Golnar there, who at this time was still in high school. They say, "Wouldn't you like to have a quick tour around the school and see what's going on?" So she goes off and Effi is left sitting out there alone.

I begin to tell the story of why I'm there, and Austin begins to get very interested. Pretty soon there's this little knock at the door. Effi hears all this going on and doesn't want to be left out. Austin says, "Yes, yes, come in." We sit there for two hours. A twenty-minute interview turns into a two-hour exchange. We discovered an enormous array of coincidences about the teaching Sisters of St. Frances, how they got to this country, how they got to Alverno College, and the fact that their school started exactly the same year as the Hillside Home School in Spring Green. Their roots are German, and they're a very independent order.

So we find out there is an enormous amount of commonality at a philosophical level about teaching, about learning, and so forth. As a result of that, we got a lot of help from Alverno. [We learned] how after Vatican II their order's whole array of institutions was going downhill so rapidly that theirs was going to be gone. And how, in fact, a very consequential few decided that they would do something to turn it around.

Here, too, was a great commonality of circumstance, even though they had already gone through the regeneration of that school. Here we were in a similar position but with different circumstances. The founders were gone, and we had the charge now to see that this school doesn't disappear. How are we going to do that? Theirs was a fairly small group, and ours was a pretty small group. Just a lot of points of contact, especially at an idea level—ideas about learning. The contact with Alverno still exists. We still depend a lot on interaction and consultation with some of the people there.

The idea of demonstrating progress was exactly the thing that Alverno was able to show us in their assessment program: how you formulate assessment, how you carry it out, and how it demonstrates progress. So, here was the answer to the charge that we were given, in more than one way. How to keep the thing going when it looked like maybe there was no rationale for it to continue and how to demonstrate how the program operates through the application of an idea of assessment.

Then you connected with Barbara and John Mickey?

Barbara and John Mickey were in a perfect position to tell us that our problem was that we were too intuitive. Taliesin had been going on so long. It's an implied situation rather than an articulated situation. What you have to do is articulate very well what you're doing in order for other people to understand it. That's the only way you're going to arrive at some level of recognition—to be able to articulate what you're doing.

They were very acute critics. They came and visited, and they said, "Okay, look. You should head this way, head that way, elaborate this or figure out how to describe what it is that's going on." And then we would do that and send our materials to them. They would critique them. Patsy Thrash was also very helpful in preparing our written material for NCA. And, bless her heart, as the English teacher she would even correct the punctuation of the things we sent in. So, these two forces—Alverno and the Mickeys—have been absolutely critical, in my view, to the success of completing the charge Patsy had given us. Of course, we're still very much in that process.[6]

This is a good time to recall that I chaired the accreditation team in March of 1992 that resulted in your receiving North Central Association accreditation for a five-year period. And now in 1994 you are starting to get ready for the next visit.

Not only that, but we have our process started now toward NAAB accreditation, and we have been accepted into candidacy with NAAB. That took some effort and required a realignment of our program, not so much in the content but in the way of describing of it—how it goes on and what its levels are—to make it fit better with what NAAB has decided are the ways that programs ought to be operated.

How do you think the pursuit of accreditation has affected the content and structure and methods of your program?

Well, I think [they are] articulated much better, so that its parts can be seen more clearly. And actually, that has been a great help to us, on the inside, to see them in a more clearly defined way. Because, just as Alverno told us, many of us have been around so long these things are kind of intuitive. They're done from an internalized kind of method. If you're forced into it, you can really put some effort into describing just what it is that goes on.

That's where we come to Barbara Mickey, because Patsy said to us after we had submitted our first self-study, "I think you need some help in the writing. You need a consultant, and I'm going to suggest you get in touch with Barbara Mickey." I was the first one to go and meet Barbara. Dick and I then met with her. We invited her to come out here. She came for a long weekend, and she got terribly interested in the whole program. She helped us construct our self-study in a more articulated fashion—exactly what Patsy knew she would do. . . . Then she and Jack, her husband, visited once in the summer. Later she came to Dick and me and expressed the desire that they would like to come and spend some time at Taliesin West. They came and they stayed for four years.

They were a tremendous help to you, were they not?

Invaluable, absolutely invaluable. Barbara, mind you, has an incredible talent for looking at everything that is going on and being able to cast it in accurate and descriptive language—far better than any of us could. In that four-year period Barbara really constructed for us a description of what happens when you come to learn something at Taliesin West. It really was, in my view, just absolutely invaluable. And we had an awfully good time with Jack and Barbara.

Of course, to come here they left their home in Estes Park, and they could go there only maybe four weeks out of the year because they were spending all their time with us here and then in the summer with us in Wisconsin. After those four years they got a little worn out with the whole process . . . so they went back home about a year ago. But we've been in continuous contact with them, and now Barbara and Jack are going to come out this spring. Barbara's going to help us also in our next NCA encounter.

After ranging over many topics (treated elsewhere in this book) and mindful of the close ties between the School and the Fellowship, I asked Tom if he had a last thought about the Fellowship with which to conclude the conversation.

Well, the Fellowship has been key to my satisfaction with the things one can accomplish during a lifetime. I have lived here a long time, spent my whole professional life here. I wouldn't change it for the world.

The idea of demonstrating progress of which Tom spoke has led to important changes in the School's practices. Julie Kardatzke remarked on the changes in the Box Projects of apprentices:

JULIE: The Box Projects have become quite a bit more formalized than they were in Mr. Wright's time. I've heard stories about apprentices in the old days starting their Box Projects the night before they were presented and that they were really just a means of expressing an idea more than developing it. Nowadays apprentices are

Apprentice Yvonne Dederichs presenting her Box Project.

required to spend nearly six months working on their Box Projects, and they do two presentations prior to the final presentation so they can show the development of the project. They're expected to give it a lot more thought and develop the idea much more. So, it's really become much more time consuming for one thing, but also a more important gauge of an apprentice's abilities.

Is it also more valuable?

That's hard to say. I think it is more valuable in terms of apprentices learning about a lot more areas of architecture by doing it, but there is also a lot of value to just being able to quickly express an idea or something. From what I've heard, some of the old Box Projects could be a lot more outrageous than they are today, particularly I've heard about some of Wes's projects where he was really sort of pushing physics to be able to express these ideas. Nowadays things tend to be pretty practical, because if the apprentices design something that can't be built they're going to be called on it.

Partly that's a result of accreditation, too, perhaps, that you're always worried about building portfolios.

Yes, that's true. I think that's something that has had both a good and a bad effect. I'm glad to see that the academic part of the education here has become stronger, but I think it's also negative in that apprentices have less time to work in the studio. And they're less concentrated when they are in the studio because they're worried about getting their portfolios and their Box Projects finished.

The Frank Lloyd Wright Archives

The Frank Lloyd Wright Archives are another critically important part of the Taliesin Fellowship. As noted earlier, Bruce Pfeiffer is the founder and director of the Archives. I asked him how he got started as a writer and archivist.

BRUCE: What started me writing was the prospect of [a book by] one of our former apprentices who wanted to publish Mr. Wright's letters to him and to other apprentices. He came here with a publisher and presented the case to Mrs. Wright, and Mrs. Wright said, "Absolutely not. Those letters belong to us. The rights are in our possession, and I don't want them to go out." And then, as I was walking out with the former apprentice and the publisher, Mrs. Wright called me back in. She said, "Don't let the publisher think that the idea is dead yet." So I took them around, and as they got into the car I turned to the publisher and I said, "There might be another possibility. We'll let you know in a few days." When I came back in to serve Mrs. Wright lunch, she said, "I want you to do that book, Bruce. Gather letters to the apprentices and write your own commentaries on them." And that's how it started.

Then we did the trilogy—letters to apprentices, and then to architects and to clients.[7] Then [Yukio] Futagawa, the Japanese photographer, wanted to do a twelve-volume monograph of Mr. Wright's work. That was very hard, to have to research each and every house and do it [to accommodate] his very quick schedules. It was almost four years of constant writing.[8] And then he wanted another series on selected houses.

He's actually a photographer, but he has his own publishing company. All around the country he photographed [for the series]. And then, of course, a lot of the photographs were of drawings—visually amplified photographs of the drawings, which we did here. We started in 1974 photographing the drawings. A friend of mine is a publisher in Chicago, and he saw an advertisement for one of the notebooks of Leonardo, which had been lost for four hundred years in Spain and was found. They'd been put back in the wrong box four hundred years ago. That's an archivist's nightmare; it's my nightmare. . . .

My friend said, "Why don't you photograph Frank Lloyd Wright drawings?" I said, "Well, it's terribly expensive for a photographer to do that." He said, "Anybody can photograph a drawing with the camera above it." I asked a professional photographer in Phoenix and he said, "In my opinion we couldn't at $100 a shot photograph 21,000 drawings." But he suggested the best kind of lens, the best kind of camera, the best kind of lighting. We began experimenting, getting the right exposure. I began with some of the more famous drawings.

About that time Yukio Futagawa came by and said he wanted to do three big portfolios of selected drawings. And he said, "Could you please send the drawings to Tokyo so my staff can photograph them?" I said, "I don't think that's possible." "Well," he said, "can my staff come from Japan and live here and do the photography?" I said, "I don't think that's possible, either, because I want to catalog [them] as they are photographed." They had been inventoried but not cataloged.

He looked sort of perplexed, and I said, "Well, wait just a minute." I went to the refrigerator and brought out a shoe box full of transparencies, which we had already made, and I said, "What do these look like?" He said, "Let me take one or two of them." Within about two weeks I got a four-color plate. He said, "They're perfect; we're in business." So that's how we started doing the portfolios of the drawings.

But other books have just come along as they were needed, like with the exhibition in Phoenix, *In the Realm of Ideas,* and *Collected Writings,* from Rizzoli.[9] We thought it would be good to put all the Frank Lloyd Wright writings back into print which had been out of print, most of them out of print totally. I mean, if you want to buy a copy of the autobiography you've got to pay $365 in a rare-book store or get it from a library—if it hasn't been stolen from the library.

As a professional archivist, did you ever go anywhere for a workshop or training in archival work? Do you belong to the Society of American Archivists?

I used to but then I canceled [our membership]. We didn't have money one year; we couldn't renew it.

One person who was like a mentor [to me] was O. P. Reed, who was the art dealer, art appraiser, and art critic living in Malibu who had known the Wrights. He sold our Japanese print collection.[10] His specialty was German expressionist art; he built up the Rifkind collection of German expressionist art. When it came time to sell our Japanese prints he spent a whole year just studying Japanese art. He's a brilliant person, a very accurate person. But he carefully worked with me—how to handle this, how to handle that, how to catalog this, how to catalog that. It was all just dipping into the collection and finding out the best way. I asked lots of people [such as] the Getty archivists. I've gone to meetings of archivists and meetings of museum people out of ICAM [International Confederation of Architecture Museums].

When I was showing Nick Olsberg, who at that time was the archivist for the Getty Center,[11] our computer system here—this was in '85—he said, "You know, you're the only archive to be on computer in the country." I said, "What about Avery?"[12] He said, "Oh, yes, their bookkeeping and their payroll, but you are beginning to put your archives card catalog [on the computer]."

Now, of course, they all do it, but the advantage of not being educated was that I had to find my own solutions. When Angela Giral, who is the librarian for the Avery, was out here four or five years ago, and the Getty gave her a computer system, she said, "You can access and find material ten times faster than I can." I said, "Yes, because I found somebody who can teach me how to write programs. I wrote my own programs."

I wondered how being part of the Fellowship affected the way Bruce had done his work with the Archives. Suppose, I asked him, that all of the materials held here had been deposited in a university archives?

Well, I wouldn't have access to them. Mr. Wright kept them here, which of course was the foresight he had in 1940 when he established the Foundation, so they wouldn't become decimated after his death—like some other archives, all dispersed. The firm wants some, the family wants some, you know. What if the six of Mr. Wright's children who survived him all wanted a piece of the pie—some of the prints, some of the drawings, and some of the real estate? No, he made a very wise decision.

So you really do have it all here?

We have the vast majority. There are bits and pieces out there, which I still get. I just got a group of letters from the Oak Park Home and Studio from Olgivanna to Mr. Wright's sister, Maginel, between '30 and '32. They're very depressing. They're lovely letters, but you realize that [Mr. and Mrs. Wright] had nothing. They had nothing. If they had two pairs of shoes they were lucky.

I asked Bruce what he would do if he could map out an agenda for himself for the next several years, and, in his low-key manner, he laid out an ambitious scenario.

Well, I'd like to see this entire imaging thing develop further. We've begun with five thousand of the drawings. I want to see the remaining 15,000 or more get imaged. We're putting them all on CD-ROM. It's being done by an outfit in California.

Then they will be accessible to libraries?

That's right, and the first tape is going to be published in a few weeks.

Will that make your books obsolete?

It will make life obsolete, won't it? I don't think so, no, because as well as photographs and drawings the books also contain a story; they contain a text. This is just data and a drawing. It's being done by a man named Michael Ester, who until last year, I think, was the director of the Getty art information program.[13] Brilliant person, two Ph.D.'s. I always call him Dr. Dr. Ester, and he calls me Nurse Pfeiffer. He's a wonderful person, lives on a yacht in a marina. A brilliant person. In fact, when he talks, as Oscar said, it's scary. You need a dictionary. Even his slang.

The Getty wanted him to image the history of art. He said, "I won't live past H." Nick Olsberg was up at the Getty at that time. Olsberg was instrumental in having the Getty give the $200,000 to complete the microfiche of the correspondence and to develop an 8x10 file of the drawings. And part of that grant was to bring in an intern each year for three years. The first one we brought in was Kathleen Cantaloupo, who worked with Penny on the Japanese textiles, and then she went to New York to work as an appraiser for fine arts. The second was Penny Fowler who stayed, and the third was Oscar Muñoz who also stayed.

Nick was talking to Michael about this imaging process that he was beginning at the Getty. This was eight years ago when imaging was just in its infancy. Nick said, "Why don't you image the Frank Lloyd Wright Archive?" It's a finite collection—21,000 drawings, 300,000 documents and correspondence, so many magazines, so many rare books, 300 tape recordings, 25,000 historic photographs, another 20,000 photographs of people associated with the Wrights. And that got Ester interested.

One time Oscar and I went over to their offices; they were in a bank building in Santa Monica. Nick's office is on the fourth floor with the archives, and Ester's office is on the twelfth floor, on the top, and I said as we were going up the elevator (they wouldn't let Oscar come; it was just Nick and myself going to meet Dr. Ester), "What's the difference between you and Dr. Ester as far as funding [is concerned]?" He said, "My office is about this size; Dr. Ester has the whole top floor, with Richard Dieberkorn prints all over the walls. I get to spend a million dollars a year; he gets to spend about a hundred and eighty million dollars a year." Both are exaggerations; they just gave us their qualifications for that.

And who is Nick again?

Nick Olsberg. He was the archivist for the Getty—English, trained in South Carolina by a man named Charles Lee, a very fine archivist.

Michael took us into this dark room and showed us the screen where they had imaged an 8x10 photograph of a Vermeer painting. Vermeer is so intense in light and dark, you know. When it came out on the screen you could not tell the difference. Then he pressed a button and out came an 8x10 color photograph of it, the same as the photograph in the book. That began it, and, of course, that was eight or nine years ago, and since then the equipment has got a thousand times better. The technology is changing every day, and I'd like to see [the imaging of the Frank Lloyd Wright materials] happen in the next five or ten years. Then, you see, everything that's in that vault will be accessible without any damage to the original.

This first set will be out. It's $1,500 for four discs.[14] You can see things on the drawing you can't see with the naked eye, because you can image in so much closer. That's one thing. [And] I want to see a center for this Archive built.

That's what the sign down there points to—a visitor center and archives.

Yes, I want to see something built there.

If they put a visitor center down there, how will they get visitors up here to take the tours?

Take them on a van. It will be so much better than all those cars parking up here, and we can control it better. And if we make the center there exciting, with a permanent exhibition—like *Frank Lloyd Wright: In the Realm of Ideas*—plus an exhibition of Frank Lloyd Wright drawings, plus a nice cafe, plus a chance to be amongst the desert [life]. . . .

And maybe building interest by including some occasional exhibitions of former apprentices.

Right, but make that so interesting that then there will be less demand on these buildings here, because it's wearing. I don't mind [the tourist traffic] because I'm very removed from it, but it is hard to be out there walking around. I can hardly walk from building to building. When I had my black Dobie, I could walk right down the pergola and the crowd of tourists just parted like the Red Sea when they saw a black Doberman.

And then, I would like to do a book—you asked about a biography. I would prefer to do *Frank Lloyd Wright: His Life through His Letters*—a twenty-volume series. It wouldn't be all the letters; it would be the pertinent ones, and it might only be sections of pertinent ones. It would not be giving you the full correspondence because you can get that on microfiche at the Getty, but it would be giving you an outlook of his life. And, of course, a text that would tie it together.

You'll see how on April 15, 1929, for example, he's writing to Alexander Chandler about the San Marcos project; he's writing to William Norman Guthrie about an apartment building in New York; he's writing to the Wisconsin Farm Bureau to sell some Holsteins and buy some hogs; he's writing to the Hoppes Water Wheel because the dam isn't pumping enough water for the reservoir; he's writing to his tailor because his suit isn't fitting. You get a picture of a man living daily, and what's fascinating is he always tended to write his letters in one day. There would be a whole group—ten or twenty all in the same day.

One of the other fellows I visited with said that what was so exciting about being an apprentice here while Mr. Wright was alive was that, contrary to impressions that you would get from other people reading about him, he was not just a bundle of eccentricities. He was a genuine, warm human being who cared about your work and about whose work you cared, and he was accessible. He went to work here every day.

I think that can only be brought out by somebody who knew him and by his own words.

I also visited with Indira Berndtson about the range of her responsibilities in the Archives.

INDIRA: In the last four years we've been concentrating on oral histories. We were given a video camera about 1989 and started interviewing people of the Fellowship, such as Wes Peters. I was very astounded that so few people from outside came to interview Wes. . . . So Greg Williams and I just started meeting with him; it was very informal. We didn't really prepare in any sense. For instance, if we were asking him about a building, that didn't mean that we would necessarily pore through all the drawings and have all these questions ready. It was more or less for Wes a time of relaxation, so we would go to his room about 5:30 and interview him for about an hour before dinner, or at other times. In some people's minds this was not the traditional way of doing oral history, and yet we are very happy that we have almost forty hours [of interviews] with Wes Peters.

I have read some of the transcriptions. They are very valuable.

Thank you. And then we just tried to get most of the other people in the Fellowship. I'm very glad you're doing this project, because there are people who don't feel comfortable talking to their own people. They prefer talking to an outsider. So at least we are getting records of their thoughts.

Aside from the oral histories, doing the interviews and doing the transcriptions, we also work with researchers from all over the world, both through correspondence and in person. I enjoy that very much. We have a number of friends who are authors throughout the United States who come to visit here. For instance, today Kathryn Smith is coming, and she's become a personal friend through the years. She worked on the Barnsdall House and Imperial Hotel and now she wants to write a book about Taliesin lifestyle. I'm actually hoping she and mother might be able to do some sort of corroboratory thing.

You mean lifestyle of people at Taliesin?

Yes, she likes to talk about our Easters and our different traditional things like that.[15]

Did you meet [Wright biographer] Meryle Secrest?

Yes, she came just very briefly. I remember that we were showing her some of the videos in the dining cove, and after just a few minutes of seeing the Mike Wallace video[16] she said that she'd had enough. She didn't need to see any more. So I was rather surprised; from my viewpoint, her research wasn't very thorough here at Taliesin. But I guess she had done a lot of it elsewhere.

Did William Storrer come here?

Oh, yes, we've known Bill Storrer for quite a long time. There are different views on him. . . . I think he did do a service by creating that first book, because we certainly use it quite a bit.[17]

Taliesin Architects

When Frank Lloyd Wright died in 1959, his architectural practice was flourishing. The Solomon R. Guggenheim Museum and the Beth Sholom Synagogue were under construction, and many more projects were in various stages of development. To carry them through to completion, the senior apprentices who had been working with Mr. Wright formed the Taliesin Associated Architects.[18] Among the projects completed were the museum and the synagogue, the Marin County Government Center (in collaboration with former apprentice Aaron Green, with whom Mr. Wright had formed a relationship that both felt free to consider a partnership[19]), the Grady Gammage Memorial Auditorium at Arizona State University, and many houses.

Wes Peters served as chief architect, and others also assumed responsible roles. Dr. Joe Rorke recalled his perception of the leadership Wes provided and commented further on him.

DR. JOE: In the drafting room he worked everybody to death. Everybody ended up "hating" him, but he held that all together beautifully. He was the driving force of the drafting room. If something had to be done he would do it. There were times he had no more right to do what he did, but he'd get out and he'd knock down walls and build up walls and he'd dig ditches. You know, he'd do all that heavy physical stuff at a time in his life when he shouldn't have been doing any of it.

He was quite a big, strapping fellow, wasn't he?

Oh, he was. But then, he began to fail, too. He got to where he couldn't [do it all] anymore. He didn't die the way Mrs. Wright did. He had a hard stroke and came out in a coma. But physically he was declining; he was a big, strapping fellow and he just crumbled. But no, he was a great, straight pillar around here, absolutely, in his early days.

Wes was not alone in the studio, of course. John Rattenbury reflected on the way things worked in the years after Mr. Wright's death.

JOHN R: We had to assume many new responsibilities. Mr. Wright had carried the flag. He designed the architecture, handled the clients, negotiated and collected fees, talked to the public, wrote books, and performed what today we call business development; that is, he brought in the work. Although he looked down on salesmen per se, he excelled in presenting himself and his ideas to the world. Now all this was in our lap and we threw ourselves into the challenge. . . . There was a great deal of unfinished work in the studio, and it wasn't long before new clients began to knock on the door. Remarkably, more senior apprentices stayed than left, and we organized ourselves as Taliesin Architects. For a while, Wes and Jack took over all the design work, but Mrs. Wright soon encouraged the rest of us to act as partners and develop our own clients.

In 1962, Jack Howe left us to open his own practice. . . . Mrs. Wright called me in and told me she wanted me to take over Jack's responsibilities in managing the studio. This was quite a task, especially since there were so many members of the Fellowship who had been here much longer than I had. None of them were about to let themselves be managed. So I worked behind the scenes.

. . . In the early '60s, new tools and techniques were becoming available to architects that we knew little about. In my function as specification writer, I made visits to other architects' and engineers' offices. I learned about their equipment— electric typewriters, copying machines, telex, filing systems and so forth. I found myself introducing all sorts of office technology to our firm. I felt it was necessary to find efficiencies to offset the huge amount of additional time that architects had to spend on the regulatory and bureaucratic systems, since nobody in the firm had any real business training, or even an interest in this aspect. There was a void.

I jumped in with all the bliss of ignorance and set up the first accounting system for the firm, a system that I invented since I had had no training in accounting. I standardized the way we put together proposals and entered contracts, kept the project records for the firm, managed the drawing and correspondence files, assigned people to work on projects, initiated time records; in short, acted like an office manager. Most of the methods were invented on the spot, customized for our needs. Soon we had about twelve registered architects, all homegrown.

I recognized that the type of client that Mr. Wright had, which was basically the patron, was being replaced by the developer. And that meant our client wasn't an individual but a group, which included investors, managers, lawyers, and accountants. Their biggest concern was the potential for profit.

As the years passed, and after Mrs. Wright and Wes Peters were no longer present to provide overall direction, maintaining the firm imposed greater responsibilities on the remaining architects. John Rattenbury continues:

I was concerned that we needed a full-time qualified person to handle the management needs of the firm. . . . Although our way was to do all the jobs at Taliesin ourselves—be it architecture, construction, farming, or cooking—I felt we would have to look outside for someone who was both qualified in management and architecture and who believed in our philosophy. In the meantime, another problem became apparent. We were developing a big gap between the young new apprentices and the senior staff. In other words, the middle group was not staying at Taliesin.

So I devoted much of my energy to attracting alumni back, to getting a strategic plan underway for Taliesin Architects, and for finding a way to put the plan into action. For years we had the luxury of not chasing after work. It sought us. But as we emerged from under the shadow of Frank Lloyd Wright, we had to compete with the rest of our profession. This meant business development. In Mr. Wright's time, words like marketing, development, management, employees, profit sharing, insurance, were all words of the Pharisees. His crusade was to raise the level of consciousness of the public to the art of architecture. To him, civilization was a way of life and culture was a way of making that life beautiful.

But he also believed absolutely in the Law of Change. As long as we hold to the principles, he said, we can and must change the ways and find new expressions of forms to stay up with or ahead of technology and changing times. There is always resistance to change, and in our group at Taliesin there is always concern that through change we don't lose sight of our principles.

John's explanation had begun in response to my question concerning what he believed to be his most important accomplishments at Taliesin. In returning to that question, he reveals a trait common among those who worked with Mr. Wright—that is, an inclination to frame the response in a quotation from their mentor.

When Mr. Wright was asked which was his best building, he replied, "My next one." So in this spirit, I would say that my best contribution to Taliesin is my continuing effort to help move the architectural firm into the next century. Not many endeavors that are founded by a charismatic and brilliant leader survive long after their death. We have lost two such leaders. What they left behind is a sensible and relevant approach to education and the timeless philosophy of a living architecture, which we call organic. These ideas are far too important to this country, to the world, not to be kept alive. Their acceptance continues to grow and Taliesin is their wellspring.

A particular challenge the architects in the firm faced was that of perpetuating the principles and ideals of Mr. Wright in their architectural work without being imitators. Stephen Nemtin addressed this and related matters

STEPHEN: My main responsibility now is to do work that is contemporary and demonstrates an architecture based on organic principle. I make the differentiation between [organic principle] and organic architecture, which I believe is an architecture that belongs totally within the framework of Frank Lloyd Wright. It's his language, his grammar, his total way of doing things. But there's a principle at work there that all subsequent architects who are interested in that work can base their work on. So that frees me to make my interpretation of what all of that means in contemporary life. And I think that's of vital importance, not to ape or imitate at a lower level the work of Frank Lloyd Wright.

How do you enunciate the principle of organic architecture that underlies your work?

Well, the term I like to use today—which I think certainly has understanding for me—is a "molecular concept" of architecture based on [the] organic principle. That means identifying all systems of construction—all of the structural, mechanical, and finishing systems—and the forms that are appropriate for the life of that particular project.

I think it can be a very sculptural approach. The major elements become sculptural elements that repeat themselves. This can be in the form of systems, or it can be much larger forms—possibly a whole room or building element that repeats itself. It has all of the major and minor axes to it, to be a molecular concept. But I think it's very attuned to the way one works on the computer and the molecular and biological world that surrounds us. By and large the building industry is a very unsophisticated approach to realizing architecture, but someday it will be much more sophisticated than it is today.

Do you see some contradiction between organic architecture being developed on such an inorganic system as a computer?

Not at all. I don't consider the computer inorganic; I consider it to be very organic because it gives you a freedom that the hand drawing, for me, doesn't give you anymore. It allows you to evolve and make the many, many changes that are constantly occurring from the time you have a design concept to the final execution of those documents that allow you to build the building. It allows you to make changes so rapidly and effortlessly, it's just a very freeing way to work.

Do you work closely with any of the apprentices yourself?

Absolutely.

Do you see yourself as a mentor?

Well, I don't get into this idea that I'm a mentor or a teacher, but I sure as hell like to work with our young people and I like the way they can teach me things. They're the ones that are teaching me how to use the computer.

What do they learn from you?

They learn everything there is that goes into making architecture a work of art, if they're open to it and sensitive to it. It's not automatic.

How do you deal with the ones who say they want to be architects but don't have the motivation to realize that nobody teaches anybody anything—that you teach yourself, drawing upon the expertise of others as you see fit? How do you deal with unmotivated ones, or don't you get them at Taliesin?

Oh, I think we get every degree [of apprentice], but by and large unless you just want to be sort of one of the components in the execution of the architectural profession, you've got to have this self-motivating, asking-questions psyche. Everything is open to question. If you don't have that you can't be a creative architect. I imagine everybody has that beginning spark when they come here. Otherwise they wouldn't associate with Frank Lloyd Wright. That is still, in my mind, a very, very individual kind of pursuit.

You get all this stuff about teamwork and so on, but that's just the current fad of talking. It's not what makes real architecture; it's not what makes the client put everything they have into the work as well; it's not what can influence, as I've experienced with the Alzheimer work, where it can really change the well-being of a family, whether it's a loved one that's in the facility or the caring wife, daughter, son.[20]

Do you do a lot of research on Alzheimer's and the conditions under which patients today live?

My research is just the direct experience with the situation, like the time I spent with Alzheimer individuals in a facility to get a sense of what it's all about, what communication with them is all about. Research in this case is really done by the client. They have all of the expertise, but I know how to translate all of that expertise to an architectural setting. We can very firmly state that the architectural environment is a component of health care. We've proven it without a doubt.

It intrigues me that so many school classrooms create conditions that are just exactly the opposite of what you would want for learning.

Well, we're going through a very interesting experience right now with a new college for the Menominee Nation. Here the molecular concept is very evident, because the modules that repeat themselves to form the long house concept is within the tradition of the Menominee people; it is an entirely new framework of an architectural setting for learning. That didn't come by my doing extensive research on the Menominee people; it came about by having a sense of what they're all about and it is being confirmed. An important part of this whole phasing of design is that you begin with something that is there for reaction to and then you really begin to understand what the nature of the thing is all about from the client's point of view.

They're telling me how it falls within their tradition. I didn't identify the idea that this represents the long house concept; they told me it represents the long house concept. There's very much an intuitive kind of learning that has to go on, and that goes on differently with each client. It may take longer or shorter with each client, and you may hit it to begin with or you may not. As long as you're open to seeing where you don't hit it and begin to evolve it to where you do hit it, then you're okay.

What you are telling me is that you listen, and then you translate the ideas you hear into architectural concepts, which you then bounce off the people you have been talking with. And ultimately, the client has to have to the last word.

Well, if you're working correctly there is no last word. Neither party has to have the last word to get it right; you've evolved it together; and that keeps happening, because you're never sure—right up to the construction documents and the bidding—where the cost is exactly [determined]. Each situation is different. I wish we had the ability as architects to gather around those contractors or those skilled people who have the understanding of the work and want to execute it. It would be a lot better for us, because it's very, very tough to do anything these days that isn't the typical thing.

The term "organic architecture" puzzles many visitors to Taliesin and students of the architecture of Frank Lloyd Wright. Stephen's explanation of its meaning and application is helpful. So are Tony Puttnam's comments in this exchange, which began with his recall of his first impressions of Taliesin in 1953.

TONY: There are a lot of buildings that have space in them, but Taliesin was like having space as a kind of energetic force moving through the building and relating to various parts of the building in various ways. The materials that this pier or this wall or that window—the materials that you found in the building influenced the dynamics of that space. And that configuration speeded it up or made it rhythmical, or other things.

Living room at Taliesin West.

So, it was a big revelation about what the possibilities were. And the works of art there, which all related to this in a sort of mysterious fashion—Japanese prints and screens and ceramics and sculptures and all that sort of thing, the ensemble of the place—was also quite overwhelming, along with the landscape and the whole way that the building managed to be both an expression of the landscape and be forceful enough almost to make the landscape an expression of it.

I once ran into a Vietnamese lady who lives over in Racine. She's a poet; she's from Vietnam. She's a factory worker and she writes poetry, in English. I met her and the second thing she ever said to me—she turned to me and said, "What is organic architecture?" Little tiny lady. And I said, "Well, it's an architecture that springs from a single, central idea," making a motion like this (from my heart). She took both hands to her heart and threw them up in big arcs overhead, and she said, "Oh, you mean like a tree," which I think is the most succinct definition of organic architecture I've ever heard.

Although there have been many communal societies in American history, few of them have lasted as long or been as successful as Taliesin. Tony identified a problem faced by the Fellowship, which in its early days had been so poor that they straightened nails to use them again. The labor of the apprentices—in construction and in the studio, the kitchen, and the fields—enabled the Fellowship to survive.

The problem has been, how do you make a transition from—at the most fundamental level—a sweat equity society to a capital-intensive society? How is that transition made? It doesn't matter how much sweat equity you put in now, you're not going to get a computer. Mr. Wright was very fortunate to have lived in a time, to have the Fellowship in a time, when that kind of leverage—being able to work to make things happen—was possible. The role that I see in all this is to try to find ways of making that transition, searching for ways of making that transition work, because the circumstances we once dealt with are just simply not here [today].

What do you see happening?

I think the world was extraordinarily simpler forty years ago; I mean architecturally. Forty years ago or thirty years ago the drawings for Monona Terrace were done in something like 125 sheets. The drawings for this version of Monona Terrace are 450 sheets. It's just that kind of difference. *[Tony is referring to the Monona Terrace project in Madison, Wisconsin, based on a design proposed more than half a century ago by Frank Lloyd Wright. Others of Wright's unbuilt projects may yet find builders, but this one is truly distinctive.]*

The drawings for Monona Terrace are all computer-generated, are they not?

Yes. Well, [whether by] hand or computer or whatever way you go at it, nonetheless it's fair [to say] that the whole thing is three times as complex as it was thirty years ago. And it really means that people, unless they're extraordinary people, do have to in some way specialize. It's hard to see that the Jeffersonian idea—the gentleman farmer, aristocrat, inventor, writer of political thought, architect [could work today]. That's awfully hard, unless you've got an incredible amount of help. But I think that's still the strength of community: that it could bring about in total the combination of those abilities, and it could then continue.

Mr. Wright and George Forster, mayor of Madison, with a model of Monona Terrace (1955).

The point of Mr. Wright's arrangement, the point of the Fellowship, was that it enabled Mr. Wright and everyone else to "sail closer to the wind," because you weren't so pushed by money demands, legal demands, an enormous amount of "worldly" things that you'd have to deal with [today]. A community today, [it] still seems to me, has the capacity of forming a working whole in an effective way that would allow it to sail closer to the wind. That is, to make it really possible to engage in a more idealistic dialogue about architecture and planning and goals.

To do that you have to lighten your load. You can't be like Thoreau's farmer pulling forty acres and a barn through life. In finding ways that the Taliesin Preservation Commission could take over building preservation, finding a way that the visitor group could take over the visitors, the accountants could do their accounting, and so on [specialization is required]. . . . For instance, there's a license person who handles the license program. You have to pay that person, but at least you don't have to do all that paper work and go out there [yourself] and try to sell things. So you've got to split off and put into responsible hands some of these things that are not essential to the mission that you're trying to accomplish. We need to find more of that sort of thing. We need to find ways to enable people in the community to pursue what their real interests are.

How did it happen that you became the principal in the Monona Terrace project? Did you work with Mr. Wright on it?

Well, lots of people worked on Monona Terrace. I certainly never had any collegial relationship with Mr. Wright working on it. I did student things—coloring walls—but I heard things that were said, as other people did. Over the years I think a number of other people had taken their turn and bloodied their nose, and it just sort of got to be my turn. Well, partially.

I think probably I more than anyone else at Taliesin have worked with government projects professionally and perhaps have more patience with it. Government is a peculiar animal to work for. You have to go into a government project and assure everyone as quickly as you can that no matter what happens to the job you're not going to blame them, and you're going to try not ever to imply any kind of responsibility on their part for something bad—that you're not going to have it end up on their doorstep.

It's just common sense in working with a certain kind of client. You're not going to get in trouble with the newspapers, and you're not going to be controversial, and you are going to listen to their constituencies very hard and not argue with them. And you're going to let them decide whether the constituency should be ignored or dealt with or assuaged. . . . The Planning and Development Department is the project manager for the building, and they're very good. The assistant planner, their principal planner of the department, actually, is someone who worked on the 1967 edition of

Monona Terrace. So he goes way back, and he knows everybody in Madison and their temperaments.

This is Monona Terrace eight, I would guess roughly. It started in 1938 with scheme one, and '54 is two—[actually], there were several in the '50s. Mr. Wright revised it several times in major ways during the 1950s. We're using the 1959 version, which I would [call] version four, and then the working drawings that I had worked on were the 1960–61 version of the building. There were several versions after that.

So you went back to '59 or so?

Well, as close as we possibly could, we used the last version that Mr. Wright worked on, where he had already eliminated the large parking terraces out in the lake which so many people [had] associated with the [earlier] design. But even in 1954, when he made the model he made the parking decks removable, and he very often showed the model without the parking terraces because he appreciated that it might simply be too expensive to build those. No one could conceive in those days of having a thousand-, two thousand-car parking lot. That wasn't anybody's fault, that they could not see that.

In the summer of 1992, people were handing out "Vote No on Monona Terrace" circulars at the Farmers' Market in Madison.

We still have people bringing lawsuits and trying to do everything that they can [to stop it].

You seem to have the temperament for dealing with all of that.

Well, Mr. Wright in the '50s came back one day discouraged from Madison and said, "You know, they're not going to build this now, but someday they will."

Monona Terrace (1997)

The Outreach Program

In 1988 the Frank Lloyd Wright Foundation began an outreach program, conceived and conducted by Shawn Rorke-Davis, who spent some of her childhood years at Taliesin. She describes the program and how it began.

SHAWN: I started the Outreach Program about six years ago, and the current summer manifestation of it is two weeks of summer camp for youngsters that was meant to be an experiment. . . . It was to be two sessions of twelve students each. The response was just phenomenal. We ended up expanding the program to three sessions, and I had fifty-nine students; we had a waiting list of about seventy-five or eighty. And that was with basically no advertising. I did a little flyer.

The purpose of the camp was to give the children a chance to do a floor plan of their own design. They had to think about where in the universe they would design this dream space. They had to think as much as they could from their experiences what kind of materials they might build it out of, given that very tight specific kind of architecture, and then translate that into a 3-D model.

Some of them had been here to Taliesin West on field trips with their school, but we started out the week with a tour of Taliesin that I gave them. I also showed them my interactive slide show with questions and answers. I bring in a lot of things in the classroom that show Mr. Wright's work and try to tell them a little about some of the underlying philosophy and present that in such a way that it's at their level. You don't have to be Albert Einstein to understand what inspired Mr. Wright. To me it was things that he observed in life, things that he then translated into structure or into art instead of lying around dreaming up things that came out of nowhere.

The reason I think that architecture is so important in the classroom is it works very well to combine disciplines. . . . In architecture you have to have science, you have to have math, you have to have art, you have to have the ability to work as a team, you have to use English or else you can't have a building. It's really an interdisciplinary thing that works well in the classroom.

Then they did this floor plan to scale, which is also something most children are not familiar with. It's such a peculiar concept that it is a real challenge for them not to make their television a thousand times larger than their bed. Anyway, they did a floor plan and then built scale models. The last hour of the last day we invited their parents to come, and each one of them stood up and gave a little "Box Project."

I had one eight-year-old and the oldest was fifteen. The dynamic of going from purely a thought process from a two-dimensional drawing to a three-dimensional model and then having to stand up and express your concept, I think, is really valuable to all of us.

I asked her if she herself had studied architecture.

Actually, it never interested me at all. I was always interested in cute students, but I had no desire to be an architect whatsoever. I was eleven when Mr. Wright died, so I have very vivid memories—from a child's perspective—of how he interacted with the group and how he interacted with me. But no, I never wanted to be an architect.

When you came back to Taliesin in 1983, did you start this outreach program right away?

No, I didn't. I worked in the front office with Dick doing bookkeeping, etc. We were noncomputerized at that time; [I was] doing all the travel arrangements for the architects, sort of miscellany. And then, of course, the community things. I immediately cooked and did all that stuff. Then I ended up working in the studio. I learned to be a pretty good draftsperson and a really good renderer. At that time Ling Po was still the only person who was a master renderer. He would do literally every perspective, the finished product for every project, because he just was a genius. He took me under his wing and said that I was very gifted in that, so he taught me how to do it. I ended up working for maybe three and a half years in the studio on specific projects, some with the senior apprentices.

That certainly gave you the background for doing what you're doing. Or it must have helped.

It helped. I think the thing about the outreach program that's particularly meaningful to me is it really combines so many parts of me: my specific education . . . education has always been of great interest to me. I taught in San Francisco for twelve and a half years. In my master's degree work, I was very interested in how children learn, how their thinking process works. Is it different than ours? So, it combines my formal training, and it combines my personality—which is very theatrical. I was very involved all during the years that Taliesin was putting on performances here. I danced big parts in that. I loved doing that. I play the flute. But anyway, I'm a very theatrical sort by nature. I think I would have been—maybe I still will be—a great actress. I've never figured out what I want to be when I grow up.

What kind of follow-through do you have with the children you work with? Do some of them show interest in continuing in architecture?

Well, there isn't really any way to quantify what I impart to them, I don't think. I'm usually a real brief part of their [experience] . . . for most of the program I go into the schools with the slide show and do that in a class or a whole grade level or whatever it is. Less often am I able to do design projects. Next year it's going to be unusual, because almost all the already-scheduled work that I'm doing is going to be long term, six or eight weeks. . . .

I think if I can help them see that they already have a lot of the skills they need to successfully complete whatever they choose to do, that that helps them in their other schoolwork and touches them in some way, which is going to benefit them in their life. So I'm really coming at it from that point of view. I love it when their finished product turns out to be outstanding, unbelievable, better than TA or our students'

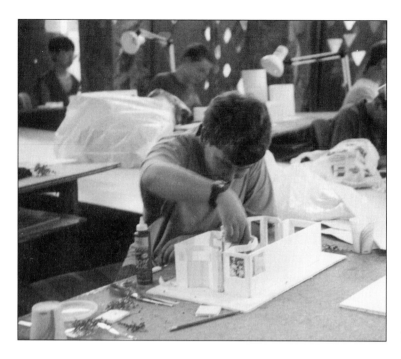

Students in the Outreach
Program.

creative architecture. That just blows my socks off. But the ones that don't do that, if
they go through the process I still think they're getting something very valuable. . . .

*Is this something that the schools contract with Taliesin for or is it a donated thing by Taliesin and
you?*

I guess you call it a public service, really, that the Foundation provides. It is an outreach.
Gail Warden works with the corporate donors.[21] She's outstanding. She really sees the
humanitarian value of what I do, but also she really appreciates how ("salable" sounds
sort of tacky) education is fundable. I don't know whether other people that we've had
before in those development positions didn't understand the program or what, but she's
been getting a lot of corporate and private foundation funding for the program. . . .

I find it unbelievably gratifying. I love what I do so much. It would probably take
a long string of adjectives to express how I really feel. Yes, I absolutely feel fantastic
about what I do. I hope it continues until the day I die.

Notes

1. The Architectural Program Report (June, 1995), 6, 11.
2. Bruce Brooks Pfeiffer, ed., *Frank Lloyd Wright Collected Writings*, vol. 2 (New York:
Rizzoli, in association with the Frank Lloyd Wright Foundation, 1992), 143–5.
3. Pfeiffer, *Collected Writings*, vol. 2, 143–5.
4. Frank Lloyd Wright, "The Taliesin Fellowship," *The Wisconsin Alumni Magazine*
(March 1934): 152–3.

5. Designed by Wright for S. C. Johnson in the mid-1930s.

6. Prior to their retirement, Barbara and Jack Mickey served on the faculty of the University of Northern Colorado.

7. Published by The Press at California State University, Fresno, they are *Letters to Apprentices* (1982), *Letters to Architects* (1984), and *Letters to Clients* (1986).

8. The first eight volumes in this monograph series include photographs and drawings, by chronological periods, and explanatory text for Frank Lloyd Wright's known buildings and projects: Bruce Pfeiffer (Tokyo: A.D.A. EDITA, 1985–88). The next three present preliminary studies and sketches of pivotal works. The final one, spanning his entire career, includes two hundred renderings designed to convey the essence of his work. See also Bruce Pfeiffer, *Frank Lloyd Wright Selected Houses*, 8 vols., photographed and edited by Yukio Futagawa (Tokyo: A.D.A. EDITA, 1988–91).

9. *Frank Lloyd Wright in the Realm of Ideas* (Carbondale: Southern Illinois University Press, 1988); *Frank Lloyd Wright Collected Writings*, 5 vols. (New York: Rizzoli in association with The Frank Lloyd Wright Foundation, 1992–95).

10. The collection was sold to raise money to pay taxes. See chap. 4.

11. The references to "Getty," unless otherwise noted, are to the Getty Center for the Study of Art and Humanities, funded by the J. Paul Getty Trust.

12. The Avery Architectural Library at Columbia University.

13. The Getty Art History Information Program is also funded by the J. Paul Getty Trust.

14. *Frank Lloyd Wright: Presentation and Conceptual Drawings*, produced by Luna Imaging, Inc. and the Frank Lloyd Wright Foundation and Archives; distributed by Oxford University Press (1995). Also produced by the same collaborators is *Houses of Frank Lloyd Wright*, which features on a CD-ROM eighty of his most significant residential works (1996).

15. Kathryn Smith, *Frank Lloyd Wright's Taliesin and Taliesin West* (New York: Henry N. Abrams, Inc., 1997).

16. Interviews with Wright recorded in September 1957; video copies remain available.

17. The most recent edition is *The Frank Lloyd Wright Companion* (Chicago: University of Chicago Press, 1993).

18. The use of the term "Associated" was gradually discontinued several years before the name was changed by legal action to Taliesin Architects, effective 1 July 1993.

19. Aaron Green was with the Fellowship from 1939 to 1943.

20. Working with providers of health care facilities for Alzheimer's disease patients, Stephen has designed residences and hospice houses for them in Ohio and Arizona. See the *Frank Lloyd Wright Quarterly*, vol. 7, no. 3 (Summer 1996): 24.

21. Gail Warden is Director of Development for the Frank Lloyd Wright Foundation.

8

Looking Back: "A Satisfying Life"

Members of the Taliesin Fellowship recall enjoyable and stimulating experiences with the Wrights and each other, reflecting their sense of having gained much from membership and contributed much in return. In our conversations, many of them about specific benefits and contributions during a life spent at Taliesin, we see that belonging to the Fellowship has affected its members differently, but sentiments like those expressed by Cornelia Brierly when I asked what had given her the greatest sense of accomplishment were a common theme.

CORNELIA: Just being a part of the group. When I was away I always felt pulled back to Taliesin. I could hardly wait to get back and be a part of Taliesin. I've enjoyed this creative, dynamic life.

[I've done] work of every description. As I was telling someone recently, I never thought of myself as having a career, although I practiced landscape architecture and also did interiors for our buildings. I never thought of this work as a career; I thought of it as part of the activities of the Fellowship. It never occurred to me to want a career. That may seem hard to understand, but I just always felt that I was a part of this group and whatever I did was in the interest of the group.

Charles Montooth came to Taliesin in 1945 but left in 1952 to start his own architectural practice. I asked him how he had benefited from being in the Fellowship—"in the communal group, eating together and living in the same general area."

CHARLES: I think it probably helped my career. I was never ambitious. In fact, Mr. Wright said that about me once. Somebody told me, or I overheard him. I was mucking around in Scottsdale then, dressed about like I am today, and then I suddenly thought, "Well, God, he's right. I'd better do something more." It's pretty hard to have a one-man office and try to keep some principles. . . . The kids were beginning to get older, and I think [Minerva] was really the instrumental person in coming back. She saw the advantages of being here.

So, for my creative life it was probably a good thing, because then when Mr. Wright died Mrs. Wright was very instrumental in pushing all of us. She recognized that we couldn't just have one or two architects. You see, first Wes did all the major buildings and Jack Howe did all the houses. She saw that that wasn't right, so she pushed us into it and gave us guidance.

Then I got involved with [designing] the school [in Racine]. Wes wanted to do it. . . . I had worked with Wes on jobs, actually at Arizona State University—in fact, one that I wanted to do very much, and I had an idea, [for] a fraternity house. The president of the college, Grady Gammage, had asked me [to do it]. Then when it came about, the way it worked out, Wes did it. I turned it over to him and he did a nice design; in my office I did the working drawings for him.

Anyway, Mrs. Wright did push, and this job came up for the school from Sam and Gene Johnson. I met them because I had been doing some school designs just for the fun of it and I had something to show. Suddenly they wanted to start, and Wes said, "Well, I've got this idea but I can't do anything about it; I've got to go to Iran. We'll wait till we get back." Mrs. Wright said [to me], "Nothing doing. You go ahead and do it." So I did, and Wes was very supportive.

. . . I tried to build on some of Mr. Wright's ideas. They didn't all materialize, because he wrote about small schools. I wanted to have the kids in biology actually growing plants, with more hands-on, more like the aunts did here [at Hillside], but that wasn't to be. Anyway, it's a lively bunch and interesting. I don't know much about

Wes Peters and Mrs. Wright at the site of Gammage Auditorium at Arizona State University in Tempe.

it academically, but it seems to be highly prized, and the kids like it. Some of our kids—like the [young apprentice] from Scotland that went over there with me last year—afterwards she said, "The place just vibrates with energy." From the kids that's what she picked up. It's fun.

Frances Nemtin describes the benefits she has derived from almost fifty years in the Fellowship.

FRANCES: Just the sense of always living in beauty and a feeling that I'm contributing to something I believe in. Raising my children in a very natural way, where they've grown up surrounded with creativity. For instance, every Christmas my son—from when he was about seven or eight to fifteen—made all his Christmas gifts here. Each year it was a different craft which he learned from someone—glass abstractions, or ceramic beads for necklaces, or whatever. So, I feel my children have had a unique childhood and benefited from those experiences in the garden, for instance, which you could never repeat.

And accomplishments that give her considerable satisfaction?

Starting a library and finding Elizabeth Dawsari. . . . She's a highly trained person and I'm really devoted to her. She's devoted to Taliesin, and the fact that she has a much smaller salary than she should have is a sign that she wants to be here more than somewhere else. And she looks out for Taliesin's interest very much. She's very active in nearby city meetings, and she keeps track of what affects us. She's very devoted that way.

I think that, and also getting the grounds, especially in Wisconsin, up to a certain state. I'm very, very interested in the gardens there, and I've made quite a big circle of friends who help me. They help me with money to buy plant material, plus work. And I want to expand that, because we need much more of the long-range planting of trees on the bank below Taliesin. . . . I've had a lot of help this summer here, from the apprentices who stay here and from professional people. My dearest friend out here is a landscape architect who for many years simply came and helped as a friend. She pruned, she gave me advice, she told me what to buy where.

Ling Po reflected on the benefits he derived from his long association with the Fellowship.

LING PO: That has to do with what I got out of living and working with Frank Lloyd Wright. Were there no such a Fellowship, I won't be able to know this great man, this great teacher. I thank the Fellowship for this opportunity.

Did he teach you art?

Not in the ordinary sense of teaching, but whatever I know about art that is worthwhile, all came from him.

Wes Peters and Ling Po working on the Court of the Seven Seas project, Santa Cruz (1961).

Have you felt that being a member of the Fellowship through the years has been a worthwhile experience for you, even in the years after Mr. Wright died?

Oh, yes, the entire duration—from beginning to the end—will be, has been, and is.

What do you think are your biggest contributions to the Fellowship? What do you feel most proud of?

Well, I'm not saying that I am most proud of, but I think that my best contribution is to be a Fellow not given full opportunity to do what he could, yet on account of understanding his own shortcomings, contented to go on.

Did you have a lot of opportunities to use your artistic ability?

Some.

You felt you had more to offer, though, than they were able to use. Has that been a little frustrating for you?

It has been.

Joe Fabris also spoke of his experiences during his years at Taliesin.

JOE: I did a lot of construction work, and I supervised a lot of jobs here like the building of the pavilion and the rebuilding of the pavilion after the fire and work around Mr. and Mrs. Wright's quarters. In general, I would say, for about fifteen or twenty years that was my main work. In Mr. Wright's time I was sent out to Los

Angeles; he was building a group of shops there, which I oversaw, and later a residence in northern Minnesota. . . .

I cooked for years and years. . . . even Mr. Wright respected the fact that you were in the kitchen and that was the main focus. You didn't have time to go out. It got to be so that it was a bit of a vacation to cook because I knew I was safe in there.

I don't do a lot now, but I still try to help the younger people and work. I sort of pick and choose where I want to work. I'm seventy-seven now. I've done a few projects, which I've designed and built—residences. I guess the last thing I did in the studio was about a year ago. But I'm still developing. I've been working up at Susan's trying to get her new studio finished. I'm very fortunate, because I can still climb around on a roof.

I've always been in the chorus, all these forty-some years. Long ago I did play the guitar and sing quite a lot. I was forced to perform one Saturday night, endlessly, while we were waiting for the movie to come.

And the personal benefits gained?

It's given me a satisfying life. Apart from working with Mr. Wright, I've enjoyed working with the younger apprentices. And for a long time the apprentices that came in were put on construction for two or three months. That was the first thing anybody did, so I had all the new apprentices. It was always satisfying for me, and I loved to get someone who really was interested and wanted to learn something. There are always the goof-offs, anywhere. And I've gotten back some response from some of them. Later on they appreciate what a great benefit it was to them.

My life has been pretty much here, and my friendships are pretty much here. I'd visit my family in Canada part of the year, but my focus was all here, so it was difficult to have a friendship outside of Taliesin.

John Rattenbury, David Dodge, and Dr. Joe Rorke all cite different benefits derived from their Taliesin experiences.

JOHN R: First of all, the opportunity to spend almost ten years with Frank Lloyd Wright and thirty-five with Olgivanna Lloyd Wright, to have them as my heroes, my mentors, to be treated as a part of the family, and to live in the beauty of Taliesin. Few people in the world get to spend time with a great inspirational genius, let alone two remarkable figures. I helped build both Taliesin and Taliesin West. I worked on many of Mr. Wright's landmark projects, and I hope I have passed something on to others along the way.

. . . I take pleasure in working with young apprentices. I know that the best way to keep learning is to constantly pass on knowledge. Every once in a while some Taliesin alumnus who is practicing architecture will show me his work and tell me how much he learned from me. That is a very fine reward. . . .

One of my avocations is the design of art glass. I loved the stained glass designs that Mr. Wright did in his early career. I made glass mosaic tables and sculpture for him and Mrs. Wright. I often get to incorporate doors, windows, skylights, and screens for the buildings that I design.

DAVID: The benefits are the learning without knowing where or how you're learning things. I have no idea how I've amassed the knowledge of the things, but when . . . somebody asks me how do we do something, I know how to do it, and I cannot tell you where I learned that. But I know it, and I did not know it before I came to the Fellowship.

So I know I picked it up here, and people have been astounded in Switzerland. They're constantly saying, "Where did you learn all this stuff? How do you know all that? I've spent my whole life learning how to be an electrician, and you know all about this." And I said, "I'm sorry, but that's the way Taliesin is, and I wasn't on the electrical crew. If I'd been there I'd know even more."

What did David think were his main contributions?

Well, certainly in the '50s, a lot of building, a lot of building. We physically helped build the buildings—an awful lot. This room [the Taliesin West Garden Room] was one of the first ones down here; well, it was the first space I worked on down here. I built that wall down there, we built that twice—in a matter of two days we built it twice. Mr. Wright wanted to see it. We built it and poured it in the morning, and Mr.

A construction project at Taliesin West.

Wright said, right after lunch, "David, get your hammer." I thought, "Oh, what's he up to now?" And he came in here and he said, "Take the form off." "But Mr. Wright, we just finished pouring that." "Oh, it's all right, just take it apart." So we took it apart and shoveled it up and put it back together again, and the next day we didn't pour it so quick—so it had overnight to sit. He just couldn't wait. He wanted to see it right away. So, I would say that was a very big contribution—helping with the construction. But the other contribution, of course, was in the drafting room, in the work, helping Mr. Wright with some of the projects that I was involved in.

DR. JOE: Just a wonderful life . . . in all respects. Spiritual and social. I enjoy the work. I never gave up my profession until I decided to retire. So I had the best of both worlds. Through all our faults, we really have a wonderful bunch of people that live here. And, in spite of it being (I don't know whether it is or it isn't) a community, they're all individuals. We do pull together when we have to. Otherwise, we never see or we never hear and we never socialize. I mean, Minerva's got her world, and Dori's got her world and Kay's got her world. But when the chips are down, and you want to do something together, well, everybody pulls together and you get it done. We've done some miraculous things in short order when we had to.

Here is how Dr. Joe summarized his contribution:

Maybe I'm being selfish in this, but I think my main contribution has been, first of all, [that] I was here to be on hand every minute for Mrs. Wright [as her physician]. Whatever was needed, I was there. And I've been that way with other people here, too. Right now I do the newsletter *[The Whirling Arrow]*, which I inherited from Indira's younger sister, Anna. I do it single-handedly. Nobody helps; nobody gives me anything. I get virtually no news from anybody. I'm very much involved with the tour program and give a lot of tours and help with all of that when I can. I'm really available to anybody, anything they need. I can't do a lot in actual physical labor. It's pretty much beyond me now. Minor things, sure, but any major construction I'd be useless.

Susan Lockhart, Dori Roy, and Effi Casey gave strikingly different responses to questions about their contributions to the Fellowship.

SUSAN: Well, I think I've always felt that Taliesin . . . as a community, should, could, and needed to be more than just the parameters of this site and the people who chose to come and be here at any one time . . . that that community of thinking, of holding the same beliefs in great esteem and espousing them and supporting them really was not exclusive to this site and this group of people and that we had to constantly nurture that larger group. I've felt this probably since the very beginning, that those interests that surround us were also very important to our community.

At one time this was not a very acceptable way of thinking or acting, and I know that in my own world that was not condoned and I was criticized for being an "outsider" because I did nurture those other relationships, which I felt not only nourished me but ultimately would nourish the whole community. . . . If I've been a part of any one thing which I think is definitely in our future it is that very thing.

DORI: With the philosophy, the Gurdjieff philosophy to develop yourself, you do anything. I'd do anything that would contribute to Taliesin. Somebody once told me, "Your talent is appreciation," and I guess that's true. I appreciated so much being here, I mean this greatness. How many people in the world get that experience?

EFFI: I consider myself as a definite link between the seniors that are really the senior Seniors today and the younger generation. I think I have . . . a capacity for enthusiasm and, to some degree, am able to pass that on to others. I take that from comments from apprentices or former apprentices who in retrospect reflect on it. Susan Lockhart is a very similar person from that point of view who can really excite people about something and get them engaged. That seems to become increasingly difficult, because people have different agendas and it's not so easy.

Although the long-time senior fellows seem secure in their niches, it sometimes takes the younger ones awhile to discover where they can best make contributions. Ari Georges is one such.

ARI: Ever since I became a senior fellow I asked myself what is the best area of contribution other than the studio, but the first thing I did was get involved in the studio. I worked with [one person] who treated me as if I were a first-year apprentice. When I challenged him with it we fell apart. I left his project. I said, "If you want me to be a colleague or you call me colleague, you have to treat me like a colleague. I'm not just a pencil, I'm not a person who doesn't know. . . ."

After that, I reconsidered what should be the best area of contribution, so I immediately thought that I should approach the Education Department. I wrote them a letter telling them what I think I can contribute, and I was invited into the Education Committee. Soon enough I was involved with revision of the publications. The rest of it is known. I was given a title [Assistant Dean for Curriculum] last February, which is just a title so far—no responsibility or acknowledgment of it. I've been heavily involved and very interested in the School. That's where I consider at least my immediate future in education is—helping the program to not only be accreditable but to be one of the good model programs in architecture. That's my interest right now, and eventually I think I will get the registration and return to the [architecture] profession.

My question to Bruce Pfeiffer about his greatest accomplishment prompted this exchange:

BRUCE: I think the staff that I have around me [is my greatest accomplishment]. I think that's really remarkable. I've acquired three people . . . who are very dedicated and very professional. That's been within the last ten years. They are what make the Archives work. I can take any letter or anything and I can just pass it on to any one of them and know it's going to be done and be done well.

And from a personal point of view beyond that? How about the books you have written?

I don't know. I never really think of that as an accomplishment. I'm just fulfilling the task they've put before me. The idea of writing never very much occurred to me. When I was in Paris I wrote. I wrote a history of my first seven years at Taliesin, just to keep the memories. I wrote for three hours every day.

[As far as my own writing is concerned], I had a New England training; public schools in Massachusetts had very high scholastics. I went to school in Worcester. Our major courses were English, English literature, writing, and public speaking, from about the sixth grade on. It was demanded of all of us. So writing was an easy thing for me; being able to express myself was easy. I've always regretted, looking back over my writing, that I had no style. You know, I read someone like . . . well, anybody, and they all have such a wonderful style. I'm just a narrator; I just simply tell a story. I don't have much of a vocabulary, and I certainly don't have any literary style.

Bruce's reflections on the past frequently lead to a story. This one he heard from Edgar Kaufmann, Jr., who was at Taliesin in 1933–34. As an apprentice, Bruce says, Edgar "brought Fallingwater with him. From his being here Mr. Wright designed Fallingwater and the other Pittsburgh projects."

In 1977 when Edgar came back for an extended visit, Mrs. Wright took him down to her dressing room, which was the little room next to the finance room. Long closet, open the doors, thirty pairs of Ferragamo shoes, beautiful Pucci dresses—the wardrobe of a very, very well-to-do person, which she had collected over many years. Edgar said, "To anybody else, this would have been showing off. But," he said, "I saw her in such poverty, that she was just saying quietly, 'Well, Edgar, it took a long time. It's as if it doesn't really matter, does it?' " And she told me they never knew where the next dollar was coming from until the Guggenheim commission in '43. They met in '24, so it was almost twenty years before they had a feeling that there was any kind of stability financially.

What do you make of Mr. Wright's comment, "Take care of the luxuries and the necessities will take care of themselves?"

Well, wasn't that Oscar Wilde's comment?

He may have been quoting somebody.

That's true. That's the way they lived. See, we had a farm, so we didn't starve. They loved beautiful things, and when he got money he bought beautiful things. When he collected a check from Kaufmann he was over in Philadelphia and he telephoned Mrs. Wright and said, "We've got some money, Mother. What do we need?" She needed a new carpet sweeper, so she said, "It would be nice if we had an electric vacuum cleaner." He said, "Well, I've found a harpsichord." And she said, "Well, for heaven's sake get the harpsichord." They both had that same feeling. You can always push an old carpet sweeper a little bit longer but you can't always get a fine harpsichord on sale.

They both lived that way, and from living that way things came to them. . . . She said that one time she said to Mr. Wright, "Frank, how much do we have in all the world in the way of cash?" He said, "Well, it's in my pocket." "What's in your pocket?" "About $65." And she said, "Let's go out and spend it, so we'll get some more." And the next morning came a letter from Kaufmann with the Fallingwater commission.

Could you live that way?

Oh yes, we do live that way. It's a little more difficult in this day and age because of what credit cards do to you, but in a way that's why people who are newer in the Fellowship can't understand the thinking process that people like Dick and I might have, because we've been through that.

Some of the good experiences enjoyed by the fellows came from travels abroad. Richard Carney describes the Fellowship's travels several years after Mr. Wright's death.

DICK: We were sitting out at the pool here, and I think it was at lunch in the spring, about 1963. Mrs. Wright said, "I think it would be nice if we all took a trip to Europe. We could just take the entire Fellowship and go to Europe." And I said, "Do you really want to do that, Mrs. Wright?" Mrs. Wright said, "Yes, I really want to do that."

So then I set about working with Mrs. Wright to see to it that that's what we did, and I (lots of other people got involved in this, but basically I organized the trip) saw to it how we could get cars to travel around Europe, what hotels we could stay in, organized the itinerary and fixed it so the entire Fellowship [could go]—we divided Taliesin up into two [groups]. . . .

We found out that we could buy cars in Europe and sell them back at the end of a certain period of time. You could go to Citroen and buy a car, and they would agree to buy it back at a certain period of time later on. So, we bought five Citroens—station wagons—and half of us went to Europe. . . . We went to Paris and picked up the cars. Then we met the rest of the Fellowship who had flown over, and we picked them up in Brussels. We drove through Europe, and eventually we brought the cars back to Paris. In Paris we met the other half of the Fellowship who had just flown over. We gave them the cars. We flew back and they took the tour around Europe, and then they brought the cars back and sold them back to Citroen.

How long were you there?

Each one of us was there twenty-one days. At that time they had twenty-one-day excursions. . . . I think if you bought a ticket for sixteen people, maybe fifteen people, you got the sixteenth ticket free. We found out a lot of things like that, and we decided that students who had only been here a year would have to pay for their own fare if they wanted to go, and things of that sort. But we worked all the details out.

We took everyone, the whole community. . . . We had to leave one or two people at home, but basically everybody went. Then the next year we started talking about it again, and we decided that twenty-one days had been so expensive, that we could spend the whole summer in Europe, and if we stayed at one place [we could stay] for about the same amount of money that it took to go to Europe for twenty-one days. So we said, "Fine."

I went to Europe and started looking for a place that we could rent for the summer. . . . I sent a message out to every apprentice we had in Europe, to every alumnus, saying we wanted to do this [and] to see if they could find a place. About three weeks later I had a place connected with the Ecole des Beaux Arts in Paris, a castle from Bavarian King Ludwig's court near Munich that was vacant that we might be able to rent. Something in Florence, something in Rome, and something in Lugano, Switzerland.

So I flew to Europe and looked at all these places, and the place at Lugano, Switzerland, was an American school that they agreed to rent to us for six dollars a day per person, room and board. It was cheaper for us to go to Europe than it was to go to Wisconsin. So we organized and moved the whole Fellowship for the summer. Then we did the same thing again the next summer. Then we decided that three summers in Europe was about enough, so we didn't do it anymore.

It was that sort of thing that I would organize with Mrs. Wright; it would move the whole Fellowship forward. Mrs. Wright and I would work together very much that way. She would tell me she wanted something done, and I would see to it that it got done.

What were the effects on the Fellowship of those summers in Europe?

Well, I think it broadened our perspective a great deal. One of the effects on the Fellowship, of course, was that the buildings in Wisconsin suffered because of our being in Europe and not in Wisconsin to take care of them. That made it more difficult in future years. But David met Anneliese in Lugano and Effi Casey joined the Fellowship there and came back, and then later on she married Tom. We really acquired two of our major members in Lugano, and it gave everybody an international sense. . . . I think it drew us closer together. It made us see if we could act in unison about something. . . .

At the beginning of the seventies we traveled to South Africa; Mrs. Wright had been asked to speak at the University of Durban. Approximately ten of us traveled with Mrs. Wright, and we made a leisurely trip down through Africa. We stopped in Addis Ababa for two or three days and then we went on to Nairobi where we spent a week. Then, on to Durban where we remained several days, after which we returned to Nairobi for a week and then back to Rome where we spent about a month.

Tom Casey, at that time, was supervising the building of the palace designed by Taliesin Architects near Teheran for the sister of the Shah, and as he needed to do business for the palace in Italy, he came and met us in Rome. The group included Cornelia Brierly, Kay Rattenbury, Davy Davison, Jason Merrit, a student from South Africa, Charles Schiffner, Mae Steinmetz, Bruce Brooks Pfeiffer, and Frederick Bingham.[1] Prince Giovanni del Drago,[2] who had been a student at Taliesin, was there all the time and seeing to it that we saw the proper things in Rome. . . .

Another time Mrs. Wright was in New York City, and she telephoned me and said that she wanted to get away for a month. I told her that I would go to Europe and look for a place to stay. I left the next day and flew to Majorca and located a hotel for Mrs. Wright. She was coming over by boat. About ten days later the boat arrived with Mrs. Wright and Kay and Dr. Rorke and one or two other people on board. We checked in at the hotel that I had picked out for Mrs. Wright, and she hated it. This happened quite frequently. Then she decided she didn't like Majorca at all, so we stayed about twenty-four hours, and then we flew to Zurich and stayed at the Dolder Grand, a magnificent hotel on a mountain near Zurich. We were there about a month.

Mrs. Wright always received very special treatment whenever she went to a hotel. We would usually be able to create a kitchen in her suite, and Kay and Minerva would be able to cook for her when necessary. The chef in the hotel would also be very particular about getting special dishes for Mrs. Wright. It was like traveling with royalty; Mrs. Wright had that air about her. It was very interesting to travel for ten years that way.

Cornelia Brierly also traveled abroad with Mrs. Wright. Here she recalls one of the trips.

CORNELIA: We went first to Rome and then Addis Ababa where we stayed for awhile; then we went to Nairobi and on down to South Africa. That was an interesting trip. I also went to Japan with Mrs. Wright when she was trying to save the Imperial Hotel. It was too late. The man who owned it was only interested in the International style and in the business of making a lot of money, because the Imperial was in a very high-rent area. He wanted to build a high-rise hotel.[3]

Occasionally, members left the Fellowship but maintained close ties and later returned. I asked Charles Montooth about the architectural firm he established in Phoenix while he was away.

CHARLES: The first time I said I was going to [leave], Mr. Wright wrote me back and said, "Mother and I think that you shouldn't go now. We don't advise it but we give you our blessing." Something to that effect.

Is that the way he referred to her when he spoke with the fellows?

He did refer to her as Mother; not always, but sometimes. He called her Olga, Olia, too. So, I didn't go the first time, I was so moved. I was staying in Arizona [year-round] at that time, because that was the way I sort of paid my tuition. I looked after the place there for three years. Finally when I did go and we were married he got me that job. We were always very close; we came back on the weekends and helped out. We had Mr. and Mrs. Wright at our little place, a tiny house, 800 square feet. . . . It was a little semicircle. . . . We sold it when we came back here.

The Korean War pulled Tom Casey away from Taliesin for a time. Here he recalls his experiences while away.

TOM: During the Korean War I got snatched back in the service again. I had to leave Taliesin for a few months and return to aircrew duty. Fortunately, I ended up going to Europe instead of the Pacific, on an exercise that the 2nd Air Force did to explore the possibility of supplying all parts for aircraft direct from the U.S. instead of trying to warehouse parts in distant areas and have major maintenance go on there—simply were testing this idea of supplying only major parts. . . . It was a great piece of good fortune, because after having spent the time in the Second World War, we were far away from any kind of wartime activities. I was in a squadron of tanker ships. At that time we were doing midair refueling. You'd refuel other levels of aircraft, either smaller, pursuit kinds of aircraft or larger aircraft, and that was a very interesting, tricky maneuver. You were in midair and you got this boom out there and you had to connect it and pump a lot of gasoline from one to the other. Nevertheless, that was another kind of learning situation. And then I came back to Taliesin.

Arnold Roy also recalled his military service during the Korean War.

ARNOLD: I went into the army; I was drafted during the Korean War—that would be in the summer of '52. Because of the little bit of experience I'd had at Taliesin I was able to put on the information form that I had some technical background in drafting and architectural engineering. It's interesting how these things happen. You sort of feel they are destined to happen. . . . I went off to training, and at that time 99 percent of the people who were in the infantry (which is what I was in) ended up in Korea.

About two weeks before the end of the training I broke a bone in my foot. I couldn't walk, so I was pulled out of training. Everybody went off to Korea, and there I was. They looked at my resume, and [saw that] I had some engineering background. I was sent down to Fort Belvoir in Virginia, the engineering center, and became part of a cadre down there for a few months. And then what they call a "levy" came down. It was a request for a French-speaking draftsman at NATO headquarters in France. I was the only one on the East Coast, so I ended up spending a year and a half in France. . . .

I was in engineering, in logistics. I was stationed at the château in Fontainebleau. Isn't it curious that the casern where I was stationed, if you go across the street and down two blocks, up one block there's a cemetery. Gurdjieff is buried at that cemetery; he was the philosopher that Mrs. Wright studied with. He's buried at the cemetery just a block or two from where I was stationed.

Johnny Hill describes the unique circumstances of his departure from Taliesin in 1953, after fifteen continuous years with the Fellowship, and his interesting experiences in the ten years he was away.

JOHNNY: Elizabeth Gordon, who was the editor of *House Beautiful,* did an issue using the Farnsworth House of Mies [van der Rohe] in Chicago as an example of a sheer horror. She got herself out on a limb and wanted help in showing what architecture she thought America should have. She called the International style Fascist architecture. I was going to New York with Mr. Wright that morning (we were in the living room, I think, having breakfast), because [work on] the Guggenheim was going to start and he wanted to put up this big exhibit on the site.

This wire came asking if he could suggest an architecture editor who would be helpful. Mr. Wright said, "Maybe you could help her." So he got us together in New York. I liked her very much. She was a fascinating, very lively, good-looking woman, and we hit it off fine. I went out and stayed with her over a weekend in her house. And so, Mr. Wright said, "If you want to do it, we'll call it a sabbatical year, and you can help her out."

Well, of course, it took me a year to know what I was supposed to be doing on the magazine, but still it did work very, very well. As a team Elizabeth and I were awfully good, and Mr. Wright, of course, felt I could do lots of good in that position because there wasn't any coverage of his work or any of his students for the usual consumer.

Mr. Wright with Elizabeth Gordon, editor of *House Beautiful.*

And nobody had published color photographs, let alone interiors. It was hard, at first, to get clients to let us do the photography.

So, as I left it with Mr. Wright, he said, "Well, as long as you feel you're doing something worthwhile, stay with it and whenever you want to, come home." So that was the situation there. A year later he took an apartment in the Plaza, which I furnished for us. There was a little bedroom for me and a beautiful big living room and a bedroom for them, and I lived there. I sort of was his official receiver in the city.

After a couple of years, Iovanna married and she wanted to live there [also], so we added another bedroom. But I didn't feel that I had to be right there all the time, because, mainly, it was important that somebody be there if he came alone without Mrs. Wright. As it worked out, eventually I got myself my own place, but when they were in town I often would stay at the hotel.

Tell me about the two issues of House Beautiful *devoted to Mr. Wright's work.*

The first one was the big explanation of what he had done for Americans' homes. That was a big effort and an enormous success. It was sold out very early. It was amazing, because the publishers didn't think that anybody would care. They didn't know anything about him. There was another issue done just after he died where we were trying to show how many people had learned from him and were practicing, and [that] it wasn't something that had died with him. In other issues we were able to support an awful lot of architects who were trying to follow his lead—getting them known, getting their work known. This was a really important contribution, I think.

Was there any negative feedback on the Frank Lloyd Wright issue?

You know, I don't think so. If there was, my head was so far up in the clouds that I didn't notice. You know, the way you feel about something that important, I wished that I could have done it better. I wasn't happy with it, yet it got done. He was nice about it, except he didn't see why all those ad pages had to be in there.

It was a wonderful time. It was right after the war; people had money; they'd started their families; and they paid attention to something that was worth reading. And we really packed that magazine. We had good writers, good authorities on any subject that was of any interest. You know, all of those things were beginning, like air-conditioning and all kinds of equipment for the kitchen—smoke cooking, you name it, there was something to write about and illustrate and study.

For instance, there were all of the cancer-producing possibilities of outdoor grilling and that sort of thing. We went into everything very, very thoroughly, and it was very thoroughly read. So, I was very proud of myself that I could fit into that thing and contribute to it. I couldn't have done it if it weren't for Elizabeth. She was the driving force, and the one who kept patting me on the back.

You went there as architectural editor and then . . .

[My title was changed] to editorial director because it had reached a point where Elizabeth wanted me to approve the angle of whatever was getting published. Whatever it was, more or less find the meat in it that I thought we should be directing people's attention to. And that put me in a position to sort of govern the content of the magazine.

What became of the magazine after you left?

It's still going. I think it's still the biggest—the number of people buying it—in the home magazine field. But it takes no stand whatsoever. Pretty pictures is more what it's doing [now]. But I don't think that the entire market is there, that demands this other thing. To give you an example of what was happening, you know Levittown that was built right after the war—those little tiny houses shoulder to shoulder. I did an article on that five or ten years later, but it was incredible what had happened to those little houses.

Many of [the residents] had hired Tommy Church to do their gardens because they'd read about him in *House Beautiful*. Most all of them had added some interesting room. Instead of identical, these became individualistic houses. They liked where they were, they had gotten used to the neighborhood, and they didn't want to go build something else. But this was an example of the times, and nowadays I don't know that people are so self-driven. They are more just imitating celebrities. Of course, I'm not in the field anymore, but I don't think I'd want to be.

You know, the name [of the magazine] came from a "House Beautiful" booklet designed by Mr. Wright. He and Winslow, his first client, printed an essay by a man named Gannett called "The House Beautiful." Mr. Wright did the page decorations. They had a press; it was a hobby for the two of them.

The format was bought by Lane publishing house. *House Beautiful* is mainly devoted to houses, and we were showing the first color publications of Frank Lloyd Wright houses outside of the professional publications—*House and Home* and *Architectural Forum*, etc.

As a matter of fact, I think that same year I did, myself, a group of rooms in the Pomona [California] art museum for the state fair which is, next to the Texas fair, the biggest in the country. It was twenty-some rooms, separate rooms facing an aisle through the museum. Mr. Wright was in Beverly Hills, and I got him to come out and see it before it opened. We had it all finished early enough so that our issue on it could come out when the fair opened in October.

He was very pleased. He had a couple of little corrections that he said he would make if it were done again. And so I dedicated that show to him. That was my first big production on my own, but this was a tremendous thing for Elizabeth to take a chance on. I set out not to do it myself, [but] I just couldn't find architects who could satisfy me. The point of the show was how to use art in your home. We had all of these students of Millard Sheets out there at the colleges that he wanted to push, and so everything was designed—hardware, dishes, fabrics—all this was artwork, in a way. That show outdrew the racetrack in attendance. It was jammed. . . .

The second Frank Lloyd Wright issue was one that we put together awfully fast when he died. This showed the last thing on the drawing boards at Taliesin, and other architects who had been trained at Taliesin, to show that there was a whole element out there working in this idiom.[4]

Johnny also explains the reasons for his return.

I left there because Gene Masselink died suddenly, and I felt I was needed. [Mr. Wright's earnings] went into the Foundation. He didn't have anything. The Foundation supplied him with clothes and shelter and food. But the whole operation of the Foundation was left to Mrs. Wright as president, Wes Peters as vice president, and Gene Masselink as secretary.

There was a question of replacing [Gene]. It seemed to me, that I should be back there helping Mrs. Wright with the support. For that reason, I left—resigned. Right away Mrs. Wright increased the size of the Board [of the Foundation]. To do this, she had to alienate many people, and that's one of the miracles. Why this community has stayed I don't quite understand, except that she got herself in a position where she held it [together], and she did everything she could to promote it.

There is something strong here that holds the group together. I think it can easily continue; it's going through lots of adjustments because of all kinds of changes. One of the main ones [is] the fact that it takes so much money to support these buildings, which we considered just houses before. But, my feeling is it's a place for creative work, and it might some day be more productive in sculpture or painting or writing or some other art, not always necessarily architecture. There needs to be production here; it's a place for people who are creating things and in no sense a place for people who want a common, community kind of an existence. It's a place for people who want to get to the heights of what's available. And that would be my conclusion—music, painting, films, anything that is valuable in the way of knowledge.

You have no regrets about coming back thirty years ago, then?

No, I don't really.

You might be retired and be living on the top of the Hancock Place in Chicago on a big, fat pension.

I don't like high places, but, yes, I know. That would be nice. But you know, I've never had to worry about money. Somehow, I seem to have enough to deal with and I've got all this.

Some of the time away from the Fellowship was spent working on the Taliesin Architects projects. As noted earlier, Frances Nemtin and Kenn Lockhart, then her husband, were assigned to the

Florida Southern College project. Later, in 1958, they were sent to New York for what was supposed to be a year, but Kenn "just didn't like city life." When they moved out to Elizabeth Gordon's "palatial" house, Frances said, the commute bothered him, and New York life was hard on the children, so they came back after six months.

Tom and Effi Casey spent much of the 1970s in Iran, and Stephen and Frances Nemtim went there from November 1973 to the beginning of 1977. Here are Frances' and Stephen's recollections:

FRANCES: Stephen and I went to Iran in November of '73. For me it was very, very familiar. It reminded me of India so much. For Stephen it was totally alien, and interesting. We had a very intense, wonderful experience there. For me it was wonderful totally, except for the hassle that Stephen had to go through with the bureaucracy of the Princess's cabinet, which impeded the work instead of helping us. And so there was a lot of—undercover kind of—unpleasantness. It was difficult for him. But the actual work was very satisfying, and the people of Iran and the landscape and the architecture and all that were wonderfully interesting.

STEPHEN: Well, the palace had been constructed. Wes had designed a complex of villas for the Caspian Sea, the little town of Chalus, which overlooks the Caspian Sea. I went there with what would be the equivalent of a developed design. It was my task to translate all of that into working drawings. We were actually supposed to go over there with working drawings, but they weren't completed. One of the ideas was that we could only complete them by working intimately with the contractor and knowing what really was available at the bazaar, because all of the materials were bought through the bazaar.

In any case—I don't recall how fast I completed them—that first winter we settled in a little area, a community of buildings that were under the auspices of Her Royal Highness, Princess Shams Pahlavi, a little community of buildings. We spent the first winter there in Mehrshar. I set up an office in our home and turned out the working drawings. And then we just stayed there and eventually had accommodations in the Chalus area at the hotel.

Were you there while the structures were built?

Yes, I took it all the way through until all the structural system was in place and all the roofing systems were in place, not the finishing. There are a lot of conflagrations that go on when working in Iran. The Princess always wanted the buildings finished very quickly, and of course they couldn't be finished very quickly. And there often was the problem of money. There actually wasn't money available, and she never wanted to hear that. She had her own bureau and people who would make excuses and all kinds of things of that nature. In the end, they pinned the slow progress on me, and so we actually were asked not to return. So we didn't finish the finishing of the buildings.

Eventually they were [finished]. Tom and Effi returned. Frances and I also did all of the landscaping work. We designed all the landscaping and oversaw its implementation, which was also a major piece in itself. It was the equivalent of forty acres; it was semiwooded. [The Princess] wanted to change the whole character of the site; we wanted to retain some of the kind of wildness of the woods. So I wouldn't let anybody cut trees unless I marked them. Whenever we would return to Iran, which was close to once a month, the Princess would always want to know how many trees we had cut down and always wanted it more clear-cut. But I would always resist that, and so we struck a balance in the end to keep some of the wild character of the site.

When the Fellowship traveled to Europe in the summer of 1966, David Dodge met Anneliese. The next summer they were married, and he opened a practice in Switzerland.

DAVID: I went to work with a Swiss architect who was here in the '50s, who had studied at Taliesin. We were good friends then. He lived in a very beautiful valley in Switzerland, and in 1961 I had seen that. I had gone on a trip to Europe, and I had seen his place and he offered me then . . . "Why don't you come to work here for awhile?" So when I got married we talked with Ernst [Anderegg] about it, and he said, "Yes, sure. Join my office."[5]

He had some twenty to thirty people working for him, so it was a pretty big office.

What did your having studied with Frank Lloyd Wright do for your credibility among European architects?

Oh, it was a bombshell; it was just unbelievable. I mean, I got invited with no ceremony, you know, no questions, no ifs, ands, or buts. I just had to show a couple of photographs of some houses that I'd built to prove that I actually built things, and I was immediately accepted in the Federation of Swiss Architects, which can be a very exclusive club. It is the only official recognition one gets in Switzerland as an architect, because an architect does not have to have a license. In fact, there is no license for him to have.

If you are a streetcar driver and you decide tomorrow you're going to open up a coiffure, you know, a ladies' beauty parlor, ha, you think you'll get away with that? Oh no, you go to jail right away. But you can be a streetcar driver and open up an architect's office; it's perfectly all right, you're not messing with Madame's hair.

I went over in '67 and I stayed from '67 until '77 and then came back here.

Have you been back continuously since then?

Oh yes, but I was continuously coming back all during that ten-year time. We were spending anywhere from a minimum of a month to two months here, and most of the work I was doing that was getting built was going through Taliesin and not through Ernst's office. Nothing went through Ernst's office, actually. I did a lot of work for him, but somehow those clients never built. But then as soon as I got back here I had a client in England to do a project there. He was anxious to have me do it, because I had this house in Switzerland, and he knew I would be coming over in the summertime.

You maintained your ties with Taliesin the whole time you were away, then.

Oh yes, oh yes. You can't give up that much of your life.

As the senior fellows look back, conversations often turn to memories of former colleagues. Some were apprentices who left Taliesin to establish their own practices and did not return. Among these, many are now members of the Taliesin Fellows organization. Also remembered are fellows who have died. The two most recent losses are Johnny Hill, in July 1996, and Kay Rattenbury in December of the same year. Although their recollections are included in this book, reflections about them by their colleagues are appropriate.

Charles Montooth wrote the following remembrance for the folder for the memorial service for Johnny. Here are excerpts.

> John deKoven Hill. An elegant man with an elegant name. The consummate gentleman. Like his mentor, impeccably dressed whether in tux or shorts. He was a hardworking, talented, gifted man. . . . Although he had to his credit important buildings and beautiful spaces, one of his last and most beautiful achievements was the simple, graceful, gradual, winding path which leads up the hill to Taliesin from the fields below. John deKoven Hill was a true extension of the work and ideas of Frank Lloyd Wright. We will miss his matchless, creative touch.

In a book of memories prepared by John Rattenbury, he remembers Kay fondly:

> In some way, each of our lives has been touched by Kay. It might have been the beam of sunlight from her lovely smile. It lit up her face, because it came right from her heart. Or perhaps you felt some joy at seeing her dressed so beautifully, in a way that complemented both the occasion and the architecture of our Taliesin homes. We remember her for her great warmth, her charm, her courage, her artistic abilities, and her love.

Two deceased colleagues who played monumental roles in the history of the Fellowship merit mention here. Many of the fellows spoke of Gene Masselink, one of the charter members and Mr. Wright's personal secretary, who died of a heart attack in 1962 at the age of fifty-two. References to him were many, and the comments by fellows were often eloquent in their simplicity. When I asked Marian Kanouse, for example, about the kinds of things Gene did, she replied, "Everything. He was a wonderful artist, and he did everything for Mr. Wright. Or everything Mr. Wright asked him to do, so far as I know, anyway." None of their comments, though, were as poignant as those by Gene's brother Ben in the tribute published by Edgar Tafel in About Wright: An Album of Reflections by Those Who Knew Frank Lloyd Wright.

> Gene was always running. Not the way I ran, to hide. He ran for just the opposite reason, to serve, to help, to become involved. I ran away. Gene ran toward. Gene broke his hip running from Hillside to the main house at Taliesin, Spring Green. It was at night. Like a horse, he stepped into a gopher hole and went down. How

Gene Masselink, secretary to Mr. Wright.

he ever dragged himself to the house, I don't know. He was taken to the hospital in Dodgeville. A new ball and socket were eventually put into his hip. But it was never right. One leg was about a half inch shorter than the other. It always hurt him, but you never knew it. He never flinched or winced; he never even limped. He covered the limp somehow, but it was a strain on him for many years, strain that finally broke his heart.

Gene died in 1962. And when he died, no one knew what to do, who to call, what arrangements should be made. Gene had always done these things.[6]

References to Wes Peters were also frequent. His death in 1991 was yet on the minds of the persons I interviewed, and they remembered him with admiration. Here Kay Rattenbury remembers Wes's role in building Taliesin West.

KAY: Wes was an inspiration to all of us. He got this idea of having two teams; one team built the forms, one team got the rocks and the cement and poured the walls. Mr. Wright chose where the stones were to be put and, of course, designed the buildings. Wes was in charge of these two gangs which competed, and at the end the gang which won, which had the wall up first—either the forms up first or the forms poured first with the concrete and rock—would buy the other team a steak dinner. In those days steak dinners were very rare, and it was quite an incentive. Wes's impulse and Wes's enthusiasm fired everybody. He did the same thing with the farmwork.

Earlier in the conversation Kay offered another good-natured remembrance of Wes:

He never did carpentry. Wes never did. He never was in the kitchen. He was in control of the farm. He was Mr. Wright's engineer; so he was extremely busy. But he never even tried carpentry. He never built a shelf in his life, and we never put him in the kitchen because he was very big—he weighed 250 pounds and [was] six foot four—and he was like an ox in a china shop. So we never dared put him in the kitchen or serving.

Here is an exchange with Frances Nemtin concerning Wes's role at Taliesin:

FRANCES: He was in everyone's life, virtually the first apprentice to come. Everyone knew him, and he was a big man in every way. His range of interests and knowledge was almost renaissance. He had a huge, huge intelligence, and was a voracious reader. He could not only read fast, he could retain it. He had a fantastic curiosity and a range of interests, and that rubbed off on everything. When we got the commission for Iran, he already knew Persian architectural tradition, so he was very respectful in all the three different buildings he did there—of the way they responded to the climate, the natural materials and the historical tradition. So he was an incredible person that way.

I think he really bloomed as an architect only after Mr. Wright's death, of course, because during Mr. Wright's life no one else designed anything except privately—for their families or for the twice-a-year Box Projects, which was the way Mr. Wright kept track of how each one was progressing as a creative architect and also as a draftsman. He encouraged people to be quite imaginative in those, and Wes was always contributing to those Box Projects, too. I remember one was a bridge over the Grand Canyon, which is really far out. But that was Wes.

Was he seen as the heir apparent, expected to take up the reins when Mr. Wright died?

Oh, yes, I think so. Mrs. Wright did designate the officers of the Foundation the first time. She wanted to structure it so she would be sure of its continuity. . . . That was her mission after Mr. Wright died, to hold this place together and to project it into the future. She was the president, Wes was vice president, Gene was secretary, Johnny was treasurer. . . . Mr. Wright had designated who he thought should be on the Board. I discovered many years later that Kenn and I were on the Board, but we had never been informed of that and it didn't function as a board. Mrs. Wright more or less set it up to function in an informal way, and then, of course, as times have changed we've got to be more structured, more legal.

Charles Montooth compared his architectural style with Wes Peters' and went on to comment further on Wes:

CHARLES: I was more plain and Wes was more ornate and much richer, which reflects his personality. He was really bigger than life. He was a local boy in a lot of ways. People liked him; they knew him; he owed them money, of course. He was kind of a legend, but he had that kind of rapport that you have with the good-old-boy network, the working people, the plumbers and people like that. He spent a lot of time in town. Also, he had cattle and stuff like that and was into so many things. . . . I think [Wes] will gain recognition. But he sacrificed his career to support Mr. Wright, which I think was wise and noble.

Ari Georges arrived at Taliesin only five years before Wes Peters' death. Wes made profound impressions on him, as he recounts here.

ARI: I knew Wes by name, having read some of the books, having read *Letters to Apprentices* and *Letters to Architects* prior to even knowing about Taliesin.

It seemed that Wes was really the kind of person who is a window to the history of Taliesin, a living window. You could see him as a man, as a character, having that strength and muscle that the Fellowship individual had to demonstrate and at the same time the fine mind. When I was reading about the history of the Fellowship in those letters books, I realized that Frank Lloyd Wright wants you to be grounded on earth with maybe your fingernails dirty from digging the ground but at the same time having a very fine mind and being able to be an aristocrat in the true sense. It's almost like this juncture of heaven and earth in man, and that attribute of character was so present in Wes, because he wasn't just talking, he really was there. That's how we first met.

I didn't work with him until the second year I was there, because the first year I was out on construction. I requested I should be all year on construction, because I had never done it before—and I had a great time. We were building the visitor center, and there was a great deal to learn there. We saw the building from foundation up.

Wes was the designer of the building, so we had him as the architect and he would come and visit. He even had made a contract with all of us that if we finished the building by the deadline he would take us all out to Trader Vic's, which was his favorite restaurant. They knew him by name there. He was famous for taking ten-member parties and paying [for them] himself. But the contract also said that if we blew the deadline, then we had to take him out to dinner to a restaurant of his choice. So we had this interesting relationship with him. We blew the deadline, but it was admittedly because he had not finished designing the building by the deadline, and we needed the drawings. So his contract was amended to say that "Since you met the second deadline, I will still take you to dinner, but since you blew the first one you have to push peanuts up the ramp of the visitor center with your nose prior to going out to dinner in your formal attire." That was in the contract, and so it did happen. It was June 10, and there were all of us in slacks and shirts down on all fours pushing peanuts with our noses and Wes laughing. He had that kind of spirit, he was that kind of motivator-leader like I would imagine Alexander [the Great] was.

Was he really the heavyweight in the studio?

Definitely. About the time I arrived, John R seemed to be doing a lot more bread and butter work, but Wes had the boldness of big design. He could handle large buildings. His auditoria were excellent examples of that.

I worked with him on St. John's church [in Spring Green]. The sketch he did for St. John's church was [done] in the hospital. Wes used to be at the hospital regularly. He used to go in every two or three months with different things—not serious. We flew together here to Spring Green to present to the committee of St. John's church. They had their old church that burned. That was the first Catholic church Taliesin . . . actually, Wes had done another Catholic church, but Frank Lloyd Wright never did a Catholic church. Wes convinced the congregation to do a fan-shaped Catholic church, which is very unusual. They usually like the long aisle, basilica-type plan. But Father Klubertanz, who had just arrived, was much more open-minded. He wanted a nice building.

Wes convinced them that he should be their architect by showing them at least eight examples of churches he had designed for different faiths, and [he] showed them that a building is a result of the faith and that he could not guarantee them what it would be like until . . . he said, "I cannot show you something that your building will look like because yours will be appropriate to your faith." The first sketch he gave me was in the hospital on a little pink slip, and I went back to the studio and started drawing. We worked a year and a half on the building, and I saw it through construction.

The acoustics are amazing. Wes had a very good intuitive sense of acoustics. He had a consultant in from California with whom we did a lot of work. The shape of the building and the composition of the geometry has a lot to do with that, and the carpet was another necessity for that because he needed to have a certain ratio of absorptive and reflective material. The church was designed for its optimal acoustics when it's full, because the bodies themselves contribute to that.

Was Wes's death a surprise?

ARI: Yes. I was in Minnesota visiting a friend, and I called in on Sunday and Pamela [Stefansson] told me Wes was in the hospital with a stroke and in a coma. I was shocked. However, that spring had been very difficult for Wes. Another person that worked very closely with Wes was Daniel Ruark.[7] He was a very talented man; he is working now with Aaron Green in San Francisco. Daniel worked with the person who, prior to TPC [Taliesin Preservation Commission], began being interested in preservation, and he is the one who initiated the whole Hill wing salvation [at Taliesin in Spring Green]. He did a lot of the drawings for the Hill wing, the as-built drawings. Daniel was a very quiet guy, a very sensitive person. He was more like Gene Masselink, I would say. He was also a graphic artist; Gene was his idol in many ways, had that kind of integrity of character, impeccable all the time. He never raised his voice, never got upset. He and I became good friends simply because we respected each other's talent. So, we ended up being Wes's boys, especially for the church, and we worked closely.

That winter, prior to the summer that Wes died, he was designing the visitor center from here. It was a competition. Actually, it was prior to the competition. . . . I was pulled away from Wes, much to his dislike, to work on the new Taliesin Architects material, because it was the year they dropped the "Associated" and all of their printed material—letterheads and everything—needed to be redone and I was asked to do all the graphics. So that winter I was doing graphics for TA, and Wes and Daniel were working on the visitor center.

In June of '91 Daniel—out of the blue, when the Fellowship was in transition from Arizona to Wisconsin—wrote a letter to the Executive Committee and departed. He parted, burning all bridges.

So Wes was left with no help, and when we arrived here they told him that TPC had a new program for the building, and he had to redesign it. That was after a full year of really struggling with it. That's when I think he really started feeling his arrhythmia much more intensely, stress-related arrhythmia, which was normal for Wes. Not having Daniel, not having me, having to redo this whole thing, for a man his age . . . I remember for a fact he was complaining, and he really didn't look very happy in early June when that happened. He complained of pains in his legs, which, I think, probably were blood clots. Eventually one of them got to his brain.

I personally didn't know how to handle [his death] internally, because I knew that it was the end of an era. I also was kind of lost personally here, because without Wes I had very few friends. And also the fact that Wes treated both Daniel and me in such a way that it was a little exclusive. In other words, we had protection with Wes. You weren't asked what you did and why; you were fully legitimate.

I worked with him overnight many times. He would spend all night going with us. He had a way of making you feel that you were worthwhile. It was a rewarding time; his work was always sophisticated, the result of exploring. You learned a lot. He was always very giving. I learned a lot from him just by driving him around and asking for stories.[8]

Sculpture of Wes Peters at the entrance of the William Wesley Peters Library.

Wes Peters will always be remembered as embodying the principles and ideals of the Taliesin Fellowship. The William Wesley Peters Library, its entrance graced with an impressive bronze bust of the man, serves as a constant reminder of his legacy. In more ways than the future will recognize, Wes Peters made possible many of the accomplishments of Frank Lloyd Wright and assured the vitality of the Taliesin Fellowship.

Notes

1. Jason Merrit was with the Fellowship from 1965 to 1975; Charles Schiffner from 1968 to 1983; Mae Steinmetz from 1967 to 1975; Frederick Bingham from 1968 to 1971.

2. Giovanni del Drago was with the Fellowship from 1951 to 1954.

3. Designed by Wright and built between 1916 and 1919, the Imperial Hotel in Tokyo was demolished in 1968. This building was notable, among other reasons, for surviving the 1923 earthquake.

4. To place Johnny's account into a larger context, see Virginia T. Boyd, "House Beautiful and Frank Lloyd Wright, *Frank Lloyd Wright Quarterly,* vol. 8, no. 4 (Fall 1997): 4–11.

5. Ernst Anderegg was with the Fellowship from 1955 to 1956. He established his own office in Switzerland in 1958.

6. Edgar Tafel, ed., *About Wright: An Album of Reflections by Those Who Knew Frank Lloyd Wright* (New York: John Wiley and Sons, 1993), 196. Ben Masselink spent parts of 1938, 1939, and 1940 with the Fellowship.

7. Daniel Ruark was with the Fellowship from 1986 to 1991.

8. As noted in chap. 7, the Archives has transcripts of lengthy interviews conducted with Wes Peters.

9

Transitions:
"The Fellowship Continues . . .
Times Change"

Communities in which the members live and work together in close settings typically experience conflict over their purposes, policies, and practices. New Harmony, the Shakers, Oneida, and Amana, for example, were all torn by conflict, particularly during times of transition; in each instance the conflict contributed to the community's decline. The survival of contemporary communities, such as Twin Oaks in Virginia, depends to a great extent upon their skills at conflict resolution.

The Taliesin Fellowship, a contemporary community with a rich history, has not been spared conflict. In times past there was an inspirational patriarch or a stern but benevolent matriarch to gloss over the differences and direct the course of action. Now, though, the Fellowship is on its own in determining its future. In our conversations, the fellows were tactful in expressing personal differences, but they left open enough cracks for the differences to be visible.

Dick Carney described the context for the debates over the Fellowship's future: after Mrs. Wright died, a by-laws change formally created the Senior Fellowship, with the fellows becoming the membership of the Frank Lloyd Wright Foundation. The fellows elect the Board of Trustees and the Board elects the officers of the Foundation. Being a membership organization means working by consensus, and that slows forward movement considerably. "You have to get everybody to agree to something," he said, "and in the past you . . . just simply went ahead and did it." That makes it "a totally different way of doing things."

It is a momentous challenge to hold a group together and use conflict creatively when the members see so much of each other. I asked Dick how he handles it.

DICK: Well, I'm not sure I handle it. I think, to a certain extent, we let it handle itself. I think there is a great deal of inner conflict, and sometimes I get involved in trying to resolve it. I think mostly people resolve it themselves, and then we have several other people in the Fellowship who have some resolving capabilities. . . . Or if it's a real problem we might bring it to the Executive Committee of the Board and have them resolve it. Or we get a group together and resolve it.

Have you ever had any sort of schism within the Fellowship, factions against factions, that threatened its future?

We have, but that's been a very minor thing. I think that right now there are some people who are never willing to go along with the main thrust. Tom pointed out to me that most of the things I've said we needed to do that have been brought to a vote have been approved pretty much by about 80 percent of the people.

There have always been three or four people who would vote no, and it's always the same three or four people. Before I take anything to the group, I've discussed it pretty thoroughly with a lot of people. In general (and I don't want to say that I alone do them, because there are a lot of people that I spend a lot of time talking to and conferring with), . . . if a group of us decides that there's a certain thing that we have to do to move forward, and we take it to a vote, it's usually voted on as "yes."

How has the Fellowship resolved conflict and used it for creative purposes? Effi Casey responds to that question:

EFFI: Well, I think at times it's not really resolved, because we are too respectful of each other or we don't want to hurt each other. . . . Whether it's in your marriage, your friendship, or your community, these are very human considerations. But I think because of these personal considerations we dilute the vision. We have to have more passion for the vision and therefore find more creative ways to deal with conflict. Otherwise, it's the wrong kind of respect for each other. I think more frank exchange would be beneficial. . . . I think since we all, in our hearts, really do have the future and the best in mind (I think we all agree on that), we want to listen to each other. We just disagree in how to move forward; we have different ideas on how that can best be accomplished.

Are there some people here who are particularly good at reconciling differences?

Yes, I think Dick is very good at that. He is so deeply, deeply devoted that he cannot function with disharmony around him . . . because of his strong desire to make peace. And I would even call myself part of that kind of group. I come from a family where there was a very, very strong closeness—very fiery arguments, political arguments. But it always had to do with the subject on the table; it didn't have to do with the people. So I think we need to learn that, to distinguish, and I think we do try. And, when things get really difficult to sort out, we get more people together.

Has the Fellowship ever been beset by factionalism—where there is faction A and faction B, not just on a given issue, but generally faction A sees things one way and faction B sees things another?

Yes, very definitely. There's a larger group that sees one way and there's a smaller group that sees another. That's the kind of a group that almost predictably will vote opposite of what the rest will. And out of those are two or three who (again, I want to make that very clear) do have a very, very deep sincere thing at heart, but I just cannot share in some of their ways of pursuing the future. They close themselves against anything that comes from outside. It's that little bit, that "truth against the world" attitude which, I think, you need to be a genius to live on that.[1]

But you are able to bridge the differences to get along well socially?

That's what is sometimes so incredibly hard. You do care so much for each other, and you're so different in the pursuit of how to run the place. I mean, at times it really tears you apart.

I can't say that what I am able to see is the right way. Who can say that about the future? . . . You have to use history as a resource for what you're trying to do. And I don't think it ever came by closing yourself off and not being willing to mold it and change it into a different thing.

Cornelia Brierly expressed satisfaction with the development of the Archives, calling it a great achievement, but she viewed other things, such as accreditation of the School of Architecture, with less certainty.

CORNELIA: The change in the accreditation system is a major change for Taliesin—to get back into any kind of academic life—because Mr. Wright was so against regimentation or any kind of academic training. It's understandable, because I see that the people who have less rigid training are the most creative. There's something devastating about just going to classes. I know this has been your life, and I don't mean that as an insult.

Having experienced it myself, I know how devastating it was; I know it didn't instill any creative feeling in the work that we were doing in that educational system. I hope things have changed in universities (maybe they have), but still there's something that is a hindrance to a real creative spirit. I'm just reading about Albert Schweitzer, how he wasn't any good in school. Well, there's some reason for that. It's because people like Schweitzer are dreaming on a different level. It isn't because they're dumb. It's because their thought is in another dimension, and I think Mr. Wright's thought was always in that other dimension. We used to be very aware of it when he started talking.

Accreditation was also a topic of conversation with Stephen Nemtin. I reminded him that my initial encounter with Taliesin came through an accrediting process and that accreditation seems to be something you cannot avoid.

STEPHEN: Well, that was the premise that started it. We didn't demonstrate that you could do it another way. There certainly was another way to do it.

What would the other way be?

Simply, I think, have a program that allowed individuals to come and experience what we do here, for a fee, and then be in the framework that we are right now which is, for the most part, we have to subsidize the apprentice in our educational program but, in a way, under real restraint. Whereas, [with] the other method, we would not have that restraint, because if they wish to continue and be a part of us and receive remuneration for their work it would be with the idea that all work leads to the same degree of illumination and knowledge and ability to understand what an architecture is based on organic principle—the living of it here and the working of it and the doing of it and so on. We wouldn't have all the restraints that are being placed on us and in which we are gradually being separated into entities, which are competing for the dollars and the people. It could possibly have been a more unified result, but we won't know that.

The problem that every institution runs into is that we live in a society that is influenced so heavily by credentials.

Right. See, we've taken on the fact that it is our responsibility to provide a setting for the credentials instead of it's the individual's responsibility. If that's what's central to them, then it's their responsibility to take that on.

If it develops in architecture as it is in law, for example, and in pharmacy, a student must graduate from an accredited program in order to be able to take the licensing exam in those fields.

But that doesn't necessarily lead to the continuity of what's central to the vitality of Taliesin, because those students leave and go on to their own working life. There is no saying that what we're involved in now is actually more fruitful to the ultimate continuity of the idea. There is nothing that says that this is more viable.

For Charles Montooth, the management of Taliesin Architects was an issue. He had written, he said, about how he would like to see the office operate.

CHARLES: It's contrary to what we're doing now. That's why I wrote it. . . . . I think we made a big mistake. First of all, there's this big drive on the part of somebody . . . most people like to have a guy on a white horse. . . . They think that's the solution, you bring [in] a manager. But the people who come to Taliesin—who really wants to be managed? I think that's why we came here, so we could be more free. That's my theory.

But if you want a businesslike atmosphere—and everybody thinks that's a good thing, to be managed and have a business. Okay, so we hired this guy—been to Harvard, the latest thing. He comes in at a time when we have the biggest architectural project we've ever had after two of the biggest. He comes in at a time of, actually, recession. We had the job but before we really got to producing income—that's

Monona Terrace, which came from Mr. Wright, which all of us at one time or other put blood, sweat, and tears into over the years. He comes in and it's a profitable year, so immediately he works out some scheme for a bonus [whereby] himself and the hired people get a bonus based on their productivity according to some formula he's developed.

Unfortunately, I was not on the Executive Committee, and we were so busy I never took the time to go into it. But in the past when we weren't such a businesslike organization we had good years and then Mrs. Wright would either take us all to Europe (which she did) or we'd do something collectively or we'd share—we'd all get some kind of a bonus at Christmastime. And that's what I think we should have done.

So what happened was, people that are hired, people that had not been here, not gone through the mill or anything, that are getting paid, they got a bonus two or three times what we got. We took some of the bonus pool, and then we decided to distribute it among the Fellowship and decided to apply it to some common good (which is fine, too). So that's your business way to do it. Those people who are perceived to be the most productive—I don't know how it's conceived—that seems reasonable. We even toyed with that amongst ourselves, thinking of a way to create incentive for people to get jobs and all that would be to go the standard business way. But it brought resentment.

Now we have more . . . I'm not talking about hired employees, I'm talking about the people in the architectural office. You take somebody like June who used to work for TA, she didn't get any bonus because she works for the Foundation, and the people who work for the Foundation didn't get any. I think that was unfair, and I think it goes against the community atmosphere.

What we've done in the past . . . obviously, with the young people and all, we don't have enough people to produce all the work that we're apt to get. Just like Monona Terrace or even the school that I'm doing. So what we've done in the past is gone to former apprentices.

I in particular have a friend—we were here together and he has an office in Denver, he's very efficient and a good practitioner—who, when he gets a job that's too big to handle, calls on us and when we get in a production squeeze we call on him. That's how we did the [Springs] hotel also. I think that's a better way to do it. Then when it's all said and done he continues his business and we don't have a big payroll to support. I think that's a better business than what we're doing. I just think it was a difference in viewpoint among our own people; I think some people were worried, they were overworked and were getting older. They were in a depression; there weren't any jobs coming in and everybody was worried—the '92 recession or whenever it was.

John Rattenbury holds a different view of the management of the firm. Here he provides background for the decision to engage a managing principal in Taliesin Architects.

JOHN R: Over the years I was fortunate enough to have many remarkable clients. Some of these became friends and I turned to them for advice on what we should do to keep the firm, Taliesin Architects, flourishing. They provided substantial support and helped shape some ideas for the future. The management problem of the firm needed to be solved. A major step was taken when a friend and client, Hamilton McRae, introduced me to Ryc Loope, a young architect who had an office in Scottsdale, served on the faculty at ASU, and also was available as a business consultant.[2]

. . . We engaged him to conduct a study of our firm and prepare a strategic plan. In 1992 we acquired his firm and brought him on board as our managing principal. He has made a big difference and we are very optimistic for the future.

It has not been so easy for Ryc because we are a group of strong individuals and we are artists rather than businesspeople. There is resistance to management in any form, but we are gradually constructing our future, and it looks healthy. I expect it will be some years before this particular effort will be accomplished, but I'm sure the time will be exciting. And by that time we will have formed more new goals.

When I asked Arnold Roy about his hopes for the Fellowship, he identified what he considers to be the main problem of the Fellowship and then turned to the matter of the management of the firm.

ARNOLD: Well, the big thing we need, and you hear it from everyone coming in, especially our nonresident employees: the organization has unbelievable potential, but we need cash. Like any other organization, you can't do anything without cash. It's much more evident nowadays. When Frank Lloyd Wright was alive, there were a lot of things he could do without any money. He just did it on sheer personality. Now, we need cash. If we want to expand the office to earn more money, we need money to build a new studio. We've got unbelievable potential, but we've got to increase the cash flow. One of the problems is that there are just a few people who feel we should go back to the way things were. . . . They want to get rid of all the high-salaried people, the hired guns, as they say. I'm very much against that, because you can just look in the record books. Two or three years ago we were operating with a $900,000 deficit. You can't last very long with an organization like that.

They are referring to people like Ryc Loope?

Yes, he did a strategic plan for us, and he's delivering on his strategic plan. Some of our people are saying, "Well, yes, if we get rid of those high salaries then. . . ." But now we've got an operating deficit of maybe $200,000 or less, in that range. That's a lot better than a million dollars, and it's going down every year. So, I attribute it to these people who have come in and told us, "Hey, guys, you'd better start acting more like professionals."

A few years ago we had a couple of big jobs which were carrying us. The future looked grim; there wasn't anything out there. And, we brought Ryc in. He's got a lot of energy, is a very, very professional man, and really has turned the curve around.

The Taliesin Fellowship has always been revitalized by the arrival of new apprentices, some of whom continued in a senior status for a number of years before striking out on their own. In the past several years it has elevated seven apprentices to the status of senior fellow. The realization that the future of the Fellowship may rest in their hands means that they seem to be looked upon in different ways than were those who preceded them. I was able to arrange conversations with four of the seven.[3]

Although the new members bring distinctive qualities and concerns to the community, it is clear that they also do not speak with one voice. In fact, on some issues they are sharply at odds. That is no surprise, of course, since there has never been a time in the history of the Fellowship when all of its members saw everything the same way.

Most outspoken in his expressions of concern over the Fellowship's transition from past to future is Ari Georges. I asked him if the Fellowship today is different than it was when he arrived as an apprentice in 1986.

> ARI: Yes, because back then we were all involved. If you see the work list now, it's all apprentices basically. There are very few of the Seniors [involved]—Effi, Susan and Indira.

You mean as far as the cleanup and the kitchen and such things are concerned?

> Yes, but that's what the Fellowship means for a lot of the people. That's what the community means. It means the chores of everyday life. I was able to make some reflection this year, because I was listening carefully to language used around this notion of fellowship and community, and all I could see was the justification of architecture as a way of life. I realized that I had a much higher intellectual understanding of what that phrase meant—"architecture is a way of life."
>
> What it means here is we live a certain lifestyle, which means architecture, which means you do what we want you to do for our lives and that's how you learn architecture. That's how shallow it is, and I haven't heard any truly activating line of thought to make you feel or think about the values of living in a community.
>
> This is not a community right now, it's a coexistence of frustrated individuals. There's a lot of anarchy in the governance, and the whole sense of commitment to one another has diminished. And it is going to continue to diminish as we're losing members, especially members such as Johnny. With Wes's passing, I think it was a turning point, a big loss of the Fellowship.

There have been three now: Wes and Kenn and Johnny.[4]

> Right, they were all pillars. Cornelia can be effective, but she has also turned older. She's not as much involved in things. She's the last, I think, true window to the early Fellowship, which was a lot more scholarly oriented.

What do you see happening?

> I'm not sure what will happen. Actually, I think the critical mass required to make sure that the School continues is not reached. When I say critical mass I mean that

theoretical framework for the philosophy of the School, which [is that] everybody is in colleagueship. . . .

Within the people who are most responsible for the School or within the Fellowship?

Within the Fellowship. There is one very characteristic attitude that even I can sometimes feel that I can exercise, and that is called passive aggression. Nobody can do anything to you once you're a Senior Fellow the way it's set up now. At the same time, you can just sit back and obstruct with no restriction other than your conscience. If your conscience doesn't let you [sit back], then you're cooperative. If your conscience is not there, then you do all kinds of things that make it very, very hard to run this program, because this program is so respectful of the learner.

The reason to have the Fellowship today is not the same as what it was when the Fellowship was founded in '32, and it shouldn't be. One should ask the question, if we have a school for learning, if you want to have learning, you have learners and you have a learning environment and you need to really be interested in what learning is. Do we need a Fellowship? All of us that belong to this organization have to be interested, and I don't see people interested in learning. I see people interested in themselves.

I'm here to serve, and the frustration is that I want to give and they aren't going to let me give. They condition my donation. That's because in their eyes I'm still the twenty-two-year-old ignorant kid from Greece who came to learn. Now, being thirty, it is like being too old to be forgiven and too young to be given full responsibility. It's this gray area. I still have the window of learning, and I'm very interested in still learning, and I am learning now but I'm learning on my own terms. . . .

For the School, as far as I am involved right now I wish to explore the curriculum and the way we work here as a group of people, get to the point where it all works. I think we need to do that before NCA gets here, because if we don't then we are not accreditable. At the same time, there is another level that has to happen before NCA gets here, and that is the clarification of where the School stands vis-à-vis the Foundation.[5] That's what Nick Muller [needs to do], because as the president and CEO he has to delegate not only a portion of the Board's resources to the School alone but also the budget required by all that. Because up until now the School was subordinate. . . .

I asked Ari, who has an M.Arch. from the Frank Lloyd Wright School of Architecture, if he was doing any architectural work now.

Not as much as I should.

Do you have a drafting table over there?

I don't. They didn't give me one.

Did you ask for one?

I shouldn't have to ask for one. I have a sketchbook, though, and that's where all my ideas go. When I'm inspired I put it down.

I also asked whether the architects in Taliesin Architects who were not trained at Taliesin worked well with the apprentices.

They work better. There is a track record already, because they're more exploratory and they're a lot less biased. They can answer questions like "I think" and not like "Mr. and Mrs. Wright thought," which is basically how any answer starts if one has a question here—with some exceptions. Some seniors have their own critical thinking. The level of inquiry, critical thinking, and analysis and perspective is not present. If you hear Frank Lloyd Wright talk, or you read a book, you see global perspective there—not only a perception of the world but also a stance, a thesis about the world. And I don't understand why that is acceptable but at the same time it is not intellectual, or it's not allowed to happen today.

This dialogue with Jay Jensen brings another perspective. I asked him what kind of future he saw for himself in the Fellowship?

JAY: Well, it's a hard question, because I didn't come here for the Fellowship. I came here for the School, and I didn't really understand what the Fellowship was nor was I too interested. It's just something that's sort of grown within me, and I have become a part of it without ever thinking I would be. So I haven't really given a whole lot of thought to your question about what the future is. I just find myself here at this point after completing school and deciding to work with the architecture firm here. . . . As I said, I do enjoy the community, but that is not my binding [activity].

Do you sing in the choir?

Yes, I enjoy singing with the choir as well.

To an observer, the Fellowship clearly is in transition now, as the ratio of people who actually studied with Mr. Wright diminishes. How can you carry on the spirit of the Fellowship that was created by Mr. and Mrs. Wright? You didn't know Mrs. Wright. Some of the younger Senior Fellows, who came after Mr. Wright died, still got to know her for another twenty-five years. I wonder if you have any feelings about what you can contribute to the perpetuation of the Fellowship or whether that's not a big deal to you.

I understand the cause that they have—the direct apprentices under Wright on our senior staff—and I understand the importance of the architecture created by Wright. That was another reason why I came here; besides the learning program, was the type of architecture that is produced here. I'm sorry, I just haven't given much thought to my participation in this bigger picture of carrying on Wright's [tradition] except in my own personal, small little world.

If your primary goal was to be an architect, then you've become that. Do you work with the apprentices now?

Yes, I do that, and in that way I am participating. I teach them.

How do you do that?

In the same way that I was basically taught here, and that's just to talk with them, be an example, try to criticize their work, and offer suggestions.

What kind of difficulties, if any, do you run into by virtue of your having been fairly recently an apprentice? Does that pose any problems now, your change of status?

There's no conflict there.

Yet another perspective is evident in my conversation with Paul Kardatzke. I asked him how he viewed the perpetuation of the Fellowship when all the people who knew the Wrights were gone.

PAUL: It's a worry, I feel, because historically it's just not happening. Without people like Paul Wagner, J. T. Elbracht, and Bill Schoettker, there are no continuities.[6]

Did you work with Paul Wagner?

I did, yes. Paul left about six months to a year after I joined.

He has taught part-time since then, hasn't he?

He maintains connections. I think I might be the one person he has worked with the most, because I took over quite a few of his responsibilities when he left—here and in the desert. I've been in touch with him quite a bit on the projects we're doing in Baraboo, Wisconsin [the University of Wisconsin center]. They were originally designed by Paul Wagner, so I've stepped into that.

Do you know why he left?

I guess I heard a little bit back then, and I've heard more since, but essentially he had married. My understanding is he was looking to continue a relationship with the Fellowship but on different terms. He wasn't planning on migrating anymore, wanted to establish a Madison office, felt that that was a very important concept for the long term—keeping a Wisconsin office viable all year long as well as the Arizona office viable all year long. That's the only way you can really bring clients in, to be there to answer the phone. Paul did that with the Baraboo project and many residences and the library here in Spring Green. There were a number of projects that he was actively securing and working on, and the Fellowship made a decision not to maintain a Madison office, not to put the resources into it. I don't know how it all broke out in the dollars and cents, but it hasn't solved any. . . .

They're trying to do that now, though, aren't they, with the Madison office?

They're putting a lot of money and effort into keeping a Madison office going.

Is he not now with the firm that is also working on Monona Terrace?

Yes. Paul Wagner is now with the Potter Lawson firm.

But he's still friendly to Taliesin?

Yes. I don't think he would ever rejoin the Fellowship or the firm, but I see him very much of a critical loss to maintaining a Spring Green office or a Wisconsin office.

You and Julie no doubt did a lot of talking about your own future when the time came to decide whether to accept Senior Fellowship status or not.

Yes. We're committed to putting our energies into keeping the Fellowship alive. We're both from the midwest, so in a lot of ways I do see the Wisconsin office as being important for our continued involvement in Taliesin. It's sort of been year-by-year for us.

It must occur to you, and to some of the other younger fellows that you could not keep the Fellowship going by yourselves, but you need a critical mass of people who have a sense of what the new Fellowship ought to be like. Is that ever a subject of conversation among you?

I discern the following distinctions in the Foundation life and work: fully-resident fellowship, semiresident employee, and nonresident employee.

Semi-resident and nonresident fellowship do occur but are not tolerated for long. The situation of a fully resident fellow having a spouse who does not participate in the work and life of the Fellowship and Foundation is not tolerable either. The rigidity with which the lifestyle of a Fellowship member is viewed makes the status of fully resident Fellowship difficult to accept.

I believe that the fully resident Fellowship will continue to have a declining control and influence over the work of the Foundation. Nonresident and semiresident employees will continue to assume the responsibilities and opportunities attached.

As the parent of children who are probably close to your age, I wonder how you and Julie can build up equity for a future, if you are to have a future beyond the Fellowship.

So do we. Even if we have a future within the Fellowship, because (I think it's a generational change that's happened across America and possibly around the world but it's happening here as well), I can't put the responsibility of my retirement on the Fellowship, i.e., the Foundation. I don't feel like it's fair.

Do they have a retirement program?

There are new things occurring. We've developed a 401(k), and Julie and I are also setting up IRAs. We're putting away as much as can conceivably be put away for our retirement.

But that still does not take care of you in the event that, say, you're here another ten years and the Fellowship folds, and then you have nothing for a down payment for a house.

Well, it's really a ridiculously pitiful amount to be putting away for retirement. I know what I was putting away before I came here, and Julie knows what she was putting away before she came here. Everything I put away before I came here has been eaten up in tuition. Talking to Joe Fabris, there were no guarantees [in the past either] that everything was secure, but I think there was more of a widespread social network in the country. There was more of a reliance that Social Security was there. They weren't worrying about retirement so much, I believe, in the '50s and '40s. Social Security may no longer be there when I retire, although it's never been something that anyone could consider to be full retirement. There are also military pensions for quite a few of the Fellowship. And, probably less than are rumored, there are a number of fortunes in the Senior Fellowship.

I see that as one major, major difference between the young Senior Fellowship members and the older Senior Fellowship members. It's one of our major concerns about staying here for a period of time, knowing that this is the time of our life when we do need to put away for [retirement]. I feel like it's a wonderful work experience. I probably wouldn't be able to get comparable work experience right away, although experience doesn't bear that out. All the apprentices I know who have left in the recent past have had fabulous work experience already.

The matter of stipends received by Taliesin fellows seldom arose in conversations. However, I asked Paul whether, when he became a senior fellow, he received a stipend in the same amount as persons who had been at Taliesin longer.

Yes. One of the things I see as being one of the unfairest is that right now I'm receiving the same stipend as Charles Montooth. He'll point out to you that he also gets social security and he was in the army and other things like this, but as far as the Foundation is concerned, Charles Montooth is treated the same as Paul Kardatzke. And Charles Montooth has a great deal more responsibility. I don't think that is fair, especially when I then compare him to some of the nonresident employees of Taliesin Architects. It's startlingly unfair that he would be receiving a small fraction of other principals in the firm. It doesn't strike me as being fair.

[In 1997, Paul Kardatzke accepted a position with an engineering firm in Wisconsin. He continued to live at Taliesin, however, and with his wife, Julie Nelson Kardatzke, participated in Fellowship life.]

What does Julie Nelson Kardatzke regard as her role in the Fellowship, as a new senior member?

JULIE: My primary focus is the studio, naturally, because I am involved in architecture. But I am also somewhat involved with the Education Committee now. I was asked to rejoin as the representative for the younger Senior Fellowship members, and that's something relatively new. I had been on the Education Committee as an apprentice, representing the apprentices, and then I got off of the committee when I was close to finishing my degree. Now I'm back on again. I've told the Education Department that my primary interest is in mentoring people in the studio, because I think that's really the core of our program here, the School program. I see that as an important function.

Apprentices in a "Group Learning Opportunity" (GLO).

And then just being a community member like anyone else and participating in the work activities and the social activities and so on.

Do you thrive on that?

To tell you the truth, sometimes it gets to be more than I'd really like. It's difficult to find time to do private activities and activities just as a couple. I guess if I had my way we would have less of those kinds of social activities and more time to pursue things on our own.

Do you see that day coming?

Well, I wouldn't be surprised, only because that seems to be a general attitude among the apprentices, and I think that it's going to be harder to sustain the community activities. We've already given up a lot of cooking duties that we had before, now that we have a professional cook who comes in five days a week. And we've turned over a lot of other activities. So now the Fellowship members only do the cooking on the weekends—well, there is also a cooking assistant who's an apprentice, and they work during the entire week.

Does that make you long for the good old days when everybody did everything?

I guess not really. I'm sort of glad to be freed of some of those things. It's a little bit sad because it indicates to me a change in the direction of the Fellowship. But on the other hand, I don't think it's possible to continue going the way that we were going. I think it is just an inevitable thing that, as the Wrights are gone, as the Fellowship continues without them and times change, that the nature of the Fellowship is going to change. I don't think there is really any way to keep it the way things were in the old days.

[In 1999 Paul and Julie Kardatzke moved to Spring Green, but Julie continues to work with Taliesin architects.]

Notes

1. A Druid symbol signifying the Lloyd-Joneses' struggle of "truth against the world" was carved into a stone set into the wall of the home of Frank Lloyd Wright's aunts in 1886. The expression became a byword for Mr. Wright's outlook on life.

2. Hamilton McRae was elected chairman of the Board of Trustees following the death of Dick Carney in January 1998.

3. Following completion of the interviews for this book, several more have been elected to the Senior Fellowship.

4. In December 1996, Kay Rattenbury also died; she had been with the Fellowship since 1935.

5. The School was reviewed in highly favorable terms by a visiting team in February 1997.

6. Paul Wagner was with the Fellowship from 1965 to 1992, and J. T. Elbracht from 1982 to 1990.

10

New Players: "Servants of Their Vision"

The Taliesin Fellowship has a long history of adapting to changing times. In its early days, the Wrights employed carpenters, brick masons, and other craftsmen to help build and maintain the buildings at Taliesin in Spring Green, and Frank Lloyd Wright had paid assistants in his studio. Gradually, however, reliance on outside employees diminished and the Fellowship sought to be self-sufficient. The spirit of self-sufficiency, egalitarianism, and sharing in the community included the practice of giving all fellows equal monthly stipends. At least it was assumed that the stipends were equal, although in Mr. Wright's day one never knew.

Among the most notable changes in the 1980s was the return to reliance on persons from outside the Fellowship in key positions in the School, the Archives, the Taliesin Architects, and the Foundation. Such a change would strain the ideals of every intentional community, but at Taliesin there is an additional worry, that is, the apparently wide disparity between the fellows' remuneration and the salaries paid to the nonresident staff. Cornelia Brierly expressed her concern thus:

CORNELIA: The Fellowship was started in an experimental way. Both Mr. and Mrs. Wright tried to find ways to deal with each problem as it arose. Whenever it came to the point where they were able to give remuneration to people, everybody in the place got the same reward, regardless of the work they were doing. Just a few years ago, it was decided to get a business manager for the studio, and it became necessary for people who lived off campus to be paid salaries in excess of the stipend Fellowship members received. I said at the time, this is going to make a very bad break with the Fellowship. In fact, it might be the elimination of the Fellowship. It hasn't been the elimination of it, but it has caused great conflict.

There was something wonderful about everybody sharing and getting exactly the same remuneration. We were one big unit. Now we're divided into many units. With the Archives we've had to rely on outside help. Naturally those people have to be paid on a different scale. It's caused a serious discrepancy to be solved.

Commenting on the changes he has seen in the Fellowship through the years, Joe Fabris referred to the employment of nonresident staff members:

JOE: Unfortunately, I'm not very happy with the changes, because I think we're losing the spirit of the Fellowship. We've become a small group, and this whole organization . . . there's just too big a proportion of hired people who don't have the same goals, I think, and the same commitment. And I don't think it works.

There's always room for some bad feelings because . . . well, take for example in the kitchen. When you get people who come from 9:00 to 5:00 . . . some of the people here believe that in order for those people to feel a part of the group we invite them to have lunch here. But then the people who are here as apprentices, if they've got to do the cooking and there are twice as many people at lunch now, they're cooking for these hired people. They have paid to come here and they're cooking for people who are being paid. Then they get a sort of resentment to that, and that sort of runs a little bit through the whole thing.

I don't think you can have a mix of people where half of them are employees and half of them are sort of family. It's a little bit like you get the family restaurant opened up and it turns out to be a great place and all the kids are working there. And then they get successful and big and they start hiring a bookkeeper and this and that. Then it just becomes a sort of business.

There's something of that going on, and I don't think it's good. And I don't know what the answer is. Obviously, there are so many of us here that are over seventy, or people in their sixties, and there are not the sort of middle-aged people here to replace us. So, it may just be that the natural course of events is . . . I heard something that Mr. Wright said, that he expected the Fellowship to last fifty years after he died. . . . So, that would be 2009. We may make it to that. There will probably be an organization of some kind here, but it won't be the Taliesin Fellowship that it is now.

The large and growing nonresident staff is by now a fact of life at Taliesin, and the continued existence of the Fellowship itself depends on the effective work of committed persons who do not hold the status of fellows.

To determine the place and importance of persons employed by the Frank Lloyd Wright Foundation, I recorded conversations with a number of them. Their voices are heard here, and they will be heard again in the concluding chapter, for they will inevitably play an important part in Taliesin's future. The conversations covered a wide range of subjects, and the recordings and transcripts will be valuable holdings in the Frank Lloyd Wright Foundation Archives, but my primary interest was to discover how these persons came to the Foundation, their observations about the Fellowship, their relations with it, and the nature of their principal responsibilities.

June Hill was among the first nonresident employees. Before coming to Taliesin, June had worked as an administrative assistant for the Aluminum Company of America (ALCOA) in the Pittsburgh area for twenty-one years. After moving to Arizona, she saw an advertisement inviting application for a clerical position at the Frank Lloyd Wright School of Architecture. That struck a responsive chord: "Wait, I know that name—Fallingwater." After an interview, she was hired.

> JUNE: The first couple weeks I thought to myself, "I don't believe this is for real," because it was like a fantasy to drive up there. Once I went over the canal area I thought, "Boy, this is a different world." And it was—and it is. Because when you drive down into the valley it's altogether different from being up at Taliesin.

Her first day of work was November 19, 1984. The date is significant, she says, because it was just a few months before Mrs. Wright died.

> I didn't know her at all. I'm sure she hired me. I don't think they would have hired anyone without her knowing, so I'm sure she was aware of me. She waved from the car as Dr. Joe would take her for a ride, but I never met the woman. I didn't have that pleasure. She had failed so much, however, that you really couldn't get to know her at all.

What is your present position at Taliesin?

> Well, I am now in my eleventh year with Taliesin. Almost three years ago I was invited to be part of the Education Department with the School of Architecture, and I am known as the educational assistant to the Deans.

June Hill

The School and the Fellowship being inseparable, I asked June what she thought communal living contributed to the Fellowship or to the Taliesin enterprises.

Well, I think probably years ago it worked easier than it does today, much easier. I was amazed . . . after a few weeks I thought, "Wouldn't this be wonderful to be living in this environment with all these people that are not unhappy with each other." And then after Mrs. Wright, their leader, died it was very evident it changed. That's not meant [to be] derogatory, but it was just very evident that they had not been the individuals that perhaps we all are, coming from the big world.

So they each had to shape a new self?

I think they found themselves. It wasn't that they were suppressed that much . . . I don't think it was suppression, I think it was wanting to have a leader. You know, some are definitely followers and some kind of like their independence.

What do you think is your greatest contribution to Taliesin?

I think one of my greatest contributions to anything that goes on here . . . is maybe I have that down-to-earth common sense, and I think that helps. I'm not caught up in the fact of living on the grounds all the time, which I'm sure is very difficult when you're there twenty-four hours a day. Now I get a taste of that up here in Wisconsin and I seem to be able to work around it, because I don't think I have any great problems. And yet I love being a part of the things I want to do.

And your contribution to the Fellowship, to the community?

Loyalty, caring about them. I guess that would be a contribution.

Elizabeth Dawsari as Dean of Libraries at Taliesin West serves the entire Foundation—the School of Architecture, the architectural firm, the Archives, and the Fellowship. How did she come to this position?

ELIZABETH: In a most unorthodox manner. I was working for the newspaper and received a telephone call from a Mrs. Frances Nemtin, who had queried the Special Libraries Association looking for a special-libraries librarian who had experience setting up new libraries, and she had been given my name. I had just returned from Saudi Arabia where I had set up the library for the University of Petroleum and Minerals. The chair of the Special Libraries Round Table, which Frances contacted, was Rosanna Miller who was then map librarian for Arizona State University, a position that I had held. . . .

Frances invited herself to my home to see how I lived and investigate me before offering me any sort of position. . . . That was in 1983. When I was hired [in 1984] and began working here—nights and weekends, because I was not going to give up my day job for something that was all up in the air—I had one carton of books and a stool and empty shelves, which were in that little reading area where the NAs [the

Elizabeth Dawsari

catalog identification for books in architecture] commence. I was told, "Here you are; here's your library."

The books were predominantly elderly engineering texts. They were part of Wes Peters' collection, and I was told this was the first carton of many yet to come. Some of them dated from the '20s and '30s. I was dismayed; I was thrilled at the quality of the material and dismayed at the dates. I informed Frances that if we were going to seek accreditation with North Central, which was why I was hired, "We're going to have to have some kind of a budget. We're going to have to really organize this like a library. We can't just take these old engineering books and put them on the shelves and call this a library."

By the time [the North Central] visit occurred [in 1985], we had made an appeal to the Fellowship to give us all of the books that individual members had possessed in their own living quarters, at their desks, etc. We had been given the next room, and Arnold had arranged for shelves to be built. . . . So now the library consisted of two rooms: the old sewing room and I don't know what this room here was. . . .

We tried to group the books in broad subject categories. Of course, no cataloging or listing or anything had been done, because we didn't have time. And strange things happened. For instance, I had placed *The Greening of America* [by Charles Reich] on the shelf with the few texts that fell into the broad category of sociology and came back in the morning and found it with gardening. Things of this nature happened to me. Everything moved around, everybody had an opportunity to go in and utilize things. I said, "This isn't going to work. This is a full-time job, and maybe it's time for me to give up my day job and get this established." So, in 1985 . . . I resigned from the newspaper and was hired full-time here. That really is the year, I would say, that this collection began as a concerted effort on the part of the Foundation and myself to develop a real library.

The most exciting thing for me has been the change in perception. When I first came here there was a strained attitude on the part of certain members of the Senior Fellowship, and I think that was associated with the misconception that Mr. Wright had said we don't have to read. Reading isn't what life is all about; it's doing that life is all about. That wasn't really true, because Mr. Wright was the greatest advocate of the book and of scholarship; otherwise, he wouldn't have written [books and articles]. At first some people said, "We don't need an outsider. What is the ALA? What is an MLS degree? Your degrees mean nothing to us. What is important is what you do and what kind of person you are and how creative you are."[1]

Those were selective voices. One member of the Fellowship came to me and said, "When I was in high school I assisted in the library, and I was prepared to be the librarian [here]. I didn't see any reason to have you here." And I said, "Well, have at it." That attitude changed as the people realized that the wonderful resources that they already possessed here could be organized and made accessible. Slowly—it took a period of years, maybe five years—the resistance eroded and people began to utilize the facility and enjoy the benefits derived from finding out information that they didn't realize existed.

I'm not going to say that everyone today is a user of this library. There are several members of the Senior Fellowship who have never set foot in it, even though they have had tea in the [adjacent] "T-Square [Cafe]." They've never been in the library, haven't a clue. But, other members of the Fellowship use it heavily, and the apprentices have really come full circle in terms of understanding that now they have to do research for their Box Projects, they need to have background information that is not derived from their own creative endeavors.

I think the accreditation process is possibly what has spurred [interest]. The fact that it has been necessary to develop this library along professional guidelines due to the fact that accrediting agencies require this has, in large part, contributed to the changes in perception and the increased funding and increased usage of the facility. I feel as though we ("we" meaning the library collection, the staff, and myself) are an integral portion of the Fellowship. We may not be considered Fellowship, but we're just one of the many legs that [support it].

Does that bother you?

Yes and no. There are times I find it very painful, and I wonder what's wrong with me, what's wrong with the years of service and the loyalty? Why isn't that good enough? And at other times I say, "Well, I have my other interests, which are professional in library science and recreational in the breeding of horses and dogs, and maybe this is for the best. So, I don't know. Yes, it does bother me sometimes; at other times, no, it does not.

Do you find yourself in sort of an "alliance" of feelings with other nonresident staff?

No, I find myself siding more with the Fellowship in understanding why it's imperative that we support this endeavor of a continued community here. I think maybe eight years ago I was more restive than I am today. I think now I see things quite differently.

At this point I observed that Elizabeth's comments on rewards in her work were mixed with remarks reflecting frustration. Had it been a mixture?

Absolutely, and there are two sides to every issue. For me professionally, the rewards have been immense; also socially and in terms of my personal life—in terms of meeting and becoming friends and a colleague of people that I consider to be interesting, affable, entertaining, and cordial.

In the academy, for a librarian life is quite different than life here at Taliesin. For one thing, the focus is administrative and task-oriented. Here, interwoven with the same needs, administering an area and accomplishing certain tasks, is a friendliness. I don't know how to put this; I haven't been down this trail before—a way of life. In other words, the accomplishments of the job contribute to a way of life and to a future for people in a different way than is apparent in the academy.

In the academy, a librarian fulfills his or her function for "X" period of years, retires, and is gone. At least that has been my experience. Or moves on to another position. When I resigned, with great sadness, from Arizona State University and moved on to the University of Petroleum and Minerals and left there with great sadness, I still did not feel that I was contributing to the way of life of the people who were trying to make both of those institutions a continued reality. I feel that here. I feel that if I were to retire from the Frank Lloyd Wright Foundation, that I would not just simply be gone, but that I would still be included amongst the people's thoughts and, hopefully, social activities.

Do you participate in things like the Easter celebration or Thanksgiving dinner?

I have been up until the last year or two. My parents are very elderly, and the past two Easters I have spent with them simply because I just fear we're losing our opportunities for future [holidays together].

Do you always feel a part of things when you do come?

I do now. I didn't in the old days, because I didn't know people so intimately. When I say intimately, I don't mean that in an improper sense at all. I think as the years have evolved and there has been a greater overall acceptance of my position and my role in terms of what the Fellowship is trying to accomplish, I think that there has been an increasing warmth. We didn't know one another in the old days; we just kind of tippy-toed around and wondered what kind of a quantity am I dealing with here. We've been thrown together, which is part of the benefits of communal life, so there is better comprehension and more affection.

The School of Architecture is a complex operation. In addition to administrative leaders, it includes on its faculty all the members of the Senior Fellowship. Moreover, its 1997–99 bulletin lists as faculty about half a dozen Taliesin architects who are not members of the Fellowship, more than a dozen "affiliate faculty," some sixteen "visiting professionals," and a "curriculum faculty" of fifteen, two-thirds of whom come from outside the Fellowship.

Working with Tom Casey in providing leadership for this interesting assembly of people (which, of course, could never be assembled at a given time or place), is John Wyatt, the academic dean of the School. My conversation with John, who was in Hawaii when I spoke with him by telephone, began with the rather standard question: How did you happen to come to Taliesin?

JOHN: Actually, I came to Taliesin through a fluke. I had been the artistic director at American Players Theatre, which is just down the road from Taliesin [in Spring Green], and I was asked to come up and give lectures on the plays that I had translated. Before that time I knew nothing about Taliesin. So I came up and I gave lectures on Chekov and Ibsen and certain things on Shakespeare. That's how I got initially to know the community. However, my interests were somewhat remote from architecture, and I guess when I left as associate director of APT they were coming to a point where they were trying to get accreditation. At that time they had no traditional academic there, and they asked me whether I would help them. And so I said yes, I would help them. Then I began to explore their mode of education and became very, very enthusiastic about it.

It came to a point that little by little my job was to try and interpret to an outside academic community what was going on within Taliesin that ultimately would make it valid for accreditation, which was no easy task. Because, ultimately what one is dealing with is trying to explain a system that is so synthesized and so dependent upon different sorts of elements that you can't really separate the School from the Fellowship and the firm. They needed someone who would cover the liberal arts. . . . Also, they had very few people who had any advanced degrees or any experience in academic administration, all of which I had.

. . . [O]ne of the things that I was most interested in was, how do you get a solid humanities program that would result in documentation in a portfolio and have a relationship to young persons who were learning their profession within the studio itself? I didn't want this to be this some kind of coffee table sort of stuff or [on the other hand] ultimately come to a point where you would have it as you would in the normal university, in the sense of grades and classes. I'm not putting that down, because I come from that tradition. I think that when you look at Taliesin you're looking at alternative schooling.

Also, you're looking for a particular type of student. The type of thing that goes on at Taliesin isn't for all people. I've had wonderful students at the University of Chicago who probably would do very poorly at Taliesin. On the other hand, I've had wonderful people at Taliesin who would probably do very poorly at the U of C.

John Wyatt

I think—at least what I came in with—that education is by its nature incredibly complex. It's like doing brain surgery in the dark, and there are many ways to do it depending upon each individual student. I just saw that Taliesin had a particular type of approach that would be most helpful and beneficial to a segment of the student population.

You're a man of many affiliations—Beloit, Chicago, Hawaii. Please say a word about them.

I'm a professor at Beloit.[2] I started off as professor of philosophy and classics and Slavic languages at Beloit. But then I have been at the University of Chicago as director of their classical and medieval language and thought program for almost twenty years now. I also am director of the Alexandria project for Montessori International, which is a program for inner-city children; in time it developed into something much more than that. Then also I am a partner in a law practice in San Francisco, which is a mediation firm where I deal with disputes over intellectual property and sexual harassment. . . . Right now we call Hawaii home, because I'm also involved in a medical school here which has been formed up in Waikiki, on the big island. It's a very interesting teaching hospital because it combines both eastern and western thought, and generally when you have those two together they hate one another and fight. But in this case, one plays off the other. I do theoretical history of western medicine and my colleague does theoretical history of eastern medicine. . . .

As far as Taliesin is concerned, what is your job description now?

Well, the job description is kind of epic. . . . I am responsible for the academic integrity of the program in the sense that what's put in the Bulletin, what we thought about, I'm responsible to see that it's fulfilled in some type of imaginative way without violating the principles of how Taliesin was founded on learning by doing. I have to be extremely loyal to both sides of the camp. When we were accredited I told the community that an obligation was imposed upon us in the sense that it just wasn't a question that we got through the series of meetings, that we got accreditation. It means that ultimately the people who came through and accredited us gave us a certain responsibility to fulfill.

I am confident we can do it, but we have to do it in our own way. So, it's just a question of making those two match and jell and that we have integrity on both sides. . . . It's kind of a juggling act sometimes, particularly when the ultimate judge of a student is the portfolio and not grades. A portfolio judgment can be subjective. I'm trying to get it to a point where, insofar as one can be objective with help from architects and peers and members of the Fellowship, it can develop the highest standards and expectations for the apprentices. I think that we're doing that.

I'm also on the Admissions Committee, and once again I have to follow two things: one, that whole tradition of Frank Lloyd Wright where people pounded on the door, and they wanted to be architects and he let them in. I have to look at their academic background, because we're in a far different world now. I don't say, "Well, grade point average means everything." But, on the other hand, I still look at it as an indicator, but I tend to look at all the stuff first—the backgrounds of both foreign and domestic students—and see what I can learn about them. . . . Now that we are accredited, both in the M.Arch. and the bachelor's programs, I don't want Taliesin to be kind of a dumping ground for people who, under the guise of learning by doing, would come to Taliesin. I think that the largest number of apprentices we are ever going to have will probably be thirty-five, at least in Arizona. Maybe we might attempt thirty-five up in Wisconsin, but that's not going to be in the near future.

We really have to be very careful of the type of young person who comes in, because ultimately they have to look upon Taliesin as a resource, they have to be tremendously self-disciplined, and they also have to be willing to work very, very hard. That order of things is rather difficult for a contemporary student, so I'm trying to get it so neither a student nor we waste our time dancing around—when what the applicant really wants is a very structured sort of program, while even though they may think that they're rebels they long for grades, and the whole thing that goes along with a formal university system. At Taliesin, of course, it doesn't work that way.

How do you fit this into your multiple obligations?

. . . It's not a question of administration from afar. If you are going to do a good job you had better be on the line some way or another. I have June and Effi and Tom, the whole Fellowship behind me, and I track those apprentices every two days to see what's happening and what they're doing.

We are not dealing with thousands of students; right now we're dealing with about twenty-two. So I can track them very well. Also, when I'm there I find out the projects that they're interested in, the projects that can also fit into the possibilities in the studio, and then I also work on the premise that I don't have to be on their backs every day. We think in terms of, "Okay, this is what you want to do. I'm here as a resource and guide; now let's see what you can do."

I talk to June every day for at least forty-five minutes, and Effi every Friday for maybe an hour, hour and a half. . . . [When I am not at Taliesin] there's a packet that goes out every Thursday evening with all of their projects and journals that I review and correct, and I also talk to them on the telephone.

You are much more involved than it would appear to be from your being there only part of the time.

It's really a full-time job in that I have to attend to all those students. I also have to think in terms of the Fellowship. Also it comes to a point of how can we develop the School in a particular way, too. We're now interested in getting it so we have seminars with schools from the outside where we might have a three- or four-week organic architecture program where people from liberal-arts colleges can send their students up there, and our students can mix with theirs. I'm working on that now; I'm also working on the possibilities of scholarships and fellowships and getting it also so Taliesin begins to have an effect once again on the academic architectural world.

Everything is there. It's just a question of how you get it so you use those resources. In fact, very often it's so embarrassing, because whenever I run into people or even prospective students, they have the impression it is so incredibly difficult to get in that no one could possibly make it. Or, people aren't even aware of the School, that there is a school there. I think maybe within the last three or four years the reputation of Frank Lloyd Wright has really zoomed. So, there's a tremendous respect for the word Taliesin, and I want the School to be equal to that respect. That means that we're going to have to have a very clear-cut idea of what we're about and also get it so all the resources that are there are in place and are ready for a young apprentice to take advantage of them.

Do you recruit the affiliate faculty?

To a point. Taliesin has a long history of dealing with different sorts of people. When I first came I was quite surprised that anyone who wanted to could come in and teach regardless of what their background was, because of the kind of notion of hospitality that Taliesin has. However, I didn't carry on that same tradition. Ultimately, what I tried to do . . . I saw those needs in the programs that had to be fulfilled, and then I would look for faculty that would fit into those slots. At this point, since we run on a shoestring budget and upon the goodwill of people, I thought we'll cover the areas that one needs for a B.A.S. or an M.Arch., but I am extremely selective about the people that I let teach there now. And I aim to be more so as we go on.

I'm interested in what you perceive to be your relationship with the Fellowship.

I knew the Fellowship for five years before I got involved, and I didn't want to get involved initially at all. When I was in Spring Green, a lot of different people in the Fellowship—even people who don't get along with one another—became very friendly toward me. I think that from the beginning it was very clear that I respected their way of life; however, I didn't want to become a Fellowship member. Since I always was very frank and tried to tell the truth to them all the time, they gave me incredible sorts of trust.

. . . I came in in a very different sense from Nick and Ryc. It's almost like I'm part of the family, but on the other hand they accept the fact that I would go to formals only when they needed me for the School. My wife, whom they all love very much, does not participate in the Fellowship per se, and I don't that frequently. I think they know that I have the greatest respect for it and they want me to come to Fellowship meetings. They know, insofar as I can be, I am a servant of their vision of the Fellowship.

I have never felt like an outsider, and, in fact, I have got up on a number of occasions and upbraided the Fellowship on Saturday morning for acting in a particular way. I think they know I care deeply about them, but on the other hand if they asked me to leave I would leave. It's no big deal.

The Frank Lloyd Wright Archives has also grown to be dependent on three staff members who are not members of the Fellowship. I asked Penny Fowler, the first of the three to arrive, how she came to her present position.

PENNY: In 1986 an acquaintance of mine was the first Getty intern, and I knew her through the Costume Society of America. It was just shortly after the Archives building had been constructed, and at that time they moved everything from off-site

Penny Fowler

storage into the new vault here at Taliesin West. At that point in time Bruce had only cataloged the drawings, manuscripts, and correspondence. So everything was being moved from the off-site storage place, where it had been since Frank Lloyd Wright's death in 1959. When they were going through the stuff that was coming into the Archives they found a suitcase that was marked "Mrs. Wright's brocades," and Bruce assumed that these were things that Mrs. Wright used as table decorations. When they opened the suitcase, they found out that these were actually Genruku embroideries, Chinese costumes and Japanese costumes, and Kosode fragments from a period of time in Japanese history that was the Edo period.

I was affiliated with the Phoenix Art Museum at that time; I was president of the Arizona Costume Institute. My friend Kathleen, who was the [first] Getty intern [at the Archives],[3] had contacted a colleague of ours who was the curator of costumes and textiles at the Los Angeles County Museum and Dale (the assistant curator) came over and she and Kathleen started to catalog the textile collection.

They ran into a time bind, so they asked me if I would come out and help. I said I didn't know anything about Japanese textiles, I just knew mostly about couture costumes. They said, "Oh, well, you don't have to do much anyway." I was in there all day helping them, and when I left Bruce asked Kathleen to ask me if I could start to volunteer on a regular basis. So she did, and I said I would be happy to, but I couldn't commit to so many hours every single day because I was married at the time and I was heavily involved with other philanthropic organizations in the Valley.

I came out when I could and continued to stabilize the textiles and store them properly. When Kathleen's internship was over . . . Bruce asked me if I would be interested in being a Getty intern. I said yes, but I couldn't do it the way that Kathleen did it, because her arrangement was that she actually had to live on the property and she had a $500 stipend and she had to be a full participant in Fellowship activities, like cooking and all the other things that fill out that bigger picture. That was agreeable with Bruce, so I just continued to live in town and come out.

My Getty project was to write a *catalogue raisonné* of the unpublished manuscripts, which I felt that I was not capable of doing. But Bruce had a lot of confidence in me, and he helped me a lot so I could do it—an in-house publication that lists the complete manuscript file and summarizes everything that was unpublished up until a few years ago, when Bruce did the five volumes of [Mr. Wright's] collected writings.

When my internship was over, the person who was the fund-raiser at that time, Elaine Freed, . . . got seed money from someone in Milwaukee to do a furniture inventory so that . . . when they went to the next phase of funding [they could] say, "Look, we've already done this to be incorporated in the Historic Structures Report." So that's how I got into the decorative arts field. While I was the Getty intern I still maintained all of my responsibility with regard to the whole Japanese collection—the textiles, the surimono, other Japanese prints, hanging scrolls (kakemono), and screen paintings.

I still do what I just finished describing with regard to the collections, and then with the furniture inventory my responsibility expanded to making sure everything would be cataloged; and the fine arts collection—much of which is *in situ* at Taliesin in Wisconsin—is also my responsibility. I catalogued all of those artifacts. Cataloging of the furnishings and art objects is ongoing.

About five years ago Dick asked me to get involved with the licensing program, and at that time my responsibility was more or less getting people together and making sure information got distributed to Dick and Bruce, and Johnny at the time. That has grown into about 95 percent of my job; we have about twenty-five licensees now and it is very demanding. Because of my knowledge of the decorative arts and the Frank Lloyd Wright decorative designs, I work with the licensees on product development, trademark issues, and write "story cards" and catalog texts. . . . I also do authentication requests of decorative objects, so if someone has a Frank Lloyd Wright window or vase or furniture, I get all those requests.

. . . Since 1990 we have participated in a lot of exhibitions, and so if anything from my area of the collection, the decorative arts, like the furniture or the actual artwork—the Japanese screens, surimono, etc.—[is requested], I am always the contact person. I enjoy it very much.

Right now we have a major exhibition that's traveling in Japan, which is twelve Japanese screens and over 120 surimonos. They have to be rotated because they're light sensitive, and probably about sixty drawings—again, which have to be rotated—of Wright's Imperial Hotel project and other Japanese architectural projects which he had.

Concerning your association with the Fellowship, do you partake in some of their dinners and other activities?

I find that my name is on what they call their "extended Taliesin family" list. And so, I'm always invited at Easter and Thanksgiving and Christmas—holidays like that or any special things that they have. I believe this year I am on the list for the formals, and of course when I'm in Wisconsin I am on the list for the formals.

You mean the Saturday evenings at Taliesin. Do you enjoy that?

Yes, it's an opportunity to meet interesting people, and it's fun to interact with the apprentices, because I don't have that opportunity when we're at Taliesin West. I don't live on the property here; I have a house in Phoenix.

After Penny, a second intern in the Archives was Oscar Muñoz. At the beginning of our conversation he talked about his long-standing interest in Frank Lloyd Wright.

OSCAR: I must have been about sixteen when I first encountered books about Frank Lloyd Wright. . . . By the time I was ready to graduate from high school I was really interested in Taliesin and the Fellowship.

I came out here with my mother and my sister to see the place in 1977. We took a tour. There wasn't a lot of information at that time—no student packet or anything like that. I was enamored with it, but my parents said absolutely not. They were willing to send me to Arizona State, which was fine for me because it was just ten or fifteen miles from Taliesin. I came up here periodically during the time I was in school.

By 1985 I had become acquainted with Effi and Susan. . . . Sometime in the following year I met Bruce and then got involved with the traveling exhibition, "Frank Lloyd Wright in the Realm of Ideas." I think everyone here was involved in some way. At the architect's office where I was working in Scottsdale things were slow, so I was coming up here, working in the Archives. Then there was a position funded by the City of Scottsdale to help Bruce curate the show, and that's how I ended up spending more and more time here.

By February of '87 it was a full-time job just keeping up with the projects and the exhibition. And then I worked in the studio that summer with Tony Puttnam, laying out the design of the panels. In 1987 Getty would fund one more internship, and Bruce asked me if I would do it. Of course I said, "Absolutely." I started that in '88; that's when we finished the show. With the idea that rather than focusing on a project like Penny did in fine arts, Bruce said, "What I would like to do for your project is that you learn everything that I know about the organization of everything in this room and become my backup." So, that's what we did that year.

What is the most interesting aspect of your work here?

The relationships, the interaction, the lack of obvious structure, and the hunt to find something. . . .

After Mrs. Wright died I think everyone to a certain extent fragmented into their own [worlds]. . . . The Archives became quite separate from the Fellowship.

Oscar Muñoz

I think within the last year we've made—and really helping that was Penny going to Wisconsin—we've started to make that connection back with the Fellowship through her.

You participate in quite a few Fellowship activities, do you not?

Actually, recently much more than I ever have. I have had a wonderful year this year, because I helped with the NAAB exhibition, and I got involved in the play that the kids did. I did a whole bunch of things. I made a commitment. I said, "I'm going to go to every formal that we have," because before that I always would say, "Well, I'll go to one or two." I hate getting into a tux and I hate getting into a crowd of people I don't know. Then I think the change I made last year was to say, "Oscar, whenever someone asks you something, just say yes instead of saying no. Just say yes and do it."

The third nonresident employee on the Archives staff, Margo Stipe, says that she came to her present position "by accident." Here is her account.

MARGO: I started out as a volunteer [tour guide] and then I was a paid docent. . . . Then at some point, I guess I had been here just about a year, when the curator of Asian art at the Phoenix Art Museum told Penny that I was here and working with the Foundation. My background was Japanese art history.

In any case, I had talked to the curator, Claudine Brown, at the Phoenix Art Museum about any possibilities of even volunteering or working sometimes at the museum, but since I was already out here and she knew about Frank Lloyd Wright's Japanese collection she talked to Penny. Penny came looking for me one day, and I started doing volunteer work down here in the Archives. And then Penny went to Wisconsin, and they were cutting back tour hours. In order to keep me on a certain number of hours so that I could stay here and would not have to go look for another job, I started working with Bruce. Bruce decided that I had skills that he could use, so by December—I guess December 1, 1990, I began full-time down here.

My official title is registrar, which means primarily I keep track of all of [Mr. Wright's] drawings. I need to know where they are at all times, and so I'm the coordinator for exhibitions. I work with the organizers; they usually make their own selection of drawings. Then I make sure that the chosen drawings get evaluated for conservation and treated at the conservation studio. Then they come back and I arrange to have them matted, framed, and crated. I work with the borrowing institutions on shipping arrangements and that sort of thing; that's one thing that I do. I also worked closely with Bruce on the publication program; I have worked with him on all of the *Collected Writings*, and the *Frank Lloyd Wright: The Masterworks* book. I do a lot of proofreading for him.

Do you do retyping then, too?

Yes, on the computer. He just copies his files over to me, and I go through and edit them and proof them and then send them back to Bruce to see if it's all okay. I make the changes as he sees fit. In the case of the *Collected Writings*, I did all the research for the footnotes and that sort of thing. And then I work a lot with outside scholars, providing some research information, but largely in terms of providing illustrative materials for publication. I have just been working with Phaidon Press on a couple different books. One in particular is new monograph on Frank Lloyd Wright that Robert McCarter is writing, and they're using about three hundred images from our Archives, so it's a pretty hefty project.

What is the focus of that book?

I guess it's just a retrospective review. Bruce has read it. He says it is very detailed, it takes you through the different houses and so it's . . . a monograph on apparently the whole seven decades of Frank Lloyd Wright's work.[4]

I'm sort of the contact for the Ken Burns documentary in that they keep coming up with more requests for material. Sometimes they just have questions and other times they are looking for other images, or they need some different materials, so I'm kind of the contact.

Did you play a key role in the Luna imaging projects?

Not so much "key." I worked to try to help put together the transparencies to get shipped. But, again, that was Oscar's. We had hired a young man to come in and re-photograph the drawings, so David [Teague] largely rephotographed the drawings and Oscar went through to check for quality and make sure that the color was okay in the transparencies we sent. To the extent that everybody does a little bit of everything, I was involved but not a whole lot.

Every time we have been around the Archives we have been impressed with the number of people who were coming through or phoning and asking for assistance. There's never a letup, is there?

There isn't. We have quiet days. Today is Saturday and the phone hasn't rung. It's really nice, because you can get a lot done without all kinds of interruptions. But I also walked in to fourteen messages [waiting]. They range from questions of—some man wanted to know what Frank Lloyd Wright's father's full name was and where he studied for the ministry. That's just one question out of the blue. Somebody else wanted to know if he could get a facsimile red signature tile that Mr. Wright would put on his buildings.

Do you answer questions like that first one or do you tell them where they can find the answers?

Well, for some like that, if it's simple enough I'll look it up and give them the answer. . . . We try to accommodate people as long as their requests are reasonable. We get some really off-the-wall requests from people, particularly from young students. Basically they're high school students who are asking you to send them all the information they need to write a paper. I usually say "Try the library" for a request like that, but if we're really the only option we try and accommodate those people to the extent we can.

One of the other things I've been doing is to catalog the slides we have gotten from the Taliesin Architects Archives. Elizabeth Dawsari and Molly have gone through the archives up there and sent down all of the slides that relate to Frank Lloyd Wright's buildings, pre-1959 buildings. There are some not-so-good slides in this collection, but there also are some really good slides that really have a lot of good color. That's something I do as I have time for it. I don't necessarily get to that very often.

How, in doing these things, do you relate to the Fellowship?

I actually have very little to do with them. I come to Easter and maybe another dinner in the year. . . . We're on friendly terms, but I don't have too much interaction with the Fellowship. . . . I see my role here in much more of a professional capacity in that I was hired to do a job, and largely what I do means working with people that are outside the Foundation as I represent the Foundation and the Archives to the outside world.

Backing up a little, I'm curious to know how you got your expertise in Japanese art.

That was kind of accidental, too. In college I needed to declare a major, and art history was the only class that I was enjoying that term; I had to make that decision. One of the courses I had to take was the oriental survey, and it was being taught that particular term by the Japanese art professor—that was at the University of Michigan. I had found my country. Within a couple of weeks I was just real excited, and I changed everything—the whole direction. I started taking Japanese history, Japanese language, Japanese literature, all the Japanese art classes I could take, and then when I graduated I went to Japan and lived there for six years.

About a dozen of the members of the Taliesin Fellowship are practicing professionals in the studios of the Taliesin Architects. Half of them apprenticed with Frank Lloyd Wright, the rest with architects trained by him. Today's apprentices in the Frank Lloyd Wright School of Architecture work side by side with these architects. However, meeting their training needs while maintaining a for-profit business compels the "TA," as the firm is known, to employ architects not trained in the Taliesin tradition or the principles of organic architecture. The managing principal of the firm, the person charged with overseeing its operations from 1992 to 1997, was Ryc Loope. Ryc resigned in October 1997 to accept the position of chief executive officer of the Durrant Group, a construction firm. As opportunities arise, he may play a consultative or collaborative role with the Taliesin Architects. Taking his place as managing principal is Bill Mims, who was with the Fellowship from 1963 to 1967 and whose Nashville-based architectural firm enjoyed a productive relationship with Taliesin Architects through the years.

When I visited with Ryc in May of 1996, he described his background as the son of a carpenter in the Washington, D.C., area. His interest in architecture began when he worked summers with his father and observed the role architects played in building. Early in his life he says, "the ideas of making and building were set in my psyche . . . it's what guided me into architecture." Excerpts from his story follow.

> RYC: I remember I was ten years old when Mr. Wright died. My father came home that evening and at the dinner table said, "A very great man died today." He talked about Frank Lloyd Wright and pulled out one of the publications of a home that Mr. Wright designed. I do not remember which home, but he said, "I always wanted to build a house like this." That was my earliest introduction, but only in coming to Taliesin did I remember that.

Ryc studied architecture at the University of Maryland under influential mentors, one of whom gave him opportunities to use his building experience. He continued his studies at Yale, earning a master's degree in environmental design. An interesting career eventually led to his becoming the chief operating officer of a large firm that was the leader in development of alternate energy sources and to the position of president of the Solar Energies Association. To develop management skills, Ryc enrolled in the Harvard Business School's Program for Management Development (PMD)—an accelerated executive training program. He then returned to the American Smelting Refining Company (ASRCO), where he gained recognition on Wall Street for "doing mergers, acquisitions and turnarounds."

After continuing his rapid climb, he took off on his own, doing turnaround and merger acquisition work for investment bankers. Interesting and challenging ventures, most of them requiring extensive travel, followed. Then:

> I got a call from a friend of mine here at Arizona State University who had read an article for which I had been interviewed about the lack of business acumen that exists within the architectural community. My basic point was, to really do good work, you had to be able to speak the full language of your client; not just the aesthetic language, the environmental language, or the construction language, but also the financial and business management and strategic management language. . . . My friend at ASU said, "Ryc, we are creating a new faculty position. We need a guy like you to organize the professional practice part of our curriculum." [This] ultimately became a concurrent MBA/M.Arch. program and [led to] other strategic links to the architectural profession and construction industry that the school had yet to establish.
>
> So I said, "Yes, I'll take the teaching position," which I did. I closed down my practice in Connecticut, closed down my practice in California, . . . and bought a practice out here with a fellow named Jack Peterson. I started networking into the Phoenix community and met a chap by the name of Ham McRae. We had lunch one day together, . . . and during a who-do-you-know-in-the-world discussion we found there were a few names in common from my turnaround days. He said to me, "Do you still do any of that kind of work?" I said, "Well, not really, I've been focusing on architecture." He said, "Well, I'm on the board of this architectural firm who could use your talents." I said I'd be happy to help out if I could. He said, "We'll do lunch one day and visit them."

Well, that day came. Ham picked me up, and we started up the hill to Taliesin. I saw where we were going, and I said to myself, "Ryc, what have you got yourself into?"—because Taliesin is the Mecca of architecture. It is the centerline, it is at the heart of American architecture. Mr. Wright's philosophical contributions, as well as his made contributions, are revered by architects around the world. So being asked to come to Taliesin was a great honor. It was also very exciting.

Initially I spent time with John Rattenbury mostly, primarily because he had some projects on which he needed help. . . . John was desperately trying to keep the firm afloat and doing a yeoman's job, a fellow who had never received any real formal business training and, quite frankly, wasn't getting a lot of support from his peers. History will show he held the firm together after Mrs. Wright's death. The organization was referred to at that time as Taliesin Associated Architects. I don't want to be pejorative about this, but the association was, basically, everybody sat under the same roof. . . . There really was no partnership intellectually or businesswise going on. No agreement to a mission for the firm or a direction. Basically there were eight separate practices underway, underutilizing the strengths or talents of each other.

John had taken it on his shoulders to shepherd the business aspects of the organization. It was an effort that I think he did uncommonly well, considering he was also the most prolific of all the architects since Mr. Wright's death, of those who stayed with Taliesin; that is, in terms of number of projects and geographical locations of the projects. So to be carrying so much water on both shoulders . . . was amazing, but it was wearing on John—mentally and physically. He was hoping for somebody like me to show up, I think—maybe not consciously, but subconsciously it was there. As you know, John is a very likable fellow, and we hit it off immediately. I could see his struggle, both technically with his work as well as fiduciarily with the firm.

So I started consulting, mostly on a pro bono basis, with the firm. We did what I call a "visioning" session in which the entire Fellowship actually participated. We set a vision for Taliesin Architects and put together a mission statement and strategic plan, which I presented to the Foundation board in October of 1992. The plan was widely embraced, to the point that Lee Cohen,[5] Dick Carney, Tom Casey, and John Rattenbury (I think primarily for the architects) approached me and said, "Is there a way you would consider coming to Taliesin and implementing the strategic plan?" I was both honored and surprised simultaneously, and I said, "If we can do this on a reasonable business level, because I have a successful firm going and I cannot just abandon my clients or my partner." We were able to work all that out. Basically, we amalgamated my practice into Taliesin Architects, and my partner came along.

How do you handle your own architectural training at Maryland and Yale and your practice with the Taliesin commitment to organic architecture?

My second introduction to Frank Lloyd Wright, after a very brief one in architectural history . . . was when I was in the Beinecke rare books library at Yale, and I was doing background research work on wind generators. I was looking at one wind tower after another or metal towers—built the same all over the world—when I came across this beautiful, wooden wind tower by Frank Lloyd Wright in a place called Spring Green, Wisconsin. It even had a name, "Romeo and Juliet." I was dumbstruck. "This architect has done everything," and before I knew it I abandoned my primary research direction to look at what Frank Lloyd Wright was all about.

I found he had done bermed earth houses, the solar hemicycle houses, all these things that my research was looking [at] . . . which I had thought architects really hadn't paid attention to because they had plenty of electricity and fuel yet to burn, but Wright had been investigating these issues and more all of his life. For example, the Jacobs I house, the bermed houses, the Usonian houses employing what he called the Korean floor heating—that is a radiant floor heating system—on and on and on. All of a sudden I was fully inspired with Mr. Wright's work, but from a very different direction than most architects; not from just aesthetic but from an understanding of a design based on ideas' being the most powerful generator of form. Designing "from the inside out" as Mr. Wright so often put it.

You no doubt face the challenge always of explaining how someone not trained by the Frank Lloyd Wright School of Architecture or the system here can legitimately lead a cadre of architects who have been.

I made it clear from day one, and still say it often, that I am an aberration at Taliesin. I am filling a void that exists, if you will, a traditional middle-management kind of void, the kind of thirty-five-to-fifty-something-year-old architects who really shoulder everything in a major practice. That middle group had just dissipated here at Taliesin

Ryc Loope

for a variety of reasons, and I think it showed up most significantly in the firm and was one of the reasons the firm was having such problems competing within the industry.

I accept that I am an aberration. If I do my job well, the young apprentices that the Frank Lloyd Wright School of Architecture is educating now will have a firm to take control of and direct. They are the next generation of leadership, and we must always be willing to "grow our own." Now that doesn't mean we shouldn't go outside when a talent is available. But all great organizations, all organizations that project themselves into the future as leaders, primarily grow their own leadership. Mr. Wright understood that in large measure when he created the Fellowship. Mrs. Wright understood it as she pushed to get the School accredited. Those at Taliesin understand it today. My being here is just one example.

How do you define organic architecture?

I will leave that to the scholars and critics. I do not believe it needs a "Websteresque" definition. It's best understood as an architecture in which design is based on ideas rather than intuition, popular theories, or a fashion of the moment. It's an architecture built upon a series of principles and tenets first espoused by Mr. Wright that continue to be explored and expanded by others, including the architects of our own practice. Principles which have to do with the propriety of place—Mr. Wright's "of the hill, not on the hill" philosophy. It is an architecture committed to be humane in harmony with its physical environment and cultural environment; it embodies the fresh spirit of its time, its place, and the people it serves. It is timeless in design, where "form and function are one," offering all beauty and integrity.

What would happen if you started calling yourself an organic architect?

Internally my partners and I have talked quite a bit about this issue. There are some who feel we ought to just drop the word organic. Bruce and I have discussions about this all the time. Bruce would like to see us drop the organic descriptor, and I tease him when I say, "Bruce, that's just because you want to corner all the publications on organic architecture." Seriously, I think it's a significant differentiation of our philosophical base and direction in our exploration of architecture that no one else can claim with the legitimacy that we can claim. We are going to keep calling ourselves "organic" architects.

But can someone not trained in it here ever gain legitimacy as an organic architect?

Absolutely. Today an architect comes to my mind immediately; his name is Santiago Calatrava. Fantastic work. I do not believe any Taliesin-prepared architect wouldn't say this man is expanding and growing the ideas of organic architecture.

The person charged with responsibility for cultivating a favorable image of Taliesin in the mind of the public is Suzette Lucas. She, too, came to the Frank Lloyd Wright Foundation as a result of prior connections. While employed at the Scottsdale Center for the Arts, she was the project administrator for the "Frank Lloyd Wright in the Realm of Ideas" exhibition that toured the country from 1985 through 1991. Around the midpoint, she proposed to the Center that she continue in that position half-time. That gave her an opportunity to accept employment at Taliesin in "a very undefined position," also half-time. I asked her about her early days with the Foundation.

SUZETTE: They were just starting to hire what they considered "outside staff" at that point. [That] probably means lots of things to lots of people in the Fellowship, and it probably also means lots of things to those of us who end up being considered outside staff—people who did not come up through the apprenticeship program. I started using the term "nonresident staff" to apply to people who were hired from the public or professional domain, so to speak.

. . . One of the things I quickly learned—and I think it's something that everyone who ever came here has learned—was that, especially back in 1988 . . . there was very little clarity in anyone's mind of the difference between the Fellowship, Taliesin West, and the Frank Lloyd Wright Foundation. . . . I think everybody who has come to work here, especially in the early days when nonresident people were first being hired, came with the idea that they were coming to work for the Foundation. Most of the resident people, I think, thought we were coming to work for the Fellowship. That's a division I'm not sure is still clear in many people's minds.

How did you gain acceptance by the Fellowship for yourself?

Well, I don't think gaining acceptance by the Fellowship was ever necessarily a goal. I really, truly did think I was coming to work for the Frank Lloyd Wright Foundation. I had worked with some people here; I had worked with Bruce Pfeiffer in the Archives in getting things together for the exhibition. Whenever the exhibition would open in any of the seven cities where it was touring, Bruce would always be there. I was doing a lot of contact with the press and he would be the public speaker, so he and I spent a fair amount of time together and I had a pretty good idea what the Archives was about. I had worked with Dick Carney a certain amount. Tony Puttnam was the person who was doing the exhibition design; I worked with him. Tom Casey had been involved in it. So I knew some of those people.

I don't think they really knew why they were hiring me. When I first came . . . I was half-time for the Foundation, but I was physically here full time. I did all the work from here. Everybody was leaving to go to Wisconsin. They parked me in the office that had been Dick Carney's. Dick said, "Go through any of the files you want to over the summer and kind of get a handle on things." It was "Here you are." . . . At some point, they asked if I would "kind of" get involved in the tour program. . . .

Pretty much what I did those initial first few months was try to figure out what was going on, try to define things in my own mind and then, basically, I think by Fall I had made up a list of things that I felt the Foundation needed to do regarding PR—

community/constituency relations and outreach. . . . [It] took me a lot of time to figure out what this place was about. They had made various attempts at fund-raising. . . .

I decided that one of the first things that needed to be done from the Foundation standpoint as an institution that wanted to get public support was to be able to articulate what the Foundation was. I came up with a list by the Fall of that year of certain things I felt we needed to do, certain things in upgrading the tour program, certain things with marketing. At that time I think the tour program was charging five dollars a person, and those in the Fellowship were complaining about too many people, and so I made suggestions to increase admissions.

Is the tour program still yours?

Yes, and that's gone through a lot of transitions. At times I've had tour managers who wouldn't speak to me. Personnel management is something that they're not real adept at handling, because the Fellowship has a peculiar way of dealing as a community that doesn't necessarily translate real well into dealing with staff. Too often they will take any kind of conflict that develops from a professional standpoint and treat that conflict as a personal issue. If somebody's not doing their job they'll treat it as if "why can't everybody just get along?" And if someone's responsible for an area and is looking to have results, well, the Fellowship is not very result-oriented. I think they are very process-oriented, experience-oriented, and the outcome of those experiences oftentimes, to me, seems to be irrelevant to them. Oftentimes I have felt they are living very much on a day-to-day basis: "We (the Fellowship) want to do this because it will be a neat experience or it will broaden us as human beings," which are very noble goals. But when you translate that into an organization that I would expect to have goals as an institution, then you have a very difficult situation.

So, do you think the Fellowship members see you now as working for the Fellowship, or do they understand the distinction between the Foundation and the Fellowship being one part of it?

I think there are certain people in the Fellowship who clearly understand the difference between the Foundation and the Fellowship. Then it's a matter of who wants to accept that difference and who wants to ignore that difference. So, it runs the gamut, depending on which person you're going to talk to and which day and what is convenient for them at the time, too.

Do you participate in Fellowship activities like Thanksgiving dinner and the Easter celebration?

No. . . . I did come to one or two Easters, but I also feel that probably, in the long run, my natural inclination no matter where I have worked has been not to particularly be that social. I think . . . it's been probably very beneficial that that was my natural inclination, because I really do believe in order to be somewhat effective as a professional [you must] establish the fact that there are professional responsibilities and there are personal kinds of things that go on. I would say, because of having traveled with the exhibition—and I did spend a lot of time in Wisconsin—I do know many of the people in the Fellowship very well. . . . I like individually most of the people in the Fellowship. As far as individuals are concerned, if they were people that I happened to meet other than having worked here, I would consider myself very fortunate to have met them because they are interesting, intelligent human beings who are just wonderful to know. As a group, as a person trying to work here, they drive me to absolute distraction.

As our conversation progressed, it was apparent that Suzette, who cares deeply about Taliesin, wished to be direct and candid in her comments about the Fellowship. She told me that there would be no surprises for anyone in them, since she had not been reluctant to say the same things face-to-face. I asked about her reasons for frustration with the Fellowship.

Well, for lots of reasons. I think they're very difficult to work with because they are not very open to any kinds of suggestions. They take any kind of suggestion regarding how professional things might be handled or how the institution might function better as an organization as some kind of personal attack on them. And if you say, "This isn't working," they don't want to say, "How can we make it work better?" They become very defensive; they fall back on the excuse, "Well, they're Fellowship members so it's perfectly okay." . . .

You know, just because I want to do my job effectively, if you expect me to bring in fifty- or seventy-five thousand dollars a year from site rentals, then I'm trying to meet that goal and being criticized for meeting it.

You have seen a lot of changes in the last nine years. You came in '86?

I came in '88. I started working with them in '86.

That was shortly after Mrs. Wright's death, and it took the Fellowship a while to adjust to that. They probably in the last few years have been trying to set their own course a little bit more.

I think in the last few years, actually, they've gotten more entrenched in some ways. There are certain elements of the Fellowship who are very much hell-bent on keeping this their private home, and they really don't care about the long-term interests of the Frank Lloyd Wright Foundation other than perhaps operating a very small school. I think there are a lot of them who don't really care too much about Frank Lloyd Wright and the Frank Lloyd Wright legacy. I really think there is a very strong element in the Fellowship that feels that the Fellowship—and I've heard people in the Fellowship say, "The most important thing Frank Lloyd Wright ever did was start the Taliesin Fellowship, that he started this wonderful way of life and got us all living together out here, and that's what is important." I've heard people say if all his buildings "collapsed to the ground and all the Archives was lost that wouldn't matter as long as the Fellowship survived." . . .

Are there rewards in your job? Do you like it?

Yes, I've had a lot of rewards. I love my job in the sense that I love the product, the product being Frank Lloyd Wright. I love the fact that I've had the opportunity to learn a lot about Frank Lloyd Wright. When I was at the Center and first got involved in the exhibit (and I was working like crazy down there because getting the exhibit ready to hit the road was just one aspect of what I was doing), I was probably working at least twelve hours a day every day from 8:30, 9:00 in the morning and getting home at 9:30, 10:00 at night and a lot of weekends and stuff, and I'd find myself sitting at home late at night reading a book on Frank Lloyd Wright.

That has been a wonderful opportunity to be working with a subject matter that I'm fascinated with. The fact that it is a national/international organization has been lots of fun, working with people all over the country and all over the world. And being able to help people who are interested in doing something related to the Frank Lloyd Wright legacy and being able to respond to their needs. I'm pleased we got the membership program going. . . . I decided that if we did a publication, Frank Lloyd Wright enthusiasts would be able to get a magazine, and that has been fairly successful.

Are you a native of this area?

No, I'm originally from Pennsylvania, and I had a pretty eclectic background. My Dad was a builder; I grew up around the building business. I knew who Frank Lloyd Wright was when I was a kid. My one son is a builder now. The environment we live in has always been something that I've been very interested in, so working with that product is something good. I think that, long-term, Taliesin West is particularly significant, because the Archives are here and the Foundation theoretically is the international resource for preserving the legacy. I think there are a lot of people out there in the world now who [have] just started seeing the Foundation as key to the Frank Lloyd Wright legacy where, I think, that's been an issue over the years.

A lot of people looked out here and said, "Who are these squatters living on the land?" because they [the Fellowship] didn't articulate a mission other than their own self-centered one: "We're superior human beings living out here, being creative artists in this wonderful lifestyle. Isn't that great?" I think that's a real tragedy for the Fellowship. I don't know why they have that, oftentimes as a group. They kind of close the circle when they talk about the Fellowship and become defensive. They have wonderful knowledge, experiences, and things like that; they all want recognition in their own funny way and they don't give much recognition to each other.

Suzette offered this final comment:

The obvious question might be, "If the Fellowship is so dysfunctional as a group, how did it survive so long?" Clearly, many communes don't survive a long time.

It can't be overlooked that one key reason the Fellowship has survived when other communes haven't is because it is well endowed in many ways. First, the Fellowship has the two properties—Taliesin and Taliesin West—to use as their homes and as a source of revenue (i.e. tours, etc.) to advance the Fellowship lifestyle. The architectural firm has the name "Frank Lloyd Wright" to use for marketing purposes, etc.

The Foundation has always been in serious financial difficulty as an institution.

But it survives in a large part because they are able to use the assets of the Foundation to do so.

The Fellowship, because it is the Board of the Foundation, has been able to make decisions that advanced the Fellowship life, even if the institutional goals of the Foundation were not being advanced. Perhaps this is even why there is so little agreement about what the institutional goals of the Foundation are.

Indeed, I believe the Fellowship has been able to be very "idealistic" in pursuing the "Fellowship life" because the Fellowship has not had to face the financial realities that most individuals—and probably most communes—must deal with. The *Fellowship* survives because they have the assets of the *Foundation* behind them, and they put survival of the Taliesin *Fellowship* as their first priority.

Responsibility for providing leadership in turning conflicting viewpoints into creative solutions has recently been handed to H. Nicholas Muller, known as Nick. The Frank Lloyd Wright Foundation Board elected him to the position of President and CEO of the Foundation in November 1995 and announced his appointment publicly in February 1996. He began to work with the Foundation around mid-June, when he became a full-time resident employee. He lives at Taliesin West where the Fellowship and the Foundation work in the winter, and in Wisconsin he commutes daily from his residence in Monona, Wisconsin.

Nick's association with the Fellowship began in 1987, when, as director of the State Historical Society of Wisconsin, he suggested to Governor Tommy G. Thompson that he appoint a commission to study the preservation of Taliesin. Governor Thompson agreed, and Nick came to Taliesin West with Secretary James R. Klauser and Nick Hurtgen, an aide to Secretary Klauser, to talk with the Fellowship about participating in such a commission. That was his first visit to Taliesin West. Ensuing events, as Nick describes them, helped to lay the foundation, not only for preservation of an architectural treasure, but for the future relationship between him and Taliesin. Here is a partial account of the events.

NICK: The Commission, in fact, became reality. It met a number of times, and it produced a report, which called for three major actions: the establishment of a Wisconsin-based corporation that would assume responsibility for the preservation at Taliesin; opening [of] a visitation program for public education, if you will, to open Taliesin to the public, a recommendation that also involved the construction of a visitor center; and the change of the ownership of Taliesin from the Frank Lloyd Wright Foundation to this independent corporation, a recommendation which has died. The independent corporation was established . . . and shortly won 501(c)(3) status.

The Frank Lloyd Wright Foundation Board includes many members of the Fellowship; they represent the Foundation on the Taliesin Preservation Commission (TPC) Board. [The Foundation Board] provided me some insights about Taliesin, and at the same time it provided them a sense of how Nick Muller operated and whether or not I had achieved sufficient trust in 1995 to bring me into the operation.

Nick Muller

The specific set of events which triggered [my] thinking about leaving the State Historical Society in Wisconsin to work with the Foundation came in the late spring and early summer of 1995 when Dick Carney began working through an episode of lung cancer. He served as the managing trustee of the Frank Lloyd Wright Foundation. Its chairman, Lee Cohen, with whom I had developed a good working relationship and for whom I had a great deal of respect, was himself dealing with bone cancer, which gave every evidence of being terminal, as, indeed, it proved to be. From the perspective of Wisconsin, the Frank Lloyd Wright Foundation could lose both Lee Cohen and Dick Carney; I judged it badly in need of leadership with administrative experience, as did a consultant hired by the Foundation.

During the summer of 1995 . . . I called him at Taliesin on a Saturday evening and told him I had given it a good deal of thought and if they were interested, I would consider taking this one on. . . . Dick and Lee and I talked a number of times. Dick gradually began to talk with all members of the Fellowship. I met with the Fellowship in Spring Green in September. Carol and I came to Taliesin West in November, during which time the Frank Lloyd Wright Foundation Board elected me CEO and President, contingent on Dick's and my arriving at a contract. We accomplished this without any real difficulty.

Nick then summarized his pre-Taliesin career. He had taught history briefly at Dartmouth College and at a Canadian University. When he moved to the University of Vermont, they asked him to teach a course in Vermont history. Lack of good resources made that an interesting challenge, and it opened the door to excellent teaching, research, and public service opportunities.

I began to realize that history had a huge role to play in public policy. History as I had originally seen it and the way I had originally learned at graduate school and taught it to undergraduates, included so much more. That got me engaged in history as a part of public policy formation. In 1978 I left the University of Vermont to become president of a school in transition. I loved academic administration and the building of Colby-Sawyer College. . . . Still, I wanted a platform to push for perspectives of the past in the formation of public policy. When the State Historical Society of Wisconsin first approached me about becoming the director, I did not really think they were serious. I was wrong. I threw my hat in the ring and had the good fortune to receive the appointment, and I worked there from October 1985 to mid-1996.

I regarded anything that had to do with the heritage of Wisconsin as fair game, and Taliesin, which stands high among the most important buildings (you might argue whether the state capitol ranks as high) I found as part of my venue and in need of attention. . . .

I take pride in my ten years [with the State Historical Society], but it seemed to me that the legacy of Frank Lloyd Wright and Olgivanna Lloyd Wright certainly merited Nick Muller's energy. If I had an opportunity to make that legacy even more solidly based so that it would remain for decades to come, if not many generations to come, I should make the effort.

What have you discovered since your arrival as a full-time person there?

I have discovered two basic things: one, that what I anticipated would occupy a good deal of my time has proved inaccurate; and secondly, how the power and the value and the importance and the enormous potential of this whole enterprise amounts to much more than I had ever dreamed.

Let me start with the second observation—or revelation. Preparing myself, I had begun to read more about the history of the Foundation, including materials from the Archives. I had begun to delve into the intellectual background of the Taliesin apprentice program, which has become the School, especially the ideas expressed in a variety of early documents. Observing the structure of the institution in 1997, and comparing it to 1932, I find it uncanny how much the educational philosophy remains, how little it has changed in sixty-five years and how successful [it has been].

We left the North Central Association exit interview yesterday, February 26, with a long list of institutional strengths, a list of institutional concerns only four long, and the announcement that they would recommend to the Commission a seven-year period before the next re-accreditation visit. I thought this confirmed what I had learned. . . .

I have lived through a lot of exit interviews, on both sides of the table, and I have never heard the people at the exit interview applaud the team—literally an ovation. A very warm feeling went both ways. We will wait to see what they say in their report, but I think they will indicate that the Frank Lloyd Wright School of Architecture has the potential, because of its strengths, if it plays its cards well, to become the "numero uno" school of architecture in the United States, teaching the nontheoretical learning by doing program.

What are some of the other discoveries you have made?

Well, I do not know if "discovery" is exactly the right word, but certainly the value I attach to the Foundation and its programs has become much higher. I had not understood fully the integration among the Fellowship, the firm, and the School. If any one of them is in trouble, the others are also in serious trouble. Without good work the architectural firm provides no place for the students in this kind of educational environment to learn architecture. If the students do not have sufficient ability or commitment, the way the firm works with apprentice help, it will not generate sufficient throughput. The Fellowship, based on the relationship of architecture to the other aspects of living, provides the continuity to make an integrated educational community work.

What emerged during the 1930s, which I do not think Mr. and Mrs. Wright fully anticipated—how the apprentice program would work—has endured. What they expected, as I read their prospectus, was that apprentices would come to Taliesin and learn and then leave. They expected to have people they called "foremen" who would be more or less permanent resident instructors. I do not think they thought they would develop those "foremen" from their own apprentices, but that is what happened. Many talented apprentices found Taliesin the most exciting place that a professional could find to work. They decided to stay and marry and raise children; they became the Senior Fellowship.

Neither the senior fellows nor the members of the nonresident staff see the latter as rescuers of the Fellowship or the Frank Lloyd Wright Foundation. All of them recognize that only by working together to perpetuate the legacies they treasure and the hopes they share can the future be promising. If the nonresident staff members are servants of the Fellowship's vision, so are the fellows themselves.

Notes

1. ALA is the American Library Association; an MLS degree is a Master of Library Science.

2. John has since retired from Beloit.

3. Getty interns are supported by the Getty Center for the Study of Art and Humanities.

4. Robert McCarter, *Frank Lloyd Wright-Architect* (New York: Phaidon Press, 1997).

5. The late Lee Cohen served as cochairman of the Board of Trustees of the Frank Lloyd Wright Foundation from May 1994 until his death in October 1995. Mr. Cohen had been trained as an architect and architectural engineer and headed a structural steel fabricating firm based in Chicago before moving to Arizona, where he owned an art gallery and provided leadership in cultural projects.

11

The Fourth Challenge:
"It Will Take Dedicated People"

W hat is to be the future of the Taliesin Fellowship?

That question is never far below the surface in conversations with senior fellows. More questions surround it, some spoken openly: If the Fellowship continues, what can be preserved from its treasured past? How can it distinguish between attempts to re-create the past and efforts to create a new future? How can the Fellowship accommodate the forces of change—or should it merely resist them? If accommodation is the choice, can the requirements of new times be satisfied without destroying the best of the old? In another vein, what will be the effects on community life of the growing tourism and other business enterprises? And more pointedly, if the Fellowship cannot be what it has been, should it perhaps be allowed to fade away, rich in memory and untainted by compromise? Or can it be reshaped and revitalized by finding new ways to carry on established missions and traditions?

If there is concern inside the Fellowship, there is puzzlement outside of it. How long, observers ask, can it last? We know the fate of other communities, each as distinctive in its own way as the Taliesin Fellowship. The Oneida Community, for example, more or less flourished from 1849 to 1880. By then it had aroused suspicion and hostility among its neighbors and its charismatic leader, John Humphrey Noyes, had fled to Canada. Internal discord reigned. Rather than disappear or disintegrate, however, it became the Oneida Community, Ltd., a joint-stock company. The business enterprises established by the community continued to prosper, and Noyes' son and grandson remained in charge for another hundred years. But the old community, held together by property owned in common and unorthodox practices known as complex marriage and mutual criticism, was gone.[1]

Between the 1770s and the 1820s, the Shakers (formally, the United Society of Believers in Christ's Second Appearing) grew from a handful of members to a total of about four thousand *residing in sixteen communities. Before long, however, the Shaker story became one of relentless decline, a consequence of internal controversies and commitment to celibacy as a way of life, among other things. An estimated 17,000 men and women joined the Society at one time or another, but as the numbers dwindled, several of the communities, according to historian Stephen Stein, "became the foundation for a vast array of commercial undertakings, many of which were linked only indirectly to the United Society." By the 1960s, he says, it "was in jeopardy of being swamped by a rising tide of commercial enterprises."* [2] *Desperate to raise cash as membership plummeted, several of the Shaker communities turned to the sale of furniture and other objects. Today, some of the reconstructed locations, such as Pleasant Hill in Kentucky, are popular tourist attractions.*

The Society of True Inspiration, with roots going back to 1817 in Germany, prospered as a communal society at Amana, Iowa, from the 1850s until the 1920s. In 1932, in what is known as the Great Decision, the members concluded that the forces of change in the world surrounding them were irresistible and irreversible. The vast majority of the nine hundred members voting favored becoming a stock company organized for profit and abandoning community ownership of property. It would be a mistake, however, to conclude that this meant the end of the Amana community. Donald Pitzer reports that when he stated in a conference paper in 1981 that the Amanas no longer fit into communal history after 1932, a community descendant asked why he had reached that conclusion. "In essence," he recalls, "she said, 'We are still a community. We still share common concerns. We still care deeply for one another. We still practice the faith of our religious movement. We still worship together. We still have an Amana Society.'" [3]

None of these communities, or any of the others that have come and gone, provides a model for the Taliesin Fellowship. While the commercial enterprises of some of them might be likened to the Taliesin Architects and the Frank Lloyd Wright Foundation's tour and licensing programs, none were integrated also with a distinctive school, nor did they possess priceless archives, nor were they housed in architectural gems like Taliesin and Taliesin West. Yet, their passing from the scene or their transformation in character and purpose serves as a reminder that perpetuating the Taliesin Fellowship in forms resembling those that have prevailed so far will be a daunting challenge.

Contemporary communities, including those established on a non-religious basis, offer further evidence that change is endemic in communal societies. For example, Twin Oaks, located near Louisa Virginia, has abandoned the behavioral principles and practices that inspired its founding in 1967. The kind of community advocated by psychologist B. F. Skinner in his novel Walden Two *simply could not prosper. Kat Kinkade, one of the founding members of Twin Oaks, has described the community's vicissitudes in* Is It Utopia Yet? *and the Twin Oaks newsletter reports on continuing adaptations dictated by changing circumstances.* [4]

The Camphill movement provides another example of the changing circumstances and directions of communal societies. This movement, founded in 1940 by Karl König on principles advanced by his fellow Austrian, philosopher Rudolph Steiner, has sought so far to work principally with mentally and socially handicapped people. It operates at several locations in the United States and at many more in England. Camphill leaders observe that the movement's "very name suggests its openness to change and its history over fifty years is witness to this. New challenges are always being presented: many are taken up either by new developments in existing centres or by the founding of new communities." [5]

In looking to the future, the Taliesin Fellowship recognizes that three major daunting challenges have preceded the one it faces now. The first, of course, was to establish and maintain the Fellowship through several trying decades—decades of Depression and war. Charismatic leaders and hardworking allies carried it through. The second challenge came in 1959 with the death of Mr. Wright. Then, however, his widow and his apprentices were there to keep it going. The death of Mrs. Wright in 1985 brought the third challenge. Her influence on those who had known and admired her persisted, and Mr. Wright's presence was still felt by those who had known and worked with him. Most of the senior fellows of the 1980s and 1990s knew the founders. They have been able to transmit their ideals and principles. But who will do that when they are gone? How will heirs of the Wrights' legacy meet the challenge they now face?

While concerns about the future exist, there seems to be a sense that life will go on and on. It brings to mind the surprise experienced when Wright died in 1959. Although he was approaching his ninety-second birthday, so powerful a presence was he, and so vigorous right to the end, that they could not anticipate the prospect of his departure. Even though he has been gone for forty years, for some of the fellows he remains at their side to this day, as the conversations in this book reveal.

There seems to be greater readiness among the nonresident staff to speak forthrightly about the future, perhaps because their appointments were occasioned in part to ensure that the Foundation and its component parts, including the Fellowship, all will have a future. Yet, they know, as do the fellows, that the future of the Fellowship will largely be determined by the fellows themselves.

Several of the fellows spoke about changing times and what the changes mean for the Fellowship. When I asked Dick Carney, for example, to identify two or three actions that he thought needed to be taken to lay a foundation for the future, his response reflected a concern that most CEOs would share, for persons in such positions know that every institution needs funds to have a future.

DICK: Well, I think we have to get to the point that we can raise funds. We haven't really been successful at fund-raising up until now, because the decision-making process at Taliesin is one of consensus and it takes a long time to make decisions. And outsiders haven't been willing to start giving funds to a consensus organization. So we have to really learn how to get a faster decision-making process if we're going to raise funds. I think until we can raise funds we're not going to achieve what we need in order to make the School a lot better right now, . . . to make the Archives better, to make the library better. In order to accomplish everything we need, we need to be a fund-raising organization, and we haven't been able to achieve that. . . . We're trying our best to make it happen, but yesterday, for instance, in the Executive Committee meeting, we were split five to five on an issue to help with the fund-raising. We couldn't move beyond that, and I'm afraid that will delay fund-raising for a year or so.

Within a month of that 1994 conversation, the fellows participated in a retreat conducted by professional consultants. The consultants recommended that, consistent with his wishes, the process for recruiting a successor to Dick Carney as CEO should begin immediately; that the Foundation should "undertake an aggressive long-range planning process designed to clarify and document a unified vision for the foundation's future"; and that the Foundation should "develop positioning and case statements to respond to institutional priorities" and "strengthen the focus of the development function to generate increased levels of support." That is what it has been trying to do.

If Mr. and Mrs. Wright aged well, so do the members of the Fellowship. One cannot but be impressed by the vigor of so many of them in their seventies and beyond. I asked Effi Casey if there was concern about the aging of the Fellowship and the lack of replenishment by new blood.

EFFI: Actually, I don't have great concern about the aging of the Fellowship. I have a concern that we manage to separate the personality of Mr. and Mrs. Wright from the vision, the thoughts and the ideas that need to go forward, because I think you cannot or should not keep the personalities [of the past] alive. That's a different chapter. But what I believe can really be propelled forward is the whole idea of organic architecture. Not just as a way of life, but it is life, and it has to filter into everything we do. With this underlying question: what is the nature of this, what is the nature of that? And really instill in young people a wonder about the order in nature and make them lifelong learners. I know that term is so overused, but you want to instill something in them that keeps them going, and that cannot be in describing the personality, I think.

So, when you ask me about the aging people, I think they have lived a beautiful arch and rich arch with these founders, and it's a natural decline of that. So, I honor and respect what they have had and what connects them to the past. That is so rich . . . and in some part I was still part of it since I knew Mrs. Wright. But, I want to make it possible for others who show excitement about this idea and the ability to see what we're after to join the effort to bring it forward.

What brings *you* here? Obviously, something attracted you enough to want to come back and dig a little deeper. I think there are many, many [such] people, and to think that you have to only grow out from within is, in my mind, a downright insult to Frank Lloyd Wright. Did I have to live with Bach to know how he was to be interpreted? Did you have to live with Aristotle or Tolstoy? These geniuses can stand for themselves; they don't need to be interpreted. . . . [You do not need] little guidebooks on how to use Frank Lloyd Wright or how to read Tolstoy. I don't think you do. Sometimes I feel that some of us think that we at Taliesin are the only ones capable of defining what organic architecture is all about. I think that's wrong.

We need to discover our *own* vision for the future, live it and share it, always infused by a deep respect for nature, spirit, and transcendence. I am confident that we *can* succeed, but I am also aware that we have the potential to kill any kind of living future.

What I meant by the aging was not the aging of ideas or anything like that, but there are people who were once very active and aggressive younger people in the Fellowship who are now stepping to the sidelines more and more, necessarily because of health and age. Between your entry and the present very few people have come into the Fellowship.

Surely that is a concern. I don't know what gives me that confidence, but I'm not as panic-stricken as some other people might be, because basically I think if we can keep open enough, people will come in. And they are coming in. Ari, for instance, has gone away and comes back. I want to concentrate on him because he has been away and wants to join. He knows why he wants to be back. I find that stronger than somebody who we desperately want to hold onto after they graduate. I would send everybody away. I would say, "Go out. Ventilate yourself and then know why you want to rejoin here." I think it's stronger.

I asked David Dodge where he thought the Fellowship would be in ten years.

DAVID: I hope we can maintain some of the intermediary ages now, the more advanced apprentices, and perhaps bring back some of those that have gone out and practiced and would be attracted to our office . . . that we could afford to give them a livelihood here. Then I think we can be a nucleus of a very creative organization working with this organic ideal.

I'm not sure they're going to commit their lives completely. I think that we're going to see many more [arrangements like mine]. Ari already wants to do something similar to what Mrs. Wright said I could do. She said I could spend three months out of the year in Europe and work here nine months of the year. Instead of going to Wisconsin I go to Europe, but I take my work with me. That's giving me a perspective, and I feel that's necessary. For me it's too much just to be with the same people, the same group, all that time. I enjoy the change, and I can come back refreshed and ready to go. Until I come back and find everything turned upside down and not in as good shape as when we left, and that gets to be distressing. But, those are things we're working on. And, of course, the fact that there is change, it's alive. It's when there's no change, then we have to ask: is this thing functioning the way it's supposed to? Or is it dead? I think it is better that there is change. Well, organic nature is alive; it's a living thing.

. . . The Fellowship must stay active and alive. Mrs. Wright was a great asset to Taliesin—and Mr. Wright, too—but they wanted to hear music made by the Fellowship. We don't have that prominence to help keep our evenings together, so it's a little bit of a forced thing now when we try to have a musical evening, musical get-togethers. We haven't found the excuse for doing that that fits with all of the instant culture that one can push buttons and have these days.

. . . The organic ideal, you see, was and is the only real cement that keeps Taliesin together. We can try all sorts of other things, but it's that organic ideal. I find it much better, I can work better, where I have the backup of Taliesin, but I need also the space *from* Taliesin. So, it works very well going to Europe and coming back again, but when I'm back here I need the assistance—both spiritually and physically—with the work I'm doing.

Frances Nemtin offered another perspective:

FRANCES: I think the most difficult time is ahead. As we see things changing so much and we're anxious to preserve the spirit of Taliesin, we cannot go back to the simplicity of the early days . . . and how to keep hold of the Fellowship feeling and the creative spirit, which is harder and harder to maintain in the face of the professionals in this field who are hired, who haven't our traditions . . . and all the jargon of the bureaucratic mind, which is in the preservation process. How to keep our own sense of our mission intact.

We want to keep a sense of excitement. That's going to be the hard part; that's one that's going to be very important. I'm very much involved in and close to it because Stephen is on all the boards and is very outspoken, very clear-thinking, a very perceptive person. So I know what he hears, and I know what's involved. He doesn't tell me anything that I don't need to know. He keeps many confidences, which I don't ask him for. It's a very serious and important time right now, and I'm concerned.

Where does Stephen Nemtin see the Fellowship going?

STEPHEN: It has two directions to go, and it's not determined yet which direction it's going to go. What I'm pressing for at the moment is that what I call the founding members of the Fellowship—those members who had significant years with both Mr. and Mrs. Wright, and I don't include myself in that because I didn't have those significant years with Mr. Wright—they need to get together and decide how they see. Not only how they see, but how they're going to permit the development of a new Fellowship. Until that happens, it's going to struggle along in this semi-, quasi-direction that's trying to have direction.

That's very important, because for the most part there certainly is the recognition that we must interject new ways in how we do things, but most situations are governed by the way it *was* done, whether it's admitted to or not. We haven't developed new ways in which we really live our life and express our culture. The format that we use is the same format. We may have lessened the frequency, but it's the same format. So there's something really missing.

I think that only when you create a vacuum does something come in to fill it. That's why it's not really happening yet; that's why we don't have a real influx of young people taking over because the vacuum is not fully there. It's going to happen. There's always one or many voices coming in and modulating the circumstance so that any individual doesn't really have a chance to explore other ways of doing something.

Can you see perpetuation of the communal life?

It's going to continue as a vital community with new ways to do things or it's going to become totally institutionalized and, for the most part, a place to come and visit whether as a tourist or as a student or as an architect or as an historian, but without the central vitality. And then it will be dead for the most part. It's not that it can't carry on in that format. It can, but people who have not lived here and simply do not have the feel of what it is all about can't step in and just bring in business methodologies of the day, which is happening to us. We're going through all the nonsense that it seems every institution is going through, with strategic plans and visioning and all that—all that stuff, all that methodology.

What we need here are the creative people who will bring in the new music we're going to play, will bring in the new theater or the new architecture but from the artist's perspective. Because it's the artist that brings in the new life. I don't see it happening otherwise. And that's what this place needs. It has to have spontaneity again.

Can you help create that?

That's what I'm trying to do. . . . My framework is what I do architecturally because I'm focusing on it, and I think I am showing a new direction, particularly now in what I'm doing.

The architectural business seems to be up quite a bit.

Yes, we had a very good year in '94, but also that year is tempered by Monona Terrace. There's this duality that goes on constantly. The work of Frank Lloyd Wright is still as contemporary as it was when he died, yet the ability to build it becomes very, very difficult and very, very costly. Fortunately for us, Monona Terrace was a large part of our success in '94. We have yet, though, to truly generate our own identity as architects within Taliesin Architects or as individuals.

As our conversation concluded, I asked Stephen if he had any final point he wished to make.

In studying this community, I think . . . it's only natural that the focus is always on Frank Lloyd Wright, and I think that's a mistake. Frank Lloyd Wright has made his place in history, and it will be for all time. We've got to make our mark. . . . The reason, for me, that we don't have a great influx of students and clients at the moment knocking our doors down is because we have not shown sufficiently what it's all about for the contemporary world. That's what we must do if we're going to regenerate ourselves from within. Otherwise, it's all going to happen from without. I don't see that as a very bright prospect.

If you had a postcard that you could mail to prospective students, what would you say on it?

That's difficult because I don't send out postcards, and I don't sum it up in a few words. . . . I would say, "This place has all the potential to have all of the excitement that it had during Mr. Wright's lifetime. It has all of that potential. Come make it happen." That might be it. We can impart and the [apprentices] can experience the totality of this whole thing, for that's where all the excitement is, in the totality of it.

Bruce Pfeiffer expressed another point of view:

BRUCE: I think we have to redefine what the Fellowship is. That was very interesting in this retreat we had last week. We could define the mission of the Foundation, of the School, of the Archives, of the Firm, but no one could define what the Fellowship was or its mission. As I said to Kay, "The Fellowship is the old codgers like you and me who are about to die." That's what the Fellowship is. There's got to be a new definition, and it can't just be the in-house people who came in here and devoted their lives to it, because we devoted our lives to it because we had two extremely powerful people. As iron filings being drawn to a magnet we were drawn to them.

I would live in a tent with a wet sleeping bag in rainy season because I knew the Wrights were going through the same thing. It was leaking on their beds also. We all were undergoing the same hardships that were somehow eliminated by these fantastic personalities. That's gone, and you can't say to new apprentices, "Now, Mr. Wright said this and Mrs. Wright said that," because you're just quoting scripture—which means nothing to them. So the Fellowship can't be what we were. Those of us who are not going to be here much longer are going to have to find something else that inspires people to be here. I think it's important that there always be a living community here, because if there isn't it would become like Monticello. I saw Monticello last month. It was lovely but very depressing. There's this charming home where there should be activity.

. . . I think that there should always be a community living here. Community is a bad word because it always has strange connotations, you know. The commune life. Of course, that's exactly what we are. It's just that words have meanings you don't want them to have. But I wish the Fellowship would expand to accept also the people who don't live here—not participating in as much a way as those who do live here, but just as a nomenclature.

You mean ones who have been apprentices and are now out on their own?

No, I'm speaking of people like my staff here. They could say, "We are members of the Taliesin Fellowship." Like a club, like an organization, rather than just being employees.

That must be a point of tension.

Well, it was discussed in the last retreat. We brought it up and people seemed more open to it than they have been in the past. The old guard is dying out, as it should, but there should be a continuum. I think the thing that would inspire people to want to come and be here would just simply be the atmosphere.

That obviously has to be a concern to people like you who care so deeply.

Yes, well you see, we lost a generation, and I think it was partly the fault of the Wrights. Mrs. Wright made no attempt to keep any contact with anybody who ever left the Fellowship. And [she] saw [them] as treacherous; they betrayed us. It wasn't until 1987 and the reunion that we began to try and get back the people who had passed through the Fellowship and develop ties with our alumni. But alumni are not the solution; the solution is to find some way of attracting people who want to be part of this organization.

The financial picture is so entirely different than it was years ago. These kids expect something—and yet some of them don't. There are people who [would work] just to live here. One of the architects we hired was a former apprentice. We probably pay him much less than he has repaid us with, but he just loves sitting in that room and working. He loves walking around these buildings, and he should be made to feel he's a member of Taliesin, not that he's an employee.

They're all worried. When Dick and Johnny and I were in Czechoslovakia two years ago, we stopped to meet an old draftsman of Mr. Wright's, and Johnny turned to Dick and me and said, "You boys have to start looking for successors." Well, successor is the wrong word, because I'm not going to find a successor. I've had almost half a century of experience in this material, so it's in the blood, you know. You don't find a successor to that.

Oscar, on the other hand, has worked very closely with me for a decade, and he knows more about the mechanics of the Archives than I do now, because I've spent most of the last four or five years intentionally writing. It's only natural that he would come into my position if something happens to me.

Tony Puttnam's comment about the future was a practical one. I asked him if, after living independently while supervising the construction of Monona Terrace in Madison, it was going to be hard to go back to a small apartment at Taliesin.

TONY: Well, I've had [a different kind of life] before, too; this is not my first experience. I think everyone agrees that more independent living, whatever that means—on the grounds or off the grounds—is an essential part of our future plan.

As recorded in the previous chapter, the process of recruiting a successor to Dick Carney as CEO of the Foundation resulted in the appointment of Nick Muller to that position. Much of my conversation with Nick dealt with his plans for the future. I asked him what he saw as his role in helping the Fellowship create a future?

NICK: Clearly one of my roles, and not the only one, is to help build the viability of the Fellowship. . . . The 1990s were the first decade in which the Fellowship did not have either Mr. or Mrs. Wright to lead. They have entered a new era, and I intend to work with the Fellowship toward ends that may preserve the notion of life in the Fellowship, including modifying the way one accesses it. It remains true that the only route into the Fellowship follows the route of an apprentice or becoming the spouse of one. I think there are a number of individuals, committed to this philosophy of a living and learning community, coming into this organization who can bring a good deal to the school, other parts of the organization, and to the Fellowship. We must consider freeing up requirements and consider those kinds of individuals who can contribute to the perpetuation of the Fellowship.

Have you found the members of the Fellowship to be quite open to you?

Yes, a variety of people frequently ask that question, especially those who find the Fellowship frustrating. All that I would like to help the Foundation accomplish is integrally tied to the success of the Fellowship. It cannot be an impediment; it must become part of the solution. People in the Fellowship have proved open and friendly. I have learned that providing them good information in a timely way, along with avoiding manipulation and instead operating through a collegial environment, earns respect.

We sensed when we were in Wisconsin for two weeks last summer, and in phone conversations, that they recognize that they needed someone like you and they have welcomed you.

I feel the welcome very much.

Is there any other matter you would like to mention?

I still have not addressed matters concerning the extent to which the people involved in Taliesin and the people closest to them have learned to articulate what the institution is. I do not really think that they have (other than intuitively) managed to talk about the tripartite institution (the Firm, the School, and the Fellowship), or that stool with three legs, the loss of any one of which collapses the enterprise. And add to that the Archives, our historic record, and the way it underwrites the fundamental programs of exhibits and publications, both of which are public education; and then the licensing program, . . . which you and I know also is an important revenue driver. Also the tour program, often seen as invading the Fellowship, can be viewed as the dues for 501(c)(3) status and the tax subsidy, which gives us the responsibility to use our assets in a public way, and I think that means the tour program. I had not anticipated how much that message needs articulation to both external and internal audiences.

When I started working with Dick and Pamela[6] and others on a full-time basis last June, I had also not anticipated the extent to which intellectual property issues would occupy my time. I had thought much more time would go toward developing the Board, rewriting or amending bylaws to reflect the contemporary conditions and needs, working through the financial situation in the Foundation and working on strengthening the Fellowship. And, at the same time, I am beginning to address some of the very serious facility needs in terms of studio space, administrative space, residential space for Fellows and other kinds of educational space, as well as the visitors' center and Archives expansion here in Arizona. Still, I had not understood how much intellectual property rests at the core of this legacy. We needed to start by putting clear policies into place; [it is] always difficult to be precise, as too little in these issues deals with the law and different interpretations of it.

You're spending more time with lawyers than you thought you would.

Yes, absolutely! However, we have made some progress on other things. I think we have come out of the woods in that we do not owe any money, and that in the past year and this year the Foundation will operate on a positive cash-flow basis. We might even balance the budget, including depreciation. That will put us in a position to invest in operations, particularly the School.

I must tell you, as February of 1997 comes to a close, I am very optimistic about the future of this organization, both as a school and a living community as well as an institution that will keep the ideas of the Wrights alive and vital and increasingly in public view. . . . In several instances (and I expect to see more of it) such as on the December Monday when Kay Rattenbury left us, the response of the Fellowship, the way the entire memorial service—the extraordinary warmth—demonstrates the extraordinary capacity of this group to rally.

My major point is the observation that pressures on people here will quickly move them beyond the little personal peccadilloes that have to happen in all communities and step up to the plate and work together with tremendous coordination. I like that; I like the way some of the apprentices do shopping, how they handle preparing food, doing it with skill and aplomb. So, they have impressed me. I speculate the Fellowship too often thinks of itself marching toward the future together, having difficulty recruiting younger members. Fellows worry about its future. I think the situation is much more healthy than it might appear—the issue of bringing younger members into it, if accepted, will add new vigor.

From the very beginning, Taliesin's reason for being has been to train architects. Consequently, it is hard to envision a Taliesin without the regular arrival of apprentices committed to learning by doing, but their arrival will continue to depend on a strong educational program. In these times, as the Taliesin Fellowship has recognized, such a program must retain the best of its traditional features and at the same time allow apprentices to gain credentials for entering the architectural profession. I asked John Wyatt what role he expects to play in the School of Architecture. He responded by outlining his vision for the School.

JOHN: I think that it comes down to this: first of all, there's a problem with an architectural faculty that only has two or three Fellowship members on it. I would like to see that people would join the Fellowship and then also become affiliated with the School in one way or another. I don't see that exactly happening at this point. I told them that I want to work myself out of this job and get it to the point where a Fellowship member should do what I do. But I also would like to see the Fellowship get back to the point where there is a notion of apprenticeship to a member of the Fellowship.

But you are dealing also with the fact that are you going to have architects who will be so fascinated by architecture and come to a point where they want to drink architecture twenty hours a day plus go into community life. . . . Now there is such an emphasis on individuality. I just don't know whether people would be interested in that. The one thing that I worry about with the Fellowship is that—and they know that I feel this way—I don't want people to get involved with the Fellowship just because they can't be employed on the outside or ultimately because they can't make it in the outside world. Taliesin offers that temptation to many sorts of people. I try to be very strong about that.

I would like to think in terms that if we're going to get architects up there, maybe we can get them from people who went through Taliesin and are older architects who have been successful. Then perhaps they can come back and teach; I don't expect them to join the Fellowship. I'm working with the ideal that we have Taliesin architects training apprentices. I live in the reality, though, that I can't see that happening in my time, and I'm trying to hold the fort until that happens. I think at this point my position is that I want to get good architects who at least give lip service to organic architecture and understand the Fellowship and will also be willing to participate and train young people.

I have had a lot of experience teaching, but I have never, ever encountered such a complex manner of educating young people. I don't say that out of despair. I'm saying it from the point of view that the standard and the vision is so compelling and so great, but to try and bring that into a system or get it to a point where you can really look at it and check it is incredibly difficult. I think we have to be extremely wise. When I use the term "wise," it's because you just have to be on it all the time. Of course, that's the excitement of it, too. I'm really, really happy that I am involved—most of the time.

The problem that I have is that you have this wonderful thing going on and very often you see what it could be, and then all of a sudden you are pushed off because of some small problem between personalities, or whatever it is, and you're dealing with this trivial matter within view of this magnificent mountain up there. But I think it is really worth all the sacrifice and havoc. I think that ultimately Taliesin can contribute a great deal to higher education.

The School of Architecture and the Taliesin Architects are interdependent. The prosperity and effectiveness of one depends upon the prosperity and effectiveness of the other. I asked Ryc Loope whether inviting students from traditional schools of architecture to study at Taliesin for a given period of time is an idea that might be implemented in the future. As noted in the previous chapter, Ryc left the Taliesin Architects in October 1997. Even so, his thoughts on Taliesin's transition from past to future and the role he played in this transition remain important in the Fellowship's story.

RYC: In a small way we are already doing just that. Many of the "apprentices" are graduates and practicing architects from foreign countries—Japan, Thailand, and Korea right now. We have several young men and one young woman here now who are fully qualified architects in their home countries. They came here to become educated and enculturated in the principles of organic architecture.

But I'm talking about the ones that graduate from Iowa State and Oklahoma State and the University of Kansas.

There is no reason we shouldn't do that also. Within our strategic plan we talk about forming virtual alliances with other architects along those lines, and we already have done that with several very distinguished firms within this country and abroad. Mr. Wright left for architecture a body of work and a body of thinking that clearly build a platform to elevate the critical inquiry into architecture well beyond where the European schools left off. We need to continue to share that with the profession.

Can you maintain the link between Taliesin Architects, then, and the traditions of the Taliesin Fellowship and the objectives of the School of Architecture?

I believe we can. I believe we must. To do so there needs to be widespread agreement to the vision. Mr. Wright created Taliesin as a place where architecture could be pursued as a way of life, not just as a means of livelihood. And, with all due respect to my colleagues—I have great respect for what they have done; they have kept alive Taliesin as a place, as a spirit, and as a living idea for thirty-seven years since Mr. Wright's death, under great adversity. It could easily have been lost. But in the process, Taliesin has become a place where a somewhat arcane way of life is being clung to. That was not Mr. Wright's vision for Taliesin.

I can see why it happened: lack of resources, the kind of cloistered life that existed, and Mrs. Wright's instructions to the architects to finish Mr. Wright's work. There were years' worth of work on the drawing boards the day he died, and, for a decade or more after that, people basically said, "Here's a project Mr. Wright started for me that I want you to finish," or "I want something exactly the way Mr. Wright did it." These architects went through that part of their lives where normally they would have established their own voice and weren't able to go very far beyond where Mr. Wright left the ideas of the work because of the nature of the way the work came through the firm and the nature of the way the place was organized.

I think right now we're at a crossroads, a threshold, an intersection, that allows us to begin to purposely advance the work for the first time since Mr. Wright's death. And so it is being advanced, and it's been advanced by many a person who has come through here—it's been advanced by Fay Jones, John Lautner, go down the list—an incredible "who's who" that's come through here.[7]

The critical community as we were discussing has perceived Taliesin Architects, at best, as doing warmed-over Frank Lloyd Wright work. I think one of the challenges we will continually face is that we will always be compared to the master, and because we put our pants on one leg at a time, we're always going to come up short. And I think it is very easy for the critical community to use that as a shot at Taliesin Architects. I mean, it's a "no-brainer."

I think we can accept and understand that and say, "Look, we're not trying to replicate Frank Lloyd Wright. What we're trying to do is advance his ideas, tenets, principles, and philosophies as he espoused and built throughout his life." I don't have any problems as an architect with somebody saying, "Well, you didn't do it quite as good as Frank Lloyd Wright would have done it." Frankly, I don't see that as very severe criticism. I'm thankful for being mentioned in the same paragraph. . . . I do believe we can elevate the critical inquiry into our own work and have begun to do so. . . .

It's been difficult, because critical evaluation of the work is not a historic practice here at Taliesin. It had always been seen, I think incorrectly, as if you're an individual you answer to no one. If you are an individual, you really answer to everyone; that's one of the things about being an individual. You're capable of answering to everyone, because you stand on your own merit. What we're trying to do is get our work to stand on its own merit.

How is it going on matters of indebtedness and the necessary financial turnaround?

Going very well, thank you. I see one of my most important contributions [as being] to have the firm successful. When I say success I mean everything from financial success to resources availability, top quality personnel, superior technological quality, as well as beautiful work. All those things fall under the big umbrella of success. I see a big part of my contribution being to lift the burdens; to get the roadblocks out of the way of our principal architects so that they can truly pursue architecture as way of life; to make sure that our firm is successful enough with the kind of resources, talent and time, that it takes to do leading-edge work, to do work of a critical nature that makes the critical embrace between theory and practice—even to the point where we're able to take on work that we know won't necessarily be profitable, but we take that work on because we know we'll have the opportunity to advance and elevate our ideas. I think that is very important for us, and we have crossed that threshold, we have arrived there. What we need to do is continually elevate the quality of our outcome and of our work now that we've begun to build a firm foundation with the resources necessary to drive that work forward.

The books were not in great order [when I came], and by the time I pulled all that together and did some consolidations, we had about a six-plus million dollar "net operating loss," meaning that the firm had managed to lose that much money through the five or six years prior to my arrival. There were a variety of reasons for that, but, nevertheless, the loss was there. We were able to get the firm to a break-even point in about six months, and we've been profitable ever since, producing the largest revenues and profits the firm ever generated.

That's not the focus of my efforts, but it certainly helps, because we've been able to fully computerize our office. We have 85 gigabits of networking computer power;

for a firm our size that's maybe unprecedented in this country. Certainly nobody here in the Valley comes close. It has allowed us to open the first new office for Taliesin Architects since Taliesin West. Tony is operating our field office in Madison; it's exclusively devoted right now to the Monona Terrace project, but that project ends in fourteen months, so we already have under way efforts for new work to fill that office.

We want to keep the office open, so we are already generating new work opportunities. It is a contemporary office, so much of the kinds of struggles we have with our historic facilities are not a challenge there. We're beginning to see clearly how much more effective we can be as architects when we have physical surroundings that support the way in which architecture is being practiced today and practiced, hopefully, into the twenty-first century.

Our goal is to define what organic architecture is going to be in the twenty-first century. We've begun some research and development efforts. We are hopefully going to get some development to do what we're calling "Usonian 21" to revisit the ideas of the unit planning and unit construction system. That's what Tom Casey is working on, and I've pitched to *Life* magazine, and it looks like we could get some support. We're all pretty excited. I've put into place a strategic marketing and PR program, which has led us to the *Life* publication[8] similar to what Mr. Wright enjoyed in his life. You know, I'm very proud to tread ground where Mr. Wright tread once before. I see it as a wonderful bellwether that we're headed down the path to where we want to go.

What do you consider to be your measure of acceptance among the organic architects of the Frank Lloyd Wright School?

I would like to think it is growing, though I must say I don't keep score. Having been a turnaround manager for a time in my life, I learned early on that the real measure of what I did was whether or not the organization prospered and not the level of my popularity at any given moment. Not being a politician, I do not need to take polls. But I must say, amongst my colleagues here at Taliesin Architects, I truly believe that my acceptance has grown and broadened. Although I guess at 6'4" I'll always be ruining the scale around here. "Waste of material," I think, is what Mr. Wright said of anyone over six feet tall. I believe all my colleagues have recognized that I make a positive contribution here, and I'd like to believe that they feel my heart and soul are for the ideals of Taliesin, the spirit of Taliesin, and that they know I'm not interested in doing anything that would detract from Taliesin.

What do you see as happening with Taliesin Architects when the Taliesin Fellowship is either gone or radically changed?

I think that right now we have in place both the people and the desire to make it survive. The form of its survival is, I think, the only thing that is in question. We all can agree on that. The degree of differentiation is the only debate that is left to have—and the speed at which that change occurs.

Are you in a position to help perpetuate the Fellowship in a different form, or do you keep at arm's length from those sorts of things?

The Fellowship, I think, has been very gracious and kind to seek my opinion about many key issues in their domain. I don't regularly attend Fellowship meetings, but I'm invited often. I've been involved in their retreats; I sit in on their management committee, attend executive committee meetings from time to time; and report to their Board. I have a good relationship with all the Fellowship members, such that I don't feel uncomfortable sharing a thought or an idea, a criticism or a compliment as appropriate. Dick complimented me greatly recently when he introduced me to some people and introduced me as a member of the Fellowship. He saw my eyebrows go up a bit and he said, "Well, I think of you as a member of the Fellowship." I felt very good about that. Any contribution I can make that allows the Fellowship to successfully make this transition is one that I'm very pleased to do.

John Wyatt, Nick Muller, and myself bring a broad, fresh, invigorated sense of renewal to Taliesin that is contagious, and I believe it is being warmly embraced. And with that embrace the continuation of Taliesin—the idea of the place and spirit—is pretty much assured. How fast, what form it will take, are the only remaining questions, and those are being addressed daily. I'm a firm believer that change is a process, not an event. And I believe our process is very clearly underway. We can point to many events, but probably the most amazing of all is my arrival, because the firm has always been the centerline, the heart of Taliesin. The decision to ask me to head the firm clearly sent a signal that the change is under way. Since then, John Wyatt coming in and now Nick Muller, the process of change is well set in motion. All the key facets of the organization have contemporary leadership that is both sympathetic as well as supportive to the ideas and spirit of this place. So I'm very positive about our future.

One of the exciting things we are doing is reaching out to the Taliesin alumni. I've been meeting with various alumni individually, and their organizations, finding ways in which the firm can collaborate [to] virtually align or strategically align our talents. I'm working to induce talent from our alumni group to rejoin Taliesin in various ways such as permanently, episodically, etc. I believe we are in a position where we can begin to start sharing our work broadly.

We have amassed a body of work, which I think is quite interesting and exciting. We've put into place a strategic marketing and public relations program that will start next year doing that, and so that "voice" we spoke about earlier will begin to be heard again. We've very carefully tried to choose certain select members of the critical community to kind of champion our work and then withstand the slings and arrows of the rest. So I think all of that is positive and under way.

The quality of the apprentices we're attracting is on an upward trajectory. That's what we need; we want the best and the brightest and we want to have an environment —physical, financial, intellectual, and creative—that's going to sustain them so that they become the next John Rattenburys, Tom Caseys, Tony Puttnams, etc., who devote their professional and personal lives to the ideas and ideals of Taliesin.

I suppose no one has ever accused you of lacking self-confidence.

No. However, I recognize that my confidence source is this place, its spirit, and the people I work with. I clearly see the opportunities, I can clearly see the talent is here or attainable, and with that I think we can be all the things Mr. Wright envisioned Taliesin to be when he first conceived it. I think anything less [and] we have let Mr. Wright down, we have let the spirit of Taliesin down, we have let hundreds of people who have devoted themselves to Taliesin down, we have let the cause of architecture down, and we've let what I think is our most sacred responsibility as architects—our cultural responsibility—we've let that down.

My conversation with Elizabeth Dawsari, who as librarian accomplished the Herculean task of acquiring the requisite number of volumes in architecture for the library in time for the NAAB accreditation visit, provides a good penultimate note for this book. What does she see as the future of the Fellowship?

ELIZABETH: I don't know. I wish I had a crystal ball. I see a great deal of work that needs to be done. I think one of the most critical things that needs to be accomplished is some sort of open forum of communication where people don't feel stressed when they voice their opinions. Where they can actually say, yes, I am in favor of this, no, I am not in favor of that and there is no personal tension. Where people can discuss issues and ideas freely and not feel threatened as a result.

When I say threatened, I think that some of the older members of the Fellowship see that there is a trend toward some sort of evolution of how things can be accomplished in the twenty-first century. And, I think that it's painful for them, because they see that they have invested their lives, their love, their blood, sweat, tears into something that they had a dream for and the world has changed. It has nothing to do with the dream, it's simply the way the world has changed.

On the other hand, I think stress has certain beneficial effects. Something which is not stressed is dead, and that alternative certainly is not acceptable, so, therefore I think we have to experience stress. And I include myself in that. I have to learn to live with the pressures of change and adapt, finding a balance of what the original dream was but how to make sure that it survives in this changing world. I think if we were to lose the Fellowship, the resident community, it would be a disaster. I think that the apprentices who apprentice to the firm would not have the benefit of the strength of that extended family. I think they would become much more like the students in the academy. And I think that some of the passion—not the professional passion, but the personal passion in terms of creativity or endeavors toward creativity—would be altered to a certain extent. I want to use the word "passion" in terms of family, in terms of the ties that bind and the fire in the belly to keep it together and we'll survive through thick and through thin. That's essential, I think, to this organization.

It's obvious that you want to play a part in that.

Absolutely, otherwise I'd be gone.

When I was here for the NAAB visit—that was my first time back since our residency here—you were a changed person.

I'll tell you what changed me. It was very simple: The Fellowship got behind my endeavor, as opposed to my continually saying, "I need, I need, I want, I want, I have to have, I have to have." Suddenly I heard, "What do you need? What do you want? How can we help you make this work?" I didn't feel alone any longer.

Marty Newland, an apprentice in the seminar I taught on intentional communities at Taliesin West in 1994, brought to the class these lines on community by writer Wendell Berry. They struck a responsive chord with fellows and apprentices.

> If we speak of a *healthy* community, we cannot be speaking of a community that is merely human. We are talking about a neighborhood of humans in a place, plus the place itself: its soil, its water, its air, and all the families and tribes of the nonhuman creatures that belong to it. If the place is well preserved, if its entire membership, natural and human, is present in it, and if the human economy is in practical harmony with the nature of the place, then the community is healthy. A diseased community will be suffering natural losses that become, in turn, human losses. A healthy community is sustainable; it is, within reasonable limits, self-sufficient and, within reasonable limits, self-determined—that is, free of tyranny.
>
> A community identifies itself by an understood mutuality of interests. But it lives and acts by the common virtues of trust, goodwill, forbearance, self-restraint, compassion, and forgiveness. If it hopes to continue long as a community, it will wish to—and will have to—encourage respect for all its members, human and natural. It will encourage respect for all stations and occupations. Such a community has the power—not invariably but as a rule—to enforce decency without litigation. It has the power, that is, to influence behavior. And it exercises this power not by coercion or violence but by teaching the young and by preserving stories and songs that tell (among other things) what works and what does not work in a given place.[9]

Wendell Berry seems to be speaking to the Taliesin Fellowship about its past, present, and maybe its future. The fourth challenge—perpetuating the legacies of the Taliesin community as the company of immediate heirs of its founders, those who worked closely with them, diminishes—will be the Fellowship's biggest one.

Notes

1. Spencer Klaw, *Without Sin: The Life and Death of the Oneida Community* (New York: Penguin Press, 1993) offers a good account of Oneida. Marion Lockwood Carden, *Oneida:*

Utopian Community to Modern Corporation (Syracuse: Syracuse University Press, 1998; orig. published Baltimore: Johns Hopkins University Press, 1969) describes the breakup of the community and the survival of its ideology in the joint stock company.

2. Stephen J. Stein, *The Shaker Experience in America* (New Haven: Yale University Press, 1992), 394–5.

3. "Preface," *America's Communal Utopias,* ed. Donald E. Pitzer (Chapel Hill: University of North Carolina Press, 1997), xvii. Pitzer traces his interest in the idea of "developmental communalism" to this experience and to his subsequent visits to kibbutzim in different stages of development in Israel.

4. Kat Kincade, *Is It Utopia Yet? An Insider's View of Twin Oaks Community in Its 26th Year* (Louisa, VA: Twin Oaks Publishing, 1994). Kinkade, *A Walden Two Experiment: The First Five Years of the Twin Oaks Community* (New York: Quill, 1973), included a foreword by B. F. Skinner. The newsletters for Twin Oaks, as well as information about many other contemporary communities, are best located through the Internet: <http://www.ic.org/>.

5. Information on several Camphill locations may be found at the same Internet address.

6. Pamela Stefansson is Executive Assistant to the Foundation Board and its Assistant Treasurer; she is also Director of Admission, Director of Financial Aid, and Registrar in the School of Architecture.

7. Fay Jones was with the Fellowship in 1953 and John Lautner from 1933 to 1939.

8. "The 1997 *Life* Dream House," *Life* (May 1997): 103–37 (with advertising interspersed).

9. Wendell Berry, *Sex, Economy, Freedom & Community* (New York: Pantheon, 1992–93), 14–15, 120.

Afterword

Frank Lloyd Wright's Taliesin Fellowship had its rather serendipitous beginnings in November 1994. We were visitors that month at Taliesin West in Scottsdale, Arizona, the winter home of the Taliesin Fellowship. In the tradition of the Fellowship, we were welcomed warmly but with little fuss. Except for the 6:30, 12:30, and 6:30 mealtimes, we made our own schedules, found our own niches, and made ourselves at home.

Our connection with Taliesin had begun when I served on a North Central Association accreditation team for the Frank Lloyd Wright School of Architecture at Taliesin West in 1992. Shirley Marty accompanied me on part of the visit, and we lingered for an afternoon after the official duties were concluded. Friendships formed led to an invitation to Taliesin in Spring Green the following summer. We also remained in touch with the Fellowship through several of the senior members who have occasionally made our home in Des Moines a way station on their semiannual migrations between Arizona and Wisconsin, Taliesin's two locations. By 1994, then, an invitation to spend time with the Fellowship while on a research leave from Drake University proved irresistible.

As a participant-observer in the life of the Taliesin Fellowship during our month-long residency, I recorded conversations with twenty men and women about their experiences as senior fellows and earlier as apprentices. Initially I simply intended to deposit the audiotapes in the Frank Lloyd Wright Foundation Archives. As a volunteer in the Archives, Shirley began to transcribe them, along with other recordings deposited earlier. Before long we realized that the tapes were filled with stories that should not be allowed to remain on a shelf, waiting to be discovered.

When our residency ended, there were yet more stories to be gathered, so the recording of conversations continued. I interviewed one senior fellow by telephone and four more in person during a brief visit to Taliesin in Spring Green in June 1995. I also began to reach beyond the senior fellows by recording an interview with a member of the larger Taliesin family—one of those referred to, for want of a better term, as nonresident staff. Additionally, I interviewed an architect who had apprenticed at Taliesin in the 1950s and was in Wisconsin for a week to work with the apprentices. In May and June 1996, in both Arizona and Wisconsin, I recorded conversations with four young persons who had recently been named senior fellows, as well as additional nonresident staff members. Since then I have interviewed by phone five more staff members—the new president and chief executive officer of the Frank Lloyd Wright Foundation, the academic dean of the School of Architecture, and three persons who work in the Archives—as well as another new senior fellow. We have also been granted permission to use the transcript of an interview with the Fellowship's longest-serving member, Kay Rattenbury, that had been recorded by the Frank Lloyd Wright Foundation Archives just prior to our 1994 residency.

Some 215,000 recorded words have gone into Shirley's ears and come out on paper by way of her fingers and the Macintosh screen. Her work as a transcriber, however, represents only part of her role in the partnership that has produced this book, just as the interviewing constituted only part of my work. Separately and together we have maintained friendships with members of the Fellowship, identified topics to be treated in the recorded conversations, debated and assimilated perceptions of the Fellowship gained through our participation in its activities during more than seven weeks of residency, determined themes to be unfolded in this book, selected and integrated the portions of the interviews to be used, written and rewritten the connecting narratives, and collaborated fully in the book's organization and production. In other words, this is a side-by-side and line-by-line collaboration.

The book reflects familiarity with the Fellowship gained through our daily life in its midst and our continuing association with it. Observing and participating in the distinctive programs of the Frank Lloyd Wright School of Architecture also contributed to our understanding of the ways of the Fellowship. During the 1994 residency, I conducted a seminar for fellows and apprentices on communal episodes in American history—the subject of an honors course I teach at Drake University. The final session in the seminar was devoted to an examination of the Taliesin Fellowship in the tradition the episodes represented. My seminar with apprentices in June 1996 explored common themes in the work of Frank Lloyd Wright and Thomas Jefferson.

Both Shirley and I benefited greatly from reading the manuscript of *Tales of Taliesin* written by Cornelia Brierly, the most senior fellow, who joined the Fellowship in 1934. Shirley gained further insights by editing Cornelia's manuscript for publication. Both of us also benefited from an opportunity to review an early draft of John Rattenbury's *Taliesin Architects: In the Spirit of Frank Lloyd Wright*. We learned much also by reading scholarly articles and books on the life and work of Frank and Olgivanna Lloyd Wright and writings by both of them. Since our residency we have remained current with developments in the Fellowship by reading *The Whirling Arrow,* a weekly newsletter published by one of the fellows, Dr. Joe Rorke. Documents prepared for recent accreditation visits have kept us informed of changes in the School of Architecture, and serving as an observer on the accreditation team of the National Architectural Accrediting Board in 1996 enabled me to see the Fellowship from yet another angle.

We acknowledge with appreciation the assistance provided by the staff of the Frank Lloyd Wright Foundation Archives, all of whose voices are heard in this book and whose cooperation made possible the inclusion of many of the pictures. At Drake University, the Cowles Library staff was always helpful, and the Center for the Humanities provided funds for acquisition of pictures and accompanying rights to publish them. We appreciate also the expertise and dedication of Paula Presley, director and editor-in-chief of the Thomas Jefferson University Press, and the encouragement provided by her predecessor as director, Robert V. Schnucker.

We are also grateful to Bonnie and Gil Daenzer, good friends who critiqued the manuscript for this book as it progressed, and to our four children—Jason, Elizabeth, Timothy, and Miriam—who have listened to Taliesin stories for more than five years. Extensive and astute criticisms by Miriam were particularly helpful, as were those offered by Elizabeth. Mildred Marty Burger and Martin E. Marty have offered us encouragement and lifetimes of example, and to them, with deep appreciation, we dedicate this book.

Our most profound gratitude is reserved for the Taliesin storytellers, without whose cordial cooperation this book could not exist. Richard Carney, managing trustee of the Frank Lloyd Wright Foundation for more than a decade after the death of Olgivanna Lloyd Wright, deserves special mention for his support and encouragement. When Dick passed away on January 14, 1998, he was chairman of the Board of the Foundation. We hope that this book will inspire his surviving colleagues to write their personal memoirs, for they have much to say that could not be said in our brief conversations.

Myron Marty
June 1998

Appendix A

Milestones in the Lives of Frank and Olgivanna Lloyd Wright and the Taliesin Fellowship

- birth of Frank Lloyd Wright, 1867
- beginning of Wright's studies with Louis Sullivan in Chicago, 1887
- marriage of Frank Lloyd Wright and Catherine Lee Tobin and the designing of the home and studio in Oak Park, Illinois, 1889
- opening of his own practice in Chicago in 1893
- birth of Olgivanna Lazovich, the future Mrs. Wright, 1899
- designing and construction of important buildings: Winslow House, River Forest, Illinois, 1893; Larkin Building, Buffalo, New York, 1903; Robie House, Chicago, 1906; Taliesin, 1911; Midway Gardens, Chicago, 1913; Hollyhock House in Los Angeles, 1917; the Imperial Hotel in Tokyo, 1916–1919
- opening of an office in Los Angeles, 1922
- construction of the "Ocatilla" desert camp near Chandler, Arizona, 1929, laying the groundwork for seeking a more permanent location in the desert later
- reconstruction of Taliesin following a fire, begun in 1925; reconstruction and preservation are ongoing processes
- establishment of the Fellowship at Taliesin in Spring Green, October 1932
- building of Broadacre City model, 1934
- designing of Fallingwater in Mill Run, Pennsylvania, 1935
- designing of the administration building for S. C. Johnson & Son, 1936
- construction of Taliesin West at Scottsdale, Arizona in 1937
- annual migrations of the entire operation, not including the Archives, from Arizona to Wisconsin each Spring and back again in autumn months, since 1937, except during World War II

- establishment of the Frank Lloyd Wright Foundation (now incorporates the Fellowship, the School of Architecture, and the Archives, and the Taliesin Architects as a wholly owned subsidiary), 1940
- beginning of the design process for the Guggenheim Museum, 1943
- installation of glass at Taliesin West in 1945, replacing canvas roofs and window coverings, a process that continued into the 1950s
- opening of an office and residence in the Plaza Hotel in New York (sometimes called Taliesin East), 1954
- an increase in the number of apprentices after World War II, reaching a peak of sixty-four at one time
- completion of the Cabaret Theater at Taliesin West, 1951
- opening of the Pavilion at Taliesin West, 1957
- installation of the first telephone at Taliesin West in the latter part of the 1950s
- the death of Mr. Wright in his ninety-second year, April 9, 1959
- formation of Taliesin Associated Architects, 1959
- a steady flow of printed words and images from the Taliesin Archives, 1980s and 1990s
- pursuit of accreditation of the School of Architecture in the 1980s, leading to attainment of accreditation by the North Central Association's Commission on Institutions of Higher Education, 1987; visits resulting in continuation of the accreditation, 1992 and 1997
- employment of tour guides at Taliesin, 1984, and Taliesin West, 1985
- construction of the building for the Frank Lloyd Wright Foundation Archives, 1985; addition of an office wing, 1991
- death of Mrs. Wright on March 1, 1985
- changes in the governance structure of the Frank Lloyd Wright Foundation, leading to its becoming a membership organization with the adoption of a new constitution and bylaws, 1989; inclusion of four public members, along with eight senior fellows, on the Board of Trustees, with authorized public membership increasing to eight in 1994 and twelve in 1995
- gradual increase of paid employees to sustain the work of the Frank Lloyd Wright Foundation and its entities, since the 1970s
- maintenance of a steady flow of apprentices throughout the Fellowship's history; retention of some of them, for various lengths of time, as senior fellows
- formal renaming of the Taliesin Associated Architects as Taliesin Architects, 1993
- attainment of professional accreditation of the School of Architecture by the National Architectural Accrediting Board in 1996

Appendix B
Locations of Buildings, Rooms, and Other Physical Resources[1]

Taliesin, Spring Green, Wisconsin

Taliesin is located on six hundred acres of rolling farmland near the Wisconsin River in southwest Wisconsin, about an hour west of Madison. The complex includes these structures:

Taliesin is the name for the house that provided living and guest quarters for the Wrights. Connected with it are Mr. Wright's studio, offices, and apartments for fellows and apprentices. The elevated portion at the west end is known as the Hill Wing.

Hillside is located three-fourths of a mile south of the house. The original part of the building was designed nearly one hundred years ago by Frank Lloyd Wright as the Hillside Home School operated by his aunts. The present structure, with additions and modifications, contains a 98'x52' drafting studio; two galleries for displaying architectural drawings, photographs, and models and providing space for small-group meetings; and living quarters for sixteen apprentices. Hillside also includes the living room, which can seat as many as seventy-five persons; the dining room and adjacent kitchen; and the theater, which is used for music, dance, and other live performances, as well as for classes, lectures, and films; the theater seats about one hundred and has a 30'x22' stage.

Tan-y-deri is used as a residence for apprentices, fellows and guests. Adjacent to it are two cottages for housing senior fellows.

Midway consists of buildings that were formerly a farmer's residence and dairy barn. Portions of Midway provide housing for fellows and apprentices; a small cottage overlooks the farm buildings.

Romeo and Juliet is the windmill tower located on the hill adjacent to Hillside. Designed by Frank Lloyd Wright in 1896, it was rebuilt in 1991 and serves as an example of innovative engineering and architectural principles.

Taliesin West, Scottsdale, Arizona

When Frank and Olgivanna Lloyd Wright established Taliesin West in 1937 it was an isolated camp in the Sonoran desert. Today the six-hundred-acre site is surrounded by the city of Scottsdale, a suburb of Phoenix. Despite being an enclave in an urban setting, Taliesin West strives to preserve its desert character. Its physical structures help serve that purpose, for they are built with materials from the desert.

A complex of connected structures includes (from west to east) the main *Drafting Studio* (96'x30'), alongside a handsome pergola; the *Kitchen* and *Dining Room*; the *Annex*, which provides office space; the *Garden Room* (or living room); offices (in the Wrights' former living quarters), and apartments for fellows.

Above the kitchen and dining room is the *Guest Deck*, with rooms for visitors and fellows.

North of this complex is the *Kiva*, a conference room.

Beyond the Kiva is a U-shaped row of apartments for fellows; also here are men's and women's locker rooms and showers. Designed initially for apprentices, the apartments surround the *Apprentice Court*.

To the east is the *Sun Cottage*, now used as guest quarters; the *Atrium*, an auxiliary drafting room; and the *Eastwing*, with rooms for apprentices and guests.

Northwest of the central complex is *Mr. Wright's Office*, now used for tour operations.

Beyond it is the *Cabaret Theater*, used for dining on formal evenings, lectures, chamber music performances, and showing films.

Adjacent to it is the *Pavilion*, a larger space for theatrical performances, concerts, lectures, and special events.

Across a courtyard from the Pavilion is the *William Wesley Peters Library*.

Forming another complex are the visitor center, the shop, a men's locker room, and a reading room.

To the south are the *Frank Lloyd Wright Archives*, and farther south, the *Crescent*, which provides living quarters for fellows and guests.

Apprentices have traditionally lived in desert shelters scattered in an area northwest of the main buildings. The *Carousel* is a women's dormitory north of the main buildings.[2]

Notes

1. The information provided here is drawn from a variety of sources, including the 1997 *Apprentice Handbook for the Frank Lloyd Wright School of Architecture*. Names capitalized here are capitalized in their common usage, a practice followed in the text of this book.

2. For photographs and copies of the original drawings of Taliesin and Taliesin West, see Robin Langley Sommer, writer, and Balthazar Korab, photographer, *Frank Lloyd Wright: A Gatefold Portfolio* (New York: Barnes & Noble, 1997).

Maps of Taliesin and Taliesin West

Here are maps of Taliesin and Taliesin West provided by the Frank Lloyd Wright Foundation, courtesy of Ari Georges.

The photographs that follow the maps show the strikingly different landscapes of Taliesin in Wisconsin and Taliesin West in Arizona.

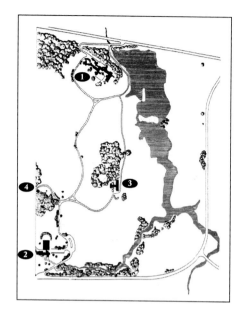

TALIESIN
1—Taliesin Proper
2—Hillside
3—Midway Barn
4—Tan-y-deri

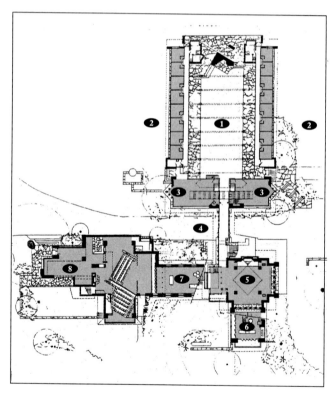

HILLSIDE
1—Hillside Studio
2—Apprentice Corridors
3—Galleries
4—Bridge
5—Living Room
6—Kitchen
7—Dining Room
8—Theater

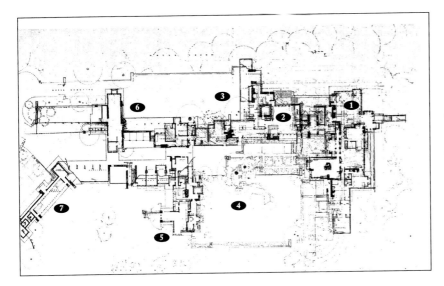

TALIESIN
1—Taliesin Residence
2—Taliesin Studio
3—Frank Lloyd Wright
  Foundation Offices
4—Hill Garden/Tea Circle
5—Education Office
6—Taliesin Preservation
  Commission Field
  Office
7—West Wing

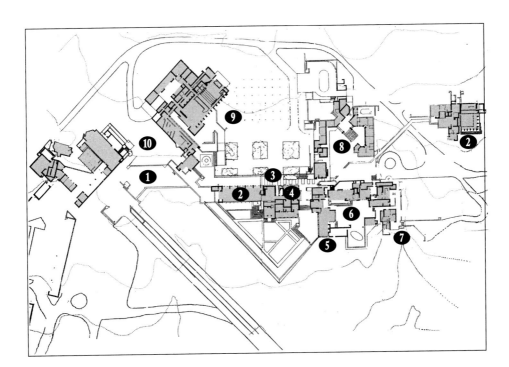

TALIESIN WEST
1—Entry Court
2—Studios
3—Kitchen
4—Dinging Room
5—Garden Room
6—Frank Lloyd Wright Foundation Offices
7—Education Office
8—Apprentice Court
9—Performing Arts Pavilion
10—Cabaret Theater

View from Taliesin of the lake and rolling hills of Wisconsin

Sonoran desert landscape at Taliesin West

Bibliography

Some of the books and articles included here offer comprehensive coverage of Frank Lloyd Wright's life and work, some relate directly to the Taliesin Fellowship, and some lead researchers to further sources of information about Wright.

Frank Lloyd Wright's Writings, Spoken Words, and Architecture

Alofsin, Anthony, ed. *Frank Lloyd Wright: An Index to the Taliesin Correspondence.* 5 vols. New York and London: Garland, 1988.

Larkin, David, and Bruce Brooks Pfeiffer, eds. *Frank Lloyd Wright: The Masterworks.* New York: Rizzoli (in association with the Frank Lloyd Wright Foundation), 1993.

Meehan, Patrick J. *Truth Against the World: Frank Lloyd Wright Speaks for an Organic Architecture.* New York: Wiley, 1987; Washington, D. C.: Preservation Press, 1992.

———. *Frank Lloyd Wright: A Research Guide to Archival Sources.* New York and London: Garland, 1983.

Pfeiffer, Bruce Books, and Yukio Futagawa, eds. *Frank Lloyd Wright.* Vols. 1–8, *Monograph*; vols. 9–11, *Preliminary Studies;* vol. 12, *In His Renderings.* Tokyo: A.D.A. EDITA, 1984–1988.

Pfeiffer, Bruce Books, text; Yukio Futagawa, editor and photographer. *Frank Lloyd Wright Selected Houses,* 8 vols. Tokyo: A.D.A. EDITA, 1988–1991.

Pfeiffer, Bruce Brooks, *Frank Lloyd Wright Drawings: Masterworks from the Frank Lloyd Wright Archives.* New York: Abrams, 1990.

Pfeiffer, Bruce Brooks, and Gerald Nordland, eds. *Frank Lloyd Wright in the Realm of Ideas.* Carbondale: Southern Illinois University Press, 1988.

Pfeiffer, Bruce Brooks, ed. *Frank Lloyd Wright: The Guggenheim Correspondence.* Carbondale: Southern Illinois University Press, 1986.

———, ed. *The Collected Writings of Frank Lloyd Wright.* 5 vols, 1892–1959 (vol. 1, 1892–1931; vol. 2, 1931–1932; vol. 3, 1931–1939; vol. 4, 1939–1949; vol. 5, 1949–1959). New York: Rizzoli, 1992–1995.

———, ed. *Letters to Architects* (1984). Fresno: The Press at California State University, 1984.

———, ed. *Letters to Clients.* Fresno: The Press at California State University, 1986.

———, ed. *Letters to Apprentices: Frank Lloyd Wright.* Fresno: The Press at California State University, 1982.

Wright, Frank Lloyd. *An Autobiography.* Facsimile edition. New York: Barnes & Noble, 1998.

———. *Modern Architecture: Being the Kahn Lectures.* Princeton: Princeton University Press, 1931; Carbondale: Southern Illinois University Press, 1987.

Works on Frank Lloyd Wright, with references to the Taliesin Fellowship

Besinger, Curtis. *Working with Mr. Wright: What It Was Like.* New York: Cambridge University Press, 1995.

Brierly, Cornelia, *Tales of Taliesin.* Tempe, AZ: The Herberger Center for Design Excellence, Arizona State University, 1999.

Einbinder, Harvey. *An American Genius: Frank Lloyd Wright.* New York: Philosophical Library, 1986.

Gill, Brendan. *Many Masks: A Life of Frank Lloyd Wright.* New York: G. P. Putnam's Sons, 1987.

Green, Aaron G. *An Architecture for Democracy: Frank Lloyd Wright, the Marin County Civil Center: A Narrative by the Associated Architect.* San Francisco: Grendon, 1990.

Guerrero, Pedro. *Picturing Wright: An Album from Frank Lloyd Wright's Photographer.* San Francisco: Pomegranate Artbooks, 1994.

Guggenheimer, Tobias S. *A Taliesin Legacy: The Architecture of Frank Lloyd Wright's Apprentices.* New York: Van Nostrand Reinhold, 1995.

Henning, Randolph C. *At Taliesin: Newspaper Columns by Frank Lloyd Wright and the Taliesin Fellowship, 1934–37.* Carbondale: Southern Illinois University Press, 1992.

Hoffmann, Donald. *Frank Lloyd Wright: Architecture and Nature.* New York: Dover Publications, 1986.

———. *Frank Lloyd Wright's Fallingwater: The House and Its History.* Second, revised edition. New York: Dover Publications, 1993.

Green, WI (608/588–7900), or the Frank Lloyd Wright Home and Studio in Oak Park, IL (1–877-848–3559 or 708/848/9518).

America's Castles: The Homes of Frank Lloyd Wright. A&E Television Networks, 1996.

Bvilding Harmonies: Frank Lloyd Wright in the Southwest. KNME Public Television, 1997.

Fallingwater: A Conversation with Edgar Kaufmann, Jr. A film by Kenneth Love, 1994.

The Frank Lloyd Wright Way: Apprentices to Genius. Gone West Publications, 1995.

The Mike Wallace Interviews. ABC, 1957; reproduced in conjunction with the Frank Lloyd Wright Foundation, 1994.

Partner to Genius: The Life of Olgivanna Lloyd Wright. Wisconsin Public Television. 1993.

CD-ROMs

Houses of Frank Lloyd Wright. Luna Imaging, Inc., and the Frank Lloyd Wright Foundation, 1996.

Frank Lloyd Wright: Presentation and Conceptual Drawings. Luna Imaging, Inc., and the Frank Lloyd Wright Foundation and Archives, 1995.

Storrer, William Allin. *The Frank Lloyd Wright Companion.* Chicago: University of Chicago Press, 1995.

World Wide Web Sites

(all with links to many other Frank Lloyd Wright addresses):
Frank Lloyd Wright Foundation *www.franklloydwright.org.*
Frank Lloyd Wright Home and Studio *www.wrightplus.org.*
Frank Lloyd Wright School of Architecture *www.taliesin.edu.*
Taliesin Preservation Commission *www.Taliesinpreservation.org.*
Public Broadcasting System *www.pbs.org.flw.*

Oral Histories

As noted in the text, Frank Lloyd Wright Archives has an extensive collection of recorded interviews and transcriptions, totaling an estimated 850 hours (363 hours of audio recordings and 587 of video). The following persons who were interviewed for this book have other recordings and transcripts in the Archives: Cornelia Brierly, Dick Carney, Effi Casey, Tom Casey, Heloise Crista, Joe Fabris, David Dodge, John deKoven Hill, Marian Kanouse, Susan Jacobs Lockhart, Sarah Logue, Charles Montooth, Frances Nemtin, Stephen Nemtin, Bruce Brooks Pfeiffer, Tony Puttnam,

Kay Rattenbury, John Rattenbury, Ling Po, Joseph Rorke, and Arnold Roy. Also Elizabeth Al-Hassam Dawsari, June Hill, and Ryc Loope. Interviews with many former fellows are also in the collection. This oral history project has been led by Indira Berndtsen, who conducted many of the interviews herself.

Also worth noting is the Frank Lloyd Wright Heritage Project of the Frank Lloyd Wright Oral History Program conducted under the auspices of the Oral History Program, the University of California Los Angeles, and the State Historical Society of Wisconsin. In 1997 the Regents of the University of California published a two volume transcription of interviews with John deKoven Hill—more than 500 pages incorporating 16.2 hours of interviews recorded in 1993 and 1995. Other former apprentices interviewed in this program are William Beye Fyfe (1932–34), John Lautner (1933–39), and Alvin Louis Wiehle (1950–51 and 1953–63).

Photograph Credits

All photographs are copyrighted by the sources providing them.

Frank Lloyd Wright Foundation: 5, 6, 39 (Dick Carney), 59, 63, 72 (John Heileman), 80 (John Engstead), 83 (Edgar Obma), 90, 92 (Engstead), 102, 112, 147, 152 (Obma), 155 (Obma), 160 (Obma), 188, 200, 210 (Engstead), 217 (Samiha Zeitoun), 221

Pedro E. Guerrero: 77, 139, 150, 202

Clarence E. Olson: 69, 189

Institut Gurdjieff, Paris (courtesy of Jacob Needleman): 7

Chicago Historical Society (Hedrich-Blessing): 8

Spencer Research Library, University of Kansas Library: 105

Additionally, these copyrighted photographs are included by permission of the Frank Lloyd Wright Foundation:

Susan Lockhart: 135

Heloise Crista: 161, 162, 163, 164, 165, 166

Kay and John Rattenbury: 16, 110, 113, 118, 198

Effi and Tom Casey: 114, 119

Tony Puttnam: 191

Minerva Montooth: 176

Ken Love: 248

Joseph Rorke: 96, 116

Shawn Rorke-Davis: 115, 194

David and Anneliese Dodge: 33, 99

Jim Wildeman: 157

Myron A. Marty: xiii, xiv, xv, 18, 20, 22, 25, 27, 28, 29, 31, 34, 36, 37, 38, 41, 43, 44, 45, 46, 48, 50, 51, 53, 53, 75, 86, 121, 123, 124, 235, 239, 241, 145, 251, 257, 264, 298, 298

Index

The names of Frank Lloyd Wright and Olgivanna Lloyd Wright appear so frequently that passing mentions are not indexed. Since the context for the stories told in this book are Taliesin and Taliesin West, these sites are indexed only when they receive special attention. Similarly, the Taliesin Fellowship is indexed only when a particular aspect of it is revealed. The names of members of the Fellowships and the nonresident staff as well as persons mentioned in the interviews are entered here as most commonly used in the text. Formal names of persons interviewed appear on pages xix–xxii. Illustrations and maps are identified by *italic* numerals.